Social Policy

University of Liverpool

For conc

Social Policy:
a Conceptual and Theoretical Introduction
(2nd edition)

Edited by
Michael Lavalette and Alan Pratt

SAGE Publications
London • Thousand Oaks • New Delhi

First published 2001

SAGE Publications Ltd
6 Bonhill Street
London EC2A 4PU

SAGE Publications Inc.
2455 Teller Road
Thousand Oaks, California 91320

SAGE Publications India Pvt Ltd
32, M-Block Market
Greater Kailash – I
New Delhi 110 048

British Library Cataloguing in Publication data

A catalogue record for this book is
available from the British Library

ISBN 0 7619 6952 7
ISBN 0 7619 6953 5 (pbk)

Library of Congress Control Number available

Typeset by M Rules
Printed in Great Britain by The Cromwell Press, Wiltshire

CONTENTS

CONTRIBUTORS

Stephen Cunningham is a lecturer in Social Policy at the University of Central Lancashire.

Iain Ferguson is a lecturer in Social Work at the University of Stirling.

Charlie Johnstone is a lecturer in Sociology at the University of Paisley.

John Lansley is a lecturer in Social Policy at the University of Liverpool.

Michael Lavalette is a lecturer in Social Policy at the University of Liverpool.

Brian Lund in a lecturer in Social Policy at Manchester Metropolitan University.

Gerry Mooney is staff tutor and lecturer in Social Policy in the Faculty of Social Sciences at the Open University (Scotland).

Tony Novak is a lecturer in Social Policy at the University of Liverpool.

Laura Penketh is a lecturer in Social Policy at the University of Central Lancashire.

Alan Pratt is a principal lecturer in Social Policy at the University of Central Lancashire.

Angelia R. Wilson is a lecturer in Social Policy at the University of Manchester.

Kath Woodward is a staff tutor and lecturer in Social Policy with the Open University.

ACKNOWLEDGEMENTS

We were both very excited when asked to prepare a second edition of this textbook. A second edition gives us a chance to thank all those people who bought and used the first edition and confirmed our original hunch that a book such as this could prove to be both popular with, and useful to, students.

The contributors were all very disciplined and met our deadlines with good grace and humour – they all made the task of editing the book (relatively) straightforward. At Sage, Karen Phillips has been patient and supportive from the beginning. When we first thought about a book like this other publishers said it would not sell. Karen took a chance on it – we are glad she did we hope she is too!

Finally, working in the university sector is not what it used to be. Mass teaching, cuts and lack of resources, the Research Assessment Exercise and spiralling administrative burdens all bring various stresses and strains. Like our colleagues up and down the country we find ourselves being proletarianized. In this atmosphere we all invariably bring work home and this has inevitable costs on social and family life. We both have partners and children who suffered, to various degrees, as the deadline approached. We would like to thank them for their patience.

Michael Lavalette
Alan Pratt
February 2001

CHAPTER I

Michael Lavalette and Alan Pratt

1.1 Introduction

Most university teachers spend some time at the beginning of first-year undergraduate courses explaining to students something about the nature of the subject(s) they are studying. This usually involves a brief foray into the origins, traditions, methods and scope of the discipline in the hope that, at an early stage, students will acquire some sense of direction, some location in the intellectual universe. For students and teachers of social policy this is a particularly difficult problem for a variety of reasons, despite the fact that since the end of the Second World War, it has become a well-established subject at most British universities. Yet, to follow a degree course in social policy is, for most students, something of a shot in the dark. Social policy now has a higher profile at pre-degree level than was the case when the first edition of this book appeared in 1997. Despite this greater presence on the curriculum for 16–19 year olds it probably remains true that most students remain to some extent unclear about what the subject is about. The simple aim of this textbook is to outline and introduce what we believe to be the conceptual and analytical tools essential to the study of the subject.

In this brief introduction we start by trying to define social policy as a subject and outline the perspectives followed in the rest of the book. Our hope is that by the end of the book, you will be more aware of the contested nature of social policy debates and recognize the need to examine carefully all positions and statements on social welfare issues, no matter how painful the experience might be.

1.2 What is social policy?

Richard Titmuss who, more than any other academic and teacher, made the subject of Social Policy an accepted and 'respectable' academic discipline wrote somewhat wearily of 'this tiresome business of defining social policy' (Titmuss, 1974: 28), and it is difficult not to sympathize with him.

One approach would be to follow the example of a multitude of books over the years and quote the opinions of the good and the great on the subject. Indeed, Titmuss himself adopted this policy on a number of occasions and it is a method adopted by David Gil (1973) in his now classic text, *Unravelling*

Social Policy. Although some 20 years old it can be argued that Gil's analysis remains one of the most authoritative and rigorous in the entire literature. He devotes considerable time to a review of then existing definitions of social policy as discipline and practice and, in the end, rejects them all as being too limited; even Titmuss himself, though afforded due recognition for his sophistication and breadth, is regarded as being too narrow. For Gil, social policy's major focal concern is the analysis of access to life-enhancing and life-sustaining resources and, as such, even foreign policy could legitimately be included within its domain. In contrast, Titmuss's observation seems to rather narrow that basically,

> We are concerned with the study of a range of social needs and the functioning, in conditions of scarcity, of human organization, traditionally called social services or social welfare systems, to meet those needs. This complex area of social life lies outside or on the fringes of the so-called free market, the mechanisms of price and tests of profitability. (Titmuss, 1976: 20)

Whatever its shortcomings for Gil, Titmuss's approach takes us to the heart of the matter and, in so doing, raises other problems which are as intractable as the definition of social policy itself and just as relevant. In essence Titmuss is concerned with the allocation of a limited range of resources to meet a range of social needs. In reality, although there have been variations between countries, these social needs are for health care, housing, education, income maintenance during periods of interruption or cessation of earnings, and that multiplicity of dependencies which in Britain are the concern of the personal social services. The market's role in meeting these needs should, according to Titmuss and the entire intellectual and political tradition he did so much to shape, be minimal. Consumption of these erstwhile commodities is far too important to be left to command over resources in markets. At this point it should be noted that there is no practical reason precluding the allocation of healthcare and the rest through unfettered private markets. An allocation of these experiences could be secured in this way and classical liberals in the past together with their neo-liberal counterparts today make exactly this point. The crux is whether such an allocation would be successful in meeting the population's needs.

Once again we are driven into the realm of definition. What constitutes need? Can anyone ever define need objectively? Is there a generally agreed definition of social need or must it be as open-ended as the definitions of social policy itself. Thus we move from concept to concept, from definitional problem to definitional problem and there is no easy way out, except perhaps to say, as the classical and neo-liberals do that the only 'things' whose allocation falls properly within the realm of public policy, and thus outside the market, are defence and law and order, the classical functions of the night-watchman state. Otherwise, when we speak of social problems and social needs we are merely giving voice to our own particular prejudices, values and opinions. Such opinions may be more or less well-informed and clearly or ill-articulated but if we move beyond the harsh and rigid logic of public goods theory we are left with little other than personal preference and tradition.

The tradition that the allocation of the experiences identified above is, in part at least, the proper responsibility of government is well-established throughout the industrial world, and rather than languish in a fog of relative values or be directed by the remorseless logic of perfect markets (which probably do not exist anyway) it might be both productive and sensible to proceed from this reality and to take it as a 'given' in our analysis. For a variety of reasons, in a variety of methods, and with varying degrees of success all countries, to a greater or lesser extent, modify the operation of market forces in the allocation of health, housing, education, income maintenance, and the personal social services. One of the continuing fascinations of social policy as a subject is the way in which debate about the propriety of state intervention itself and the relative merits of particular strategies and tactics of intervention has changed and developed over the years. Significant advances in conceptual and theoretical sophistication have been made over the last 50 years (many of them covered in this book) as the subject has grown and matured but the objects of analysis remain much as Titmuss discussed them almost 30 years ago. Thus:

1 The analysis and description of policy formation and its consequences, intended and unintended.
2 The study of structure, function, organization, planning and administrative processes of institutions and agencies, historical and comparative.
3 The study of social needs and of problems of access to, utilization, and patterns of outcome of services, transactions and transfers.
4 The analysis of the nature, attributes and distribution of social costs and diswelfares.
5 The analysis of distributive and allocative patterns in command-over-resources-through-time and the particular impact of the social services.
6 The study of the roles and functions of elected representatives, professional workers, administrators and interest groups in the operation and performance of social welfare institutions.
7 The study of the social rights of the citizen as contributor, participant and user of social services.
8 The study of the role of government (local and central) as an allocator of values and of rights to social property as expressed through social and administrative law and other rule-making channels.

(Titmuss, 1976: 22–3)

Titmuss was, of course, as aware as anyone of the significance of occupational and fiscal welfare, indeed he pioneered their study (Titmuss, 1962) but the long quotation above is limited to the extent that it omits three areas of concern. First, there is no mention of the role of the market. To Titmuss and his colleagues market failure was both a historic fact and an article of faith. He shared with Myrdal (1972) the conviction that the long, postwar progress of the social democratic welfare state was an immutable reality. While the occasional tactical retreat might be necessary at times of transient political crisis, the strategic conquest of the market was secure. The history of industrial capitalism had demonstrated the market's unsuitability as an allocative agency for those resources essential to the experience of a full and complete life. Any possibility that a return to the market might be seriously advocated was minimal. Organizations like the Institute of Economic Affairs, founded in 1957, which canvassed such ideas were regarded as amusing, marginal irritants with nothing serious or substantial to contribute to the intellectual and political debate.

Second, there is a failure to recognize that social policies can be instruments of social control. Inherent to this Fabian complacency (although specifically rejected by Titmuss) was the idea that social policy would always tend to be beneficial, humanitarian and progressive. That in a world changed for ever by the intellectual revolution personified by Keynes and Beveridge discussions about the future of the welfare state would focus on points of administrative and technical detail rather than the institutional model of welfare itself. It was left to the theorists of the Marxist left and the neo-liberal right to point out the control and oppression of individuals and families present in relatively undemocratic and unaccountable welfare structures. The Fabian tradition of social administration, organized by and delivered to a relatively powerless population, was always susceptible to charges of paternalism. Authority and power did not rest with the citizen but with the bureaucracy which operated at several removes from those who received education, healthcare, housing, and so on. It also became clear that much of this provision was structured on lines of class, 'race', and gender. The terrain of social policy was an area of contention and struggle. On an altogether different plain, confirmation that social policy could be literally destructive and evil was to be found in the very recent example of Nazi Germany where the torture and murder and mass destruction of millions of Jews, homosexuals, gypsies, and the physically and mentally impaired was accomplished in the name of a clearly conceptualized and articulated social policy.

Finally, social policies are intimately bound to the societies in which they develop and reflect the priorities of those systems. Social democratic thinkers like Titmuss found this relatively unproblematic as we now lived in welfare societies where meeting the basic needs of the majority was paramount. But for other traditions in social theory this is not the case. For Marxists social policies exist within capitalist socio-economic systems and for neo-liberals within free market economies. In both these paradigms social policies are inherently problematic reflecting, on the one hand, the contradictions of class divided societies and, on the other, the futility involved in attempts to control the free play of market forces.

1.3 Social policy or social policies?

One of the most useful questions that we can ask of social provision is whether it represents a social policy in the singular or simply a collection of ill-related social programmes. For us, to speak of 'a social policy' implies that a government or political party has a clear vision of what constitutes the good society. Whatever characteristics this good society might possess each of the programmes in the discrete areas of health, education, housing, economics, taxation and so on has to be structured in such a way that it enables the consummation of the overall vision. Without such a vision as an organizing totality there is the probability that social provision will proceed through a series of incremental adjustments. Policy will happen by accident rather than be created through directed, political will. We have already suggested that the Third Reich possessed a social policy, and we can point to periods in British history when a similar sense of clarity and purposiveness has existed. Thus, the 1834 Poor Law Report together with the Poor Law Amendment Act it inspired were designed primarily to create a free, national labour market through the implementation of a harsh, deterrent system of poor relief based on the principles of less eligibility and the workhouse test. In this way British industrialization was supposed to proceed unhindered by the sentimentality and relative generosity of the 'Old' Poor Law.

The long break-up of the post-1834 Poor Law was finally and officially concluded by the National Assistance Act in 1948 which in its turn was a manifestation of the liberal collectivist social policy encapsulated by the Beveridge Report in 1942. Beveridge's initial brief was to examine, and suggest reforms to the chaotic and complex collection of income maintenance schemes in existence at the beginning of the 1940s. By introducing his three 'assumptions' of a national health service, a system of children's or family allowances, and full employment he transformed his task into what became the project which created the Keynesian-Beveridgean welfare state, which in its turn was challenged by the Thatcherite project whose neo-liberal foundations represent an attempt to resurrect the economic and social philosophy of 1834.

From this perspective social policy can be seen as an intensely political project and, as such, an immensely important arena in which competing ideologies can clash. Consequently, politics matter a great deal and political activity is afforded no little significance in the policy making process in particular and the shaping of social policy in general (Ringen, 1986). In this regard it is important to bear in mind that the one thing which unites the various contributors to this book is their rejection of the primacy afforded to the market as an institution of resource allocation by the Conservative party and, increasingly, by New Labour. The authors occupy a variety of left of centre positions and, it should be noted, disagree with each other at least as much as they do with the main thrust of New Labour social policy. Given that one of our major objectives is for you to understand the contested nature of the ideas and concepts dealt with in this book it is probably an advantage that it is a multi-authored text. Whatever our personal opinions about the merits of the examples of social policy referred to above, that they represent a unified and purposive intent cannot be in much doubt. They enable us to see social policy as a manifestation of political economy in the sense that Hutton (1995) uses the term. 'It has economics and the economy at its heart, but attempts to line them to the wider operation of the social and political system' (Hutton, 1995: xi).

1.4 Implications for studying the subject and the organization of this book

From the little that has been said so far about the domain of social policy as activity and practice it will be clear that students of social policy are presented with a challenging and exciting task and therefore need a variety of intellectual tools and approaches if that task is to be accomplished. As an academic discipline social policy is concerned with the critical analysis of social provision in the public, private, occupational, voluntary, and informal sectors. That is, with a comparative, historical and theoretical examination of healthcare, education, housing, social security, the personal social services and other related activities in what was commonly called the 'welfare state'. As a subject it has clear and close connections of methodology and substance with the other social sciences, although possibly its most distinguishing characteristics are its eclecticism and its normativeness. Social policy has always been concerned with a wide field of activities and, at its best, it has managed to operate in a distinctively integrative fashion. It has never been as restricted to relatively narrow and discrete boundaries in the way that some other subjects have. While social policy may still lack the variety of theoretical refinements that distinguish cognate subjects such as economics, politics, and sociology (a feature not nearly so marked as formerly) this characteristic is balanced by its capacity for selecting, developing, and deploying existing theory in the examination of a significant area of human activity, social provision. This is its eclectic strength.

Our belief is that important dimensions of any analysis of social welfare are that it be comparative, historical, and theoretical. Each of these dimensions is demanding in itself and together they can only begin to be achieved through the entirety of an undergraduate course. Obviously, even to attempt such a project within the pages of a single introductory volume would be impossible. All we do in mentioning these characteristics is to indicate what we believe to be essential requirements of a sophisticated and comprehensive approach to the subject. This book is intended to make a contribution to this end although it is also fair to suggest that the theoretical perspectives discussed in these pages, as well as the problems and issues of policy they treat, are likely to be relevant to the investigation of social policy in any society.

This belief underpins the structure of the present text. The book is divided into three sections: theoretical approaches; critical perspectives, and issues and debates. In the first section we outline competing interpretations of the social world based on the perspectives of social democracy, neo-liberalism, and Marxism, and attempt to ascertain where social welfare fits into these broad paradigms. These theoretical traditions cover the political spectrum and emphasize our contention that social policy is an inherently political activity where decisions about the extent, nature, and form of welfare provision are intimately connected to our political values and judgements regarding what we perceive to be 'right' and what we think it is possible to achieve. At heart these competing perspectives diverge over whether they think we should structure modern societies to meet human needs (Marxism), whether we should free individuals to pursue their own wants through market mechanisms (neo-liberalism), whether we should try to combine elements of both of the above via the workings of a 'social market' (traditional social democracy) or whether a new 'third way' is necessary (New Labour's social democracy). Whatever conclusion we come to each of these has something important and interesting to say about social policy and welfarism and as a result it is important for students to engage with each of them.

In Part Two we move on to look at some critical perspectives on welfare provision. Here we have grouped together a number of views which emphasize the range of inequalities which social policy often fails to acknowledge. We start with the feminist critique of welfare (Chapter 5) which looks at the way in which welfare practices and social policies make assumptions about the role of women in society and, both consciously and unconsciously, reinforce women's oppression. We then proceed to analyse the way in which social policies also make assumptions about notions of race and hence act in an institutionally racist way (Chapter 6), and about our sexuality and the institutional discrimination that takes place against gays and lesbians (Chapter 7). The analysis of each of these forms of oppression has grown out of and developed from the political movements for the liberation of women, blacks, and lesbians and gays. In their most recent form, these movements arose out of the movements of 1968 and reflected a demand for the extension of equality and liberation to these oppressed groups. As these political movements have gone into decline however, they have engaged with a politics of difference and diversity. These themes have been affected by various postmodern concerns and approaches and hence to end this section we include a chapter that looks at postmodernism – although one that suggests its emancipatory potential is limited. The chapter is an explicit critique of postmodernist approaches.

Finally in the last section we move on to look at a number of issues and debates within social policy. Again in this section the ideas and debates being discussed build on, refine, apply or take issue with the various approaches and perspectives covered in the first two parts. Here we look at a range of issues which continue to inform debates within the subject (such as what we mean by contested concepts like distributive justice), look at issues traditionally at the core of the subject (such as poverty, the 'underclass' and social exclusion), and discuss the form of welfare provision (universal versus selective provision). In this section we also include an examination of structural factors like demographic structure which have traditionally been given insufficient attention; the growing importance attatched to managerialist solutions to service delivery and re-emerging areas of concern such as the position of children on the wider social policy agenda. There are undoubtedly important issues which have been left out due to restrictions of space but it is our contention that the debates included here will always have a resonance for students of the subject.

In each chapter, in order to aid reflection and understanding, the authors have included a range of activities. Sometimes these are simply questions which can be answered from the text itself but on other occasions students are asked to carry out tasks of a more practical nature drawing on experience and practice in the outside world. We offer this book in the belief that the sooner students begin to engage with debates of this nature the more complete and enjoyable will be their experience of social policy as a subject and their understanding of social policy as practice.

PART ONE

THEORETICAL APPROACHES

In this first section we introduce the three paradigms which have traditionally structured discourse in the social sciences in general and social welfare studies in particular: social democracy, neo-liberalism, and Marxism. These traditions all focus primarily on the broad and general features of social life and attempt to provide holistic interpretations of the social world and historical developments based on the utilization of universally applicable categorizations (such as concepts like equality, justice, freedom and class). As such they are not primarily concerned with the specifics of social policy or developments in welfare provision but, nevertheless, each includes social welfare (its cause, developments, and consequences) within its remit.

In Chapter 2 Alan Pratt examines the ways in which social democratic theorists have responded to the challenges and opportunities presented by the apparent triumph of a free market version of free market capitalism. He discusses the extent to which this new social democracy has responded to the social and cultural changes present in modern society and whether or not this emergent political and social philosophy has succeeded in reflecting the traditional concerns of old social democracy, not least of which is the idea of a reciprocal approach to distributive justice.

In Chapter 3 Alan Pratt examines those aspects of neo-liberal theory which have made such an important contribution to the explanatory power of New Right ideology in general. After a discussion of the behavioural assumptions on which neo-liberal theory is predicated he focuses on the claims of the free market as an allocative institution and the nature of politics in a mass democracy, and goes on to consider those characteristics which provide much of the clarity and edge of the entire perspective.

Finally, in Chapter 4 Michael Lavalette looks at Marxism and social welfare.

Perhaps more than any other perspective Marxism produces most student apprehension. The concepts, terminology, ideas, and language used by Marxists are 'new' to students and sometimes the language used by academic Marxists is unnecessarily complex. Nevertheless Marxism remains a crucially important tradition with which students need to engage. Further, as Lavalette argues, recent developments in the world have led a number of academics to reconsider the importance and relevance of Marxism as a social theory committed to understanding the world with a view to changing it. Are we witnessing a return to Marx?

CHAPTER 2

TOWARDS A 'NEW'
SOCIAL DEMOCRACY

Alan Pratt

2.1 Introduction

In the first edition of this book which was published in April 1997, Kearns noted in his chapter on 'Social democratic perspectives' that the social democratic tradition was 'once again on the march and that its adherents no longer feel that they have lost the intellectual initiative' (Kearns, 1997: 27). Just a month later the British Labour Party ended 18 years of opposition by securing its largest ever victory in a general election, perhaps the most spectacular and symbolic event in a political revival of the centre-left which had begun with Bill Clinton's success in the US presidential campaign in 1992 and which, by the end of the century, had seen parties of the centre-left either in power by themselves, or as the major partners in governing coalitions, in a majority of the leading industrial nations of the OECD. The intellectual self-confidence discussed by Kearns has developed apace and much work has been done by social democratic theorists to create a 'new' social democracy, one more suited to a modern society allegedly characterized by economic globalization, cultural and political diversity, the diminution of the importance of social class and greater individualism. The main purpose of this chapter is to offer an assessment of this theoretical work and to consider the extent to which it represents a potentially coherent and effective challenge to the currently dominant neo-liberal paradigm.

However, before we begin this task it is sensible to remind ourselves of the main characteristics and concerns of what might usefully be termed 'old' social democracy.

2.2 Old social democracy: a brief review

Old or traditional visions of social democracy were rooted in the belief that significant degrees of autonomy and political power rested with national governments. They could, if they wished, take action to modify the operation of market forces and change the initial allocation and distribution of resources produced by market operations. In other words, politics mattered and could be used to achieve a variety of economic and social ends. (For a definitive account of the possibilities of politics see Ringen, 1986.) Armed with a range of more or less Keynesian policy instruments and intellectual insights, supported by a majority of electoral opinion (Fraser, 2000), and operating within a relatively stable international financial order based on the Bretton Woods agreement of 1944, national governments could run their economies in ways that would deliver economic growth, full employment, and tolerable levels of price inflation. For most western industrial economies, including the UK, the result was the longest sustained period of economic growth in history. Although there is disagreement about the precise role of Keynesian demand management policies in securing this outcome, one undoubtedly made possible by the restocking and investment booms that sought to remedy the damage caused by the Second World War, there can be no doubt that, thanks to Keynes and his followers, governments now had the ability to iron out the worst excesses of the trade cycle.

The resources generated by this long boom in capitalist economies made it possible for governments to satisfy their populations' expectations of rising levels of real personal disposable income as well as their desire, expressed through the ballot box, for greater collective consumption in the form of high quality, decommodified health, education, housing, social welfare and income transfers in generally non-discriminatory and non-stigmatizing ways.

This economic agenda was accompanied by an equivalent social philosophy which informed citizens' access to collective social consumption. It was a philosophy founded on notions of solidarity and citizenship, and Wolfe and Klausen (2000) have recently reminded us how important these two ideas were in the construction of the classic welfare state in the 1940s. Thus:

> a sense of solidarity creates a readiness to share with strangers, which in turn underpins a thriving welfare state

while

> citizenship rights, especially social ones, promoted what Marshall called 'class abatement'. He accepted a certain amount of economic inequality as inevitable. What he wanted eliminated was the badge of inferiority associated with a class system as rigid as that of 19th century Britain. (Wolfe and Klausen, 2000: 28–9)

We will have cause to return to these ideas later in the chapter.

2.3 Social democracy in the new world order

The decline, fall, and recrudescence of social democracy as philosophy and political practice are intimately bound up with the rise of neo-liberal orthodoxy as the ruling idea, together with the creation of a global economy driven by a quantum leap in technology, especially in information processing and communications. The real world now is a very different place from that in which traditional social democracy achieved its greatest triumph: that 'compromise between capitalism and socialism which was hammered out in Europe this century and which produced the actual product of the mixed economy and the welfare state' (Self, 2000: 281). This section of the chapter attempts a brief examination of the nature of the major changes in the external environment which transformed the modern world and demanded that social democracy itself change if it was to have a future as a political vision.

Economic globalization and neo-liberal orthodoxy

Since the dramatic collapse of the Soviet Union and its satellites in Central and Eastern Europe it has become part of conventional wisdom that there is now only one viable economic model, only 'one game in town'. That game is capitalism, and in the last decade of the twentieth century it has manifested itself as a triumphalist, free market doctrine which can simply ignore the attempts of individual nation states to articulate some vision of the national interest through political debate and action. Contrary to the beliefs of some adherents of globalization this is not the first time in history that there has been a high degree of transnational economic power developed in the interests of a relatively small but hugely powerful group of corporations. Before the cataclysm of the First World War interrupted the process the world economy had acquired many of the characteristics of globalization. The technology of the 'second wave of industrialization' had produced the means through which a new level of economic integration and dependency could be achieved, then as now, fuelled by an intellectual orthodoxy which preached the virtues of free trade (Atkinson and Elliott, 1999).

The difference between then and now is one of generality and speed. Undoubtedly there is now a greater degree of integration than there was in 1914. All of the leading contemporary international financial and trading organizations such as the International Monetary Fund, the World Bank, and World Trade Organization, are:

strong supporters of the development and further expansion of the global economic system. They are naturally influenced by the strongest member states, especially the USA, and their financial contributions. They also are open to direct lobbying from major business and financial interests. This is particularly true of the World Trade Organization, whose network of advisory committees is dominated by the representatives of big corporations, and which is highly pro-active in spreading the gospel of freedom of trade and investment. (Self, 2000: 151)

Because these corporations control most of the world's investment decisions, national governments have felt obliged to compete with each other in an often unseemly scramble to attract the investment that would bring scarce jobs to declining regions and developing nations. The ability of these same corporations to damage communities and nations by transferring production across national boundaries to maximize profits and shareholder value is demonstrated now on what sometimes seems an almost weekly basis.

Another dimension of this particular version of liberal capitalism can be seen in the operations of the foreign exchange markets. Following the breakdown of the system of fixed exchange rates achieved at Bretton Woods in 1944, which provided the industrial world with the stability necessary to its expansion after 1945, there was a switch to floating exchange rates validated in the Smithsonian Agreement of 1971. Speculation has always been a feature of the world's financial markets, but since the Smithsonian Agreement the volume of such speculation has increased enormously, and instability has become a permanent feature. The amount of speculative capital flows across the world's financial markets has taken on a new dimension with the development of new technology. Trade in currency has become a 24 hours a day, seven days a week activity. There is always at least one major foreign exchange market open and decisions to trade currencies can be taken and transmitted instantaneously. These same financial markets have been completely liberated during the last two decades as national governments have abandoned a whole range of controls over capital movements. The instability generated by these developments is obvious; as is the influence such markets can exercise on the decisions on economic and social policy taken by democratically elected governments. The threat to economic stability and the independence of national governments is profound.

This transition to a deregulated, global form of capitalism has led to major changes in the occupational structure and a significant decline in the manual working class. In Britain especially there has also been a sustained attack on the legal rights of trade unions, so serious in its consequences that British workers, regardless of occupation and skill, have fewer rights than any workforce in Europe. For social democracy as an ideology this decline in the size and potency of the manual working class has serious implications since it was this class which throughout the twentieth century had provided the heart and muscle of the movement, it was this class whose vulnerability in capitalist market economies social democracy was invented to remove. The protection and security afforded by a mixed economy, full employment, and the welfare state has been much reduced in the last two decades, a process led and informed by a new and confident neo-liberal orthodoxy, and the economic and political agenda in Britain is dominated by ideas and policies redolent of the heyday of classical liberalism in the nineteenth century. How has this occurred in a society with an advanced economy and a mature parliamentary democracy?

For Crouch (1999) the answer lies in 'the fate of class in British politics, and in particular the parabola of class politics during the course of the twentieth century which parallels and is a major cause of the parabola of policy' (Crouch, 1990: 71). At the beginning of the twentieth century the manual working class was the 'coming' class, the class of the political future. During the twentieth century, helped by the growth of new, Fordist forms of production and the development of Keynesian theory, it became a force that no government could afford to ignore. With greater economic prosperity and higher disposable real income, as a collectivity of individual consumers it also acquired a significant presence in the overall structure of demand for goods and services. In representative democracies political parties had to compete for the votes of this class, and its preferences inevitably found a presence in the programmes of all mainstream parties, especially in Europe. Below the surface of the mindset of the political and administrative elite (and in many cases, not far below the surface) was also a lurking fear that, if it were so minded, this class could overturn the whole system of capitalist social relations. Keynes's challenge to neo-classical political economy came at just the right time and made it possible to construct a more inclusive and regulated capitalism. In this new form of capitalism the interests of the manual working class were a vital consideration and in Britain all governments had the search for economic and political stability as their major strategic objective (Middlemas, 1980).

The decline in the size of the manual working class which Crouch refers to has meant that, 'it is a central mantra of the contemporary political elite that class no longer exists' (1999: 71). Its significance has been overtaken by 'new' concerns and cleavages such as ethnicity and gender, indeed to a general fixation with diversity, difference, and individualism. In this new world there is no place for a politics of class, especially a politics based on the interests of a class whose size and influence have been massively reduced by the creative destruction of technology driven global capitalism.

We are constantly being told by members of the contemporary political elite, and by theorists of difference and diversity, that the concerns which led atomized workers in unstable capitalist market economies to seek a new ideology which would remove or modify their insecurities are now irrelevant. Currently existing capitalism is alleged to have produced a growing prosperity for all with an increase in individual opportunity. People see themselves as consumers not workers, as men or women or black or white or gay or straight or young or old or disabled; as anything in fact but members of a particular social class, least of all the working class. All this means that the need for a social democratic politics, certainly one characterized by social democracy's traditional concerns of equality, social justice, solidarity and citizenship, has disappeared. The decline of the traditional manual working class has been matched by an equivalent rise in the power of capital. Moreover, many of the jobs in the service sector industries which have replaced manufacturing jobs are insecure and filled by subordinate workers with little or nothing by way of effective trade union representation. The men and women who fill these jobs are working longer hours, and, as more and more women are drawn into the labour force, there are growing problems for the maintenance of stable family life. (See, for example, Hutton (1995).)

Thus, it could be suggested that this growth in insecurity means that ordinary people need more protection not less, that:

> . . . to argue objectively these needs no longer exist is quite specious. Needs for means to restrain the pressures of the market, including those of work, remain high on any objective political agenda, at least for any party stemming from the left. All that might have diminished is the capacity of those worried about such questions to place them on the political agenda. (Crouch, 1999: 72)

We now turn to a consideration of how the theory and practice of social democracy might respond to the changes and challenges discussed above, and the possibilities of constructing a political programme which represents a continuity with social democracy's traditional past and which resonates with an electorate whose dispositions and preferences have been influenced by the neo-liberal orthodoxy of the last 20 years.

Activity 2.1

1 What are the major economic, political, and social changes to which social democracy has had to respond?
2 Why has it been obliged to change?

2.4 Towards a new social democracy

Social democrats believe that the only valid means of securing political power is through electoral contest in representative democracies. Therefore the programmes which social democratic parties present to electorates must be sufficiently appealing that there is a chance that power can be achieved. The record of the British Labour Party in this regard has not been good in the twentieth century. Between 1945, when postwar general elections were resumed, and 1997 the Labour Party has only been in office for a total of 17 years: that is, from 1945–51, 1964–70, and 1974–9. Even during the halcyon days of the classic welfare state, Conservative governments were preferred at least as much as Labour.

From 1979 to 1997 the Labour Party had an even worse record, rejected by the electorate in four successive elections, those of 1979, 1983, 1987 and 1992. As in the 1950s the party engaged in a long and painful reappraisal of its purpose and programme, one that created much bitterness between competing factions. These self-evident splits intensified the electorate's distaste for Labour, although it must be noted that for a few years the Social Democratic Party, led by a core of Labour defectors such as Roy Jenkins, David Owen, Shirley Williams and Bill Rodgers, enjoyed a lot of public support. For the British Labour Party, the message was clear. The electorate had no fondness for disunity (as John Major was to discover so painfully in 1997), nor any liking for fundamentalist, left wing agendas such as the one on which Labour lost so ignominiously in 1983. After 1983 the party was to write no more suicide notes as it began its attempt to reconnect with the electorate. Neil Kinnock and John Smith were to play key roles in this process but it was left to Tony Blair, who succeeded Smith after his untimely death in 1994, to complete a transformation which received its reward with a stunning victory in the 1997 general election.

Whatever one's views about the merits of the four successive Conservative governments which held office in the 18 years from 1979, there can be no denying their impact on national life and national politics in altering our perceptions of the relationship, between the public and the private, between the state and the individual, between government and civil society. Perhaps their most remarkable success can be found in the revolution they achieved in the management and delivery of collective provision, a revolution which has been eagerly embraced by Blair's government and, indeed, taken even further. All this is simply meant to say that social democracy is bound to have been influenced by this experience. Has there been a Thatcherization of the centre-left or does contemporary social democracy offer an analysis of society and a set of prescriptions which are consistent with its long traditions? It is to these, and related questions, that we turn next.

2.5 A contemporary social democracy

Although we will have cause to make quite frequent references to the 'Third Way' and to New Labour it is not our intention to suggest that these terms are necessarily synonymous with the new social democracy. That they do, on occasion, overlap is certain but this should not constitute a major problem. The basic purpose of this chapter, it must be remembered, is to establish the contours of the new social democracy as political philosophy, as perhaps a new manifestation of the old social democratic impulse in very new times, and to see if there is any coherent policy agenda consistent with this vision.

The choice of the phrase 'new times' is not entirely accidental because it draws our attention to one of the major intellectual sources of Third Way politics. In a short but important article Finlayson (1999a) sheds a great deal of light on the nature of Third Way theory and its relationship to both New Labour and the new social democracy. He notes that New Labour began to use the term 'Third Way' before Blair or Anthony Giddens had published their work on it. He writes that as a consequence of this lack of considered theory it (the Third Way):

> . . . could only appear vacuous or gratuitous, and that analysts were left considering not how useful or coherent it was, but what it might actually be. The only certainty seemed to be that 'old' models of social democracy and the conservative right had failed and something new was in need of development. (Finlayson, 1999a: 271)

New Labour's position does not rest on 'a substantial moral claim about the nature of society and the distribution of its resources' (Finlayson, 1999: 271) but on a sociological claim about the real nature of modern society. While the world has been transformed by the economic, technological and cultural forces described above our political ideas about the world have not altered to the same extent. The Third Way is an attempt to provide this new political compass.

Finlayson argues that the Third Way has been shaped by two major intellectual influences: one associated with the analyses developed by Stuart Hall, Martin Jacques and others in the journal 'Marxism Today' in the 1980s, and the other in the sociology developed primarily by Anthony Giddens. The key ideas of what we might call the 'Marxism Today' perspective are to be found in Hall's analysis of Thatcherite neo-liberalism as a hegemonic project, and in the articulation of the concept of 'New Times'. The first of these is a theoretical critique in which Hall claims that political explanations and accounts derived from class analysis (the general approach adopted by Marxists and social democrats) were wrong theoretically and therefore the challenge for the left was to 'develop new strategies beyond a simple appeal to class allegiance that would generate a wide enough constituency for a hegemonic project of socialist renewal' (Finlayson, 1999a: 273). The New Times strand was empirical rather than theoretical and argued simply that Marxism and social democracy were both 'empirically in error'. They did not correctly understand existing economic and social patterns. 'Post-Fordist flexibility created and required a new individualism and autonomy that should be enabled, not interfered with by the state.' (Finlayson, 1999a: 274). The left should respond by recognizing these new realities and develop a version of politics that could accommodate them.

Giddens's analysis demonstrates a similar general understanding of the nature of the new world created by contemporary capitalism, a world which has changed in unpredictable and surprising ways in which old ideas about Keynesianism and socialism are dead: one which is too 'complex, fluid and diverse to be managed by a central state' (Finlayson, 1999a: 274). According to Finlayson, Giddens argues the need for a new 'life politics', one concerned with the emancipation of lifestyle, identity and choice, and his analysis of contemporary social relations ultimately provides:

an alternative ethical basis to that of socialist anti-capitalism. This is a 'philosophic conservatism', concerned with redeveloping and repairing social cohesion and solidarity. (Finlayson, 1999a: 275)

2.6 A political philosophy of 'new' social democracy

Whatever its strengths may be Third Way theory is:

> not a political theory in a conventional sense but an attempt to think through the emerging social complexity of contemporary society. (Jayasuriya, 2000: 282)

Given this lack of concern with political philosophy in Third Way writing, and in theories of diversity in general, where do we look to for such a political philosophy? What attempts have been made to recast social democracy in a way which is consistent with the complexity and diversity of modern societies? Is there, in fact, anything resembling a political philosophy (and political programme) of the new social democracy?

Clearly such a philosophy would need to bear in mind existing electoral preferences and traditional social democracy's history of defeat in the recent past. Although it must recognize these preferences it must also avoid the charge of being opportunistic and thus seen as simply a continuation of Thatcherite neo-liberalism by other means. It must also be able to demonstrate a genuine and strong sense of continuity with the traditional values and concerns of historical versions of the ideology. This presents an immediate and fundamental problem as Wolfe and Klausen (2000) have vividly demonstrated in a recent important article in the journal *Prospect*. They remind us that:

> For the 100 years preceding the 1970s progressives in Europe and America pursued a politics of solidarity. The left demanded the creation and expansion of the welfare state. Public policy should redistribute income and subsidize, if not deliver directly, essential services such as education and health. The ideal was a society in which the inequalities associated with social class would fade away. (Wolfe and Klausen, 2000: 28).

Since the 1970s this ideal has been supplemented by the promotion of diversity: individuals and groups should not suffer because their gender, race, sexuality or physical status is different from that of the majority. As Wolfe and Klausen note:

> Herein lies the progressive dilemma of the twenty-first century. Solidarity and diversity are both desirable objectives. Unfortunately they can also conflict. A sense of solidarity creates a readiness to share with strangers, which in turn underpins a thriving welfare state. But it is easier to feel solidarity with those who broadly

share your values and way of life. Modern progressives committed to diversity often fail to acknowledge this. (2000: 28).

A resolution of this dilemma has been suggested in the very recent work of a number of thinkers writing in the general tradition of social democracy (e.g. White, 1999; Vandenbroucke, 1999; Coote, 1999; Jayasuriya, 2000).

White's (1999) essay seeks to establish the ideas of rights and responsibilities as central themes of the new social democracy. Together these constitute the doctrine of civic responsibility, a doctrine which Blair and his government have been most concerned to stress as a central element of their economic and social philosophy. The idea of civic responsibility is very controversial in centre-left politics. Some have argued that it conflicts with the traditional libertarian values of British social democracy, while others have claimed that:

> the commitment to balance rights and responsibilities expresses a conception of fairness and mutuality that has deep roots in the social democratic tradition. (White, 1999: 166)

White's concern is to offer an interpretation and defence of civic responsibility from a specifically social democratic public philosophy, one defined by three core values; reciprocity, equal opportunity and autonomy. For White such a tradition is already present in broadly social democratic thought, specifically in the 'liberal socialism' of Hobhouse, Tawney and Crosland. Economic justice in this tradition is about a principle of reciprocity, 'according to which entitlements to income and wealth are properly linked to productive contributions' (White 1999: 166). As a theory of distributive justice it asserts that:

> those who willingly share in the economic benefits of social cooperation have a corresponding obligation to make, if so able, a personal and relevantly proportional productive contribution to the community in return for those benefits. (1999: 168)

Is the possibility that this obligation to contribute might be enforceable consistent with social democracy? White's answer is unequivocally 'Yes' and he cites writers as varied as Hobhouse, Tawney, Laski and Crosland to support him. He also makes the very important point that left wing political culture might have moved too far away from this tradition in recent decades, perhaps because of a fear of blaming the victim. However he concludes by suggesting that this departure from an important principle of centre-left distributive justice might now have gone too far and that:

> this is to be regretted, because the reciprocity principle does seem to capture a deep and widespread intuition about distributive justice. (White. 1999: 170)

For a full discussion of the wider concept of distributive justice see Brian Lund's chapter in this book.

White's attempt to restore the idea of reciprocity to the heart of social democracy's renewed understanding of distributive justice is vital for reasons other than political theory. There can be little doubt that many of Labour's traditional core voters deserted during the 1980s because of their feeling that far too many 'free riders' were battening on to the welfare state without making any contribution to the funding of that provision. The decline in the income tax threshold since the 1940s had drawn into the tax population millions of workers (and voters) who themselves were not particularly affluent, indeed, whose earned incomes were only a little, if at all, above benefit levels. Their resentment at what they felt was a gross injustice not only cost the Labour Party crucial votes but also resulted in significant damage to their attachment to a non-discriminatory, institutional model of welfare. Marquand (1996) has also noted the importance of reciprocity in old or traditional social democracy. In an important essay he has argued that the usual distinction between individualism and collectivism has been accompanied by a further distinction, one between two different conceptions of the good life. Thus:

> On the one side of the divide are those who see the Self as a static bundle of preferences and the good life as one in which individuals pursue their own preferences without interference from others. On the other are those for whom the Self is a growing and developing moral entity, and the good life is one in which individuals learn to adopt higher preferences in place of lower ones. (Marquand, 1996: 20)

The first of these are 'hedonist' or 'passive' and the latter 'moralist' or 'active'. This provides four possible groupings: hedonistic collectivists; moralistic collectivists; hedonistic individualists; and moralistic individualists. Since 1945 each of these has taken turns as the dominant influence on policy. What the centre left forgot, or never knew, in the 1970s, 1980s and 1990s is the similarity between the moral collectivism of the Attlee government, a government which preached a doctrine of civic responsibility, and Thatcher's posture of moral individualism. By arguing for the return of reciprocity as a defining feature of a new social democracy, White is, in an important way, seeking a return to one of old social democracy's animating principles.

Notions of reciprocity do not exist in a void. They are conceptualized and articulated in real-world patterns of resource distribution and life chances. In this regard we should bear in mind that egalitarian and libertarian values are both important in liberal socialism. White's argument is that these egalitarian values demand that we look at the existing distribution of opportunity against which 'citizens' putative reciprocity-based obligations are enforced' (White, 1999: 167). Thus, the real concern for social democrats should be to ensure not just reciprocity but *fair reciprocity,* and fair reciprocity demanded the operationalization of 'a robust principle of equal opportunity' (1999: 171). Equal opportunity itself demanded some redistribution of initial market allocations and distribution of resources. If the state insisted on the application of an idea of reciprocity on the basis of unmodified market allocations, the chances are, as recent US experience demonstrates, that social policy would become entirely punitive. Thus:

> it is vitally important to stress that the reciprocity-based contract between citizens and community is a two-sided contract: that the community must do its bit by securing certain standard threshold distribution conditions, at the same time as the individual citizen is required to do his/her bit. (White, 1999: 171)

This might require that individuals have access to meaningful and non-stigmatizing work for a decent, minimum income. It is interesting to note with regard to this latter point the extent to which the Blair government has become wedded to the idea of wage subsidization through policy instruments such as the Working Families Tax Credit. That which was anathema to the Labour Party when the Family Income Supplement scheme was introduced in 1971 is now entirely consistent with its principles in the 'new age'. The introduction of a national minimum wage, major increases in Child Benefit and a serious attempt to provide decent and more generally available access to high quality childcare demonstrate the strength of Labour's commitment to the idea and reality of work and, perhaps, to the idea of 'fair reciprocity'. Perhaps all that is required to secure the kind of background redistribution White demands as a pre-condition of fair reciprocity is for the state to act as 'employer of last resort' in areas with long standing and deeply rooted economic problems, together with vertically redistributive taxation of inheritances and other wealth transfers to preclude economic free-riding by the wealthy. A commitment to the creation and maintenance of full employment would also be useful.

White goes on to argue that his understanding of fair reciprocity is not the same as the 'New Paternalism' of American intellectuals such as Lawrence Mead who argue that the imposition of obligations is good for the moral well-being of recipients. By combining vertically redistributive taxation, a more equal opportunity to access decent income levels through work and/or benefits, and the obligations on citizens to make an acceptable, reciprocal contribution of some socially useful kind, White believes that social democracy can re-connect with the general public's instincts about distributive justice.

Autonomy is the third of White's core values and he is insistent that the idea of civic responsibility must be clearly separate and distinguished from 'a concern to promote or enforce a sectarian conception of personal morality' (1999: 167). A respect for individual autonomy would satisfy the libertarian impulses in social democracy which find their most powerful expression in the liberal tradition exemplified by John Stuart Mill. This tradition counsels us to refrain from activities that produce significant harm to our fellow citizens by, for example, avoiding intimidation, some forms of discrimination (such as gender, ethnicity, age etc.) and economic exploitation. Otherwise the state should leave people alone:

It must itself respect our spiritual integrity by giving us the autonomy to pursue our own good in our own way. We may refer to this idea as the autonomy principle. (White, 1999: 174)

In those instances when the state does act to define what we can or cannot do legally we need to be assured:

1   that this is indeed necessary to prevent a genuine harm;
2   that the gain in this respect is sufficiently large and sufficiently certain as to outweigh any damage to civil interests that may result from the state's new policy. (White, 1999: 174/175)

Jayasuriya (2000) has also recognized the need to recast the social democratic commitment to equality and freedom so that they reflect the complexity, diversity and plurality of modern society in his attempt to develop a normative rationale for new social democratic politics. Like White he bases his understanding of the new social democracy in 'a liberal conception of individual autonomy' and contends that: '. . . the key project . . . is to reconcile the social commitment to equality with a liberal emphasis on individual autonomy' (Jayasuriya, 2000: 283). He follows Sassoon (1996) in defining freedom as 'the material ability to make more choices. The role of the state is to ensure that everyone possesses such material ability' (Sassoon, 1996: 738). Thus for Jayasuriya, the key normative principle is *capability*. The enhancement of individual capability is viewed as central to the agenda of the Blair administration, specifically to the whole notion of social exclusion. He suggests that to think in terms of capability implies a notion of *complex equality* which is contrasted sharply with traditional egalitarian ideas of equality. Complex equality as an idea recognizes the need 'to take into account differences in circumstances and individual locations and the diverse ends of individuals' (Jayasuriya, 2000: 283). Capability therefore suggests a normative commitment 'to a notion of freedom defined in terms of the capability of people to make effective choices' (2000: 283). Jayasuriya draws on the work of Mark Latham (1998) as implying that at the heart of the new social democracy is an attempt to reconcile traditional egalitarianism with negative liberty and that 'it is this liberal socialism that is inherent in the new social democracy' (Jayasuriya, 2000: 284).

An important part of Jayasuriya's work is his critique of Giddens's approach to Third Way theory. Giddens, he argues, is preoccupied with redeveloping the welfare state in ways that respond to the new risks generated by a form of capitalism which has undermined the basis of traditional forms of welfare. In his analysis of the welfare state since the end of the Second World War Giddens distinguishes between negative welfare and positive welfare. Negative welfare is understood as action taken to compensate people for the costs and diswelfares they experience as a consequence of economic and social change. Positive welfare incorporates negative welfare but also attempts to develop:

the capacity for risk taking and integrating welfare institutions within the broader economic system. (Jayasuriya, 2000: 284)

This, in essence, is what Giddens means by the term 'social investment state'. The positive welfare state (and, by implication, the social investment state) are intensely concerned with the processes of inclusion and exclusion which facilitate or prevent individuals from taking part in economic activity, especially in labour market participation. A technology driven global economy creates the risk that certain groups such as the unskilled and the poorly educated may be permanently excluded from such activity. Traditional or negative forms of welfare, because they seek solely to compensate for diswelfares, may exacerbate social exclusion. Positive welfare, in sharp and marked contrast, would encourage capability and help prevent exclusion: inclusion would be a dominant objective of such a policy. This has clearly become the leitmotif of the Blair government, and for the government as well as Giddens:

> inclusion and exclusion have become important concepts for analysing and responding to inequality because of changes affecting the class structure of industrial countries. (Giddens, 1998: 103)

The new global economy, obeying its technological imperatives, demands welfare policies structured to develop individual capability and the capacity to participate in the rapidly changing labour markets of contemporary capitalism. The old manufacturing industries with their largely male, full time labour force have been replaced by industries and technology which thrive on flexible labour markets (helpfully de-regulated by government) demanding part-time or fixed-term or casual labour. The new welfare state according to Third Way theorists must reflect these changes and do all in its power to encourage labour market participation. As Jayasuriya observes:

> In the new global economy, employment is likely to be transitory, and therefore the new social welfare is designed to facilitate the re-inclusion of the unemployed into the economic mainstream. (Jayasuriya, 2000: 285)

How relevant are these ideas of negative and positive welfare states, social inclusion and social exclusion, and even Jayasuriya's concepts of capability and complex equality, to a new social politics that is genuinely in the social democratic tradition? There is nothing which is fundamentally problematic in Third Way theorists' identification of the implications of economic, cultural and social change for social democracy or the welfare state. It makes perfectly good sense to change the pattern of provision, perhaps even the nature of provision itself, in recognition of the significance of these contextual changes. What might be more difficult for a mainstream social democrat, one for whom ideas of reciprocity, equal opportunity and autonomy have genuine substance, is the nature of the analyses which have been made and the content of the policy suggestions. Contrary to the apparent assumptions and understanding of Third Way theory, insecurity is not a new phenomenon. People who exist by and through the sale of their labour in capitalist labour markets have their only access to the resources necessary to even an approximation of a full and civilized life determined by the nature of the bargains they can strike with potential employers. The vast majority of working people are still only a job loss away from poverty. It was an awareness of their inherent insecurity and vulnerability in capitalist economies that caused ordinary people to combine together in labour organizations and political parties so that they might possess a collective, countervailing power to deploy in their negotiations with employers and their dealings with politicians. There has been an objective change in capitalist economies and insecurity has increased, but that insecurity has increased because the dominant intellectual and policy paradigm of the last two decades has been one of neo-liberal orthodoxy. It has been a politics which has clearly and deliberately sought to increase the power of capital vis-à-vis that of labour. The intent of much of the policy agenda suggested by Third Way theory has been to fit workers for capital's purposes: not to modify capital so that its consequences no longer initially and ultimately rest on the shoulders of those made poor, vulnerable, and unemployed by its operations. State action to shift the incidence of the costs of economic change from the poorest and most marginal members of society on to those more able to bear these costs was always a primary objective of the social democratic welfare state.

We may also add that concepts such as the social investment state, capability and capacity themselves are hardly new ideas. From this perspective:

> ... welfare is viewed not as an end in itself, but as an investment by which people's capacity and choices can be enlarged; in other words this version of welfare places more emphasis on the positive role of welfare in helping individuals deal with risk, rather than playing a passive role as an instrument to provide security. (Jayasuriya, 2000: 285–6)

It is sometimes difficult to see why security should be regarded as 'passive.' It is not too outrageous to suggest that most people's lives are characterized in one way or another by a search for security. This is not surprising because with security comes confidence, optimism and, ironically, the willingness to take risks. In other words security is not such a debilitating condition after all. Perhaps those who have never known real insecurity find it difficult to understand the attraction it has for the majority of the population. It is appropriate to remind ourselves at this point of Michael Foot's note that one of Aneurin Bevan's favourite words in describing the power of the NHS was that it gave people a sense of 'serenity' at a time (illness) when they most needed it.

It would take a rather particular and perverse view of welfare practice in the UK to believe that, in general, the state has not been keen to secure people's re-attachment to the labour force. This has been done through a variety of policy instruments incorporating positive work incentives as well as strict disciplinary mechanisms. The problem for public policy has always been to secure an appropriate balance between compensating individuals and families for the diswelfares they experience through one or other contingency (unemployment, sickness etc.) and ensuring that everyone takes seriously her/his obligations and responsibilities to make a contribution, of whatever kind, to the public good. As White (1999) and Deacon (2000) have both suggested, in recent decades some on the left (Marquand's 'collective hedonists') have got this balance wrong, but the recognition that there is this form of reciprocal understanding has always been a central plank of social democratic philosophy. Thus, there is no real need to invent a 'Third Way' (Self, 2000).

It may well be that Third Way critics of traditional social democracy do not really understand it. On occasion they seem to misunderstand Keynesian theory, which was about far more than demand management, and they underestimate the capacity of national governments and regional or supranational organizations to modify or challenge market triumphalism in the globalized economy. Theirs can be regarded as a defeatist politics, and, in this sense, not deserving of being included in a new and genuine social democracy. One is also left to wonder about the historical accuracy of assertions such as Jayasuriya's claim that:

> technological innovation, productivity and competitiveness have entered the lexicon of social democracy, taking pride of place over – if not replacing – the traditional Keynesian vocabulary of macro-economic management and distributive issues. (Jayasuriya, 2000: 286)

Social democrats, by the very nature of their analysis, have always argued that a competitive, innovative and high productivity capitalist economy was an essential pre-requisite for increasing levels of real personal disposable income and the creation of a comprehensive, generous institutional model of welfare. This is why social democratic intellectuals like Crosland took as their model the achievements and programmes of their counterparts in Sweden and the Federal Republic of Germany in the 1950s and 1960s. For them social democracy was essentially about the socialization of consumption not the socialization of production. The greater the volume of resources generated by a competitive and successful private sector economy, the greater would be the pool of resources the state could call on for its social agenda. On this agenda education and training had a very prominent place given their potential contribution as forms of economic and social investment. 'Education, education, education' was a social democratic mantra long before Tony Blair.

2.7 What kind of programme?

So far our main concern has been to examine the ways in which the new social democracy has reacted to the changes associated with globalization and advanced modernity at the level of normative values, of political philosophy, and we have noted the new emphasis given to ideas about fair reciprocity, autonomy, equal opportunity, complex equality and capacity. We now consider what economic and social policy agenda might best reflect this newly conceptualized social democracy.

Vandenbroucke (1999) argues that the second half of the 1990s witnessed a developing convergence in centre-left European literature on the welfare state. After making due allowance for national differences in circumstance and culture he suggests that this literature reflects a general agreement about a number of fixed points and focal concerns. Foremost amongst these is the conviction that employment policy is the key issue in welfare reform. Unlike the traditional concern with securing full employment for men, the social challenge today is full employment for men *and women*.

> It points to the need to rethink both certain aspects of the architecture of the welfare state and the distribution of work over households and individuals as it spontaneously emerges in the labour market. (Vandenbrouke, 1999: 37)

The emerging welfare state should also cover new risks such as lack of skills and single parenthood, along with a recognition of new social needs, including the reconciliation of work, family life and education, and the negotiation of changes in both family and workplace over a person's 'entire life cycle' (Vandenbroucke, 1999: 37) An intelligent welfare state should respond to new needs and risks in an active and preventive way: it should be about social investment and not just the provision of compensatory social spending. Greater priority than hitherto should be given to active labour market policies tailored to individual needs and situations, policies which should seek to achieve a correct balance between incentives, opportunities and obligations. These policies should also try to avoid the poverty and unemployment traps associated with the disincentive effects of targeted taxes and benefits. (For a fuller discussion of this see the chapter on universalism and selectivism by Pratt in this book.)

Perhaps the newest element of the converged policy agenda discussed by Vandenbroucke is the much greater importance given to the augmentation of low paid work through minimum wages and wage subsidization. The apparent assumption that the state will continue to provide cash subsidies to low wages has attracted very little comment which is, perhaps, surprising given its intellectual and political significance. When this practice was first revived in 1970 in the form of the Family Income Supplements Act it attracted the wrath of the British Labour Party, then in opposition. Labour's concern was the traditional one that it would subsidize bad and inefficient employers and, in effect, represent the institutionalized pauperization of a significant proportion of the low paid. If Vandenbrouke is correct in his claims about the generality of wage subsidization it surely represents a major departure for political parties of the centre-left: a genuine reflection of the triumph of pragmatism over principle. The market will always produce low-paid jobs and better these than no jobs at all: all the state should do is to raise the incomes of the low paid in ways which take account of the family demands on the low wage, through a combination of minimum wage legislation and wage-subsidization. The continuing presence of these policies is again reflected in Vandenbrouke's observation that the new social democracy requires an economy which has not only a sector exposed to international competition, but also a private service sector not exposed to such competition in which the unskilled can find new jobs, probably subsidized by the state. Thus far, continental Europe lags behind the UK in this regard.

What is not so apparent at the moment in this revived and reconstructed social democracy is any general understanding of, and commitment to, the need for national governments, international economic organizations such as the IMF and the WTO, and regional agencies like the European Central Bank to respond to the normal fluctuations of the trade cycle. Notwithstanding the wishful thinking of the proselytizers of the 'new economics', the trade cycle has not been abolished. Unless there is collective and concerted action to respond to the decline in economic activity during cyclical downswings, unemployment will rise and there will be a reduction in the jobs available for the newly trained and re-moralized beneficiaries of active labour market policies. This is not a call for a return to the debased form of Keynesian demand management pursued by successive British governments during social democracy's earlier ascendancy, but a recognition that supply-side economics by itself is not enough. It is a call for social democratic politicians to recognize the validity of the claim that:

> The basis of Keynesian thinking is law, i.e. the one thing the Euro-left considers to be politically unimportant. It is about the intelligent application of the law and the adaptation of the legal framework to right the wrongs of the market. It is, above all, a recognition that the economy is a human creation, not a force of nature, and that what has been created can be adapted. (Atkinson and Elliott, 1999: 43–4)

Social democratic political leaders need to moderate their uncritical worship of the market as an institution and rediscover their commitment to the possibilities of politics for effecting significant changes in the distribution of resources and life-chances.

2.8 What kind of state?

A consistent theme in the new social democracy is a belief in the need to reconstruct the relationship between the state and civil society. It is argued that the traditional top-down approach typical of British social democracy, where the state decided what was good for people and then delivered it, resulted in a failure to meet the real needs and preferences of individuals and families. Similarly, neo-liberalism's attempts to break up public monopolies themselves led to a range of unacceptable consequences as service standards declined and inequalities spread. Thus a new set of mechanisms for service provision is required which avoids the failings of old social democracy and neo-liberalism, and which also reflects the growth of individualism and diversity. To use a current cliché: the state should 'steer more and row less'. As Coote says:

> One of the key features of a modern social democracy is that it has strong social objectives but a weak set of levers for achieving them. (Coote, 1999: 117)

Techniques and approaches are required which will actively involve people more in programme development and delivery rather than resting content with their role as passive recipients of public policy. The image is of myriad possibilities of form and mechanisms in an expanded and genuine mixed economy of welfare, one in which the interests of consumers/users/citizens are paramount.

The idea that an over-mighty state might abuse and ignore individuals and families is not new in left politics and theory. It brings to mind the distinction between the 'mechanical' reformism of the Fabians, with their insistence on expert, scientific solutions, and the 'moral' reformism of liberal socialism which always insisted on the need to involve the active support and involvement of civil society. However it must be remembered that centralized, top-down solutions were, in part, chosen as policy instruments because of the gaps and deficiencies that existed in social provision before the creation of the institutional model of state welfare. If we move to a more pluralistic model of welfare provision, one which actively seeks to involve the community and other agents of civil society as partners in programme development and delivery, what happens then to the idea of territorial justice, the belief that people have the right to roughly the same standard of service regardless of where they live? Does this mean that government will take on greater responsibility for laying down national standards of service and become a very active regulator as it seeks to secure compliance with these standards? If so, what price then for local autonomy and responsibility?

Although one of the reasons for looking to self-activating individuals and groups is to use their physical and organizational resources, thus reducing demands on the public purse, it is inevitable that government will continue to contribute a major part of the income needed by local groups, voluntary bodies and community organizations. It is very likely that this will bring with it serious questions of accountability which cannot be ignored. How is this problem to be overcome? Moreover, there can be no guarantee that newly empowered local organizations will not use their authority to discriminate against one or other section of the population. It may also be the case that unpopular causes (mental impairment, lone parent families for example) will find their needs ignored or marginalized.

If the concern of the new social democracy is to secure a much greater role for individual and group involvement is the appropriate answer necessarily to be found in the resources and agencies of civil society? Might a more appropriate solution not be found in a re-energized and democratized form of local government, one given responsibility for all areas of social provision (health, education, housing, social care etc.) other than income maintenance? With coterminous spatial boundaries, and with a legal requirement to involve citizens and civil society at all levels of policy development and delivery, this revived local government may be a more effective mechanism for meeting the genuine interests and needs of local populations than anything else yet suggested. It could more easily guarantee territorial justice; meet the demands for a transparent accountability; involve citizens and groups as active participants in a genuinely democratic political process; and create a renaissance in civic life. With expanded power and greater and more democratic participation, there is every chance of increased voter activity and, with this, a greater legitimacy of the whole enterprise. British social democracy could secure a return to its old convictions that local solutions were the best solutions, especially if they had democratic legitimacy and authority.

2.9 Conclusions

It is likely that the nature of the new social democracy outlined above will not be attractive to some, perhaps many, people who regard themselves as natural supporters of centre-left politics. With its emphasis on civic responsibility, earned rights, fair reciprocity and individual autonomy it will be criticized on the grounds that it concedes too much to the demands of global capitalism, and that it is imbued with a repressive moral authoritarianism. However, although these fears can be understood and recognized, the position adopted here is that it is possible and justifiable to claim that much of this new thinking is entirely consistent with the best traditions of social democracy.

Whether we like it or not the world has changed and social democrats are confronted by the realities of globalization, new technology, diversity and individualism. What matters surely is the nature of the response developed by those on the left who would challenge prevailing orthodoxies. Third Way theory offers little in terms of normative political principles and is too accepting of the market's demands: it makes too many concessions to be regarded as properly social democratic, but the other ideas examined in this chapter point to a new vision of social democracy.

This is a vision which is sensitive to the realities of the modern world but combines this sensitivity with a continuing attachment to recognizably social democratic values. Through its newly regained focus on fair reciprocity as a defining approach to distributive justice it reconnects with the moral collectivism of the Attlee government of 1945–51 and resonates with the instinctive beliefs of a majority of the population. Combined with a reconstructed approach to the state's relationship with civic society and a willingness to delegate accountable powers to a renewed local democracy this is a vision of politics with rich potential in the twenty-first century.

CHAPTER 3

NEO-LIBERALISM AND SOCIAL POLICY

Alan Pratt

3.1 Introduction

The purpose of this chapter is to consider one particular strand of liberal theory, that of possessive individualism, and its part in the rise of that set of ideas and values generally grouped together as the 'New Right'. Thus it is not an account of the full range of 'New Right' ideas, and consequently says nothing (except in passing) of neo-conservatism's espousal of monogamous sexual relations and the traditional two-parent family nor of its hostility to abortion, easier divorce laws, and same sex relationships, all of which have found a sympathetic home in the Republican Party in the USA and, to a lesser extent, in the British Conservative Party.

Instead, it attempts a synthesis of the economic and political theories, and the behavioural assumptions on which they rest, which have played such an important role in the sustained attack upon institutionalized welfare provision in Britain and the rest of the western industrial world. Although Britain will be the heart of our analysis it must be remembered that the ideas and theories we will be considering have had a resonance even in Sweden, that quintessential social democracy committed to the socialization of consumption.

This analysis is located in the changed economic circumstances of the early 1970s which saw successive western governments fail to maintain the full employment and economic growth which together provided the under-pinnings for the construction of post-1945 welfare states. It discusses the key individual components of the whole intellectual system, such as rationality, the supremacy of the market as an allocative mechanism, public choice theory, the public burden theory of welfare, government overload, and the superior morality of individual responsibility and self-reliance over the culture of dependency. After considering the consistency and coherence of these ideas the chapter concludes with an assessment of the extent to which this ideology has succeeded in creating a momentum towards a convergence of welfare systems based on a residualist model of state welfare and a larger role for voluntarism, the private market, and occupational welfare.

3.2 The context

> Consensus policies became increasingly inappropriate to Britain's evolving needs. They had to be either reformed or replaced. In the mid-1970s, they were, of course, to be replaced – ironically, by policies which closely resembled the very ones which had been perceived to fail in the 1930s. (Lowe, 1990: 182)

This extract from Lowe's essay on the historiography of the postwar consensus provides us with the basis of our agenda, which is about tracing and explaining the replacement of one intellectual paradigm by another. Although significant, if unplanned, progress had been made in British social provision during the inter-war period, it was chronic, involuntary unemployment that was the dominant problem of economic and social policy. It dwarfed every other aspect of domestic politics and, notwithstanding the work of revisionist historians of the period, <u>unemployment remains as the single most potent image and memory of that age.</u> The then dominant neo-classicism failed to provide any solutions and only slowly did a coherent and rigorous non-Marxist alternative emerge, and even then it took the transforming experience of total war to force even the smallest break in Treasury orthodoxy.

At the heart of social democracy was Keynes's critique of a central assumption of neo-classical economic theory, that full employment was a general case. In *The General Theory of Employment, Interest and Money* (1936), Keynes demonstrated that equilibrium could exist at a less than full employment level of output and, because the system was in equilibrium, unless exogenous intervention occurred chronic, involuntary unemployment would persist. If governments had the desire to reduce unemployment they now, thanks to Keynes, had the tools to do the job. Whatever its equivocations and failings, the 1944 White Paper on employment policy seemed to promise that henceforth public policy would be very different. The commitment it contained to 'a high and stable level of employment' can be seen as the most important single event of the reconstruction of the welfare state achieved by successive governments in the 1940s. Among other things it met the most important of the three 'assumptions' on which Beveridge executed his plans for social insurance and allied services. (The other two, of course, were the creation of a national health service and the introduction of a system of children's or family allowances.)

Just as the 1944 commitment to full employment symbolized the dawn of a new collectivist age with an active, interventionist government at its heart, so the abandonment of full employment, and the economic theories which had contributed to its creation, by Callaghan and Healey after 1976 can be seen as the harbinger of a new-old world, a world shaped and informed by exactly those theories which Keynes had apparently dethroned some 40 years before. In a very real sense the world had come full circle. Hayek, perhaps the twentieth century's most articulate and important classical liberal

voice, emerged from relative obscurity and became the single most important intellectual influence on the Conservative government which took office
in 1979. Hayek's influence was particularly significant on that government's
most creative thinker, Sir Keith Joseph. The ability of ideas by themselves to
effect significant changes in the strategic dispositions of public policy is necessarily limited by the objective realities of economic and social structures.
Hence Kavanagh's recollection of John Stuart Mill's observation that 'ideas
must conspire with circumstances if they are to be successful' (Kavanagh,
1990: 64).

3.3 The collapse of consensus

That the circumstances alluded to by Kavanagh altered in the 1970s seems
unquestionable, and in a relatively short period a paradigm shift occurred.
Moreover, there is general agreement about the nature of those changed circumstances. One of the most important achievements of international
economic policy after 1945 was the creation of an ordered pattern of relationships between trading nations based primarily on the system of fixed
exchange rates that emerged from the Bretton Woods Conference. Co-
operative and relatively free trade governed by institutions and structures
such as the World Bank and GATT, designed to prevent the competitive
devaluations and economic autarky that compounded the depression of the
1930s, was seen as the best hope for humankind. However, this ordered world
system could not cope with the instabilities generated by the fiscal demands
of American governments engaged in a war in Southeast Asia and a domestic war on poverty. The Smithsonian Agreement of December 1971 failed to
contain the pressure and in 1973 a new system of floating exchange rates
was introduced.

If, to these important institutional arrangements, we add the reality of
major technological change, an explosion in commodity prices (especially of
oil) and the ending of the long postwar boom, the sudden collapse of the
Keynesian system becomes understandable. As a consequence, a crisis in
state authority developed throughout the western industrial world and the
search began for a new analysis and for policy prescriptions more in tune
with this new world order. Britain, as the weakest of the world's major capitalist economies, experienced this crisis probably earlier and more intensely
than anywhere else. The failure of the corporatist attempts at modernization
in the 1960s meant that 'the existing policy regime was severely discredited
by the dramatic worsening of performance on unemployment, inflation, economic growth and the balance of trade' (Gamble, 1987: 192).

3.4 Neo-liberal theory: the substance

Although there are differences in emphasis and approach reflecting the predilections of individual writers, neo-liberal theory in general offers a coherent and consistent explanation of the way the world works and ought to work. Departures from the ideal can be quickly remedied if the old verities are reasserted and the proper relationships re-established between government and economy, between state and individual, between state and civil society, and between individuals themselves. Drawing especially on economics, politics, and philosophy, a powerful theoretical synthesis has been forged, one whose influence in the last 20 years has been immense across the whole range of industrial economies, offering a sense of direction and purpose in a world whose economic foundations have been transformed by revolutionary changes in technology and trading relationships. This section offers a synopsis of these ideas.

Assumptions

Although detailed aspects of neo-liberal theory can be intellectually complex the totality is relatively clear and simple, resting as it does on a very particular set of assumptions about human behaviour and institutions. Of these assumptions the most important are methodological individualism, rationality, and the supremacy of the free market.

Methodological individualism asserts that 'all phenomena are reducible to individual behaviour; organic entities such as "society" or the "state" are comprehensible only in terms of the activities of their constitutive individuals' (King, 1987: 94). In Margaret Thatcher's memorable phrase, there is no such thing as society. Free individuals go about their business within the general framework of the 'rule of law', knowing wherein their best interests lie, pursuing pleasure rather than pain. Embodied in contractual exchanges these individual pursuits produce a set of collective outcomes, which by themselves are neither good nor bad. They simply are. Others may take a moral position on these outcomes but methodological individualism would suggest that such positions are irrelevant. They belong to another realm.

The individual pursuit of self-interest only makes sense if individuals act rationally. So important is this assumption that without it the whole edifice of neo-liberal thought would be endangered. For, if individuals do not always behave in a rational fashion in all circumstances, what should we conclude about the nature of the outcomes of such behaviour? In this universe rationality is understood as the pursuit of perfectly informed self-interest. Any other kind of behaviour is inconceivable.

The perfect arena in which rational, self-interested, perfectly informed individuals should meet is the market. Markets as institutions are good; perfect markets are perfect. Markets are about exchange, and for neo-liberals exchange relationships are supreme, far outweighing the claims of other kinds of relationship such as political transactions. Although sometimes mistakenly understood as being a synonym for capitalism, markets long pre-date the capitalist mode of production. They have existed since the first act of trade took place. They make trade possible and are the best institutional setting for the generation of wealth. Given these assumptions we can now move on to a consideration of the major elements of neo-liberal thought.

Economics

The market

In essence, neo-liberal theory hardly differs from the classical political economy developed by Adam Smith, David Ricardo, and their disciples in the late eighteenth and early nineteenth centuries. At its heart is a belief that the market is the best institution yet created by human agency for the conduct of economic activity. Individuals bring their preferences to markets and the aggregate weight of consumer preference can compel suppliers of all kinds of commodities to comply with consumers' demands. Failure to comply will guarantee the failure of any company foolish enough to behave in such a way. Given freedom of entry into the market, other potential suppliers are always available who will recognize the fact of consumer sovereignty. These characteristics make markets efficient, sensitive, and speedy signalling mechanisms, doing spontaneously that which is impossible for the planning structures of command economies. Modern industrial societies are such vast and complex entities that the idea of a government taking responsibility for the myriad decisions necessarily involved in the allocation of resources is foolish. It is beyond the capacity of governments to do what markets do. Hayek (1944) derided the whole concept of government planning, and argued that any and every attempt to replace the market with a system of politically administered decision-making was bound to end in tyranny and disaster. The collapse of the economies of the former Soviet bloc, the enormous changes that have taken place in the economy of the People's Republic of China, and the retreat of managed economies everywhere all testify to this. Capitalism has triumphed, and free market capitalism in particular.

In markets decision-making is delegated to the lowest possible level, that of the individual consumer and firm, and this decentralization of decision-making not only renders unnecessary the complex and overstaffed public bureaucracies of non-market economies (at a great saving in public expenditure) but also produces outcomes which are autonomous, spontaneous and, because they represent the choices of free, perfectly informed, and rational individuals, valid. In markets, freedom of choice is guaranteed and respected; not to respect it would result in loss of profit and potential bankruptcy. As Marquand notes, 'in the market-liberal ideal, free men, freely exchanging goods and services without intervention by the state, maximize the general interest by pursuing their own interests' (Marquand, 1987: 66). For neo-liberals the question is not so much what goods be allocated through the market but what goods can the state, and the state alone, provide. It is concerned with the nature of public goods. If we can clearly establish the identity of truly public goods then it must follow, given the superiority of the market as an institution for the allocation of resources, that all other goods can, and should, be provided through the market. Although there are differences of emphasis in the work of individual neo-liberal theorists, the general outlines of agreement are clear. Typical of them is Seldon, who argues that public goods have characteristics that distinguish them from other goods. Public goods are:

1   supplied collectively rather than separately to individuals or small groups;
2   provided by general agreement to pay jointly, 'that is, they require voluntary collective arrangements to coerce one another and also individuals who do not want the services at all but who cannot help benefiting from them' (Seldon, 1977: 17);
3   non-rival in the sense that until full capacity is reached they can be used by more and more people at no additional cost;
4   for Seldon though, 'the essential characteristic of public goods is that they cannot be refused to people who refuse to pay, and who would otherwise have a "free" ride if they were not required to pay. Public goods, to be provided at all, cannot therefore be produced in response to individual specification in the market: they must be financed collectively by the method known as taxation' (Seldon, 1977: 18–19).

Given the validity of the criteria advanced by Seldon, is it possible to establish a list of functions which only the state can perform? Through the application of the 'free rider' principle Seldon identifies the commodities and services which can properly be described as public goods. It is not a lengthy list, and comprises defence, a system of law and order, protection against contagious disease, and what he describes as 'a not obvious but important one: the production of knowledge and information' (Seldon, 1977: 19). Street lighting, lighthouses, and externality problems such as pollution, together with provision to protect children and the mentally infirm, are sometimes added to extend the list slightly.

The expansion of the state's role to include the provision of services other than true public goods is the hallmark of what has been termed the 'interventionist state' (Hall, 1984). This expansion, which normally includes education, healthcare, housing, a variety of income maintenance programmes and the personal social services, has led to a very substantial increase in public expenditure's share of national income in all OECD countries in the twentieth century but especially since the end of the Second World War. The implications of this rising trend of expenditure for public finances, and for the efficiency of the market economies within which this expansion has been located, is a particular concern of neo-liberal political economy.

The problem of public expenditure

In 1979 the first public expenditure statement of the incoming Conservative government asserted that 'excessive' public expenditure lay at the root of Britain's economic problems. In this it was no different from its predecessor led by Edward Heath in 1970, which came to power armed with exactly the same economic philosophy as that which later became known as 'Thatcherism'. The manifestos on which the Conservatives fought the 1970 and 1979 general elections share the same economic analysis and advocate the same prescriptions for recovery, with the exception that in 1970 monetarism had not yet become politically fashionable (it never became very popular among economists at British universities who, by a substantial majority, remained broadly Keynesian in disposition).

Public expenditure is invariably seen as a major problem, a real and present threat to economic efficiency. Hence the popularity of the public burden theory of welfare with all neo-liberal theorists. As governments moved further and further away from their proper concern with the provision of public goods and took on responsibilities that ought to have remained with individuals in markets they inevitably found themselves engaged in a competitive conflict with the private, productive sector of the economy for available scarce resources. In this conflict there could be only one winner. Governments could offer a guaranteed return on the loans they sought from the financial markets; the private sector could not. The public sector was also in competition for skilled and educated labour, and even though it could not always match the salaries available in the private sector, both job security and guaranteed, inflation proof pensions could always sugar that particular pill. In brief, wealth creating activity in the traded goods sector was, 'crowded out' (Bacon and Eltis, 1976). If this process was allowed to continue, negative sum welfare-efficiency interactions were a certainty (Geiger, 1979). In other words, the productive ability of the economy would be compromised by the public sector's excessive demands. Taxation and government expenditure are regarded as burdens having to be borne by commerce and industry in the private sector, the only real source of genuine wealth creation.

The expansive and expensive welfare regimes of social democracy place a great strain on governments' revenue raising capacity. Impelled by the insatiable demands of greedy electorates and self-interested bureaucrats intent only on empire building, governments have to tax and borrow more and more. The level of direct taxation is of particular concern to neo-liberal economists. If personal and company taxation is too high at the margin, incentives will be damaged. Why should employees work harder and take on more responsibility if they know that the net advantage to them of the marginal pound they earn is going to be significantly reduced by the government's depredations? In neo-liberal theory there is the certainty that high marginal rates of income tax and high rates of corporation tax reduce work incentives and discourage risk taking. The end result is bound to be an economy in which productivity declines, output is reduced, and innovation and investment are both discouraged. Negative-sum welfare efficiency interactions are the norm. In order to reverse this debilitating decline it is essential that governments reduce the rates of these direct taxes on individuals and companies. Incentives would then be restored and augmented, and risk taking and investment both encouraged. As a consequence, output and real incomes would both increase and Britain's long, relative decline would be halted.

For neo-liberals the dismal reality of a high-tax, low-growth economy is compounded by the consequences of a benefit-earnings ratio skewed in favour of benefits. It has been argued that one of the avoidable causes of high levels of unemployment is that people in receipt of benefit will not consider taking one of the large number of low-paid jobs that are available because the wages such employment would generate are not noticeably higher than benefit income levels and would not compensate them for the effort, time, and energy they would have to expend in the labour market. Being rational, they will tend to prefer the leisure of unemployment to the demands of work. The neo-liberal solution to this dilemma is not to increase earnings through measures such as a minimum wage (this would only add to the costs of employers, especially small companies, in what are usually very competitive sectors of the economy and create more unemployment) but to reduce benefits and make them more difficult to claim (Minford, 1987). The labour market implications of income maintenance programmes have always been a critical concern for all types and forms of political economy, but for the neo-liberal this concern is definitive.

The labour market

Labour is a commodity like any other and therefore susceptible to market operations. The larger market contains a market for labour, and that market can be cleared if the price of labour – that is, its wages – is determined by the normal market forces of demand and supply. If the market is left to its own devices and not distorted by government intervention (through the provision of a minimum wage and the operation of wages councils) and the activities of powerful trade unions equipped with significant legal immunities, the tendency would be towards little or no involuntary unemployment. There would always be frictional and structural unemployment of course; these are the desirable and natural features of any dynamic market economy as people change jobs and employers in their search for better wages and conditions and as old industries decline and new ones emerge in response to new technologies and changing tastes. If involuntary unemployment does exist it is because of 'artificial' rigidities in the labour market occasioned by the behaviour of organized labour. Therefore, for the neo-liberal, the battle against unemployment should be dominated by an assault on the bargaining power of trade unions and their privileged position in law. This would assist the necessary progress back towards a 'natural' rate of unemployment in a deregulated and flexible labour market. Any other approach is doomed to failure in the long run. Keynesian inspired attempts to force unemployment below its natural, market-determined rate might secure some temporary success but in the long run there would be greater inflation as governments resorted to deficit financing and pump-priming to stimulate aggregate demand, and ultimately higher unemployment. As Hayek put it, 'unemployment has been made inevitable by past inflation; it has merely been *postponed* by accelerating inflation' (quoted in Marquand, 1987: 86).

Inflation

The suppression and control of inflation is the key policy objective of neo-liberal economics. Secure it and a multitude of benefits will flow. Regular, sustainable increments to economic growth, low unemployment, rising disposable real income, and even improvements in the quality of justifiable public services can only be secured if inflation is conquered. If this means temporary hardship and suffering for some, as the toxin of Keynesianism is expelled, it is a necessary experience. As Norman Lamont said, unemployment is a price worth paying.

The precise nature of the alleged relationship between excessive public expenditure and inflation has varied over time. All that neo-liberals are sure of is that there is a causal relationship. If governments cannot raise all the revenue they need to fund their welfare commitments from taxation and charges then they have to resort to borrowing. If the public sector borrowing requirement (PSBR) is high and/or rising as a percentage of GNP, the government may be forced to raise interest rates to induce the finance markets to take up the stocks and bonds on offer. A general increase in the cost of borrowing will have potentially serious implications for business activity as costs increase, and for the politically sensitive housing market as well. If market conditions permit manufacturers will be tempted to pass on their higher costs to customers in the form of higher prices. If market conditions are depressed it will not be as easy to increase prices and business operations may have to be scaled down. Either way the news is bad. Similarly, an increase in housing costs could lead to potentially inflationary wage claims as workers seek to make good this implicit cut in their real incomes.

If governments are unable to meet their borrowing requirements in this way they have the option of resorting to a form of borrowing which can be used by the banking system to expand its credit base and thus increase the supply of money in the economy. For economists such as Friedman the most significant long-term cause of inflation is an expansion of the money supply beyond that dictated by market-led economic activity. After a time lag of around two years an increase in money supply generated by avoidable government borrowing will lead to an increase in the general price level: there is a mechanistic, causal link between money supply and the price level.

In their earlier years the governments led by Margaret Thatcher were particularly enamoured of Friedman's version of monetarism, an attachment which manifested itself in the adoption of a Medium Term Financial Strategy (MTFS), which incorporated clear, fixed targets for monetary growth, targets which were in line with expectations of growth rates in the real economy. While monetary aggregates are clearly an important feature of any economic theory, and have always been recognized as such, for neo-liberal economists they are critical. However, this aspect of neo-liberal economics in many ways has proved to be the most disappointing feature of the theory as a whole. There was much discussion, and no general agreement, about what constituted a proper definition of M (the money supply) in monetarists' equations, and in the real world of economic policy it proved very difficult to control any definition of M at all. Eventually the MTFS was abandoned and with it went one of the central planks of monetarist theory.

Despite this failure the control of inflation remains the key objective of neo-liberal economic theory. Inflation, as measured by the Retail Price Index, is at its lowest level for over 30 years and only a fraction of the peaks reached in the 1970s. There is even a suggestion that inflationary pressures have been squeezed out of the system completely. British inflation still remains at the top end of the range for nations within the European Union and, as we have noted, it is very unlikely that the government will relax its stance.

Activity 3.1

In what ways do neo-liberals' behavioural assumptions affect their views on the economy?

3.5 Neo-iberalism: aspects of political philosophy

'When properly presented, their arguments strike at the heart of the normative assumptions of the post-war welfare state' (Plant, 1990: 7). Inevitably, the
value premises of neo-liberalism are determined by its assumptions.
Methodological individualism, rationality, and a preference for the free
market are as important here as they are in its economics. Indeed, economics
and philosophy are part of the seamless web that is neo-liberal political economy. Plant's analysis of the normative content of neo-liberalism provides a
perceptive and coherent framework which we can use to develop a relatively
complete synthesis of neo-liberalism's values and preferences (Plant, 1990).

Liberty

For Hayek liberty was the supreme value, far outweighing any other, be it
democracy or social justice, or fraternity. The great tragedy of modern
European civilization was the gradual retreat from the understanding of liberty developed by British liberals from Locke onwards in face of the advance
of the German tradition of an authoritarian, interventionist state possessed of
a belief in its right to shape the economic and social destiny of its citizens. It
posited a belief in the existence of a discernible 'national' interest which could
be pursued and achieved through a range of specific programmes and instruments. For the classical and neo-liberal, 'market relationships are freer, more
spontaneous, in a strange way more authentic than political relationships:
market power does not exist, while the state is, by definition, the realm of
power and domination' (Marquand, 1987: 67).

Hayek argues that after 1870 the tide turned against liberalism; increasingly, planning and regulation became the new lodestones, deployed in the
interest of a chimerical equality and social justice. Possibly Hayek chose 1870
because it marked the triumph of Prussia in its war with France and the consequent emergence of a new, unified German state under Prussian leadership
and with Prussian traditions (Hayek, 1944). As an emigré Austrian intellectual
Hayek was well qualified to point out the dangers of authoritarian collectivism, especially in conditions of mass unemployment, and its attendant
social tensions. His passion for liberty and suspicion of democracy are characteristics present in a great deal of neo-liberal writing, and, as we shall see
later, they are characteristics which present neo-liberal theorists with some
very real dilemmas. Hayek, though, had no doubts; liberty should triumph in
every contest.

Since the emergence of liberal collectivist thought in the last quarter of the
nineteenth century in the work of Green, Hobson, Hobhouse and Ritchie,
there has been an assumption about the relationship between liberty and

welfare. Liberal collectivists moved beyond the formal, procedural notions of liberty central to classical liberalism such as those attached to civil, political, and legal rights, and asserted a positive as opposed to negative concept of liberty. In the twentieth century the idea has become associated with the notion of an equal worth of liberty (Plant, 1985). Thus, liberty is inextricably bound up with access to those resources and experiences essential to the living of a full and civilized life, like education, health, housing, and a guaranteed income, in fact those resources whose distribution is perhaps the most important feature of modern welfare states. To paraphrase Tawney (1931), the pauper and the prince are both formally free to dine at the Ritz. In reality, of course, one can and the other cannot because, in markets, access is determined by command over resources. If we substitute education, health, housing, and a guaranteed income for dinner at the Ritz, then the conclusions are obvious. Just as war is too important to be left to the generals so is access to the formative experiences of modern life too important to be left to the market. Hayek recognized the significance of linking the freedom to act with the ability to act. It provided a powerful basis for arguing that vertical redistribution of resources should be sought, because to do so would increase the worth of liberty enjoyed by those at the bottom end of the initial, market-determined distribution of income by enhancing their ability to act. This switch from a negative to a positive concept of liberty within the liberal tradition was a significant factor in the growth of the interventionist state in late nineteenth-century Britain with the consequent movement from the free market and minimal state ideal of classical liberalism.

Neo-liberals reject the idea of positive liberty, liberty as power and opportunity, and reaffirm their commitment to the older interpretation. Their position has nowhere been better expressed than in the following statement: 'Liberty is liberty, not something else. And the slave is a slave: you do not set him free by feeding him' (Joseph and Sumption, 1979, quoted in Pope et al., 1986: 221). Negative liberty therefore is the only valid approach. Liberty means the absence of coercion and market outcomes are unforeseen. They are not the consequence of a deliberate political judgement made by those with the authority and power to determine such outcomes. The free market cannot restrict or otherwise impinge on liberty. Market outcomes are the consequence of individual choices made by rational beings with the intent of maximizing individual satisfaction. These individual decisions in markets become powerful aggregates whose signals cannot be ignored by suppliers. The results may mean that some people get more than others, that there is inequality, but there is no compulsion involved; no political authority has intervened. As Hayek has observed, individuals are still free to try to improve their position by any means open to them provided that such actions are legal, do not coerce others, and that all such actions are governed by the overarching 'rule of law' providing transparent, known, and generally understood procedures. Life may be unfair. Some may be luckier than others. Talents and resources may be unequally distributed. There may be suffering, but in market economies people are always free to try again using whatever abilities and energy they possess.

Social justice

The positive liberty of liberal collectivism demands a rigorous, clearly articulated and generally accepted concept of social justice to serve as the criterion through which resources can be allocated by non-market mechanisms. If market forces are to be modified or dispensed with, the least that is needed is a valid basis on which to intervene. Neo-liberals reject the possibility of such a notion. Hayek was contemptuous of every attempt to develop an operational concept of social justice and dismissed them as self-indulgent posturing (Hayek, 1944). Because market outcomes are unintended they cannot be unjust since social injustice can only be caused by intentional acts. Consequently, 'the moral demands of social justice evaporate' (Plant, 1990: 11). Social justice as a concept lacks specificity. There are many possible criteria of social justice (need, merit, desert and so on), but in a free society there can be no general agreement about which criterion should be used as the operational basis of resource allocation. Therefore:

1 Because of the absence of agreed criteria, allocation through non-market methods will be arbitrary and discretionary. 'This will mean that at the very heart of the public policy of a welfare state will lie the arbitrary and discretionary power of welfare bureaucrats and experts charged with the impossible task of distributing resources according to intrinsically unspecific criteria' (Plant, 1990: 11).
2 Because of the absence of known and agreed criteria there will be selfish and destructive competition by interest groups for resources. It is the relative power of interest groups that will be significant in the allocation of scarce resources. The powerful will inevitably win.

For all these reasons illusory ideas about social justice should be abandoned and the market liberated from government intervention. If a welfare state had to remain in place then it should be a residual one providing a minimum safety net for those who were not able to compete or operate in the market.

Consistent libertarians such as Nozick would, of course, dispense with any kind of welfare state (Nozick, 1974).

Rights

The idea that people possess welfare rights as a constitutive element of citizenship is essential to the liberal collectivist/social democratic view of the welfare state (Marshall, 1950). In contrast, neo-liberals totally reject the idea of social or welfare rights. They see a clear and fundamental distinction between the civil and political rights at the core of classical liberalism and the more recent claim of alleged rights to welfare. These traditional rights which liberals have asserted for centuries all imply negative duties of forbearance rather than the commitment of resources to substantiate them. The reality of scarce resources implies a limit to the exercise of rights which demand that resources are made available to fulfil them. The resource implications of recognizing that citizens have rights to a certain amount of healthcare, education, income and so on are immense. On the other hand, civil rights are categorical and absolute. To claim that people have rights to welfare demands that we have a view of needs, and the probability is that such views will tend to be open ended with clear consequences for governments trying to decide between the validity of a range of competing claims on resources. There is certain to be intense interest group competition for these resources, and opportunity cost means that meeting one group's claim will lead to the neglect of some other group. The lack of agreed criteria to distinguish between these claims must lead to anger and frustration, and possibly to the erosion of faith in the political institutions of liberal democracy.

Poverty

Neo-liberals adopt an absolute concept of poverty rather than a relative one. Given this, their belief is that there is very little, if any, poverty in modern Britain (Joseph and Sumption, 1979). A free market economy, liberated from the debilitating effects of government intervention, an institutional welfare state, and the burden of high taxes is much the best mechanism for helping the poor; more precisely, of helping the poor to help themselves. Market economies do generate inequalities; in fact the existence of inequalities is a significant part of the motive force of market economies, but they are far more successful than any other form of economic system for the generation of wealth and jobs. The greater productive power of market economies will do more than anything else to improve the real living standards of the poor, not least through the trickle-down effect and the greater demand for labour. Poor people need the opportunity to work their way out of poverty and to break free from the culture of dependency which disfigures their humanity.

Culture and values

If the poor are to be weaned away from welfare dependency and reintro-
duced to the world of enterprise, risk, and work, it is essential that the role of
the free market is expanded and the values of the enterprise culture prosely-
tized. Neo-liberals believe that poverty is not caused by a dysfunctional
economic system, nor by a dysfunctional social system. Poverty is culturally
determined through the values, mores, attitudes and lack of aspirations transmitted across generations. Ergo, if the policy objective is to improve the
conditions of the poor, then the behaviour of the poor themselves must be
changed. Welfare dependency saps initiative, enterprise, autonomy and the
sense of being responsible for one's own destiny. If we remove the resources
that encourage dependency and restructure social policy so that people are
moved off welfare and prepared instead for the world of work, then we can
begin that process of cultural transformation essential to a real attack on
poverty – real because it treats the causes and not the symptoms. Such a
change might result in some initial discomfort but the prize of an economically dynamic and remoralized society is one worth securing.

3.6 Public choice theory: the apotheosis of the rational egoist

It has been argued that both the novelty and the real cutting edge of neo-
liberalism is to be found not in its economic theory, which, as we have seen,
is not new anyway, but in its view of politics. The promises of Keynesian
social democracy were based on the belief that government was inherently
benign and inherently competent. 'The real originality and power of present
day neo-liberalism lie in its attempt to turn that central presupposition on its
head' (Marquand, 1987: 75).

The economic consequences of liberal democracies are determined by the
nature of political activity in these societies, the major features of which are
the existence of competitive party politics, mass electorates, and well-
entrenched, well-organized interest groups. In this situation, market failure (a
reason for government intervention in the first place) is less likely than government failure. Although neo-liberalism is not a monolithic creed it can be
understood as a cluster of related ideas and attitudes which share the same
underlying theme of 'overload'. The system cannot cope with the excessive
demands generated by the politics of Keynesian social democracy. As governments provide more, electorates demand more. In consequence,
governments overreach themselves.

'The result was a paradox. Big government turned out to be ineffective
government. The more it tried to do, the more it failed. The more it failed, the
more it lost authority. The more authority it lost, the more it failed'

(Marquand, 1987: 73). Public choice theory is a microcosm of neo-liberal political economy, resting in a particularly intense way on the same behavioural assumptions. In King's words: 'The emphasis is on the micro-economic assumptions of actors (egoism, self-interest) and context (a perfect political "market"), with utility maximization and rational action by the parties also assumed' (1987: 100).

Downs's (1957) central assumption was that political parties develop policy objectives in order to win elections rather than to consummate some vision of the public good. They are reactive rather than proactive.

Given the assumption of rational self-interest the sceptic can be forgiven for asking why individuals can safely be left to express their own wishes in the economic market place but not in the political one. Surely, what is good for the consumer is also good for the voter? They are, after all, the same people, and rationality is a general assumption. The neo-liberal response is that there is a fundamental difference between the economic and political markets. In the former, consumers are constrained by an awareness of their own resource limitations; therefore they can be relied on to act with caution. In the latter, voters are under no such inhibition since in democracies majority opinion will prevail. Voters do not directly pay as individuals for the policies they 'buy' (vote for). Even if a voter prefers cheaper policies to expensive ones, she or he will have to pay her or his share of the expensive policies, if that is what voters want. Marquand illustrates the problem well with his restaurant analogy:

> He is like a skinflint, dining in an expensive restaurant with a party of friends, who have agreed to share the bill equally between them. However tight-fisted he may be, it is not rational for him to order the cheapest items on the menu. If he does, he will probably end by subsidizing his fellow diners. It makes more sense for him to opt for the caviar and champagne. (1987: 76)

This destructive pursuit of self-interest by individuals as voters creates a dilemma for public choice theorists. Liberty is the prime value and the free market is the institution most likely to protect economic freedom. Similarly, democratic politics, based on universal adult suffrage, is in one sense synonymous with liberty. We choose our rulers in free elections and, if they fail to please us, we can remove them. However, the selfish, if rational, behaviour of individuals as voters is an important cause of the system overload observable in all liberal democracies. How then can people be prevented from damaging or destroying that institution, the free market economy, wherein they can find the best opportunity of fulfilling themselves as individuals and which is also the best guarantor of that liberty which is the supreme political value?

In public choice theory bureaucrats cannot be expected to lay a restraining hand on the excesses of democratic politics. After all, they share the same behavioural characteristics of all the other actors in the drama, voters, parties and interest groups. The idealized norm, characteristic of received wisdom, of the disinterested, objective public servant, impervious to any shred of self-interest, is a fiction. Bureaucrats are just like the rest of us; greedy, vain, ambitious, and keen to follow their own interests. Occasionally those interests might coincide with the public good (if such a thing exists) but the bureaucrat is more likely to judge success by the size of the departmental budget and the number of people on the payroll.

Many neo-liberal writers have proposed a series of institutional changes which would transform the nature of political life in liberal democracies. These include constitutional amendments to enforce a balanced budget and the establishment of an independent commission to control the money supply. Not unexpectedly, Hayek has made the most radical suggestions with his scheme for limiting the suffrage to those over the age of 45 and excluding civil servants, old-age pensioners, and the unemployed. The legislature elected through this process of less than universal suffrage would have its members in place for 15 years and would content itself with laying down general rules for the conduct of business. Administration would be left to a subordinate assembly whose decisions would only be binding if they conformed to the general rules of the legislature. As Marquand goes on to note, if 'the source of the problem is democracy, how can it be solved democratically?' (1987: 81).

Activity 3.2

After reading the last two sections:
1 What services do you think a neo-liberal would argue should be the state's responsibility?
2 What, in their view, should be the responsibility of the individual?
3 How do they justify these allocations?

3.7 From idea to practice: the role of 'think tanks'

Ideas may provide penetrating insights into the nature of economic and social reality, but they also need effective transmission mechanisms to ease their progress from university departments to public policy initiative. Politicians need to be captured and bureaucracies permeated. One of the most significant features of the political landscape in the last 20 years has been the proliferation of neo-liberal 'think tanks', impelled not just by a desire to proselytize but also by a determination to destroy the social democratic/liberal collectivist paradigm. Of the major liberal democracies perhaps only Germany has been free from their influence, an influence which has become paramount in the politics of Australia, Britain, Canada and the USA (see, for example, King, 1987; Kavanagh, 1990; Self, 1993).

Equipped with substantial financial backing from big business they have succeeded in creating networks of formal and informal contacts linking intellectuals, the media, bureaucrats and politicians. In so doing they have been equally successful in changing the policy agenda in many countries. Their ability to do this has been facilitated by the failure of the left to create similar structures. In Britain, for example, the Institute for Public Policy Research, so active in the proceedings of the Commission on Social Justice, was founded only in 1988, by which time the neo-liberal critique was already well-established and successful in shifting the policy terrain to the right.

Although the British think tanks all share a profound distaste for the interventionist state, they have favourite individual themes. Thus, the Institute of Economic Affairs (IEA), founded in 1957, initially provided an organizational base and publishing house for bringing the individualist, free market ideas of Hayek and Friedman to a wider audience. Later on the IEA publicized the public-choice theorists such as Niskanen and Buchanan. The Adam Smith Institute, created in 1977, is libertarian on social and political issues and is particularly associated with the policy of privatization of public sector industries and services. The Social Affairs Unit, set up in 1980 by Digby Anderson and his associates, shares the same philosophical assumptions as the IEA and from the outset has applied this analysis to the public provision of social welfare. In Anderson's words, 'just as it [the IEA] attacked a sclerotic consensus in economics, we wanted to do something similar on social policy' (Kavanagh, 1990: 85). The remaining important body, the Centre for Policy Studies, was formed in 1974 by Margaret Thatcher and Sir Keith Joseph with the specific intent of pushing the Conservative Party towards a free market, individualist line after what they regarded as the disastrous betrayals of the Heath government, of which, it should be remembered, they were both leading figures.

The ideas and programmes advocated by these organizations have informed every single area of economic and social policy in Britain since 1979 and have helped to shift the centre-left to a much more pro-market, low tax position.

3.8 Neo-iberalism: summary and concluding assessment

How are we to assess the success or failure of the neo-liberal critique of the Keynesian-Beveridgean welfare state? To do this we need to form some judgement of the approach in its own terms, of how successful it has been in achieving its general and particular objectives.

A good place to begin is by asking whether there has been a paradigm shift. Do intellectuals, politicians, policy makers and the public in general now view the world in a different way than they did 20 years ago? The evidence would suggest that the answer must be a qualified 'yes', although the extent to which this change is a consequence of structural imperatives such as economic globalization and the continuing revolution in technology, or the superiority of neo-liberal theory itself in explaining the significance and meaning of these structural changes must remain to some extent a matter of personal choice. As evidence of this sea change we can point to the acceptance by left-of-centre political parties of the market as an allocative instrument with much to recommend it, indeed in many cases as one to be preferred over non-market mechanisms. To some extent this change has taken place everywhere but is perhaps most obvious in France and Spain, and latterly in Australia, and Britain where under the leadership of Tony Blair, New Labour has become a social democratic rather than a socialist party (see Chapter 2). So significant has been this transformation that some political scientists have felt it appropriate to talk in terms of the 'Thatcherization of the Labour Party'. In this view the Labour Party is attempting to present itself as the party of low and fair taxation: of being opposed to any significant increase in public expenditure as a share of GNP; of accepting the creation of quasi-markets in health, education, and the personal social services; and of being opposed to the return of the privatized utilities into public ownership.

At a general theoretical level, then, neo-liberalism seems to have been successful in changing the nature of mainstream political debate and in recasting the ways in which we think about the respective responsibilities of the individual and the state. We turn now to a brief assessment of neo-liberal ideas in two of the most important substantive areas of policy concern, the economy and the welfare state.

In order to address this second general issue it is perhaps appropriate to consider a statement made in 1979 when the first of Mrs Thatcher's governments, in its first public expenditure White Paper, asserted that excessive public spending lay at the heart of Britain's economic problems, and expressed its determination to reduce state spending. That public expenditure takes up a similar share of GNP now as it did in 1979 is not so much a consequence of neo-liberal theory as an indication of the demands generated by structural factors such as an ageing population.

Having looked at public expenditure it is now time to turn to taxation. Although there has been a significant reduction in levels of direct taxation with a basic rate of 21 per cent and a highest rate of 40 per cent, this reduction has been matched by a significant increase in indirect taxes such as VAT and the duties levied on petrol, tobacco, and alcoholic drinks. Taxation as a proportion of GNP is now about 1 per cent higher than it was in 1979, but the structure of that taxation, the balance between direct and indirect taxes, has altered profoundly, a development which reflects the importance of low rates of direct taxes in neo-liberal theory.

After reaching consistently high levels for much of the 1980s and much of the 1990s, under the chancellorships of Kenneth Clarke and Gordon Brown unemployment has fallen significantly over the last five years, and has been accompanied by the creation of a flexible, deregulated labour market, one in which casual and part-time employment have become widespread. Industrial relations in this labour market have been transformed by a series of eight Employment Acts whose collective impact has been to reduce trade unions to their weakest position since before the First World War. These changes to the labour market and the reform of industrial relations are a direct consequence of the application of neo-liberal theory.

Perhaps the greatest success of neo-liberal theory can be found in its colonization of much of New Labour's economic policy. Thus, notwithstanding mounting evidence of the failure of many aspects of the privatization programme, the present government is determined to extend that policy into hitherto uncharted areas such as the air traffic control system. Despite opinion survey evidence that there is majority support for taking the rail industry back into public ownership there appears to be very little evidence that the government is even thinking about such a measure. New Labour seems to have absorbed into its bloodstream all of neo-liberalism's belief in market mechanisms and its rejection of public enterprise.

Thirdly, in the arena of social policy, although the institutions of the welfare state (in the shape of the National Health Service, education free at the point of use, a social security system, personal social services and a much reduced social housing sector) remain intact, there have been great changes in the nature of the policy instruments used to deliver public social provision. Neo-liberal theory, particularly in its themes of markets and choice, has been the major motive force in securing these changes. These have been considered in some detail in the third section of this chapter.

We began these conclusions by suggesting that at the intellectual level there has indeed been a paradigm shift and that neo-liberal ideas now dominate in policy discussion. We have also noted that there are signs that neo-liberalism's dominance is now beginning to be challenged in a serious and sustained way. It is profoundly ironic that this challenge has been nowhere as systematic as in New Zealand where a Labour government has been attempting to overturn years of neo-liberal policy through the application of distinctly 'old' Labour policies. Whether this presages a more general change in political attitudes must await the unfolding of events throughout the world.

CHAPTER 4

MARXISM AND SOCIAL WELFARE

Michael Lavalette

4.1 The world today: the billionaires versus the billions

The modern world is richer and produces more wealth than was thought possible even a generation ago. In 1848, in the *Communist Manifesto*, Marx and
Engels wrote: 'The bourgeoisie, during its rule of scarce one hundred years,
has created more massive and more colossal productive forces than have all
preceding generations together' (1998: 15). Today this quotation seems almost
quaint. When Marx and Engels wrote these words, capitalism existed in
Britain, parts of Western Europe, and the eastern seaboard of America – today
it is a truly global system, dominant everywhere. As Susan George notes:
'The world now produces in less than two weeks the equivalent of the entire
physical output of the year 1900. Economic output . . . doubles approximately
every 25 to 30 years' (1999: 7). Such wealth creates fantastic possibilities.
Improvements in agricultural techniques, for example, make it possible to
feed the world's population several times over. Technological developments
and medical breakthroughs mean we could eradicate many killer diseases.
The world wide web creates the possibility of significant spread of information, education, and knowledge. The production of a range of basic
commodities mean we could easily provide people across the globe with
decent, well-built, insulated homes, with appropriate sanitation and running
water. It gives us the possibility to provide high speed, publicly owned, and
integrated transport systems that are environmentally friendly. And it could
allow us to cut working hours, improve working conditions, and expand
and improve upon leisure facilities for all.

Yet despite the world's wealth it is common to turn on our televisions and
see people starving, or being forced to migrate from their homes, or their children dying from preventable and curable illnesses. The tragedy is that
society's vast wealth is not used to improve the lives of the overwhelming
majority. Instead the priorities of the system are to protect the wealth and
power of a tiny minority of already wealthy and powerful individuals.
At the top of the heap are the 450-dollar billionaires, at the bottom the 3
billion who live on less than £1.30 a day – the assets of the top 200 richest
people constituting more than the combined wealth of 41 per cent of the
world's population (Health Matters, 2000: 2). At the end of 1999, when the

World Trade Organization (WTO) met in Seattle to discuss how best to expand and deepen world trade for the benefit of multinational capital and the already wealthy advanced capitalist economies, the *Observer* (28 November 1999) noted that if the richest 200 people gave up a mere 1 per cent of their annual income, every child across the globe could have a fully funded primary education. And yet, to protect the wealth of the wealthy in the USA, one of President George W. Bush's first commitments was to a multibillion dollar 'missile defence system', in addition to a $1billion pay increase for the military and a $20 billion boost for other high-tech weaponry (*The Guardian*, 9 January 2001). At the same time 840 million people worldwide are mal-nourished; 2.6 billion people lack access to basic sanitation and one quarter of the global burden of disease is due to preventable or easily curable diseases such as measles, worm infections, and malaria (Health Matters, 2000: 2/3). Table 4.1 presents a stark breakdown of annual expenditure of various goods to emphasize the point.

Table 4.1   The world's priorities (annual expenditure)

Basic Education	$6bn
Cosmetics in the USA	$8bn
Water and sanitation for all	$9bn
Ice cream in Europe	$11bn
Reproductive health for all women	$12bn
Perfumes in Europe and the USA	$12bn
Basic health and nutrition	$13bn
Pet foods in Europe and the USA	$17bn
Business entertainment in Japan	$35bn
Cigarettes in Europe	$50bn
Alcoholic drinks in Europe	$105bn
Military spending in the world	$780bn

(*Source*: United Nations Development Programme, 1999)

Table 4.1, in part, emphasizes the spending priorities in the world today – but global poverty and inequality is not created, or even made worse, by indi-viduals buying one or two ice-creams in the summer. Rather, the poor are poor because the rich are getting richer and the wealth of the minority is built on the impoverishment and exploitation of the majority.

Economic inequalities between countries have been widening steadily for 200 years. Yet, it is not simply a case of global inequality divided along the lines of a rich North and an impoverished South as inequalities within coun-tries (in the North and the South) are also widening. The transition to market capitalism in Eastern Europe has produced, according to the United Nations Development Programme: 'the fastest rise in inequality ever. Russia now has the greatest inequality – the income share of the richest 20 per cent is 11 times that of the poorest 20 per cent' (Callinicos, 2000: 2).

Britain is one of the richest countries in the world, yet as Carole and Alan Walker note:

Since the late 1970s, the UK has experienced an increase in income inequality that is unparalleled, with the sole exception of New Zealand, in the industrialized world . . . Between 1979 and 1993/4, the real incomes . . . of those in the poorest tenth of the population fell by 13 per cent . . . while the richest enjoyed a huge increase of 63 per cent. (1998: 46)

One of the clearest indicators of this rise in poverty over the past three decades is revealed in figures of the proportion of children living in poverty. In 1979, 9 per cent of children in Britain lived in households with an income below the average, by 1996/97 this had increased to 35 per cent (DSS, 1998). The fact that more than 1 in 3 children now live in poverty is perhaps one of the starkest indicators of the extent of inequality in Britain today.

At the same time in the USA, by far the wealthiest country on the planet: 'The personal wealth of Microsoft chairman Bill Gates alone, at $85 billion, is greater than the combined holdings of 40 percent of the US population' (Smith, 1999: 15). Over the past generation living standards of working families in the USA have been under constant downward pressure, leading Jeffrey Madrick, the liberal commentator, to argue: 'The average real income of families was only a few percentage points higher in 1993 than in 1973, and that largely because so many more spouses were working' (1997: 16). While conservative theorist Edward Luttwak writes:

The United States is on its way to acquiring the income distribution characteristics of a Third World country, with a truly very rich top 1 per cent, and a significant minority (roughly 12 per cent) which remains below the official poverty line even though fully employed, forty hours a week, fifty weeks a year. (1999: 67)

So although modern capitalism has given us the potential to escape misery, disease, ill-health, and poverty, and to meet human need across the globe, these needs remain unfulfilled and we are witnessing more, not less, inequality. Why is this?

The answer is not simply because of the greed and avarice of the rich. Rather it is a consequence of the very nature of capitalism itself, a system that is wracked by two great divisions. The first of these is the division between a class of people who own and/or control the means of production (the offices, factories, machines and resources) needed to produce societies' wealth (Marx termed them the bourgeoisie), and the vast majority, the working class (Marx termed them the proletariat), who have no means of surviving beyond their ability to work for a wage. These two classes confront each other in an antagonistic relationship. It is in the interests of the bourgeoisie to make workers work harder for less so they can increase their profits, but it is in the interest of workers to get higher wages, work fewer hours, have better conditions at work and longer holidays, for example. These two great opposing classes, and the inevitable conflict between them, shape the modern world in its entirety.

The second great division is internal to the bourgeoisie itself. They are, to paraphrase Marx, a 'band of warring brothers'. They have a common interest in ensuring that the working class is kept in its place, but they are also competitors, constantly trying to put each other out of business and obtain a greater market share for their product. This competition means they must constantly reinvest their profits in new machines, new factories, and new forms and techniques of production, because 'he who hesitates is lost' and to lose means bankruptcy. It is this competition that drives each company and employer to try and force up their profits and to try and make their employees work harder and longer for less money. It is not individuals that are the problem, but the very logic of the system of capitalism itself.

The greatest theorist of the logic of capitalism was Marx – hence his continuing relevance to our understanding of global and local inequalities and how they are structured by capitalism itself.

4.2 A return to Marx?

In the 1980s and early 1990s Marxism went out of fashion within academic circles and some academics would have questioned the relevance of the present chapter for students studying social policy. For these critics, Marxism was viewed as 'old fashioned' and flawed, unable to cope with the critique of postmodern theorists who dismissed its claims to offer an insight into the world in its totality.

By the end of the 1990s however, this was beginning to change and Marxism was, once again, obtaining credence as a theory of understanding the world with a view to changing it. At its most surprising and most populist was the successful nomination of Marx as 'Greatest thinker of the millennium' in a BBC Internet poll in 1999. The same year saw the publication of a well-received, sympathetic biography of Marx by Francis Wheen (1999). The 150-year special edition of the *Communist Manifesto* was on Waterstone's best sellers list for several weeks during 1998 and the *Independent on Sunday* (7 December 1997) and the *Financial Times* (25 March 1998) both ran complimentary pieces on Marx and his work. At the same time within academia, critics like the postmodern theorist and French academic Jacques Derrida claimed: 'the Marxist inheritance was – still remains, and so it will remain – absolutely and thoroughly determinate' (1994: 14).

The obvious question is, 'Why the change?' The answer has probably less to do with academic fashion than changes in the world of global capitalism. The beginning of the twenty-first century saw a number of countries facing economic crisis. Japan and the South Asian 'tiger' economies were facing severe problems – yet during the 1980s and early 1990s these were being promoted as the most dynamic economies who offered a model for advanced economies (certainly Britain) to follow. Further, the former command economies of the Eastern Bloc had undergone rapid marketization – which brought, as a consequence, crisis, poverty, and vast inequality. During 2001 increasing numbers of economists and analysts were discussing the probable onset of an economic crisis within the USA and its impact across the globe – their disagreements being primarily over the timing of the slump, rather than its likelihood (Harman, 2001). Finally, in many parts of the 'second' and 'third' world, neo-liberal 'structural adjustment programmes', ushered in under the auspices of the International Monetary Fund and the World Bank (and which required the deregulation, privatization, and marketization of their economies, including their welfare services), brought devastating consequences for the poor of these countries – while both further reinforcing these countries' indebtedness to banks and governments in the advanced economies, and making their economic problems more intractable (Harman, 2000).

Secondly, it became increasingly clear that the unrestricted expansion of free market capitalism – the pursuit of profit at all costs – was creating innumerable environmental problems. Developments such as global warming, the destruction of rainforests, and GM foods, all pointed to the negative impact unfettered capitalism was having on our lives and questioning the long-term sustainability of the planet (McGarr, 2000).

Thirdly, there was the claim that the 1980s marked 'the end of history' (to use the conservative philosopher Francis Fukayama's phrase) – meaning that liberal democracy had 'won' the ideological struggle, and war and conflict were things of the past. Yet the 1990s were a decade of war when Britain, the USA, and their allies intervened to assert their authority in the Middle East and Yugoslavia. In both cases advanced technology was used to wreak havoc on Iraq and Yugoslavia's infrastructure and uranium tipped weapons caused death, injury, and malformation to the civilian populations on the receiving end of supposedly 'humanitarian intervention'. Instead of the end of history, the 1990s seemed to mark a new level of barbarity (Ali, 2000).

Fourthly, the intensification of global capitalism brought with it the very obvious and intolerable levels of inequality already noted in section 4.1. But linked with this was the growing realization that as the rich were getting richer, the poor were being sweated more in factories across the globe, that child labour was expanding and that some of the most respectable 'logo' manufacturers were making their vast profits by ruthlessly exploiting the most vulnerable (Klein, 2000).

Finally, each of the above was partially responsible for the rebirth of mass protest that was signalled in Seattle in November 1999 during the demonstrations against the World Trade Organization's Third Ministerial. Throughout the year 2000 large 'anti-capitalist' demonstrations took place in Washington, Melbourne, Millau, Prague and Nice as people protested against the inequity and barbarity of global capitalism and its consequences for both people and planet. But the year 2000 also saw the return of the organized working class as a potential agent of social change. Towards the end of the year 2000 the Yugoslav revolution saw mass conflict on the streets of Belgrade and other major cities. Central to the events were the miners in the Kolubara region of Serbia. As the *Observer* correspondent Jonathan Steele commented: '[Milosevic's] downfall was not won on a battlefield or by NATO pilots. It was won among the black dust of the Serbian coalfield, under the vast arc lights of Kolubara pit among the miners who had been his most loyal supporters' (*Observer*, 8 October, 2000). The World Development Movement (Woodroffe and Ellis-Jones, 2000) reported that in the first six months of the year 2000 strikes and demonstrations against neo-liberal policies took place in Argentina, Bolivia, Colombia, Costa Rica, Ecuador, Honduras, Paraguay, Kenya, Malawi, Nigeria and Zambia. The significant rebirth of the union movement in the USA and the continuing conflicts in France emphasize that these developments are not merely 'second' or 'third' world events.

The combined effect of these developments has led some academics back to a reconsideration of Marx, his critique of capitalism, and his vision for a freer, more open, and more democratic society committed to the rational, planned production of goods to satisfy the needs of the majority, as opposed to a society run by a tiny minority to expand the profits and enrich the lives of the few.

But if there is evidence of a 'return to Marx', what kind of Marxism is on offer? The American writer Hal Draper (1966/1996) has drawn a distinction between what he terms the 'two-souls' of socialism. On the one hand are various forms of 'socialism from above' – ushered in by various groups from enlightened politicians to red army tanks – on behalf of 'the people', but without their active involvement in the political process. On the other is 'socialism from below' – the self-emancipation of the working class, the movement of the vast majority in the interests of the vast majority. Marx was a theorist of this second camp.

Any return to Marx should involve a rejection of 'Soviet Marxism' and its like. The Marxism of the former Eastern Block had little to do with the liberation of the vast majority. Indeed working class rebellions against the ruling classes of these countries took place in East Germany in 1953, Hungary in 1956, Czechoslovakia in 1968 and Poland on several occasions during the 1960s and 1970s, culminating in the challenge from the Solidarity trade union in 1981. Furthermore, oppression of women, minority nationalities, and gays was not uncommon in these societies. By 1989 when they were swept away by popular rebellion it was clear they had nothing in common with socialism as envisaged by Marx.

But there has always been another tradition within Marxism, one that Perry Anderson called the 'classical tradition', committed to the self-emancipation of the working class and sweeping away all forms of oppression. It is a tradition that can be traced through the works of Marx and Engels and then on through Lenin, Trotsky, Luxemburg, Lukacs and Gramsci. Within the writings of this group is a grounded social theory committed to understanding the world in order to change it, they bring with them some powerful analytical tools.

4.3 Four key concepts: totality, class, alienation and class struggle

Central to Marxism, especially in its classical form, are four concepts that can fruitfully be applied to the study of social welfare, these are: totality, class alienation, and class struggle. Here we give a brief definition of each and an indication of their relevance.

Totality

Marx's method developed by expanding upon some of the insights of the German philosopher G.W.F. Hegel. From Hegel he took three main points: (1) the world is in a constant process of change, (2) the world is a totality, and (3) this totality is internally contradictory (and that it is these internal contradictions that produce change).

Viewing the world as a totality means insisting that the various, apparently separate and discrete elements that compose the modern world are in fact linked and related to one another. In modern society we face an array of apparently disconnected and separated social institutions and practices – in the academic world this separation is solidified into distinct academic disciplines. But for classical Marxists each of these areas is interconnected. For example, welfare development cannot be adequately understood unless we acknowledge the various elements of control, social wage, commodification and investment in labour power that it involves; the state is portrayed as neutral, yet it reinforces and maintains the power of the already rich and powerful. Rees continues:

> Poverty and crime, unemployment and suicide, art and business, language and history, engineering and sociology cannot be understood in isolation, but only as part of a totality . . . [W]hen we bring these terms into relation with each other, their meaning is transformed. Once we understand the relationship between poverty and crime, it is impossible to look on either the criminal justice system or those who live in poverty as we did when they were taken to inhabit two separate realms. (1998: 5)

To see the world as a 'differentiated unity' is to note that each sphere of social life is interconnected. But this does not mean that the diversity of the social structure is eliminated or everything can be reduced to its 'economic logic' – each sphere has its own processes and laws which must be understood and grasped in their own terms while being located in, and related to, the rest of the social world. This is part of the process of 'mediation', in other words, the ways in which the parts and the whole mutually condition each other. Thus, as Rees notes:

Marx's notion of the dialectic . . . necessarily requires that he reject reductionist for-mulations and give full weight to the mediating contradictions between different elements of the totality . . . The dialectical method involves analytically separating a chaotic social whole into various constituent economic formulations, classes, insti-tutions, personalities, and so on. It then involves showing how these factors *interrelate and contradict each other* as part of a totality.(1998: 107, 275, my emphasis)

In the sphere of welfare studies the concept of totality means rejecting those approaches which portray social policy and welfare developments as in some way separate or disconnected from the central drive and direction of capital-ism.

Class

For Marx, capitalism is a system dominated by two main classes in direct opposition to each other. They are the bourgeoisie, who own and/or control the means of production but who rely on others to work in their factories and offices to produce goods and create wealth, and the working class, the vast majority, who have no means of supporting themselves except by selling their labour power to the bourgeoisie: to work for a wage. Thus class, for Marxists, is an 'objective category', it is determined by your relationship to the means of production.

Yet this perspective has been rejected by many academics. They claim that Marx's picture is too simplistic and the social world, and with it the class structure, is more complex than his simple dichotomy suggests. This is based around the claim that, for Marxists the 'working class' refers to industrial workers in the productive sphere, but that this group is declining numerically.

The Marxist response to this criticism is two fold. First, it is to deny that the working class is only made up of industrial workers. Marxism offers a rela-tional model of class not an occupational or sectoral model. Capitalism as a system is constantly changing and adapting. As part of this process new tech-niques of production are developed, new jobs created, and old jobs become redundant. For example, in the early nineteenth century hand loom weavers were a substantial part of the working class in Britain, now they do not exist. The growth and expansion of capitalism has brought complexity to the divi-sion of labour; it has created large numbers of white-collar jobs in, for example, telesales, services, local government and welfare work – but these workers have little control over their work process. They are wage labourers, often working in poor conditions and very often join trade unions to fight for better conditions. These types of jobs have become 'proletarianized' and these workers are an integral part of the working class of advanced capitalism.

Of course as capitalism has changed and become more centralized this has brought changes to the class structure. The head of British Gas or General

Motors may work for a wage (and a share package) rather than own their particular company outright – but they do have effective control over the direction followed by the company, including control over the labour of its workforce. Further, a range of tasks have been delegated to managers – at various levels – whom the American sociologist E.O. Wright describes as occupying 'contradictory class locations' between the working class and the bourgeoisie and whom we may refer to as the 'new middle class'. Nevertheless these developments have led Alex Callinicos (1987a) to suggest that the bourgeoisie are a 'tiny minority' and the new middle class 20 per cent (at most) of the population of the advanced economies, leaving the overwhelming majority as part of the working class.

The second response to the criticism is to suggest that the outlook is very Eurocentric. Actually the industrial working class today is more numerous than it has ever been. It exists in towns and cities across the globe from Beijing and Seoul to Buenos Aires and São Paulo, from Cape Town and Harare to Cairo and Tehran – and it still remains numerous throughout Europe and North America.

Class is the basis of the inequality we started with in section 4.1, and study after study shows that class is a central determinant of 'life chances'. If you are born into a working-class family you are likely to end up working in a working-class job (your parents may work in a factory, you may work in an office – but you are likely to stay in the same social class). People from working-class backgrounds are more likely to suffer ill health and die younger than those from bourgeois or new middle class backgrounds (Shaw et al., 1999). Those from working-class backgrounds are more likely to live in poverty (or live in poverty at particular points in the lifecycle) (Oppenheim and Harker, 1996), face periods of unemployment, perform relatively poorly within education (Adonis and Pollard, 1997; Plewis 2000) and are more likely to be victims of crime (Goldson, 2000) and both domestic violence and sexual abuse (Corby, 2000).

We live in a class divided society and class invades our lives in innumerable ways. Thus to study social welfare necessarily means taking account of class (see Ferguson and Lavalette, 1999).

Alienation

Alienation is a concept that is at the heart of classical Marxist theory – Istvan Meszaros, for example, has called it 'the central idea of Marx's system' (1970: 96) – yet it has not figured significantly in writings on social welfare (even Marxist writings). For Marx alienation is a consequence of material and social processes at the heart of capitalism. Humans, according to Marx, are naturally social and productive animals, yet within capitalism the worker is forced to sell her strength and skills to the capitalist. As a result she neither controls the product of her labour, nor her labour itself. What should be her 'life-activity' through which she reaffirms her humanity or 'species-being' becomes a mere means to an end. Indeed the product of her labour is turned into a commodity and sold in the market place, beyond her control, possibly outwith her financial reach, and now confronting her as an 'alien object'.

Alienation under capitalism is reflected in the lack of power and the lack of control we experience in so many areas of life. Power is a central theme in much current social welfare writing. Reflecting the influence of poststructuralism (see Chapter 8), power within this body of literature is usually conceived of as omnipresent. The microrelations of men and women, blacks and whites, gays and straights, are seen as being saturated with power. It is a view of power which fits with 'common-sense' experience – after all, large numbers of individual men clearly do assault and abuse women; many whites do behave in racist ways towards black people. In this view, it is male power that is responsible for sexism; white power for the racism experienced by black people and so on (Ferguson, Lavalette and Mooney forthcoming).

The Marxist starting-point is very different. For while there clearly is a small group of people in our society who do wield enormous power over the lives of millions – the ruling class – the experience of the vast majority of people is not one of power but rather of powerlessness, of having little or no control over the major areas of their own lives. It is this lack of power which often leads people to behave in violent and anti-social ways towards others and themselves, and which breeds the despair and frustration that contribute to drug and alcohol abuse, mental health problems, and family breakdown.

It is the lack of power and control which working-class people experience over all aspects of their lives that is at the heart of Marx's theory of alienation. While that lack of power is experienced most acutely by those whom capital does not regard as even worthy of exploitation – those excluded from the labour market on grounds of age, disability or lack of skills – it is in the process of the production and circulation of commodities that the roots of alienation are to be found.

Class struggle

Class location, as we noted above, is objectively defined, yet class also has a subjective element to it – that is the degree to which people identify themselves as having common class interests and the extent to which they actively pursue those interests through political struggle. For Marx there was a distinction between 'class in itself' – the objective element – and 'class for itself' – the subjective element of class consciousness. The importance of this, for Marx, is that when 'fully conscious' the working class has the potential to reshape society anew. It is potentially a collective social actor – the 'grave digger' of capitalism – who, because of its location within social production, has the power to abolish capitalism and establish a better world.

But class consciousness is not static; it can develop and dissipate. Throughout the history of capitalism there have been periods when substantial class conflict took place followed by periods when little seemed to happen. The Chartist conflicts of the late 1830s and 1840s were followed by the relative calm of the 1850s and 1860s. The 'Great Unrest' in the years 1911–14 was followed by the First World War, the postwar rebellion of the early 1920s by the defeat of the General Strike, the upturn in workers struggles of the early 1970s by the defeats and 'downturn' of the 1980s. Thus while in Britain at the end of the twentieth century the level of open class conflict has been relatively low, history suggests this will not always be the case.

Such conflicts represent the open struggle between the classes under capitalism but 'class struggle' permeates capitalism in myriad ways. There are several points to note. First, the class struggle is a consequence of the basic antagonistic class relationships of capitalism. Capitalism is like a pressure cooker: companies are forced (because of competition) to increase the level and rate of exploitation – but the increasing intensity makes it more likely that workers will respond.

Secondly the struggle involves (at least) two classes in conflict. This means that although open conflict may be missing, the dominant class will still try to force its agenda onto a (subservient) working class. Thus the 1980s in Britain may have been an era of defeat for the organized working-class movement but that did not mean it was a period of social harmony. Indeed, the dominant class in Britain used their position to restructure significantly welfare provision, trade union legislation, economic policy, and so on.

Thirdly, in order to avoid conflict and disruption to the production process, sections of the dominant class within society will try to 'legitimate' the system by making it appear that workers have a substantial stake in the system and that capitalism brings benefits for us all; while others may argue for strategies to enforce the authority of capital on to working-class communities. Here, in a sense, the very presence of the working class is significant, leading some sections of the dominant class to look towards social reforms and others to advocate directly controlling strategies.

Thus the class struggle, in its widest sense, shapes the context within which debates over social welfare take place and policies develop.

These four concepts distinguish a Marxist approach (at least in its classical form) to the study of social problems and social welfare, but Marxist approaches to social policy involve other themes as well. The specifics of a Marxist approach to analysing social policy is developed in section 4.4.

4.4 Marxism and the analysis of social policy

For Marxists, social policy developments take place in the context of capitalist societies. As Jones and Novak have noted:

throughout the history of capitalism, the existence of some form of 'social' policy has been determined in part by the fact that capitalism as a system of production depends upon a workforce that has neither property nor security. Those who, for whatever reason, are unable to work have nothing to sustain them, and the relief of their necessity, for both obvious political and economic reasons . . . [has been central to social policy development] . . . In relieving poverty, however, the State has not only assumed part of the responsibility of the maintenance of labour for industry . . . but it has also . . . served to reproduce the conditions and necessity of labour. (1980: 145)

There are two issues to which this quotation draws our attention. First, social policies are policies that are introduced, implemented, and organized by the state. Second, social policies have developed in response to the problems created by the structure and operation of capitalism in the area of labour reproduction. It will be useful to explore each of these propositions in more detail.

To claim that social policies are 'state policies', may seem rather obvious, but what do we mean by the term 'the state'? The first point to emphasize is that Marxists would reject the narrow liberal perspective that depicts the state as merely the government (made up of the executive and the legislature) and the judiciary. Marxists would argue that the state is much more ubiquitous than most liberals would admit: it includes sections of the civil service and various state administrators, the army and the police (protectors of the existing social order), various local and regional organs of government and a range of ad hoc quasi-autonomous semi-public bodies. Further, the state is not a neutral entity, equally predisposed to the interests of all individuals and groups within society. For Marxists the state performs a number of roles, but its primary activity is to maintain the conditions for the existence and expansion of capitalism as a socio-economic system. This involves the state in the reproduction of the dominant social relations of production, legitimation of the operation of the capitalist system, and the facilitation of the self-expansion of capital. In turn these may involve the state in:

1   the creation and maintenance of an adequate legal framework to allow business contracts to be maintained and fulfilled;
2   direct economic activity to support its national currency or aid or run major manufacturing interests;
3   the amelioration of the worst manifestations of poverty and hardship faced by the working class and generated by recurrent economic slumps, and
4   the development of social policies to support and discipline particular groups within society, partly to legitimate the present form of society and partly to control those who may threaten the economic workings of society.

Moreover, through the provision of social policies, the state also relieves individual capitalists of the burden of maintaining and reproducing labour –

doing so in a more rational and efficient manner than would otherwise be the case. These roles may involve the state in conflict with certain sections of capital (in the short term) and its activities will be open to alteration and debate over appropriate strategies. Nevertheless the parameters of such debates and strategic decisions are that the state cannot undertake policies and activities that will undermine the economic and political basis of capitalist society (of which the state is a part). In other words, the state is intimately bound up with the socio-economic interests of society and the 'economically' dominant class will also be the 'politically' dominant class. As Marx and Engels stated in the *Communist Manifesto*, the state is 'but the executive committee of the *entire* bourgeoisie'.

The second issue that we identified at the start of this section related to 'how' and 'why' social policies have developed in response to the problems generated by capitalism. Social policies and spending on social services and welfare provision is only part of any state's activities which are geared to enabling capitalism to exist and expand. States are actively involved in economic policy (from direct investment in industries to macro-economic planning), public policies (such as providing a transport infrastructure), and law and order strategies aimed at obtaining internal control over their own population. Social policies are linked to each of these but are primarily concerned with those activities that are concerned with the reproduction of labour power and the maintenance of non-working groups within society. Thus the development and expansion of social policies and welfare provision has been intimately bound up with the consequences, problems, and social conditions created by capitalism. The expansion of capitalism has resulted in large numbers of people living and working in close proximity and these features have created a number of social problems which have threatened the very existence of the system itself. Yet the development of social welfare has not simply reflected the needs of the system or the bourgeoisie. Rather social legislation and the creation and activity of welfare institutions reflect the outcome of the interaction of five competing and conflicting pressures. We will look at each of these in turn.

The first pressure could be termed the 'structural needs of the system'. For capitalism to exist and expand there is a requirement for certain activities to be performed and for certain services to be provided. Capitalism needs relatively fit and healthy workers to work efficiently in the offices and factories. It needs some sort of support mechanism for non-labouring individuals (and this may include basic financial provision) and new workers must be trained in the skills they will utilize while at work. These provisions can either be provided by individual capitalists (or groups of capitalists), be based on some form of 'insurance scheme' with payments being given to private companies to provide these services, or they can be provided by the state. An example of state provision can be seen in the development of the education system in Britain which partially reflects capitalism's need for more educated workers (Simon, 1960).

The second pressure is the international context of policy developments. Capitalism is an integrated, competitive, international social and economic system. Economic pressures are felt (with differing degrees of intensity) throughout the system. Governments copy economic and social policy experiments from each other – an activity sometimes called 'policy transfer'. Dominant ideologies and political strategies spread across the globe, while a range of international financial institutions and transnational bodies intervenes, both directly and indirectly, to shape policies within various nation states. In the international context of social policy it is increasingly important to understand welfare developments as reflecting global economic and political pressures. The international role of institutions like the World Bank, or individuals like Tony Blair, as promoters of certain approaches to welfare cannot be underestimated.

The next two pressures reflect the impact of individual or collective political activity or agency. Thus the third element is that some policy responses reflect the political activity of certain sections of the bourgeoisie or are the result of intra-class conflict between sections of the bourgeoisie. Historically there have been considerable intra-class divisions amongst both the bourgeoisie and the working class over the form welfare provision should take. This can be illustrated by taking the example of educational provision. With regard to the development of the education system we can locate a number of perspectives. Throughout the nineteenth century many textile owners were hostile to developments because they threatened to deprive them of a cheap source of (child) labour (Lavalette, 1994, 1999). Other sections of the bourgeoisie saw such developments as being vital if Britain was to maintain its pre-eminent position as the 'workshop of the world' in the face of growing competition from the USA and Germany (Hay, 1975). Within the working-class movement there were sections who demanded and supported educational facilities as a means of educating workers as to their plight, the source of their misery, and the possible political solutions to such questions, while at the same time these groups were often hostile to the form and disciplinary nature taken by state schooling (Simon, 1968). Other sections of the working class objected to the loss of earnings and costs of schooling and hence the material hardship full-time schooling brought with it (Frow and Frow, 1970), while many working-class children objected to the process of schooling in toto (Humphries, 1981). There are, therefore, different perspectives between and within social classes, and these help shape policy outcomes.

The fourth identifiable pressure is collective working-class activity. The working class itself has on occasion been able to assert collective demands for social welfare legislation to either protect or improve its living conditions. Welfare provision can be identified as part of a 'social wage', that is not a direct wage payment paid by an individual capitalist but one which refers to the: 'sum of the collective benefits which are transfered to individuals or families in both cash and kind via the state' (Bryson, 1992: 32). In other words, it is services provided by the state which meet or provide certain social needs. As such it can be a necessary part of the working class's living requirements and without it living conditions would be worse and the struggle for basic survival that much harder. In these circumstances it is not surprising that the working class has occasionally fought to obtain or maintain state welfare provision.

Such popular struggles demanding welfare are often devalued or dismissed from histories of social policy (see Lavalette and Mooney, 2000). But despite being 'hidden from history' they remain important as the following example emphasizes. During the First World War there was a significant rent strike on Clydeside (Glasgow). The move to a war economy meant that there was a rapid expansion of war related industries in Glasgow. Labour was sucked into the city to work in the shipyards, engineering factories, and related industries and as a result there was a severe housing shortage. Landlords now had control of a valuable and scarce resource and put up their rents. The response from sections of the working class in Glasgow was to go on rent strike. This was led and organized by working-class women and quickly gained the support of a wide range of working-class activists and trade unionists. When the strikers were pulled in front of the debtors' courts there was a mass walkout from many workplaces on Clydeside. The women were released and the government introduced the Rent Restriction Act that pegged rents to their prewar level and prohibited landlords from increasing rents for the duration of the war (Melling, 1983). The more recent struggle against the Poll Tax in Britain between 1989 and 1991 emphasizes that such struggles are not merely historical.

Finally, the capitalist mode of operation is, as we saw in section 4.3, one that depersonalizes and alienates individuals. On occasion social policies have been developed to give the working class the impression that they have a stake and a say in the system. Social policies, therefore, have a role in the 'legitimation process' within capitalist societies. As Lord Hailsham said in Parliament in 1943: 'if you do not give the people reform, they are going to give you revolution' (quoted in Birchill, 1986: 49). The interaction of these five sources is not always easy to dissect and generally policies cannot be assigned as easily to any one category as our examples above may suggest. Nevertheless, they each remain important tendencies shaping the development of welfare institutions and social policies.

Thus policy developments are the outcome of a complex process of struggle and conflict which takes place within a context: the structural needs and requirements of capitalism and the uncertainties (economic, political, and social) created by social life within capitalist society. The operation of these elements means that policy outcomes often take the form of an 'uneasy compromise' either between factions of the bourgeoisie and/or these and the working class. Resultant legislation can often be contradictory in its operation and on its impact on the working class. Thus, most welfare institutions and social policies can be seen to reflect, in different measures, elements of both 'care', however loosely and widely this may be defined, and 'control'. Yet any policy developments will, as state policies, reflect the contradictions of capitalist society and the values of the bourgeoisie. Hence all such developments affect and structure our lives. They embody different 'proposed solutions' to any crisis but do so in a way which embodies ideological commitments: assumptions about how we live (or should live) our lives (see Chapters 5 and 7 for example), about the causes of poverty and inequality (solutions which blame individuals as opposed to the social structure for example, see Chapter 10), or targeting on welfare provision (see Chapter 14). Finally given such 'ideological commitments' it is not surprising that policies become another 'factor of struggle'. Thus the assumptions, inadequacies, and/or failures of policies and welfare institutions have often created new crises and struggles and have been part of the process establishing new policy proposals.

Activity 4.1

1 What benefits do the working class receive from:
   (a) the NHS;
   (b) education provision;
   (c) social services;
   (d) the social security system?
2 What benefits do the bourgeoisie obtain from the provision of each of the above services?

It will be possible to look at these features in more detail by considering some of the social problems and predicaments created by capitalism and to which social policies are partially addressed. This can be done by identifying four interlinked 'social crisis tendencies' which capitalism inevitably generates. These are issues associated with:

1 the conditions of social existence;
2 the reproduction of labour;
3 technological innovation, the labour process and the division of labour; and
4 the problems of social control, order and harmony.

The conditions of social existence

Capitalism brought with it the commodification of labour, industrialization, migration and urbanization. These linked processes meant that, as capitalism developed, there was a growing class of proletarians who had no means of support but their ability to labour. They were drawn into the rapidly expanding towns and cities to look for work. Housing was scarce, poorly built,

overcrowded, expensive, with inadequate (if any) water and sanitation facilities. In these conditions poor and ill health were the norms. Work, if it could
be found, was hard and long, conditions bad, and wages pitiful. In order to
meet their subsistence needs entire families went out to work. Men, women,
and children, the old and the young, worked for up to 15 hours a day, but
still wages did not provide enough for adequate food and clothing. Further
there was no support for the unemployed, injured, sick, frail, elderly or very
young. These circumstances produced a number of severe problems for the
working class who had to live in such conditions but it also created problems
for the bourgeoisie and capitalism as a system. First, the living conditions
forced on to the working class produced ill health and bred disease. But
these problems did not only affect the working class. Although diseases like
cholera started in working-class slums they quickly spread out of the ghet-
tos to the more prosperous parts of the towns and cities. A comparison of the
age of death in Manchester and rural Rutland in the mid-nineteenth century
emphasizes that geography was almost as important as class in determining
the age of death.

Table 4.2   Average age of death

Profession	Age in Manchester	Age in Rutland
Gentry and Professional Classes	38	52
Tradesmen	20	–
Farmers	–	41
Mechanics and labourers	17	38

(*Source*: Rogers, 1993: 8)

Not only were the city dwelling bourgeoisie under direct threat but there
was an economic price as well: the early death of skilled labour was a waste
of an economic resource. Moreover, replacing such skilled labour was not
only expensive but it was a risky exercise. According to Chadwick, the
replacements would be 'young, inexperienced, ignorant, credulous, passion-
ate, violent and proportionately dangerous, with a perpetual tendency to
moral as well as physical deterioration' (quoted in Rogers, 1993: 8). Thus the
living conditions of early capitalism prompted action to improve basic living
conditions and sanitation levels.
     Second, the long hours of work were problematic on three counts. Long
working days, combined with inadequate nutrition meant that workers were
physically exhausted and hence less productive creating an inefficient use of
labour power; the employment of children and women clashed with bourgeois ideological notions of family organization and responsibility, and,
finally, such conditions fed the growth of trade unionism and political opposition to industrial capitalism. The combination of these elements promoted

the gradual growth of (albeit inadequate) factory and employment legislation (see Lavalette, 1994).

Finally the lack of adequate support networks for the elderly, sick, and unemployed led to concern from some sections of the bourgeoisie over the operation, uneven burden and costs associated with the Poor Laws, and promoted the enactment of the Poor Law Amendment Act (1834) which enshrined a national response to poverty, although one based on the concept of 'less eligibility' and had an important role in the creation of a national labour market. The eventual collapse of the New Poor Law in combination with continuing problems of under employment and unemployment lie at the root of the social security system we have today. As Jones and Novak note:

> The need to do something about social conditions, about unemployment, poverty and disease, was thus set by the recognition that under the need for growing productivity and efficiency, labour was not simply a commodity that could be used up and discarded: that capitalism had both an immediate and long term interest in its healthy maintenance and reproduction. (1980: 147)

Thus the very conditions of existence within capitalist society promoted the development of social policies. The problems of living and existing in capitalist societies today mean that the 'conditions of existence' remain an important factor in social policy developments.

The reproduction of labour

One central problem in early industrial capitalism was the daily and intergenerational reproduction of labour. There is some evidence that the process of proletarianization in the early to mid-nineteenth century was undermining the existence of the working-class family (Engels, 1845; German, 1989). The long hours of work, combined with shift patterns meant that in some districts family life was completely disrupted. In these circumstances child rearing was problematic and domestic labour (cooking, cleaning, personal support) was left inadequately fulfilled. This created problems for both the bourgeoisie and the working class.

For the bourgeoisie it threatened the existence of a future workforce: while existing profits could be guaranteed on the basis of the cheap labour of men, women, and children (at least to the extent that they can ever be guaranteed given the anarchy of the market system), the creation of surplus value in the future required the existence of a new generation of fit, healthy, and disciplined workers. The break-up of family life threatened all of this.

From within the working class there were concerns that mass proletarianization was having the effect of 'overstocking the labour market' and hence reducing wages. In these circumstances there were attempts from within both the bourgeoisie and working class to re-establish the family. From the bourgeois perspective this matched their ideological commitment to the family while providing a network that would be responsible for child rearing, support for the elderly, sick and unemployed and would have a role in maintaining and supporting the existing workforce while socializing future generations of workers (Creighton, 1980 and 1985). From the working-class perspective it was suggested that by establishing a 'family wage' (that is a wage earned by men and large enough to support an entire family) first children and then women could be withdrawn from the labour market. This would protect children from the worst horrors of the factory (Lavalette, 1994) and allow women to engage in domestic labour to support the family. There was then an apparent material reason why such a demand was raised and supported (German, 1989). Here we see a possible convergence of interests around this issue among both the bourgeoisie and the working class. The result was the growth of family related social policy. These were policies which initially restricted the hours of work and sectors of employment available to children and women but by the end of the nineteenth century such policies had become much more interventionist, attempting to structure and control working-class family life.

Finally it is worth emphasizing that while such policies were supported by many women as well as men they represented a significant defeat for women, removing them from the public arena and isolating them within the home. Furthermore, while the 'family wage' demand was ideologically important it was rarely obtained in practice (Barrett and McIntosh, 1980). Family policy remains, however, a crucially important area within social policy and one where the conflict between the elements of 'care' and 'control' are most visible. Further, the ideological assumptions regarding the perceived role of women as 'natural carers' is clearly expressed within social policy, such as present day community care legislation.

Technological innovation, the labour process, and the division of labour

Technological innovation has been a feature of capitalist development. But such innovation brings with it social costs and, as the writer Harry Braverman argued, has been partly shaped and developed by the concern to assert control over the labour process and the workforce. Improvements in technology have a number of consequences within capitalist societies. First, it generally results in job losses as old skills are made redundant. This need not be the case, of course; the technological advances could be utilized to cut the working week on the same rates of pay but under capitalist structures of organization such strategies are rejected because they are not 'profitable'.

Unemployment brings with it social and economic costs which will be borne by many welfare institutions.

Secondly, such technological advances can 'deskill' some tasks while changing the skill requirements of others. In general terms such changes have the effect of cheapening labour. Again this has implications for the reproduction of labour. Thirdly, the outcome of these changes is often a more complex division of labour which can introduce divisions within the working class (these may be based on skill, race, or gender). Finally, such divisions may be reinforced by various occupational welfare benefits which some core or better organized workers may obtain (Mann, 1992).

Such changes to technology and work organization have also led to debates about appropriate methods of skill training. In particular there have been demands for a flexible education system able to cope with changing work patterns. The recent rapid expansion of higher education partly reflects the changing composition of the working class and the new skills required to work in the offices and welfare institutions of advanced capitalism. But the state also plays a role in employment training for young and old, whether this is to impart new skills or to encourage workers to accept lower wages in the growing number of deskilled tasks.

Historically both unemployment and insecurity of employment have had an effect on the creation of the social security system, a system which has been structured as much by considerations of controlling the unemployed, as it has by concerns of providing relief from hardship. The existence and operationalization of the division of labour has the effect of institutionalizing divisions within the working class. The consequence is that often social policies 'act on the divisions created by capitalism as a whole . . . By acting on these divisions, supporting and reflecting them and often creating further subdivisions, social welfare measures have had their greatest success in maintaining and effecting a marked ideological impact' (Jones and Novak 1980: 162).

The problems of social control, order and harmony

As has been emphasized, within social policy the 'control' element has been as vital and as central as any element of 'care' policies may contain. For example, although Income Support (IS) in theory provides a safety net against poverty it is increasingly stigmatized and used to discipline groups within society. The rules and regulations which govern the operation of the DSS. or the Social Services Departments, for example, may only directly affect a minority of the population but it is a substantial minority. Further, such rules, regulations, and institutions remain a threat to many more as the problems of poverty and hardship encroach on our lives and economic insecurity becomes a more pervasive threat. In these circumstances such disciplinary activities only need to be applied to a minority within society to have an effect.

Concerns over present and future order have been important in attempts to socialize children within the education system. At times this has been expressed via emphases on rote learning, classroom discipline, or the wearing of school uniforms. Thus Cunningham (1990) has argued that one of the central arguments promoting universal compulsory education in the 1870s was that it would take working-class children off the streets and solve the order problem created by working-class youth. While today the National Curriculum clearly expresses government views regarding what is 'legitimate knowledge' (the history of kings and queens, for example) and what is not (the social history of riots, rebellions, and revolutions). Finally, attempts to obtain social harmony have often been constructed via commitments to welfare provision or expansion and are part of the legitimation process.

Activity 4.2

1   What problems, for capitalism, do social policies attempt to solve?
2   Why does the working class have an interest in expanding welfare provision and what contradictions may this bring in capitalist societies?

4.5 The Marxist critique of 'welfare regimes'

This section looks at existing Marxist critiques of what may be termed 'welfare regimes', that is that amalgam of welfare services, institutions, and political commitments which produce different forms of welfare settlements within a range of capitalist societies. Any such critique will involve an acknowledgement of both the state and its social policy developments discussed here. However, prevalent within Marxist writings is not only an acknowledgement of the contradictory constitutive elements to social policy and welfare formation but a recognition that such developments bring forth their own contradictions for the capitalist system as a whole. We will start by outlining four key points to which Marxists adhere:

First the term 'welfare state' is generally rejected. This terminology gives the impression either of a concerned post-capitalist socio-economic system or of a separation of economic and political power. For Marxists no matter the particular form of any welfare regime it remains a part of the capitalist system.

Second, the development of welfare regimes has not reduced class inequalities nor has it significantly redistributed resources in favour of the working class. Several studies have emphasized that existing welfare systems essentially redistribute resources horizontally (that is within the working class) rather than vertically (that is from bourgeoisie or petit bourgeoisie to the working class) (Gough,1979).

Third, as we noted in the last section: (a) social policies and welfare systems have developed as a result of the conditions and conflicts inherent in capitalist societies: they reflect structural needs, conflictual outcomes and are part of the legitimation process; (b) the state provides services which would otherwise not be available or provides services on a more rational and/or cheaper basis than would otherwise be the case, but (c) the costs of an expanding welfare system eat into surplus value. Resources spent on welfare can not be utilized in other directions, such as directly aiding the self-expansion of capital.

Finally, Marxist writers do not suggest that welfare regimes and their associated costs are the cause of generalized economic crisis. Despite the suggestion given in some reviews of Marxist theories of welfare (Mishra, 1984; George and Wilding, 1994) neither O'Connor (1973) nor Gough (1979) give state welfare spending such a pre-eminent position. The causes of economic crises are located elsewhere for these writers (for O'Connor it is essentially the result of 'overproduction' in an era of monopoly capitalism and for Gough it is the 'distributional struggle' over wages). However, in the midst of such economic crises both writers argue that the welfare system becomes a major contradiction for capitalism: it fulfils certain essential functions and plays a role in socializing and placating workers, but the resources it demands become increasingly more difficult to provide (because the state's revenue is squeezed at times of crisis and such expenditure is directed at 'non-productive' welfare outlets instead of productive economic ones).

It is these last two points which identify the major contradictions associated with capitalist welfare regimes. According to O'Connor the state must perform two linked roles: accumulation and legitimation. With regard to the first of these, O'Connor argues the state undertakes more than merely creating and supporting a framework for capitalist expansion, it must become an increasingly active actor in economic life. Thus he notes that the state attempts to regulate and co-ordinate the economic workings of the system and support and direct economic investment and growth to ensure (or at least attempt to ensure) profitability. Historically state intervention arose as a result of the failure of the market system but, according to O'Connor, while such intervention could be successful in terms of managing economic crises in the short term it could not manage the crisis tendencies of capitalism indefinitely. This was because such strategies failed to alter the underlying class divisions in society, its economic structure, and organization. Further, the reassertion of economic crises could be made worse as a result of the state's second role: legitimation. We have already discussed this concept. According to O'Connor legitimation refers to those sociopolitical activities, performed by the state, which give the appearance that the capitalist social order is just and fair and by doing so help maintain social harmony.

As O'Connor notes, it is not always easy to separate the accumulation and legitimation functions of the state and the need to fulfil both these functions has led to a dramatic increase in state activities and expenditure. O'Connor argues that we can divide the resultant state public spending into two sets of components: 'social capital' (which is primarily concerned with 'accumulation' and can be further divided into 'social investment' and 'social consumption') and the 'social expenses of production' (which are overwhelmingly connected to the state's 'legitimation' function). This means we can identify three types of state expenditure:

1　Social investment: this expenditure is 'indirectly productive' and covers services and projects that increase the productivity of labour. For example, the cheap supply of electricity to industry, spending on roads and infrastructure, and educational spending are all forms of 'social investment' spending.
2　Social consumption: again this is 'indirectly productive' and involves spending on services which will lower the reproduction costs of labour, for example Family Credit payments.
3　Social expenses: these are completely 'non-productive' but are necessary for social stability. This includes expenditure on aspects of the welfare system, such as social security payments, but not national insurance benefits which have to be earned through work. The aim of this expenditure is to maintain social harmony.

From our examples we can see that welfare spending falls into all three categories and indeed O'Connor recognizes that nearly every state agency is involved in both the functions of accumulation and legitimation and that most state spending is part social investment, part social consumption, and part social expense.

O'Connor proceeds to argue that while the state can fulfil these functions during periods of sustained economic boom (such as occurred in the 1950s and 1960s) in periods of economic downturn it becomes increasingly difficult for the state to meet these requirements. There are several reasons for this. First, in periods of boom, full employment can fulfil the functions of both aiding 'accumulation' and providing 'legitimation'. But in periods of crisis these functions can more easily and openly conflict (the requirement to obtain legitimation may suggest more welfare spending, while 'accumulation' strategies may be based on reducing government expenditure in an attempt to control inflation, for example).

Second, throughout the twentieth century there has been a tendency for state activity to increase dramatically in scope (in the social, economic, and politico-military fields for example). But while the public sector has expanded, it has rested on the private sector (both commercial and individual) to provide its revenue, primarily via taxation. This has produced a tendency for 'state expenditure to increase more rapidly than the means of financing them' (O'Connor, 1973: 9). Such explanations may be less helpful than simply suggesting that increasing state activity is paid for out of surplus value and such expenditure means that there is less available for directly productive investments both by the state and by capital.

Following from the last point, Gough has noted the expanding costs and scope of welfare. He argues that there are four reasons for the growth in social expenditure. These are:

1 Rising relative costs: the social services are labour intensive and because there is less possibility of raising productivity to offset higher wages then there is a tendency for the relative costs of the social services to rise faster than the average. As a result a higher level of spending is required year on year simply to maintain services at their pre-existing level.

2 Population changes: there has been a growth in the size of the population and also significant changes in its structure. In particular there has been a growth in the 'dependent' population (children and elderly), and these groups tend to be the heaviest users of welfare services.

3 New and improved services: there are two elements here. First, there has been an expansion of welfare services and secondly various technological and/or bureaucratic improvements or rationalizations have provided more services to wider groups. The National Health Service, for example, has been quite successful at expanding its activities and providing, often expensive, life saving operations.

4 Growing social need: there are two aspects here. First, for example, the growth in unemployment since the mid-1970s in Britain has meant that there has been an increasing need for unemployment and social security benefits. But secondly, needs, like poverty, are relative to the age and the society in which we live and capitalism is constantly generating new needs. As society becomes wealthier then the basic requirements to live and take part in that society (one's basic needs) expand. As a consequence there are demands on welfare to meet these basic needs (although the demands may very well not be met).

The result of these developments, according to O'Connor has been uncontrolled state expansion and increased costs of government. Further, within the state bureaucracy there are individuals and groups who will tend to pursue their own particular ends, the result of which is the duplication of state activities. As a consequence these pressures have all been instrumental in producing what O'Connor calls the 'fiscal crisis of the state': the state increasingly spends more than it earns. But, crucially for O'Connor and Gough, any attempt to solve this crisis by reducing state expenditure will (a) affect economic activity, either immediately or in the future; (b) potentially undermine the legitimation process, and (c) possibly provoke a working-class response in defence of such state spending. Thus while the fiscal crisis may be economic in origin, solutions to any such crisis have directly social and political consequences.

The arguments presented by O'Connor and Gough are complex and both writers utilize substantial data to emphasize the political and economic contradictions of the welfare regimes of modern capitalism. Although we do not have the space to develop their arguments further the important points to note are:

1   that they recognize the economic, political and social factors driving welfare provision and expansion in capitalist societies, and
2   that such expansion becomes one factor in the general ongoing crisis of capitalism, and thus, for the ruling class, one element which must figure in their crisis management.

This does not mean that either of these writers suggests that there will be an inevitable collapse either of capitalism or of welfare provision. But they do note the contradictions associated with welfare provision in capitalist societies and the struggles that welfare and attempts to restructure welfare provision can produce.

Thus to summarize we can note the following:

1   There has been a tendency for state activity to expand and for states to play an increasingly active role in economic, social, and political life.
2   There is a tendency for welfare expenditure to increase as a result of
    (a)   rising relative costs;
    (b)   population changes;
    (c)   new and improved services, and
    (d)   growing social needs.
3   The costs of financing increasing state activity comes out of surplus value. Such expenditure can have benefits for capitalism (and can be indirectly productive) but it is also a drain on resources (such expenditure cannot be used in directly productive activities).
4   Such tendencies promote the fiscal crisis of the state.

Activity 4.3

Why, and in what circumstances, may welfare expenditure produce a 'fiscal crisis' for the state?

4.6 Marxism and welfare: an assessment and summary

The key themes of a Marxist approach to the study of social welfare can be summarized by suggesting that Marxism provides a perspective that orientates on to the totality of capitalism. This involves at least three elements.

First, social welfare must be placed in its appropriate national and international context – global capitalism, structural adjustment programmes, economic crises, the role and activities of the IMF, World Bank, and World Trade Organization, the structural needs of capitalism – all shape the context within which welfare develops, expands, or retracts. Second, social welfare must be located in the activities, decisions, disputes and disagreements between political parties, different sections of the bourgeoisie, and state agencies over social welfare problems, directions, and solutions. Politics matters. What governments do impacts in very real ways on all our lives. Third, state policies have concrete consequences on people's lives (they make gendered assumptions, reinforce particular practices, criminalize, stigmatize, and criticize various modes of living) but equally, people respond to these developments in a range of ways for example, by undertaking collective action to defend existing welfare arrangements or resist new impositions or by setting up alternative, non-state, mutually supportive welfare forms (for example, food co-operatives, credit unions) (see Lavalette and Mooney, 1999a). Social welfare is not a separate, non-conflictual, part of society but an integral part of capitalism, reflecting the conflicts and contradictions of capitalist society in its entirety. Finally the Marxist concepts of totality and mediation, alienation and class, are powerful explanatory tools. They help us understand and explain the social inequalities and contradictions of modern capitalism and the isolation and powerlessness felt by many welfare clients. The concept of class struggle emphasizes the optimism within Marxism – it points to the possibility of a better world, built upon the transformatory potential of the working class as a collective actor with the social power to abolish capitalism.

PART TWO

CRITICAL PERSPECTIVES

In the following section we introduce a number of critical perspectives. By utilizing this terminology we are not suggesting that the approaches which follow are less important or less theoretical than those which were discussed in the last section. Indeed it is important to stress that the four chapters which follow offer a critique on two levels. First, they question the assumptions of social policy and welfare practices. Welfare institutions and social policies operate in ways which assume things about how we live, or should live, our lives. But by making such assumptions they can have the effect of reinforcing the subordinate position of groups within society. Thus social policies make assumptions about our race and who is British and as a result who is deserving of welfare service support or whose needs should be met, about the correct or appropriate role and activities to be performed by women in society and about the types of families we live in, and about legitimate or normal sexual orientations. But such assumptions are social constructions, artificially created by historical processes and should not, therefore, be uncritically accepted or go unchallenged.

The chapters which follow, however, are also radical critiques in a second sense. That is they are critiques of, and challenges to, those paradigms outlined in the last section. Thus what follows covers a range of theoretical perspectives which have grown up in response to what is often termed the gender, race and sexuality 'blindness' of the traditional theoretical perspectives. In other words, by talking in terms of broad historical structures and periods and utilizing wide all-embracing concepts like 'class', 'citizenship', or notions of 'abstract individuals', Marxism, social democratic and liberal and neo-liberal paradigms underplay or ignore the role of specific power relations in society which shape the lives of black people, women, gays and lesbians.

However, we should also introduce a note of caution. Although the chapters in this section are critical of the theoretical approaches already discussed this does not mean that they necessarily reject these paradigms. Some perspectives, like radical feminist or black nationalist theories may dismiss these approaches as being male centred or Eurocentric and thus of little relevance to women or black people, but others depict the feminist critique, the anti-racist perspective, the focus on sexuality as necessary elements widening the appeal and areas of concern of the 'traditional' theoretical perspectives. Thus to take feminist writers as an example, we can identify both socialist feminists, combining insights from social democratic perspectives, Marxist philosophy and feminist concerns, and liberal feminists who develop traditional social democratic and liberal concerns with equality and justice and apply them to the position of women in society. Thus the aim of these writers is to adjust the priorities and concerns of these traditions (liberal, social democratic, Marxist) to include the previously excluded (women) and their main concerns.

Hence in Chapter 5, Kath Woodward introduces the feminist critique of welfare. She looks at the important role played by early social policy legislation in re-creating the family around the concept of the male breadwinner. She then proceeds to look at the way the welfare state and social policies have developed to de-prioritize the concerns of women and to devalue women as secondary welfare citizens.

In Chapter 6 Laura Penketh looks at the assumptions of race and the role of racism in shaping social welfare. She starts by challenging us to think about what is meant by terms such as race and racism and then applies a committed anti-racist perspective to an analysis of the legislative framework and the operation of social welfare.

Angelia Wilson, in Chapter 7, introduces a number of themes which have been marginalized within social policy for too long. The emphasis on the family within social policy clearly discriminates against those who are perceived to live in inappropriate families or whose lifestyle challenges the moral assumptions of family policy. But institutional heterosexism spreads beyond simple family policy. It is present in a range of social services and is shown in the way that social policy and welfare institutions consciously or unconsciously discriminate against gays and lesbians.

Finally in Chapter 8 Iain Ferguson and Charlie Johnstone look at postmodern perspectives on welfare. In the 1980s, postmodernism became a dominant intellectual fashion within various academic disciplines. In social policy, a number of writers have claimed that postmodernism offers an explicitly 'emancipatory' perspective on oppression, diversity, and welfare theorizing and some of these themes are developed in the chapters in this section (see especially Chapter 5). In Chapter 8, however, Ferguson and Johnstone argue against postmodern perspectives developing an astringent critique which harks back to some of the themes outlined in the political economies discussed in Part One.

CHAPTER 5

FEMINIST CRITIQUES OF SOCIAL POLICY

Kath Woodward

5.1 Introduction

This chapter outlines feminist approaches to social policy, starting with some of the shared concerns of feminist critiques and moving on to an exploration of different perspectives within feminism. Feminist critiques are primarily concerned with two themes. First, the ways in which the gendered nature of social practices and institutions have been ignored and gender neutrality assumed within society and social policies, and secondly, the ways in which issues which are of particular relevance and importance to women have in the past been marginalized or excluded from the welfare agenda. In particular, feminists have drawn attention to the patriarchal structure of the welfare state and the different ways in which women and men have been incorporated into the role of citizens (Pateman, 1988). Increasingly feminist concerns have included the diverse concerns of different women and focused on difference as well as equality.

Particular aspects which have been the focus of feminist critiques are discussed here in order to illustrate the impact of feminism and its different strands. The first of these is the family, which has been a major target of state intervention in the implementation of welfare policies and a key concern for feminist research and analysis (Segal, 1987, 1993). Linked to discussion of the family are the issues of domestic violence and sexual abuse, which have become major concerns in recent debates, having been put on the agenda as social, and not individual, problems by feminist activists and researchers with their insistence on listening to the voices of women within families and as survivors (Saraga, 1993). Citizenship is addressed as an example of an important concept in discussion of social policy, which feminists have argued is gendered and not universal or gender neutral.

Thus, the main aims of this chapter are to provide an understanding of the major concerns of feminist analyses, to explore some of the differences between these analyses, to show how the different approaches focus on gender difference as a structuring principle in the provision of welfare, to suggest strategies for the analysis of social policy, and, by using the variety of feminist approaches, to develop a critical perspective on other theoretical positions.

5.2 Historical context

As Lewis (1992) argues, one of the key elements underpinning historical changes in welfare provision has been the shifting relationship between women, men, the family and the state. Women have long been the target of state intervention, often where concern with women as mothers was linked with state anxiety about children especially and family life in general. This can be traced back to the intervention of the state in the private arena of the family and notably to the development in European societies from the eighteenth century onwards of policies which were concerned with the body and health in a trend which Foucault called 'biopolitics' (Foucault, 1987). The idea of state intervention into the family began to be taken for granted, with the notion that women were 'man's salvation, the privileged instrument for civilizing the working class' (Donzelot, 1980).

State intervention has been two-pronged. On the one hand it has been concerned with the regulation of sexual relations and in particular the enforcement of heterosexuality, and on the other it has focused on the family and family-centred legislation, particularly targeting mothers and children. Let us look at each of these in turn.

Enforcing 'appropriate' sexual relations

The two main targets of state policy have been homosexuals and prostitutes, each seen as a danger to the British race, motherhood and the population, and with legislation structured by Victorian concerns about purity and pollution. Homosexuality was seen as a social threat, with the potential to affect the birth rate adversely and to undermine the patriarchal family and, by implication, the hierarchical social order and male authority. Debates about homosexuality in the nineteenth and into the twentieth century related to men, since women were defined by the state as asexual (Weeks, 1977), except as reproducers. The negative public image of the homosexual constructed, for example, by the trials of Oscar Wilde (Weeks, 1977) put pressure on men to marry and have children in order to be seen to be heterosexual, thereby creating a notion of normal sexuality as heterosexual and taking place within the traditional family. This had repercussions for women even if lesbianism was not named in legislation. Lesbians have also been portrayed as a social threat, especially to the normal family. Consequently, although motherhood is seen as women's natural destiny and women are much more likely to be granted custody of their children in divorce cases, even when the woman has committed adultery, the lesbian mother is still less likely to be awarded custody (see Chapter 7). Such values also inform current access to new reproductive technologies where suitability is often defined in relation to a white, heterosexual, middle-class norm (Woodward, 1999).

Explicit and direct attempts were made to categorize and control women's sexuality. This had a moral dimension, where the dichotomy of the 'good' (respectable) woman and the 'bad' (immoral) woman operated. The most obvious instances related to prostitution. The trigger to state intervention was fear about the spread of venereal disease among troops. This was clearly a serious health threat, although anxieties about physical well-being were conflated with those about moral degeneracy. Male sexuality was construed as an imperative which demanded relief. Unlike for the civilian population marriage was not the solution, as in the military population marriage was discouraged because the loyalty of soldiers was to their country and their command. Denied marriage and homosexuality, in theory if not always in practice, the only outlet for men's sexual urges was the prostitute. The Contagious Diseases Acts of 1864, 1866, and 1869 put the entire onus of responsibility and blame for the spread of venereal disease on women (Walkowitz, 1980). Women identified as 'common prostitutes' by the police would then be subject to fortnightly examinations and would be interned in a lock hospital if found to be suffering from venereal disease. There was less emphasis on medical treatment than on moral reform in the lock hospitals. As a result, lock hospitals subjected female inmates to a repressive moral regime (Walkowitz, 1980: 61). The operation of these laws gave the police the right to stop and caution almost any women, thus allowing in particular for the regulation and control of working-class, single women. Male protection through marriage and the respectability thus afforded became even more pressing for women. Needless to say, the Contagious Diseases Acts had no positive impact on the spread of venereal disease, which actually increased between 1876 and 1882, because men were not inspected, and thus freely carried and spread the disease without any preventive or interventionist action by the state directed at them.

Family policy

Family policy, including the identification of women as mothers, with its underlying assumptions about what constitutes the 'normal' family – namely, the traditional, patriarchal, heterosexual family form – has been a particular focus of state intervention and welfare provision. The other main focus has been the idea of the male breadwinner. The 1834 Poor Law Amendment Act which reasserted the Elizabethan Poor Law was based on a major concern with labour and, in particular, the male worker. Women were on the whole considered to be dependants if they were married and non-workers if they were single. The main aim of legislation was to reduce unemployment and promote industry, the assumption being that much unemployment was voluntary. Men were divided into two categories, able-bodied and non-able-bodied, so that male, and hence family, entitlement to support depended on their capacity for work. Women's position was defined according to their marital status. This produced a three-fold categorization, with the first and largest group being married women who were constructed as dependants of their husbands, the breadwinners. The second category included women without a man to support them, seen initially as a homogeneous category (Daly, 1994), to which the state was reluctant to give any support, but later subdivided into the 'deserving' (such as widows) and the 'undeserving' (such as single mothers). Unmarried mothers, who were actually mentioned in the 1834 Report, were themselves to bear sole responsibility for their illegitimate children, although in 1844 it became possible for them to sue for an affiliation order against the father. In the nineteenth century it was women in this group who were more likely to be sent to the workhouse rather than granted outdoor relief, suggesting something of the contribution of moral discourse to the production of a female identity associated with shame and stigma. Single, childless women comprised the third category, which illustrates a division between women based on marital status that has echoes in British income maintenance to the present day. Such single women were regarded as having a duty to work, especially by 1869–70, when Poor Law administration was reviewed.

The notion of a male breadwinner is closely tied to the of that family wage. This idea is bound up with the historical development of the relationship between the family, social production, the modern labour market and industrial production. With the advent of protective legislation such as the Factory Acts of the 1840s, children were excluded from factories and from paid work outside the home. Women were increasingly employed in specifically female sectors of work and married women became less and less likely to be in full-time waged employment, becoming marginalized within the labour market (Barrett and McIntosh, 1980). The financial dependence of carers is implicit in the structure of a society in which responsibility for children and the elderly rests within the family and in which caring for children restricts access to paid work. The family wage assumes women's dependence on men. In the wage bargaining situation it gives men the authority to claim higher wages because of the needs of their dependants. Women do not need outside, paid employment because they have domestic responsibilities and because they are provided for by the male breadwinner; any income they provide is supplementary or 'pin-money'. The family wage undercut arguments for equality of pay and employment opportunities between women and men. Campbell and Charlton are quoted as saying, 'The Labour Movement has managed to combine a commitment to equally pay with a commitment to the family wage' but 'you can't have both' (in Barrett and McIntosh, 1980: 52).

Feminist critiques have not only pointed to the contradictions within the family wage demand, and its incompatibility with demands for equal pay, but they also question the extent to which male breadwinners actually did earn an income sufficient to support a family (Barrett and McIntosh, 1980). Hence, not only did the concept not serve women's interests but neither did it provide the support for working-class families which it purported to do.

Although feminists have adopted different positions on the benefits or otherwise of the family wage it remains a central concept in explanations of social relations, the construction of the modern family and women's place within it. Hartmann argues that the principle behind the family wage, of women's financial dependence on men, and men's rights to women's labour inside the home persists.

> Women's lower wages in the labour market (combined with the need for children to be reared by someone) assure the continued existence of the family as a necessary income-pooling unit. The family, supported by the family wage thus allows the control of women's labour by men both within and without the family. (Hartmann, 1979: 18–19)

State intervention developed throughout the nineteenth and into the twentieth century. Measures included giving Poor Law guardians the power to remove children from unsuitable, 'bad' mothers (the 1899 Poor Law Act), along with more positive initiatives such as the provision of school meals and campaigns for maternity insurance. Women were also to be educated in the art of mothering (Holdsworth, 1988; Sapsford and Abbott, 1988). The 1918 Maternity and Child Welfare Act which led to the provision of infant, and later ante-natal, clinics aimed to improve the quality of mothering. As Gittins points out, however, help was not given to the mothers themselves through this improvement in state support to children (Gittins, 1985). While trade union pressure led to more protection and security for men at times of illness or unemployment, mothers received virtually no support. The 1911 National Insurance Acts which introduced flat-rate subsistence benefits as of right on the basis of contributions in cases of unemployment, sickness, disability and workplace accidents did not cover married women (Gilbert, 1970), a demonstration of how, in the provision of welfare, women are identified primarily as mothers with little, if any, visible independent existence and identity.

After the end of the Second World War state policy sought to encourage women to leave the workforce and return to the home (Richardson, 1993). The Beveridge Report, although written in 1942 when women were actively participating in the public arena – for example, in the armed forces, in munitions factories, and as land workers – assumed that in peace time women would revert to traditional roles. Thus Beveridge stated: 'in the next thirty years housewives as mothers have vital work to do in ensuring the continuance of the British race' (Beveridge, 1942: para. 117).

Key notions about family life, and women's place within that family,

There would not be the same for men only women! ↙

embodied in the Beveridge Report are important in that they set the agenda for British welfare policies and underpin much of what follows. They are mentioned here in order to illustrate that agenda and the implicit assumptions which feminist analysis sought to reveal. Wicks summarizes the assumptions of the Beveridge plan as being:

(a) that marriages are for life . . . the legal obligation to maintain persists until death or remarriage;
(b) that sexual activity and childbirth takes place, or at least should take place only within marriage;
(c) that married women normally do no paid work or negligible paid work;
(d) that women not men should do housework and rear children;
(e) that couples who live together with regular sexual relationships and shared expenses are always of the opposite sex (Wicks, 1991: 93).

Beveridge makes quite explicit reference to the domestic, supporting role of women as mothers. Elsewhere, women are subsumed as a category into the family, but while such universal categories appear to be gender neutral, in reality they rest on assumptions regarding women's perceived position within society. Women are defined in familial terms as carers and nurturers, as in the Beveridge Report, or ignored and not mentioned specifically at all, as in discussion of citizenship as a universal category. One of the objectives of feminist research as been to show how.

> Women are precisely defined, never general representatives of humanity or all people, but as specifically feminine, and frequently sexual, categories . . . Being a man is an entitlement not to masculine attributes but to a non-gendered subjectivity. (Black and Coward, 1981: 83)

Activity 5.1

Look back over this section and try to establish
1 what was assumed about women's position in the family;
2 the workplace;
3 the nature of women's sexuality. How have women been defined by state intervention and what sort of divisions characterize women's and men's social positions?

5.3 Feminism

One of the distinguishing features of the sexual division of labour and of women's social position has been the division between the public and the private arenas and a failure to identify the connections between the two. Demands of the private arena impact on women's participation, or lack of it, in the public arena for example. Women have been located within the private arena of the family, home and domesticity and men defined by their public role, especially in relation to the paid work from which women have often been excluded although this is changing. In the UK although their pay is still only 70 per cent of men's women constitute 44 per cent of the labour market (Social Trends, 2000). This section looks specifically at the kind of questions which feminists raise in response to these questions, and suggests some of the conceptual tools which feminists have developed to explain how women's role has been constructed by state interventions.

Feminist perspectives locate gender as a structuring principle of social policy and the provision of welfare. Feminism puts gender first when defining social problems in explaining their causes or exploring appropriate levels of state or voluntary sector intervention. It contains different perspectives from which to address questions of gender, but what unites all feminist approaches is their concern with the question of how social policies affect women in particular. Initially, feminism can be seen as highlighting the differences and inequalities between women and men, focusing on the different experience of, for example, a social problem such as poverty. Poverty can be seen as a generic social problem, but feminist research demonstrates the different experience of women and men. For example, the use of the term 'family poverty' obscures gender differences and in particular the 'feminization of poverty' (Millar and Glendinning, 1987). Feminist research draws attention to the ways in which women and men view household income differently, with women tending to spend their earnings on domestic items and men retaining some income for their own purposes (Payne, 1991). In poor households women are more likely to deny themselves rather than any other family member (Graham, 1987). This illustrates how feminist approaches ask questions about the different experiences of women and men and challenge definitions of social problems, especially the notion of gender-neutral categories.

Another illustration of this is presented by the apparently gender-neutral concept of 'community care', which feminists have shown to be a euphemism for the unpaid work of women for their family members. Community care is, on the whole, care by women (Finch, 1988). Such policies are based on the assumption that there is a gendered distinction between what Dalley has called 'caring for' and 'caring about' (1988). Whereas men are allowed to care about their families – that is, to feel an emotional bond, without having to care for them (that is, to undertake the practical work of caring) – women are expected to show that they care about family members by caring for them. Thus it is argued the conflation of 'caring about' and 'caring for' operates to ensure that women will continue to provide unpaid community care, with the added constraint of guilt which is experienced by those women who fail to fulfil their 'obligations'.

But feminist critiques are concerned about more than simply exposing the gendered nature of social policies and the definition of social problems with a particular emphasis on women. Feminism also involves some commitment to action to redress the inequalities which empirical enquiry reveals. In the above example of community care, Finch makes a plea for change, and argues, 'Women must have the right not to care and dependent people must have the right not to rely on their relatives' (Finch, 1988: 30). Thus, as well as drawing attention to gender differences and inequalities, through the deconstruction of categories and concepts and through empirical research which emphasizes the need to listen to women's voices and women's accounts of their own experiences, feminism involves a call for change.

Challenging the assumption that it is 'natural' for women to serve and care for others would involve fundamental policy shifts in the provision of care for children, the sick, those with disabilities and the elderly as well as the care of the male workforce within the private arena of the home. It would also necessitate drastic alterations in employment practices. Finally, a further challenge linked to this commitment to action which feminism has presented is a questioning of the traditional orthodoxy of organizations and practices, notably of their hierarchical structures. Feminism has been associated with the collectivist, democratic, non-hierarchical forms of organization of women's groups which reject traditional organizational practices and structures. Women's greater participation in the labour market is leading to challenges to traditional structures and working relationships (Franks, 1999).

Notwithstanding the different approaches and emphases which exist within feminism, there are clearly a number of continuities and shared concerns which include:

1   giving gender a high priority;
2   asking questions about the position of women in particular in relation to the definition of social problems and levels of state intervention;
3   listening to women's voices;
4   drawing attention to gender differences and inequalities;
5   having a political dimension which includes strategies for change; and
6   challenging hierarchical forms of organization.

Activity 5.2

1   Make a list of tasks generally assumed to be performed by men and those generally assumed to be performed by women.
2   What do you think would happen if it could no longer be assumed that women would provide the unpaid care on which community care depends?

All the perspectives have their view on what
u discriminating against women — meanthon
for essay

5.4 Feminist perspectives

Although feminists might agree about the existence of gender inequalities and seek to highlight women's experience, both empirically in their research methodology and in deconstructing 'gender-neutral' categories, they do not agree on the causes of gender differences and inequalities, nor on the form which commitment to change and strategies for effecting change might take. The search for explanation is considered in what follows. This section outlines some of the differences between perspectives in what has been called 'second wave' feminism (Rendall, 1985), a category used to describe developments in the women's movement linking political activity and feminist theoretical work mainly in Europe and the USA, which began in the early 1960s. Some of these positions draw on the repertoires of the 'first wave' feminism of the nineteenth and early twentieth centuries, especially liberalism, and rearticulate conceptualizations drawn from mainstream – or what Daly (1978) has called 'malestream' – social theory. Others, especially those of black feminism have developed in response to perceived limitations of 'second wave' feminism.

Liberal feminism

'First wave' feminists seized on the language of liberalism and demanded formal equality and equal rights to citizenship with men. In its campaigns, liberal feminism has sought to secure equal rights for women within the public domain, focusing on changing legislation. The concerns of this approach since the early 1960s have been about equality and civil rights, with the emphasis on the reform of existing institutions. Explanations of gender inequalities are located within the systems of social and political institutions which can be reformed through the actions of individuals. Organizations such as the National Organization of Women in the USA and the Equal Opportunities Commission in the UK are examples of this strand, with the policy paradigm based on the supposition that, given some reform of social institutions and practices, especially in employment and education, women could attain equality with men.

They have tried to limit discrimination by campaigning to change legislation. They feel this will have the biggest impact.

Socialist/Marxist feminism

Marxist and socialist feminism have been more important in Britain than in the USA, possibly because of the stronger tradition of class based politics. This perspective links the position of women to the dominant mode of production,

of work + having children

and employs a Marxist analytical framework which presents a critique of capitalism (see Chapter 4), along with a feminist critique of patriarchy, as a form of power in which adult men oppress women through their authority and domination over everyone else, including boys and younger men (Rowbotham, 1969). Subsequent debates have engaged with the interrelationship between capitalism and patriarchy. This has involved focusing on women's 'dual role': first, their involvement in the reproduction, not only of the workforce, but also of social relations through their role in the private arena as they produce the next generation and care for the current labour force; and secondly, their activities in the public arena as a reserve army of labour, drawn in and out of the labour market to meet shortfalls in the labour supply (Rowbotham, 1974, 1989). This branch of feminism retains the Marxist emphasis on the unequal distribution of economic power, and thus class divisions within capitalist society, as a source of gender inequality, and stresses the interrelationship between public and private spheres of economic relations and those of gender, sexuality, and domestic living.

Radical feminism

Whereas socialist and Marxist feminists stress class relationships and argue for a fusion of class analysis with an understanding of sex inequality, radical feminists argue that it is patriarchal relationships which provide the central division upon which other forms of oppression are based. The term 'sexual politics' (Millett, 1971) was used to describe unequal power relations between women and men, and patriarchy (that is, men's power), was seen as the source of women's oppression whether institutionally or personally. Radical feminism does not prioritize the economic structure and class relations as Marxists do but views the economy as one institution among many through which men exercise control over women. All social institutions, including the family, education, the law, the police and the military, as well as ideologies of romance (and, at the other extreme, representational systems such as pornography), are seen as part of these patriarchal relations. Some radical feminist positions developed out of what has been called the 'woman-centred' stage of second-wave feminism (Lerner, 1979), which gave priority to female experience as the focus of all study and the source of social and cultural values. Motherhood was a major concern of such approaches (Rich, 1977; Chodorow, 1978). While celebrating motherhood as an essentially female experience, accounts such as Rich's present extensive critiques of motherhood as a social institution under patriarchy which distorts women's experience. In the 1980s and 1990s radical feminist approaches extended Millett's focus on patriarchy to include heterosexuality as a social institution which oppresses women (Rich, 1980; Jeffreys, 1986), and in both, empirical research and political campaigns and practice have often focused on sexual

which is proven in the pay difference which still exist today

women can do same jobs as a man but get paid less.

* *People's perspective!*

violence and support for survivors (Kelly, 1988). The women-centred approaches of radical feminists have been important in establishing alternative 'self-help' welfare services outside the confines of the traditional welfare state. An example of this is the women's refuge movement, the establishment of safe homes for women victims of mental and physical abuse by men.

Black feminism

Boundaries between the different feminist approaches became blurred in the 1980s and 1990s, and other perspectives have developed from the theoretical positions outlined above. Most notably, feminism has had to take on board the critiques of black and minority ethnic women, many of whom have challenged the ethnocentricity of what has been seen as a predominantly white women's movement (Lorde, 1984; Aziz, 1992). For example early second wave feminists' demands for free contraception and abortion on demand were challenged by black women denied the right to have children.

These approaches are briefly outlined here in order to indicate some of the differences between feminist positions. The main differences lie in the emphasis which is given to the factors contributing to gender inequality and in the tension between equality and difference. Should the policies advocated by feminists seek to promote equal treatment of women and men and equality as their goal, thereby assuming that there is a single category 'woman'? Or should such policies acknowledge both what is different about women (that is different from men) and the differences among women? Black feminists, for example, have challenged the ahistoric, blanket category of patriarchy which was the focus of early radical feminism – they point to the weakness of race blind versions of equality, which are defined by people who are white (1998). Race and ethnicity are not irrelevant; they are key components in making up identity. Also if equality involves gender neutrality, Anne Phillips suggests, that would appear to eliminate the possibility of affirmative, positive action, such as those which promote women's greater participation in public life (1999). Arguments which stress economic factors focus on the workplace and include the possibility of shared struggles between women and men, whereas the radical feminist position views men as the source of women's oppression. The liberal position is distinguished by its optimism about reform of the system, even of individuals negotiating their own more egalitarian relationships, without recourse to a revolutionary overthrow of existing social relations. All perspectives give some weight to the social and institutional sources of inequalities between women and men, and each offers some challenge to the imperatives of biological determinism which have often been used to confine women to the private arena of the home and to domestic, caring duties. This discussion also illustrates the close ties between feminist theory and social and political practice. It is through campaigns that feminists have put women and women's concerns on the public agenda, and the explanations which feminists offer for what their research and struggles reveal derive from listening to women's voices.

Activity 5.3

1 What do you think are the causes of women's oppression according to
   (a) liberal feminists;
   (b) Marxist/socialist feminists;
   (c) radical feminists;
   (d) black feminists?
2 What social policy initiatives and wider political solutions do you think each group would promote to secure women's greater independence and liberation?
3 Would these policies involve treating all women equally or recognizing difference?

5.5 Feminism turns to culture

By the 1990s feminism can be seen to have taken a 'cultural turn' and to move from grand theory to local, cross-cultural studies of the complex interplay of sex, race, and class from notions of a female identity to the instability of female identity and the active creation and recreation of women's needs. A new focus on discursively produced meanings about sexual and sexualized identities emerged. For some feminists their concerns became sexual difference and the creation of complex identities. As Michele Barrett and Anne Phillips have argued 'in the past twenty years the founding principles of contemporary feminism have been dramatically changed, with previously shared assumptions and unquestioned orthodoxies relegated to history' (1992: 2). This 'turn to culture' has involved a concern with how meanings are produced, through language and practice and notably, following the work of Michel Foucault, through discourse – women as the targets of social policies and as the recipients of welfare and constructed as 'good' or 'bad' mothers, as the 'dependent lone mother' through the language and practice of welfare provision (Woodward, 1997). This can also be seen as arising out of earlier political campaigns which have been called 'identity politics'. Claiming an identity through membership of a marginalized group is the starting point for political activity. Identities of race, sexuality, disability are produced through how we see ourselves and how we are seen by others and social movements involved in identity politics have sought to reconstruct these identities through more

*why should be seen as "bad momerhood"-father
does it, + has worked for centuries. - mother's shud aw
write to.

Feminist critiques of social policy   93

positive representations and through the celebration of difference. Identities
are given social meanings through the processes whereby they are represented. Culture and the production of meaning about who we are, are seen
as very important. Thus the processes through which meanings are repro-
duced become key sites of investigation. Here the concern of some feminists
is to deconstruct these processes, which appear to be fluid and changing,
rather than fixed or static (Pringle and Watson, 1992). An example of a
changing identity, which has particular resonance for women is that of the
'working mother'. Recent shifts in government policy in the UK have reconstructed the association of paid work and lone motherhood into a notion of
desirable independence. Women, including lone mothers are encouraged to
achieve greater autonomy by engaging in paid work. No longer is paid
work and motherhood construed as signifying irresponsibility and 'bad
motherhood'. It is seen as a desirable move away from dependency on the
state. Whilst feminists might have argued for the removal of women's
dependency on men or on the state through access to paid work, such policies are based on the availability of that paid work and of affordable,
appropriate childcare. –▷ Is needed for mother's to be able to wk.

(margin note: More away from dependency on state & girls save money ↓ they shud encourage this.)

Does this 'turn to culture' mean a retreat from economics and material
inequality? Lynne Segal, arguing from a socialist feminist position, says not.
She suggests that the cultural and the material are not exclusive opposites and
that feminists need both in their analyses (1999). As we have seen in different
examples in women's lives, in the family, in relation to paid work and the
state and sexual identity in this chapter, material circumstances shape experience and are themselves given meaning by cultural processes. However a
focus on social exclusion and the diversity of identities may shift explanations
from material inequalities which does not serve women's interests.

5.6 Feminist critiques of the family

As should be clear by now, the family is a key social institution, a major focus
of social policy, and of feminist research and analysis. Given the family's pivotal social position it is perhaps not surprising that feminists should see it as
the key site for the exercise of male power and authority. As Millett notes,
'Patriarchy's chief institution is the family. It is both a mirror and a connection
to the larger society' (1971: 55). However, although the family is changing,
changes have often led to women being targeted as the source of social ills,
ranging from boys' under-performance at school to criminality and even
marriage breakdown and the increase in teenage pregnancies.
Women's position within the family has previously been taken for granted
as universal and 'natural' and hence not worthy of investigation (Beechey,
1985). Second-stage feminism sought to rectify this, and the family has been
the focus of many feminist critiques, moving from fierce criticism of the

family – notably the patriarchal nuclear family – through powerful celebration of women's role as mothers, to diverse analyses reflecting positions which seek to address differences between women as well as those between women and men (Segal, 1993). Feminist critiques of motherhood have ranged from Firestone's demands that women be freed from their biology and 'the tyranny of reproduction and childbearing' (Firestone, 1970: 221) to Adrienne Rich's vision of a time when 'woman (as mother) is the presiding genius of her own body . . . and thinking itself will be transformed' (Rich, 1977: 285–6). What is important for analysis of social policy is the feminist questioning of dominant ideologies of family life and the focus of the patriarchal family as the source of women's oppression.

At the start of second-wave feminism, following the sustained attempt after 1945 to reconstruct and impose the traditional family, with women firmly positioned at its centre (as illustrated by the Beveridge Report), the main concern of feminists was to investigate that familial form, to challenge the view that the family was a safe haven, 'a little world immune from the vulgar cash nexus of modern society' (Barrett and McIntosh, 1985: 28). Friedan (1963) in the USA exposed the experience of the 'problem with no name' and the depression of housewives in the 1950s. Gavron (1966) described the feelings of frustration and isolation of housebound wives in Britain, and attention has been drawn to the despair, and even violence, experienced, by women within the family. The alienation and despair experienced by many women within the nuclear family and within marriage was well supported by empirical research – for example in the USA (Bart, 1971; Bernard, 1973) – and Britain (Oakley, 1974). Evidence was produced by listening to women's voices and by exploring those areas of the private arena, hitherto invisible and unquestioned, such as housework, previously not classified as work (Oakley, 1974).

Feminist research set the context for future methodological and conceptual debates as it fought to expose the gender specific nature of apparently universal concepts like the family. The research challenged the assumptions of the Beveridge Report and, albeit less explicitly, of social policy initiatives such as community care which assume that the family can be conceptualized as a single unit. The internal organization and functions of the family have to be investigated and the interconnections between the family and the wider social, political, and economic context disentangled, exploring the interrelationship between the public and the private arenas.

The aims of many feminists in the early 1970s were to seek gender equality, through, for example, improving the conditions under which women experienced family life, because 'the socialization of housework, paid maternity leave, proper collective childcare, publicly funded, and decent jobs with shorter working hours were the solutions advanced' (Wilson, 1989: 15). This could include more involvement by men in childcare and domestic labour, stressing liberal notions of equality, where women and men should be able to participate in public life and in the labour market as well as being parents and carers.

The later 1970s saw the emphasis shift, with a move within feminism to revalue the female and celebrate uniquely female attributes and qualities, notably women's mothering. Rich makes a distinction between the repressive, patriarchal social institution of motherhood and women's mothering abilities. Dinnerstein and Chodorow explored the psychological effects of the fact that it is women who mother (Dinnerstein, 1976; Chodorow, 1978). Other feminists brought together these notions of a maternal identity, suggesting some universal characteristics of 'maternal thinking' and 'maternal practices' (Ruddick, 1980) and women's separate styles of moral reasoning (Gilligan, 1982). Such approaches have been more popular in the USA than in Britain, although some work using psychoanalytic theory, notably based on the Object Relations School, has informed analysis of the mother-daughter relationship and the work of feminist psychotherapists such as Eichenbaum and Orbach (1982). For other writers this emphasis on motherhood has been seen as reactionary and essentialist in its stress on a biological role and thus as colluding with a traditionalist view of women within the home (Segal, 1987).

This examination of the two facets of feminism in the 1960s and 1970s shows that it has ranged from critique to celebration of women's maternal role. However, both approaches include the need to explore the diversity of family forms, to challenge the notion that the nuclear family of 1950s ideology was universal and natural, and to argue for a deconstruction of the family as a natural unit and its reconstruction as a social unit (Rapp, 1979). Difference and diversity have increasingly become recognized following the critiques by black and Asian feminists of the ethnocentricity of white feminism's stress on the particular examples of white, middle-class women. Many black women might well have welcomed more leisure time at home freed from the demands of their low-paid work (hooks, 1984) and would not have experienced the boredom of Friedan's housewives. Others sought to secure their fertility rights against enforced sterilization and contraception rather than struggling to obtain rights to abortion on demand as expressed in the demands of the Women's Liberation Movement (Aziz, 1992).

Feminist analyses have also had to engage with the realities of profound demographic and social change in a world whose economics and politics have been transformed since the crises of the 1970s (see, for example, Chapters 3 and 4). In Britain, as elsewhere in Europe, an increasing number of children were born to unmarried mothers. In 1999 38 per cent of babies were born to unmarried women. The number of children living with a lone parent has trebled in 25 years to reach 2.8 million in 1999. Families are becoming smaller, and the average number of children among married and cohabiting couples in the UK is 1.7, with many more women choosing not to have a child at all. The OPCS estimates that nearly 25 per cent of women born in 1980 will not have any children. Britain has an ever escalating divorce rate, the highest in Europe, estimated at 40 per cent of marriages in 1999, with three-quarters of all divorces instigated by women. More women, including mothers, are participating in the labour market, albeit often in low paid and part-time

work. In 1998, 48 per cent of women and 64 per cent of men were in employment in the UK, with women constituting 44 per cent of the workforce (data
from Social Trends, 2000). All of these factors create a very different pattern of
domestic living for women from that represented by the familial ideologies of
the 1950s. This changing climate coincided with the Thatcher years in Britain,
when social policy involved a retreat from state welfare provision in favour of
a market-led system, a retreat which has created difficulties for many women,
including the growing numbers of lone parent families, most of which are
headed by women, living in poverty (Social Trends 2000, and also see Chapter
12). This has persisted in the UK with different responses to the so-called
problems of the 'dependency culture' of lone parenthood (McIntosh, 1998).
Feminist critiques of the family and social policy over this period have
stressed material factors as the major contributors to the problems of single
mothers (Campbell, 1987), in contradiction to the rhetoric of New Right politicians who have constructed single motherhood within a moral discourse and
sought to reinstate the traditional two-parent family. In the words of the
Conservative family campaign, 'putting father back at the head of the table'
(Webster, 1986).

[handwritten margin note: In Thatcherism s. pricy. created many difficulties for lone parents (women)]

Activity 5.4

1 It would be useful to stop at this point to consider the main features of
   the feminist critiques of the family which have been discussed here. Which
   factors do such critiques take into account in analysing the family? What
   distinguishes feminist critiques?
2 How can feminists respond to recent policies of encouraging lone
   mothers into the workplace?

5.7 Violence and the family

In this section we explore two examples of violence within the family which
have been 'rediscovered' in the last 20 years, and consider their implications
for social policy.

Domestic violence

Feminism has contributed to the exposure of domestic violence and has challenged assumptions about the privacy of the home, showing that these
assumptions are based on the idea that members of a family have a right to do

as they please within that family, and that families should resolve their own problems if any occur and not appeal to outside, public agencies. Feminists have shown that such principles fail to address the unequal rights of different family members, and argue that the family structure reflects and reproduces men's power over women, Empirical investigation indicates that domestic violence committed by men against their female partners accounts for a quarter of all reported acts of violence and that 70 per cent of violence takes place within the home (Pahl, 1985). Feminist research has put this violence on the public agenda and has investigated women's perceptions of their experience.

facts

Feminist explanations of the phenomenon vary, though in general radical feminist explanations see domestic violence as a feature of patriarchy and men's control over women: 'although there are many ways that men as a group maintain women in oppressed social positions, violence is the most overt and effective means of social control' (Yilo and Bograd, 1988). Such feminist approaches and studies of male violence, and especially feminist campaigns including the work of the Women's Aid Federation, have been very important in increasing awareness of gender inequalities, abuse, and violence against women which had hitherto been concealed within the private arena of the family and personal relationships (Kelly, 1988). Women's campaigns have led to the establishment of refuges where the victims of violence can escape with their children and receive support and advice, and to increased recognition of the extent of domestic violence against women and the need for intervention – for example, by the police.

Socialist feminism sees domestic violence as resulting from class related, economic factors, including poverty and material deprivation, which have been identified as significant contributory elements. The poverty which women and children experience is linked to the notion of the male breadwinner and to the construction of women's dependency. The lack of childcare, and hence the difficulty experienced by single mothers in participating in the labour market, has ensured women's dependency on the state and on men. The gendered construction of income maintenance produces a system where men's eligibility depends on their labour market characteristics, such as age, invalidity, and unemployment, and women's, in contrast, is determined by their marital and family situation. Unless women are single and childless, their access to income maintenance is determined by whether they are seen as having a man who could, or should, support them. Married women were encouraged to rely on derived insurance rights until the late 1970s and were barred from claiming means-tested Supplementary Benefit for the family until the early 1980s. The entitlement of mothers who are not married, or those who are separated or divorced, has been governed by moralistic directives over a period of time extending from the New Poor Law to Beveridge (Daly, 1994). Women's dependence on men or on the state, especially through non-contributory, means-tested provision rather than insurance provision in their own right, has tied women into social and familial relations which have often provided the site of their experience of domestic violence. Feminist per-

Reinforced discrimination.

spectives challenge individualistic and psychological explanations of domestic violence and locate it within the broader social context.

Child abuse

The emergence of child abuse as a social problem in the last 20 years has attracted considerable media attention, sometimes leading to moral panics about the breakdown of family life, or perhaps more frequently, the scapegoating of social workers (MacLeod and Saraga, 1988). Feminist research in this area has again challenged existing assumptions about the privacy of the home, the responsibility of individuals, notably mothers, and the ideas of 'mother blaming'. Feminists have been concerned to explore the complexity of this phenomenon and to disentangle some of the assumptions about what constitutes child abuse, who is responsible and why it occurs.

In order to address these questions the distinction has been made between physical abuse and sexual abuse, and empirical research has been conducted which suggests that sexual abuse of children is mainly perpetrated by men, without specific characteristics of age, class, or culture. Physical abuse is more frequently committed by women, although it has to be noted that women are much more likely than men to have responsibility for children (Saraga, 1993). Physical abuse is linked to cases of domestic violence (Finkelhor, 1983) and to class and poverty.

Feminist research raises questions about the definition of child abuse which reflects problems about what is considered normal and what abnormal, what is the boundary between the two, and who decides the location of this boundary. Feminist research has concentrated on the experiences of women and children as survivors of abuse, who had hitherto largely been excluded from research studies. This has raised questions about who should be investigated. Should it be victims or parents (for whom read 'mothers')? The last, and most important question is that of explanation, and it is in this area that the feminist contribution has been most significant. Feminists go beyond describing what happens and, in the case of domestic violence and child sexual abuse, ask questions about why men should seek to exercise power and control over women and children. Feminists do not see this violence as exceptional or deviant masculine behaviour, but rather as an extension of the social construction of male sexuality which is articulated through the language of power and domination (*Feminist Review*, 1988). Even though it can be argued that feminist critiques do not achieve full recognition, they have put domestic violence and child abuse on the public agenda where they have since been acknowledged as social problems. It is no longer possible to dismiss these issues as private concerns or even individual problems, although 'blaming the victim' and 'mother blaming' have not entirely disappeared from explanatory frameworks and interventions.

> **Activity 5.5**
>
> 1 What behavioural traits would you characterize as:
>   (a) masculine; and
>   (b) feminine?
> 2 Look at your list and think about which, if any of these are
>   (a) biologically based or determined; and
>   (b) which of them are social constructions.
> 3 Has public policy been responsive to problems stemming from 'masculine identity'?
> 4 How are the biological and the social connected? Can you think of examples of where the one affects the other?

5.8 Gender and citizenship

This section explores the concept of citizenship upon which the British welfare system is based. In it we widen the debate and examine the concept of citizenship which is accorded a significant role in some theoretical accounts of the welfare state. This section should be read in conjunction with Chapters 2 and 10.

The majority of writing on citizenship does not include the dimension of gender (Marshall, 1950; Mann, 1987; Turner, 1990). A great deal of debate about citizenship has been concerned with social class and draws on the work of T.H. Marshall, with its three components of civil, political, and social citizenship (1950, 1975, 1981). Criticisms of Marshall have included discussion of his ethnocentricity and even of his failure to acknowledge the public/private dichotomy (Turner, 1990), but gender as a concept is significantly absent from these critiques. The fact that women did not achieve many of the features of either political or civil citizenship in Britain before 1928 might suggest that women have simply been slower to attain full citizenship status, but that it is still possible. In the liberal view, all that is required is the removal of legislative barriers and overt discrimination. A whole range of other civil rights have been won by women in western nation states: for example, access to education, the right to own property, to terminate a marriage and to professional employment (see Walby, 1988), some before suffrage rights and some in the years afterwards.

Feminist critiques of the second wave have challenged the unified notion of citizenship as a model to which women can aspire on equal terms with men. They locate citizenship within the broader social context and stress the gender differences which a unified concept obscures. Although most theorists include class – and the key debate has been about the relationship between class and citizenship in a capitalist society – the structural factor of patriarchy has not been addressed. Feminists argue that 'democratic theorists fail to recognize the *patriarchal* structure of the welfare state; the very different way that women and men have been incorporated as citizens' (Pateman, 1992: 223). The structuring of the public and private spheres is crucial to the position of women and their citizenship status. 'The patriarchal division between public and private is also a sexual division . . . The public world of universal citizenship is an association of free and equal individuals . . . of men who interact as formally equal citizens' (Pateman, 1992: 226).

Walby argues that the patriarchal institution of the 'male-dominated household is incompatible with full citizenship' (Walby, 1994: 391) and that the solution to the exclusion of women from full citizenship rights is the socialization of women's domestic role, just as other aspects of work in the domestic arena have been socialized – through schools, nurseries, and hospitals, for example.

Feminists have shown how social citizenship depends largely on being a paid worker in order to obtain full rights. Women whose primary responsibilities lie with care of children, husbands, and the elderly tend not to have access to the higher levels of income generated by occupational pensions. Many women are in part-time employment, and Lister (1990) argues that the demands on women as carers, and their availability for unpaid work, limits their full participation in political citizenship while their financial dependency is an obstacle to civil citizenship. Overall, it is women's domestic and caring duties, part of the institution of patriarchy, which exclude them from full citizenship rights, making clear the gendered nature of the concept of citizenship. However, this also presents a dilemma for feminists. On the one hand it seems that to obtain full civil citizenship rights women should participate in the labour market and abandon the constraints of domestic duties, and on the other that women's caring roles should be recognized and supported. Lister calls for changes 'so as to reflect the value to society as a whole of caring work, whether it be done in private or public sphere' (1990: 464). Do women join the world on men's terms or seek recognition of 'women's work'?

As Pateman (1992) points out, this is a false dichotomy, as is the opposition between men's independence and women's dependence, and it is essential to recognize the interrelationship between the public and private arenas. She argues for the construction of a welfare society instead of a welfare state to accommodate the changes which are taking place in employment and in patterns of domestic living in the late twentieth century. This challenge to mutually exclusive binary oppositions, such as male/female and public/private, upon which much of our understanding of gender has been based, is a feature of recent postmodernist feminist approaches which seek to address and understand difference and diversity.

Activity 5.6

1 Given the discussion of feminist critiques in this chapter, what challenge can be mounted to the liberal claim that women's achievement of citizenship rights has merely been slower than men's?
2 What are the problems associated with policies which treat women as equal to men? Does this mean treating women and men the same?

5.9 Summary and conclusion

This chapter has mapped out some of the shared concerns of feminist approaches as well as some of the differences between them. It has been argued that it is no longer possible to talk of feminism, but only of 'feminisms' (Crowley and Himmelweit, 1992). However, all feminist approaches include a concern with gender and with asking questions about the position of women in relation to social policy. They go further than this and question the basis of universal categories such as citizenship and equality and of naturalistic concepts like the family, and in deconstructing these conceptualizations reveal their gendered features. Often, as has been shown here, the universal category is largely male and women's exclusion has passed unobserved, until feminism drew attention to this. Feminist critiques have challenged traditional categories and oppositions such as the natural and the social, the material and the cultural and have engaged with the tension between equality and difference. Feminist theories have developed out of political action and campaigning and are born of the interrelationship between theory and practice.

CHAPTER 6

RACISM AND SOCIAL POLICY

Laura Penketh

6.1 Introduction

This chapter will explore the relationship between race and social policy, specifically analysing how racist assumptions and race-related policies have influenced, and continue to affect the lives of Britain's black population.

Across Britain black people face violence and abuse against themselves, their families, their homes and their properties. This was shown most graphically in the 1990s in the murders of Stephen Lawrence, Michael Menson, and Ricky Reel.

Less conspicuous is the manifestation of institutional racism in society that affects the representation, treatment, and systematic discrimination that black people face in the labour market and within a range of state institutions. For example, the 1997/1998 Labour Force Survey revealed that: 'Unemployment rates were 6% for whites, 8% for Indians, 19% amongst the black community and 21% amongst Bangladeshis and Pakistanis [and that] . . . More than 40% of 16 to 17 year olds from ethnic-minority groups were unemployed compared to 18% of their white peers' (*The Guardian*, 21 February 2000). Discriminatory processes also operate in relation to the earnings of black and white workers in equivalent jobs. For example, the Institute for Social and Economic Research found that between 1985 and 1995: 'On average, Pakistani and Bangladeshi men earned just over half the salary of their white peers' (*The Guardian*, 21 February 2000). In relation to other aspects of social life, black people are more likely to live in inferior housing in run-down areas (Ginsburg, 1992; Law, 1998), experience higher mortality and morbidity rates (Skellington and Morris, 1992), differential health provision (Mason, 2000), and are often subject to differential treatment in terms of educational provision (Troyna and Hatcher, 1992; Gore, 1998). For example, the Children's Society in 1999 revealed that black children are six times more likely to be expelled from school than white children (*The Guardian*, 21 February 2000). These statistics were reinforced in the Macpherson Report that published the findings of the Stephen Lawrence inquiry. Housing departments were seen to be too slow and bureaucratic in response to racist tenants, and in schools there was disturbing evidence of widespread racist attitudes amongst very young children, and a failure to implement anti-racist policies (*The Guardian*,

25 February 1999). While Statewatch noted that within the criminal justice system: 'Black people are between four and seven times more likely to be sentenced to prison terms, and nearly eight times more likely to be stopped and searched by the police' (*The Guardian*, 21 February 2000). However, as well as recognizing these facts, the student of social policy needs to obtain a critical understanding of why such inequalities exist. Thus, the first half of this chapter will explore these concepts in the appropriate political, economic, and historical context, and will critically assess the nature of postwar race-related legislation and the development of political ideologies and explanations underlying legislative change.

The second part of the chapter, using state social work and the criminal justice system as examples, moves on to examine how racism manifests itself in specific state institutions. These are important examples, for they provide an opportunity to assess the nature of institutional racism within organizations and the difficulties in tackling it effectively. In relation to social work provision, the Central Council for Education and Training in Social Work (CCETSW) found itself under pressure to tackle racism effectively during the 1980s and attempted to develop an anti-racist strategy in the early 1990s. Within the criminal justice system, it was the Macpherson Report that exposed the nature of institutional racism within the police force, and provoked a fierce and controversial public and political debate regarding the validity of its findings. In both cases, the professional and political backlash that resulted, demonstrates that whilst anti-racist initiatives are clearly relevant in a society structured by inequality, they are vulnerable to counter-policies from political opponents hostile to anti-racist perspectives.

6.2 Race and the origins of racism

Following the Second World War, scientists and social scientists were asked by the newly established United Nations to examine the question of whether racial difference as expounded by the Nazis had any scientific foundation. They concluded that it had none. More recently the developing science of genetics has further confirmed this view by demonstrating that there is more statistically significant genetic diversity within population groups than between them. To geneticists, the physiological differences associated with race have no more significance than hair or eye colour. Thus, race is a social construct and not a scientifically valid reality. However, most people think that races exist, institutions consciously and unconsciously discriminate against people on the grounds of 'race', and hence the concept motivates action, behaviour, and discrimination, which we can understand as racism (Miles, 1984), which occurs: 'Where a group of people is discriminated against on the basis of characteristics which are held to be inherent in them as a group' (Callinicos, 1993: 17). In short, although biologically discrete races do not exist, racism certainly does, and millions of people's lives are blighted by racist discrimination. In order to understand why this is so, we need to critically explore and analyse how notions of racial superiority and inferiority developed historically.

At this juncture however, it is also important to note that we need to distinguish the term 'racism' from 'prejudice' and 'discrimination.' Prejudice means irrational attitudes and beliefs held by individuals, and discrimination concerns action on the basis of these beliefs. However, although visible minorities in society may suffer from the prejudiced views of individuals, which may result in unfair discrimination, racism is not merely the sum total of the actions of prejudiced individuals. As the following section reveals, any analysis of racism needs to go beyond individual and cultural prejudice to recognize the structural and institutional nature of racism. Structural analyses see notions of natural inferiority and superiority arising in the conditions of capitalism, and institutional racism describes the systematic discrimination that black people experience, in, for example, jobs, housing, and education. In short, racism is an institutional feature integrated into the history and social, economic, political and ideological fabric of British society (Sivanandan, 1982; Miles, 1989; Divine, 1991).

6.3 The roots of racism

Racism is a relatively modern phenomenon that grew up with the development and expansion of capitalism (Miles, 1982; Fryer, 1984; Callinicos, 1993). According to Fryer (1984) it developed in Britain through three distinct phases that he terms, the 'racism of slavery', the 'racism of empire' and the 'racism of postwar migration'.

The racism of slavery

The racism of slavery developed in the seventeenth and eighteenth centuries in order to justify the systematic use of African slave labour in the great plantations of the New World, when, during the eighteenth century alone, some twelve million African captives were transported to work on the plantations of North America and the West Indies (Blackburn, 1997). Racist ideologies were constructed based on the view that humankind was divided into races reflected in distinct biological characteristics, with white races being superior to black races. They constructed, promoted, and disseminated images of black populations as, for example, savage, unintelligent, dirty, and licentious (Fryer, 1984). Edward Long (the son of a Jamaican planter) wrote in his *Universal History* (1736–65) that Africans were:

proud, lazy, treacherous, thievish, hot, and addicted to all kinds of lusts, and most ready to promote them in others . . . as . . . revengeful, devourers of human flesh, and quaffers of human blood . . . It is hardly possible to find in any African any quality but what is of the bad kind: they are inhuman, drunkards, deceitful, extremely covetous . . . (quoted in Fryer, 1984: 154)

Further, he stated that there was a continuous chain of intellectual gradation from monkeys through varieties of blacks, 'until we mark its utmost limit of perfection in the pure white' (quoted in Fryer, 1984:159).

Notions of race and of biological superiority and inferiority were expanded upon during the mid-nineteenth century when there was the greatest migration of peoples in history, revealed in the mass migration of European immigrants to America, and to a lesser extent, Australia and South Africa (Hobsbawm, 1977). During this period, as a result of poverty, repression, and famine in Ireland, there were high levels of Irish migration to Britain, when the Irish were described as, for example, 'human chimpanzees', charged with 'backwardness'. Notions of inferiority were based on the view that the Anglo Saxon blood of the English was superior to the Celtic blood of the Irish (demonstrating that racism is not always an anti-black issue).

The racism of empire

The racism of Empire can be traced through the expansion of colonial conquest at the end of the nineteenth century, and further reinforced inequalities within the social structure. By 1914 the British Empire covered 12,700,000 square miles, and had a population of 431 million, consisting of 370 million black people, but only 60 million of the white self-governing population. Britain's rulers therefore needed a racism more subtle and diversified, but just as aggressive, as that used to justify slavery (Fryer 1988). As a result, from the 1840s to the 1940s, scientific theories reflecting notions of inferiority and superiority emerged to justify this exploitation. For example, phrenology, a pseudo-science that deduced people's characters from the shape of their skulls, was used to explain that the skulls of Africans clearly demonstrated their inferiority. Anthropology was also used to demonstrate to the British that black people were closer to apes than to Europeans, and that they were intellectually inferior. As Anglo Saxonism, racism claimed that God had fitted the British to rule over others – even though for most of human history Britain (and the North west of Europe generally) remained a remote and backward place, far behind the advanced societies of the Mediterranean, Indian subcontinent, and China (Harman, 1999). In its popular version, the message that black people were savages, who could be rescued from heathenism by British rule, was transmitted through schools, newspapers, literature and popular entertainment. The main political function of all these theories was to justify British rule over black people (Fryer, 1988).

The racism of postwar migration

The third phase discussed by Fryer (1984) was the racism of postwar migration. In the postwar period, Britain experienced an acute labour shortage, and politicians actively sought labour from Commonwealth countries. As a result, during the 1950s and 1960s, economic migrants from Britain's Commonwealth entered the country because of the demands of the job market, and as a result of poverty and lack of opportunity in their country of birth (due to the immiseration of the colonies under the British Empire). Workers were particularly needed in sectors of the economy characterized by the poorest pay and conditions, such as textiles, catering, and public transport, which white workers could afford to reject in an era of economic expansion and full employment. But precisely because of the history of racism and the way it was deeply embedded within British society, migrants arrived to face harrowing levels of discrimination and abuse. This is very important in understanding the position that the black population came to occupy both geographically and economically in Britain. The location of the black workforce within already overcrowded conurbations where they occupied the largely unskilled and low status jobs resulted in their also occupying very poor housing in inner-city areas. It also contributed to, and reinforced notions of white superiority, for racism offered white workers the comfort of believing themselves to be superior to black workers, and during economic crises enabled employers and politicians to scapegoat black workers and blame them when levels of unemployment rose (Husband, 1980).

Activity 6.1

1   How can we explain the emergence of notions of white superiority and black inferiority during the seventeenth century?
2   In what ways have economic and political developments since then reinforced these ideas?

6.4 The racialization of politics

The growth of black migration to Britain in the immediate postwar period provoked a series of racist responses. First, prejudice was widespread and:

More than two-thirds of Britain's white population . . . held a low opinion of black people or disapproved of them. They saw them as heathens . . . as uncivilized, backward people, inherently inferior to Europeans . . . and suffering from unpleasant diseases. They saw them as ignorant and illiterate . . . they believed that black men had stronger sexual urges than white men. (Fryer, 1984)

The most prejudiced strongly objected to mixed marriages, would not allow black people in their homes, and refused to work with them.

This prejudice led to many incidents of verbal abuse and physical violence, which for many years, were treated with complacency by the government, state institutions, and the population as a whole. However, in August 1958 in Nottingham, after a series of attacks on individual black people in the Nottingham streets, and an incident of fighting between blacks and whites, anti-black race riots took place. There were calls for the black population to 'go back to their own country' and be banned from social venues such as pubs. On one occasion, thousands of white people took to the streets shouting, 'Let's get the blacks' (Fryer, 1984: 377), and there were incidents of physical harm against black people and attacks on their property. There were also disturbances and riots in London in 1958 where racist attacks against the black population were commonplace. Gangs of white teenagers armed with iron bars, sticks, and knives went out, as they put it, 'nigger hunting'. As a result, many black people were seriously injured, yet the police, demonstrating their own hostility to the black population, offered no effective opposition to these groups and their activities.

However, discrimination can be direct and indirect, overt and covert, and during this same period, state social policy was imbued with racism. Labour and Conservative politicians, both fearful of losing votes and seats, progressively accommodated themselves to racism. They blamed the black population for 'race relations' problems rather than the racism of the white population, and called for restrictions on black immigration. As a result, racism became institutionalized and legitimized, enshrined in the law of the land, reflected in the development of state immigration controls whose aim was to limit black entry to Britain. An exploration of race-related legislation from the 1960s onwards demonstrates how the migration of labour to Britain, became increasingly tangled up in the politics of race, and was mediated by the role played by politicians. For example, the Conservative politician Enoch Powell, who had encouraged black migration when there was a shortage of labour in the British economy, later warned the British population that as a result of increased immigration: '. . . their wives (were) unable to obtain hospital beds on childbirth, their children were unable to obtain school places, their homes and neighbourhoods were changed beyond recognition' (quoted in Sivanandan, 1981: 82). In the postwar period racial discrimination was legal, and employers and other groups such as landlords could simply state that 'no coloureds' were wanted. In the mid-1960s however, in an atmosphere of increasing racist political activity, the government responded by adopting two related strategies: integration and restriction. Integration was to be achieved through a number of policies to promote appropriate relations between the races. In 1965, the Race Relations Act made it unlawful to discriminate on the grounds of race, colour, or ethnic or national origin in public places such as hotels, restaurants, and swimming pools. The Act also set up the Race Relations Board to receive complaints of discrimination. Three years later, the Race Relations Act of 1968 made discrimination in the area of employment, housing, and the provision of goods and services unlawful, and made it possible to bring cases of discrimination to court. The 1976 Race Relations Act replaced the 1968 Act, and for the first time the law was extended to cover indirect discrimination. That is, unlawful practices, which whatever their intentions, were shown to have a disproportionately adverse effect on the minority ethnic communities. The Commission for Racial Equality replaced the functions of the Race Relations Board at this juncture. Another piece of relevant legislation was the 1966 Local Government Act which provided funds for what became known as 'Section 11' workers, who were employed to promote the integration of new Commonwealth immigrants into British society in areas such as education.

The second strand of government strategy was 'restriction' of black entry to Britain. The Conservative government in 1962 introduced the Commonwealth Immigrants Act which limited entry from the 'coloured' Commonwealth by making workers apply for different categories of work vouchers based on their occupational skills. Although the Labour government bitterly opposed this whilst in opposition, the degree of popular support for the measure caused serious problems for them during the 1964 election, and they reversed their position. Instead, they not only kept the Act on the statute books, but passed another such Act in 1968 at the time of Enoch Powell's notorious speech on race matters, and the crisis caused by the expulsion of British passport-holding Asians from Kenya (Penketh and Ali, 1997). In 1971 the Conservative government further tightened restriction on black migration by passing the Immigration Act, the consequence of which was British passport holders from the new Commonwealth were no longer guaranteed entry to Britain. As Miles and Phizacklea (1984) note, the progressive tightening of entry requirements had a clear political implication; the black presence was viewed as creating political and social problems and the solution was to limit the numbers entering the country.

Since the 1980s, legislation associated with race and immigration had become increasingly punitive as a result of economic recession, rising levels of unemployment, and the election of a right-wing Conservative government. The Conservative Prime Minister, Margaret Thatcher, voiced the following opinion, during the 1970s: '. . . you know, the British character has done so much for democracy, for law, and done so much throughout the world, that if there is a fear that it might be swamped, people are going to react and be rather hostile to those coming in' (quoted in Miles, 1993: 76). She and her government reinforced notions that the black British presence was a threat to Englishness or

Britishness, reflected in the 1981 British Nationality Act, and by Margaret Thatcher's positive references to Britain's history as an imperial power.

These sentiments have been resurrected more recently in relation to the debate regarding asylum seekers and refugees, and in the context of increasing global instability, the growth of oppressive regimes, and an escalation of internal conflict in areas such as the Balkans. The debate over immigration has now been expanded and applied to groups such as Kosovan refugees, who face the same direct and indirect abuse that Asian and Afro-Caribbean migrants faced in the past, portrayed as 'economic migrants' seeking to abuse the hospitality of European states, a view reinforced by politicians and sections of the press. For example, Michael Howard, the then Conservative Home Secretary, stated that: 'We are seen as a very attractive destination because of the ease with which people can gain access to jobs and benefits . . . only a tiny proportion (of asylum seekers) are genuine refugees' (cited in Cook, 1998: 152). As a result, legislation such as the Asylum and Immigration Act (1996), instead of focusing on the legal and welfare rights of immigrants, is increasingly involved in criminalizing them. The 1996 Act has included withdrawing asylum seekers' rights to income support, child benefits, and public housing, and anyone not satisfying entry clearance requirements is liable to detention, leading to concerns that a form of welfare apartheid is being established. There is evidence of scathing and vitriolic attacks by politicians and sections of the press. For example, in the British press refugees have been described as 'scum of the earth' and 'human sewage' (Marfleet, 1999: 75), and by the mid-1990s, a network of prison camps and holding establishments had been set up across the European Union, with the British state imprisoning asylum seekers at a rate of 10,000 a year (*The Independent*, 28 June 1999). Yet, these debates fail to acknowledge that, in fact, Britain is a net exporter of people.

The tone of political and public debate regarding refugees and asylum seekers has been strongly criticized by Nick Hardwick, Chief Executive of the Refugee Council, who recently stated that: 'It beggars belief that one of the richest countries in the world cannot deal with the tiny proportion of refugees who come to us without becoming hysterical. We all have a responsibility to restore some sanity to the situation' (*The Guardian*, 11 February 2000). The *Observer* editorial (13 February 2000) also expressed its disgust regarding the treatment of asylum seekers when it stated that:

The widespread view is that Britain is a soft target for asylum seekers. The truth is different. Britain has so tightened up its asylum rules that the country is effectively impenetrable, with among the lowest rates of asylum seekers in the West. The level of financial support is miniscule and the welfare state is so inadequate it hardly offers protection for native Britons, let alone asylum seekers . . . People need to be desperate to leave the country of their birth; most asylum-seekers are *bona-fide* applicants fleeing from oppression . . . And when they enter, we need to ensure that natural justice is applied. That their claim is genuine unless proved otherwise, and, if accepted, that they have every right to be treated as properly as we would if the same tragedy befell us. The implicit racism [in the coverage of asylum seekers] expressed last week from the floor of the Commons to the *Nine O'Clock News* disgraced and belittled us all.

This is evidence of the continuing hold of racism, and the extent to which structural and institutional racism is embedded in British society.

Activity 6.2

1   What do we mean by the 'racialization of British politics?'
2   Since the 1950s, what form has direct and indirect discrimination taken in relation to Britain's black population?

6.5 Anti-discriminatory perspectives

Since the 1950s, there have been political attempts to address, what are considered, 'race-related concerns'. These have, in turn, been influenced by underlying assumptions regarding the black population, public anxiety, and the emergence of racial tensions, as described above. The 'race-related' perspectives that have emerged have produced various attempts to control or manage the situation. For some, this has been a problem of regulating relations between 'races'. Others have promoted social-democratic notions of multiculturalism, while a minority current has been motivated by anti-racism. It is to these competing perspectives that the chapter now turns.

Assimilationist/integrationist perspectives

Assimilationist perspectives are based on the belief in the cultural and racial superiority of white society and the associated belief that black groups should be absorbed into the indigenous homogenous culture. That is, they are expected to adopt the British 'way of life' and not to undermine the social and ideological bases of the dominant culture. Integrationist perspectives also subscribe to assumptions of cultural superiority, and therefore place the responsibility on black communities to learn 'new customs' and ways of behaving in order to be accepted by the indigenous population. However, they also believe that there has to be some attempt on the part of the host community to understand the difficulties faced by black groups. Integration was described by Roy Jenkins in 1966 as 'equal opportunity accompanied by cultural diversity in an atmosphere of mutual tolerance' (quoted in Troyna, 1992: 68). However, both these 'race-related' perspectives have endured historically. For example, during the

1980s the Conservative politician Norman Tebbitt described what he called the 'cricket test,' when a test of Britishness was whether or not black cricket supporters supported the England cricket team. Assimilationist perspectives also tend to ignore the fact that most black people are British born and therefore quite competent in negotiating the dominant culture. For example, research carried out by the HMSO (1994) revealed that 75 per cent of the British black population are UK born, and at least a quarter of a million are of 'mixed race'.

Multiculturalism

During the 1970s and 1980s 'multiculturalism' was reflected in government initiatives associated with race. Multicultural perspectives are based on the notion that learning about other peoples' cultures will reduce prejudice and discrimination in society, and are mainly about doing things such as celebrating cultural diversity within a theoretical framework which is informed by integrationist perspectives. They incorporate the belief that contact with other cultural lifestyles will reduce the ignorance and prejudice of the white population. However, they can be criticized for focusing on individualistic and cultural analyses rather than structural analyses to explain the discrimination which black people experience in society. As such, they fail to explain how and why black groups are disadvantaged. As Sivanandan stated:

> There is nothing wrong about learning about other cultures, but it must be said that to learn about other cultures is not to learn about the racism of your own . . . unless you are mindful of the racial superiority inculcated in you by 500 years of colonization and slavery, you cannot come to cultures objectively. (1991: 41)

Analyses based on individuals and cultures led to the development of Race Awareness Training (RAT) within state organizations, whose aim was to challenge racism by enabling professionals to 'discover' their personal prejudices. But as Husband observes, RAT: 'reduces racism to human nature and individual fallibility, thus leaving the world of the state, the world of politics and major structural aspects of contemporary life out of focus' (1991: 50). The implementation of RAT not only reinforced the view that tackling individual prejudice was the major route to eliminating discrimination within professional institutions, but also had a tendency to intensify the defensiveness and guilt that white professionals experienced around issues of race and racism. Thus, although it represented a significant change in seeking not to pathologize black people, it created an atmosphere that made many professionals wary of subsequent anti-racist initiatives.

Despite the flaws inherent in these race-related initiatives informed by cultural pluralism, they dominated the political agenda throughout the 1970s, until the election of Margaret Thatcher in 1979 who wanted to dismantle all race-relations legislation and multicultural programmes. Despite the Conservative Party's commitments however, as the 1980s progressed they utilized a range of 'race-related' initiatives in response to uprisings in Bristol, Brixton, Toxteth and other parts of Britain in the early 1980s, which provoked a high-profile public and political debate about racial violence, race riots, and the emergence of ghetto violence (Jenkins and Solomos, 1989). Although The Scarman Report, which published the findings of an inquiry into the disturbances, called for urgent action to tackle racial discrimination and social conditions underlying the disorders, the Conservative government chose an alternative response. They elected to give more resources, more training, and more equipment to the police in order to control the symptoms of urban unrest, and revived Section 11 funding (specialist funding to support local government initiatives aimed at promoting the integration of the black community). They also promoted 'equal opportunities', often by putting black people in bureaucratic positions of power, which for some, led to their alienation from the black community. For example, Sivanandan stated: 'All the system did was make more room for the rising black petty-bourgeoisie – to get them into the media, the police force, local government, parliamentarize them – to deter extra-parliamentary protests' (1981: ii).

Anti-racist strategies

In the late 1970s and early 1980s anti-racist perspectives began to emerge, which in contrast to previous policies based on assimilationist/integrationist and multiculturalist perspectives, went beyond a concern with individual prejudice and culture in order to expose the structural and institutional nature of racism in society. This perspective was supported by a major survey published in 1984 by the Policy Studies Institute on the position of black people in Britain. It demonstrated that black people were still generally employed below their qualifications and skill levels, earned less than white workers in comparable jobs, and were still concentrated in the same industries as they were 25 years earlier (Brown, 1984). It also revealed discrimination in areas of welfare provision such as housing and education.

Anti-racist perspectives offer a much more radical interpretation of discrimination within society. They point to the ways in which racism is built into the structures and institutions of capitalist society, and how the state and a range of state institutions have played crucial roles in disseminating and mediating race and racialization processes.

Thus, they are sceptical about the extent to which legislative reform alone can successfully challenge racism, or improve the lives of the black population. These doubts reflect a belief that the state is not neutral or independent, but is an expression of an economic, social, and political system that benefits from racism by oppressing black people and dividing workers along racial lines – that it is a structural and institutional phenomenon within capitalist societies.

Consequently, strategies to tackle racism have involved external challenges by anti-racist organizations and coalitions within the communities, the workplace, and within state institutions. Some anti-racists however, believe the fight against racism can only be carried out by the black community itself. Their argument is based on two premises. First, that the black population, as a result of their experiences, are particularly insightful regarding the roots and consequences of racism. Second, that the white population is inherently racist – their history, their culture and their social practices are built on racism, and therefore, no matter how well-meaning certain individuals may be, they can never eradicate all the vestiges of racism in their behaviour.

There are three possible counter-claims to these assertions. First, while it is certainly true that all black people in Britain experience racism and this has a detrimental impact on their life chances, this does not necessarily mean that they have an inherent understanding of the institutional and structural nature of racism. There have been examples where different groups within the black community have come to see each other as rivals competing for scarce resources, occasionally leading to violent conflict. In these circumstances division rather than 'racial unity' has been dominant within the black community. Thus there is nothing inevitable about a 'unified racial consciousness'.

Secondly, the black community constitutes a small minority of the British population as a whole, and simply looking towards the black community for political change would seem to limit the potential power and mobilizing effects that anti-racist struggles can generate.

Finally, it is not the case that the black and white communities cannot stand together. Over the last 20 years in Britain, there have been a number of important examples of black and white groups standing together to defeat racist policies and practices, and to confront racist organizations. For example, in the mid-1970s the Grunwick strike led by Asian (mainly women) workers, became a central focus for the working-class movement at the time. The predominantly Asian workforce was supported by a series of mass pickets of overwhelmingly white trade-unionists, and the factory was boycotted by local post workers (Ramdin, 1987). In the late 1970s Rock Against Racism and the Anti-Nazi League were able to mobilize large numbers of black and white youth and various political activists in the struggle against both racism and the far right. In a series of uprisings in the 1980s and 1990s, black, Asian, and white youth fought together against poverty, deprivation, and state policing (Hassan, 2000). While more recently, in 1999 at the Ford plant in Dagenham, an overwhelmingly white workforce went on strike against the racism meted out to black workers by supervisors, and the struggle of the Lawrence family was supported by various trade unionists such as firefighters, postal workers, and council workers This last example led black writer, Darcus Howe, to comment that there had been greater solidarity for the Lawrence family from the white working class than the black middle class (Ferguson and Lavalette, 1999), leading us again to question the notion that all members of the black community understand each other's plight and that they will always stand together. These and similar events are often ignored or dismissed within the anti-racist literature, but they remain important occasions which demonstrate the possibility and potential of black and white unity in the anti-racist struggle.

Anti-racist activity has also been evident in other parts of Europe. For example, in the 1990s in France there were massive mobilizations of black and white youth demonstrating against racist attacks, and in Paris in 1997 there was a demonstration attended by large contingents of anti-fascists from other European countries that attracted 100,000 protesters (Marfleet, 1999). On 19 February 2000, there was a demonstration of over 300,000 people, protesting against the inclusion of the fascist Freedom Party within the Austrian government, a protest that included black and white people from across Europe.

Activity 6.3

What are the dominant assumptions underlying assimilationist/integrationist, multicultural and anti-racist perspectives, and what strategies do they offer to deal with racism?

6.6 Tackling institutional racism within the criminal justice system and the personal social services

Institutional racism is concerned with social structures and institutional practices rather than personal psychologies, and it focuses not upon the intentional acts of individuals but rather upon systematic outcomes of institutional systems and routine practices (Williams, 1985). It occurs when the routine practices of a profession or an institution produce outcomes which in their effect discriminate against members of minority ethnic populations. Husband states that: 'It leads to the unhappy consequence that nice people can be accused of being culpable of participating in generating racist outcomes. It can be very disquieting for anyone to be told that independently of their own sense of personal agency they are perpetuating a form of racist practice' (1991: 53). In the last decade or so, two state institutions have both been confronted with evidence of the manifestation of institutional racism within their professions, and both have been forced to examine their race-related policies and practices. It is to these two institutions, the Central Council for Education and Training in Social Work (CCETSW) and the Metropolitan Police, that the chapter now turns, with an examination of the manifestation of institutional racism and attempts to deal with it.

The personal social services

During the 1980s, pressure to tackle institutional racism had become a major objective within the Personal Social Services, and CCETSW began to seriously address the issue. This led to the incorporation of anti-racist learning requirements into the Diploma in Social Work in the early 1990s. The aim was that eventually social workers in the field would be conscious of the nature of structural and institutional racism in British society, and would be able to support clients faced with such oppression. For the first time, a state institution had acknowledged institutional racism, and there was a concerted attempt to develop a more radical anti-racist approach. There was increasing recognition and concern that the black population were under-represented both as workers and clients in social work agencies (Cheetham, 1987), and that when they were represented, they were often pathologized using negative and damaging assumptions, endorsing the superiority of white culture over others.

The direction taken by CCETSW came about from discussions that took place amongst black and white sections of the social work academy and profession during the 1980s, in workshops, conferences, and publications. As a result of these pressures and activities, in 1989 CCETSW introduced the 'Rules and requirements for the diploma in social work' (Paper 30), which made it a compulsory requirement for students undertaking social work training to address issues of race and racism, and demonstrate competence in anti-racist practice. As a consequence, university courses and social work agencies were required to facilitate anti-racist training for students with the aim that, eventually, social workers in the field would be conscious of the nature of structural and institutional racism in British society, and would be able to support clients faced with such oppression.

In many ways this was a remarkable initiative, which represented a significant and important step forward. It emanated from a government agency and contained within its remit a recognition that Britain was an institutionally racist country, and that social work education and training should, as a consequence, be structured by anti-racist concerns and principles.

CCETSW, in 1988, formally adopted an anti-racist policy that stated:

> CCETSW believes that racism is endemic in the values, attitudes and structures of British society, including that of social services and social work education. CCETSW recognizes that the effects of racism on black people are incompatible with the values of social work and therefore seeks to combat racist practices in all areas of its responsibilities. (CCETSW, 1991: 6)

The Diploma in Social Work further stipulated learning requirements in relation to anti-racist social work which included:

> Recognizing the implications of political, economic, racial, social and cultural factors upon service delivery, financing services and resource delivery.

> Demonstrating an awareness of both individual and institutional racism and ways
> to combat both through anti-racist practice.
>
> Developing an awareness of the inter-relationships of the processes of structural
> oppression, race, class and gender. (CCETSW, 1991: 6)

Those providing courses (programme providers such as universities) were also expected to implement and monitor anti-racist policies and practices.

However, the successful implementation of CCETSW's anti-racist agenda was seriously impaired by a political, and in some cases, professional backlash, which denied the structural and institutional nature of racism. CCETSW increasingly found itself under attack by right-wing politicians, sections of the social work profession, and the media, who all denied the assertion of the institutional nature of racism within British organizations. In 1992, Virginia Bottomley, the then health minister, took CCETSW to task for too great an emphasis on anti-discrimination in qualifying training, and this set the tone for a series of other attacks. There was the accusation that CCETSW had been taken over by groups of obsessed zealots whose major concern was to express rigid 'politically correct' values. Professor Robert Pinker, a prominent academic in the area of social work and social policy, was particularly vociferous in his condemnation of CCETSW's anti-racist developments, and his views reflect criticisms being articulated in other quarters. He stated: 'It was clear to some of us in the academic community that radical political elements had taken over the whole of the council's planning process' and that 'there would be no avenues of escape for either staff or students from this nightmare world of censorship and brainwashing' (Pinker, 1999: 17–18). He accused those involved in developing CCETSW's initiatives of believing that 'oppression and discrimination are everywhere to be found in British society, even when they seemed to be "invisible"' (Pinker, 1999: 18–19). However, such a perspective necessarily involves underestimating the levels of discrimination in British society described earlier in this chapter.

As a result of these criticisms, there were moves to undermine the relevance and importance of CCETSW's anti-racist recommendations. Jeffrey Greenwood, in taking over as chair of CCETSW in Autumn 1993, defined himself as a supporter of equal opportunities, while publicly committing himself to 'rooting out politically correct nonsense' (quoted in *The Independent*, 28 August and 19 November 1993). He then ordered a review of CCETSW's anti-discriminatory policies, and the Diploma in Social Work was published with the formal commitment to anti-racism dropped.

It is perhaps no surprise that more recently, the Macpherson Report has experienced a similar response from the Metropolitan Police, right-wing politicians and media commentators.

The criminal justice system

It was the inquiry into the death of Stephen Lawrence, culminating in the Macpherson Report, that placed the issue of race and racism high on the political agenda in relation to the policing of Britain's black population. The report was significant in its acknowledgement that institutional racism had been a key factor in the police response to Stephen's murder, thereby moving away from an interpretation of racism based on personal prejudice.

Stephen Lawrence was murdered in 1993 by a group of white youths, and it was the endeavours of his parents, Neville and Doreen who exposed the racism of the Metropolitan Police in dealing with his death. In early 1997, a coroner's jury, after just 30 minutes of deliberation, returned a verdict of unlawful killing 'in a completely unprovoked racist attack by five white youths' (*The Guardian*, 14 February 1997), and in July, 1997, the Home Secretary, Jack Straw, set up a judicial public inquiry into the case to be chaired by Sir William Macpherson.

The findings of the Macpherson Report were revealed in February 1999, and concluded that racism exists within all organizations and institutions and is: '. . . deeply ingrained. Radical thinking and sustained action are needed in order to tackle it head on . . . in all organizations and in particular in the fields of education and family life' (*The Guardian*, February 25 1999). During the inquiry, Michael Mansfield QC, acting on behalf of the Lawrence family stated that:

> The magnitude of the failure in this case . . . cannot be explained by mere incompetence or a lack of direction by senior officers or a lack of execution and application by junior officers, nor by woeful under-resourcing. So much was missed by so many that deeper causes and forces must be considered. We suggest that these forces relate to two main propositions. The first is that the victim was black and racism, both conscious and unconscious, permeated the investigation. Secondly, the fact is that the perpetrators were white and were expecting some form of protection. (Norton-Taylor, 1999: 22–3)

The conclusions of the Macpherson Report, that racism was institutionalized within British society, were a radical departure from recommendations enshrined in the Scarman Report (1981), the last major investigation into police racism in Britain, commissioned after the Brixton riots of 1981. The Scarman Report denied the existence of institutional racism and instead defined racism as individual prejudice concluding that: 'The direction and policies of the Metropolitan Police are not racist. [I] totally and unequivocally reject the attack made upon the integrity and impartiality of the senior direction of the force' (Para 4.62, cited in Barker and Beezer, 1983: 110). In short, the Scarman Report denied the existence of institutional racism and defined racism as individual prejudice. Not surprisingly, in contrast to the response to the Macpherson Report, it was well-received by superiors within the police force, reflecting their belief that the problem was one of a few 'rotten apples in the force' rather than a 'rotten barrel'. Furthermore, the police claimed that the behaviour of officers was itself occasioned by the street culture of black youth who:

> spending much of their lives on the streets . . . are bound to come into contact with criminals and the police. Police 'misconduct' was then blown out of all proportion into a 'myth of brutality and racism' by the 'West Indian habit of rumour-mongering and their flair for endless discussion of . . . grievances'. (quoted in Sivanandan, 1981: p. ii)

During the course of the Lawrence inquiry, political commentators and the media were supportive of Neville and Doreen Lawrence, and were vociferous in their calls for justice. However, after the publication of the Macpherson Report their tone changed and, like CCETSW's anti-racist initiative, the revelation of institutional racism within the police force was ridiculed and undermined.

However, despite this hostility, racism has been identified as a causal factor in other deaths during the 1990s. The deeply entrenched institutional nature of racism has been emphasized in the deaths of, for example, Ricky Reel, Michael Menson, and Christopher Alder. In all these cases, the police were accused of behaving in a racist manner during the investigative process, demonstrating once again, how institutional racism is deeply embedded in the criminal justice system.

In both these case studies a similar pattern emerged. There was an increasing emphasis on racism within the two professions, which led to some attempts to challenge the dominant institutional culture and redirect practices and procedures. Yet, almost immediately there was a backlash initiated by professional interests, politicians, and the media. This emphasizes the contentious nature of anti-racist initiatives and the fact that they challenge dominant political and cultural interests. However, these dominant interests are not passive in this process, but actively operate to reassert 'older values and assumptions'.

For example, in December 2000, William Hague gave a speech to the right-wing Centre for Policy Studies suggesting that, because of recommendations enshrined in the Macpherson Report black offenders are getting away with crimes because the police are not allowed to stop them, and pledging to overturn the tide of liberal 'political correctness' which had brought the criminal justice system to its knees. It led John O'Farrell to comment that: 'For the sake of perceived narrow party advantage between now and election day, he is prepared to stir up racism with a poisonous speech packed with prejudice, factual inaccuracies and straightforward lies' (*The Guardian*, 16 December 2000). William Hague made these comments despite research carried out by the Joseph Rowntree Foundation that found a range of agencies received almost 42,000 reports of racial harassment between April 1999 and March 2000, double the number of incidents recorded the previous year before the findings of the Stephen Lawrence Inquiry were published (*The Guardian*, 22 November 2000).

This analysis reveals that debates regarding racism are not static, but are an ongoing site of struggle, both in the community, and for professionals, and academics committed to anti-racist work.

Activity 6.4

1 What role do state institutions play in reinforcing racism in British society?
2 What obstacles do they face when they attempt to challenge racism within their ranks?

6.7 Conclusion

This chapter has emphasized the following points:

Although there is no scientific or genetic basis for the idea of race, and it is a socially constructed term, it continues to have meaning in society, and racism has a negative and damaging impact on the lives and opportunities of Britain's black population. For example, they experience disproportionate levels of poverty and deprivation, and there is continuing evidence of the discrimination which they experience in the health service, the education system, and in terms of housing provision.

Racism is a relatively modern phenomenon that emerged with the development of capitalism, and we can identify three major stages in its growth and expansion. First, there is the racism of slavery, second the racism of Empire, and third the racism of postwar migration.

In the postwar period British politics became 'racialized'. Relationships between the black and white communities were perceived as problematic by politicians. Both major political parties pampered to racist sentiments in society and there was a bi-partisan agreement which moved discussion on this issue towards the political right. As a result 'race-related' legislation was introduced which pathologized and had a discriminatory impact on the black population.

From the 1950s onwards, different perspectives have been adopted in order to deal with racial tensions and improve the nature of race-relations in Britain. In the postwar period assimilationist/integrationist perspectives were dominant. Multicultural approaches became popular in the 1970s, whereas from the 1980s onwards, a minority of activists and academics promoted an anti-racist perspective. All three perspectives continue to have varying degrees of influence in contemporary society, and should not be 'chronologically compartmentalized'.

Increasing evidence has emerged regarding the nature of institutional racism within state institutions, which has been given a high political and public profile as a result of the inquiry into the murder of Stephen Lawrence, and the attempts of CCETSW to introduce and implement anti-racist social work initiatives. Both examples provide evidence of the difficulties associated with such developments and their vulnerability to counter-attacks from political opponents.

Debates around 'race' and racism remain contentious in contemporary society, and the struggle for racial equality is ongoing.

CHAPTER 7

SOCIAL POLICY AND HOMOSEXUALITY

Angelia R. Wilson

7.1 Social policy and homosexuality: imposing and challenging hetero-normativity

Few social policy textbooks specifically address the way in which normative policies acknowledge heterosexuality as the only, or the only morally acceptable, sexuality (recent examples include Alcock et al., 1998; Alcock et al., 2000; Baldock et al., 1999, Lewis et al., 2000). While issues of discrimination based on race or sex have become familiar topics for social policy students, many are not acquainted with critiques of sociopolitical discourse that discriminates against gay men, lesbians, and bisexuals or gives preferential treatment to heterosexuals. This chapter seeks to provide a brief look at the historical construction of criminalized homosexuality, the emergence of gay and lesbian identity politics, and the moral and ideological issues underpinning policies regulating homosexuality. This will provide a backdrop for considering contemporary policies that, for the most part, continue to privilege heterosexuality.

Mainstream political debates tend to rest upon polarized categories of sexuality as 'homosexual' or 'heterosexual' (for a discussion of the construction of oppositional categories in relation to sexuality see Butler 1990; Foucault 1978; Phelan 1997; Weeks 1977 and 1985 and Warland 1992). Such labelling privileges heterosexuality leading to heterosexism – 'the system by which heterosexuality is assumed to be the only acceptable and viable life option' (Blumenfeld and Raymond, 1993: 244). This assumption of heterosexuality as 'normal' linguistically places non-heterosexuals in the resulting opposite category 'abnormal', for example, lesbians, gay men, and bisexuals. When such assumptions inform policy, the result is social exclusion.

> Though not direct or overt, heterosexism is a form of discrimination. Its subtlety makes it somehow even more insidious because it is harder to define and combat. Heterosexism is discrimination by neglect, omission, and/or distortion, whereas often its more active partner – homophobia – is discrimination by intent and design. (Blumenfeld and Raymond, 1993: 245)

Homophobia, on a personal level, is often violent taking the form of 'gay bashing', which includes verbal harassment and physical assault. Unfortunately homophobia extends beyond the personal attack. As we will see below, institutional homophobia dictates codes of behaviour through a system of penalties and rewards that actively discriminates against gay men, lesbians, and bisexuals through social, political, and business practices that sanction heterosexuality exclusively.

Social policies and practices that either directly discriminate against homosexuality or indirectly discriminate based upon heterosexual privilege are justified by myth or moral positioning that has not withstood examination by biologists, sociologists, psychologists or reasoned political activists. Recalling the two most vivid examples of contemporary institutional homophobia, the section below illustrates the extent to which prejudice, myth, and fear can be the sole basis for implementing health and education policy. Both examples appeared on the political agenda in the late 1980s: the government's initial response to the AIDS epidemic/crisis and the ratifying of Section 28 of the Local Government Act of 1988.

Activity 7.1

1 What is heterosexism?
2 What is homophobia?
3 How are they similar or different?
4 Can you think of instances when you have witnessed each?

7.2 Contemporary homophobia

The discovery in the early 1980s of a virus in some gay men, which had affected the immune system leaving the body defenceless against infections and cancers, quickly became a medical justification for discrimination against an already stigmatized group (for a history of the AIDS crisis see Duberman 1991; Grmek 1990, Shilts 1988; Watney 1987). Doctors first referred to the new disease as the 'Gay Plague', later officially labelling it 'Gay-Related Immune Deficiency' (GRID). Only after gay activists protested that such a name perpetuated discrimination and hostility towards only one group affected by the disease was the name changed to 'Acquired Immune Deficiency Syndrome' (AIDS). Unfortunately the initial label, supported by 'medical' proof that gay men were the largest number of sufferers in the west, acted as vindication for already existing homophobia. At an AIDS conference in Britain in 1986 the Chief Constable of Manchester, James Anderton, informed the audience that AIDS was a 'self-inflicted scourge' and that homosexuals were 'swirling about in a cesspit of their own making' (cited in Jeffery-Poulter,

1991: 196–7). While sexual relationships outside the confines of heterosexual marriage had become a socially acceptable part of heterosexual life, similar activity for gay men was constructed as sinful promiscuity. As a result, the stereotype of oversexed gay men and a fear of HIV and AIDS combined as a breeding ground for attitudes like Anderton's to become commonplace. AIDS became, for those on the right, nature's or God's way of punishing unnatural sinful behaviour. This insensitivity to those affected by AIDS, and prejudice towards homosexuals, was reflected on a national level as the Thatcher government failed to respond to the crisis: not until September of 1985, over four years after the first reported British case, did the Department of Health commit funds for treatment and counselling (Department of Health, 1985: 176–98). One would assume that a disease of this magnitude, known to be transmitted through blood and some body fluids, would be a high priority for state action such as mandatory blood screening, information campaigns, and funding for treatment. The delay in this case can easily be linked to apathy, lack of concern, and disgust towards homosexuals.

In the wake of the AIDS crisis, homophobia became a habitual political position of the Thatcher government. The introduction of Section 28 clearly defined the second-class status given to homosexual citizens. It attempted to force local governments to perpetuate homophobia and heterosexism in every policy forum. While New Labour promises change, Section 28 remains on the statute books in the new millennium. So far, attempts to repeal Section 28 have met with a formidable, and well financed, opposition. Before considering the contemporary debates, it is important to remember the political context that gave birth to such overt, publicly sanctioned discrimination.

Throughout the 1980s, conservative interest groups such as the Responsible Society and Family and Youth Concern and later the Conservative Family Campaign (CFC), had campaigned for the Department of Education to allow parents to withdraw children from sex education classes. They believed that sex education in schools led to promiscuity, abortions, and homosexuality, all of which would undermine the centrality of the nuclear family. In response, the 1986 Education Act relocated responsibility for the sex education curriculum away from local authorities (perceived by the Thatcher government to be liberal) to school governors (perceived to be more conservative) (for discussion see Thomson, 1993). In addition, the media orchestrated a national outrage over Haringey Council's 'positive images' campaign, which included, amongst other oppressed groups, promoting positive images of lesbians and gay men. Conservative MP, David Wilshire, worded an amendment to the local government bill 1986 to prevent councils from 'promoting' homosexuality or the teaching of its 'acceptability' as a 'pretended family relationship' (original amendment tabled by Lord Halsbury, for a full account see Jeffery-Poulter, 1991; Cooper 1994). Section 28, as it became known, rested upon the belief that homosexuality was 'unnatural', 'subversive', and 'spread disease'. The CFC insisted that if children were taught that homosexuality was an acceptable option and/or were exposed to positive images such as homosexual teachers, they might become homosexual. While gay and lesbian activists mobilized strong opposition, in March 1988, with the support of Margaret Thatcher, the amendment became law under the Local Government Act.

Policy summary

Section 28 of the Local Government Act 1988:

Part 1 – A Local Authority shall not:

    a) Intentionally promote homosexuality or publish material with the intention of promoting homosexuality,

    b) Promote the teaching in any maintained school of the acceptability of homosexuality as pretended family relationship.

Part 2 – Nothing in subsection 1 above shall be taken to prohibit the doing of anything for the purpose of treating or preventing disease.

The impact of Section 28 is difficult to measure. This is primarily due to the vague language and broad scope of the policy. What does it mean to 'promote' homosexuality? For most school governors, now responsible for the sex education curriculum, it means that classes should not include discussions about homosexuality. Moreover, given that the initial public outrage was over 'positive images', gay and lesbian teachers remain unsure what 'promoting' homosexuality means – maybe they should not offer advice or pass on a helpline number to students seeking someone to talk with about homosexual feelings, maybe they should not be 'out' for fear of providing students with a 'positive image'. The fear of conservative interpretations of 'promoting homosexuality' leaves many teachers and governors avoiding discussions of homosexuality altogether. As a result, students are unable to discuss prejudice or homophobic bullying or the possibility of homosexual desires. Beyond the school gates, support for social services directed at gay men and lesbians suffered a serious decline in the late 1980s and early 1990s (see Thomson, 1993 and Cooper, 1994). Local authorities tried not to promote homosexuality by cutting funding for HIV/AIDS education amongst gay men and for lesbian and gay help lines.

Undoubtedly the election of New Labour in 1997 signalled a shift away from the institutionalized homophobia of the Thatcher government. As we will note throughout this chapter, some Labour policy initiatives have been more inclusive. However any attempt to repeal Section 28 has been consistently challenged by the House of Lords. For example, in an effort to calm fears about homosexuality appearing in the sex education curriculum, the Labour government amended the learning and skills bill to stress the importance of marriage and stable relationships. The House of Lords refused this wording because 'stable relationships' could include gay and lesbian families. Instead they approved an amendment by Lady Young placing heterosexual marriage at the heart of sex education. New Labour has issued guidelines for sex education in schools that fails to mention homosexuality but does acknowledge the need to have an 'understanding of difference and an absence of prejudice' (Sex and Relationship Education Guidance, July 2000). However, in England and Wales the battle to repeal Section 28 continues.

In Scotland, Labour has successfully managed to repeal Section 28 (or 2a as it is in Scottish law). However, it had to overcome fierce opposition to do so. Scottish entrepreneurs such as Neil Hood, Gill Hughes, and Sir Tom Farmer, former owner of Kwik-Fit, funded the campaign against the repeal. Religious leaders such as Cardinal Winning provided the call to arms labelling gay people as 'perverts'. At the helm was the Scottish millionaire owner of the Stagecoach bus company, Brian Souter, who believed that the democratically elected Scottish Parliament did not have the electorate's mandate in repealing Section 28. So, as a private citizen, he funded a nationwide Scottish referendum on the subject. His 'Keep the clause' campaign included billboards, leaflets, ballot papers, vote counters, and full media blitz. Of the 1.2 million votes cast, 86 per cent agreed that Section 28 should stay on the statute books. The referendum was hardly objective or well organized: the electoral register used was out of date; all those aged 18 and 19 were deemed ineligible to vote. Many ballot papers were sent to people who had died and some houses received multiple ballot papers while others received none. The tremendous result only reflected the manipulated outcome of a privately funded hate campaign. In a separate, but related, campaign the Christian Institute funded the first legal challenge against Glasgow City Council for violating Section 28. They claimed that the City Council was promoting homosexuality by funding an HIV/AIDS support group, an HIV carers' group, and a lesbian and gay counselling helpline. While the Christian Institute eventually withdrew the case, the threat of legal action did cause Glasgow Council to suspend payments to support agencies for a short time. Such uncertainty surrounding the interpretation of Section 28 continues – as does the potential threat to funding for HIV/AIDS organizations and gay and lesbian support groups (Powell, 2000).

A brief consideration of the sociopolitical discourse around AIDS and Section 28 enables an understanding of how normative social policy can legislate homophobia. It also highlights the need to analyse policy within a historical and theoretical framework. So, the following section offers a survey of British policy regulating homosexuality and of the rise of gay and lesbian politics. Neither of these serves the topic sufficiently and it is suggested that students acquire a more comprehensive historical analysis from further reading (see Weeks 1977, 1981; Hyde 1970; Jeffrey-Poulter 1991; Cooper 1994; Evans 1993; Healey and Mason 1994). The final section of the chapter turns to current policies regulating the lives of gay men, lesbians, and their families.

> **Activity 7.2**
>
> 1 How might homophobia inform health services for people with
>   HIV/AIDS?
> 2 Describe the heterosexism that underpins education policy.

7.3 Sexual history/sexual identity

The western Christian tradition serves as the bedrock of condemnation of sexual activity between men found in English law. The stories of Sodom and Gomorrah are understood to warn that such behaviour would lead to the worst of punishment from God. In the Middle Ages the English ecclesiastical courts were responsible for punishing such sins. Translating these sentiments into law, Henry VIII in 1533 declared the vice of buggery, with man, woman, or beast, a criminal offence punishable by death. Over 300 years later, in 1861, the death penalty was replaced by ten years to life imprisonment. In 1885 the Criminal Law Amendment Act broadened the scope making all male homosexual acts short of buggery, committed in public or private, illegal. In a significant shift in language homosexual acts were described as 'gross indecency' rather than only acts of 'buggery'. In other words, 'gross indecency' is the criminal offence that includes buggery as well as all other sex acts between men such as kissing, oral sex, and mutual masturbation. The offence of 'gross indecency' remains on the statute books today.

As noted in Chapter 5, the late nineteenth century was marked by the formal recognition of the nuclear family as the paradigm of a stable society. Homosexual acts were seen as a moral abomination and as such a threat to the role of the family – a role that was becoming increasingly important to the success of the capitalist economy. The result of this emphasis on the nuclear family was that the penalties outlined in the 1885 Act became known as a 'blackmailer's charter' because those suspected of homosexual acts were targets for blackmailers who preyed upon fears of public scandal and prosecution. Jeffrey Weeks argues that the criminalization of same sex acts, along with public trials, such as that resulting in Oscar Wilde's conviction, began the process of socially constructing a homosexual 'identity' which then came into fruition in the late twentieth century (1977).

In his influential history, *Coming Out*, Weeks suggests that a number of elements came into play in the late 1950s and 1960s which led to a review of laws regulating homosexuality and eventually to significant reforms (1977). The emphasis on the nuclear family unit in the postwar years made it clear that this model of family 'by its nature, must exclude homosexuals except as aberrations' (Weeks, 1977: 157). He points out that around this time homosexuality became known as a 'disease', a 'severe mental sickness which usually requires long analytical psychotherapy', a 'mental disorder', or more generally, a deviation from the polarized sex/gender norm (Weeks, 1977). Probably not unrelated to this emphasis on the family, the postwar years saw a dramatic increase in indictable homosexual offences. For example, those charged with gross indecency rose from 316 in 1938 to 2,322 in 1955 (Weeks, 1977: 158). During this period the police used agents provocateurs, usually in public toilets, to catch homosexuals. Some of those arrested were public figures, including Labour and Tory Members of Parliament as well as actors such as Sir John Gielgud. One such trial, that of Lord Montague and Peter Wildeblood, sparked intense publicity and led to a review of the laws regulating homosexuality. In 1954 the Home Secretary, Sir David Maxwell-Fyfe asked the Vice-Chancellor of Reading University, Sir John Wolfenden to head an inquiry into the issues of homosexuality and prostitution. The final recommendations of the Wolfenden Report encouraged legislation which would decriminalize homosexual acts between men, aged 21 or over, in private. However, members of both Houses believed that public opinion of the late 1950s would not tolerate homosexuality (Hyde, 1970: 237). Indeed, it was another 10 years before the Wolfenden recommendations were enacted. Finally, in 1967 the Sexual Offences Act decriminalized homosexual acts in private between consenting men, over 21, who were not members of the armed services.

This legislation did not grant equality – it decriminalized a few sexual acts between men (see section 7.5 for recent changes to the 1967 stipulations). For example, it applies to same sex acts taking place in private – a hotel room, a friend's home, or anywhere a third person could be witness to the activities is not understood as private. In addition, as the Act does not mention lesbians or sexual acts between women, one might assume that lesbians cannot be prosecuted. However, the failure to mention lesbianism does not indicate legal approval. As the charge of gross indecency has yet to be repealed, gay men and lesbians continue to be harassed, and prosecuted, for public sexual acts such as kissing in the street or having sex in a public place.

The supporters of the 1967 Act hoped that decriminalization would remove this issue from the public agenda. They advised homosexuals that the change in law was not an indication of approval but an 'act of toleration'. The original sponsor of the Bill, Lord Arran, warned that, 'any form of ostentatious behaviour now or in the future would, I believe, make the sponsors of the Bill regret that they have done what they have done' (Hyde, 1970: 274). Even the Wolfenden Committee had commented that 'it is important that the limited modification of the law which we propose would not be interpreted as an indication that the law can be indifferent to other forms of homosexual behaviour, or as a general licence to adult homosexuals to behave as they please' (cited in Weeks, 1981: 243). But the late 1960s and early 1970s were not a time for quiet thankfulness and private sex; it was a time of sexual revolution.

By the latter part of 1967 the Manchester-based North Western Homosexual

Law Reform Committee set up the Esquire clubs to provide social facilities for homosexuals (Jeffery-Poulter, 1991: 85). By 1970 the Spartacus *Gay Guide*, the first publicly available magazine catering for gay men, listed 60 gay venues in London and more than 200 throughout the UK. The next 10 years witnessed the birth of numerous organizations focusing on the variety of aspects of the gay community, for example the Gay Labour Group, the Gay Christian Movement, the Gay Business Club. Gay historians locate the birth of the gay and lesbian movement from the Stonewall Riots of 28 June, 1969. The police raided the Stonewall Inn, a transvestite bar in Greenwich Village, New York, on a regular basis arresting anyone not conforming to appropriate gender norms. On that night the customers fought back, taking their protest into the streets. As Rosa Parks, who refused to give up her bus seat to a white person, had set in motion the 1960s Civil Rights Movement in the American South, those taking a stand that night inspired others to challenge prejudice based on sexuality. By November 1970 the Gay Liberation Movement had spread to Britain. The Gay Liberation Front's message was 'that every person has the right to develop and extend their character and explore their sexuality through relationships with any other human being, without moral, social or political pressure . . . we demand honour, identity and liberation' (GLF pamphlet, in Jeffrey-Poulter, 1991: 100–1). This revolutionary theme found a cultural resonance with the Women's Liberation Movement (see Millett, 1971; Jeffreys, 1990; and Rich, 1980). Some lesbians who had been a part of the women's movement also lent political support to the fledgling gay and lesbian movement. And while differences of opinion and political objectives are a part of all new social movements, gay and lesbian activism in Britain worked towards a goal of anti-discrimination and respect.

As noted above, the 1980s AIDS crisis and Section 28 challenged gay and lesbian activists to consolidate an organized opposition. In May 1989 a few well-known artists, such as Sir Ian McKellen and Michael Cashman, experienced activists like Lisa Power and Peter Ashman, as well as former Tory MP Matthew Parris, organized a professional lobbying group, Stonewall, to monitor the legislative process (see: www.stonewall.org.uk). Other activists groups such as OutRage! emerged around this time and focused on public protests in order to heighten awareness about prejudice and to encourage large numbers of gay men, lesbians, bisexuals and transgender people to join the growing political community. This in your face activism also proved successful for Act-Up, which campaigned for government support for research and treatment for those with HIV and AIDS. These organizations built upon the 'gay culture' which had developed in the late 1970s and early 1980s, and mobilized the power of the 'pink pound' – a phrase which has come to define the economic impact made by some gay men and lesbians with significant disposable incomes. As this economic and cultural gay and lesbian community began to flex political muscle, it became a constituency commanding the respect of all political parties. For example, Prime Minister, John Major, signalled a small shift from the previous homophobic

Conservative government by meeting with Sir Ian McKellen, one of the founders of Stonewall. Unfortunately, this conversation did not lead to changes in policy. Only with the election of New Labour in 1997, came a real expectation of social inclusion. And although the situation of gay men and lesbians may have slightly improved, equality remains out of reach. Moving from a place of discrimination, social exclusion or social damnation to a place of equal citizenship is a slow and arduous journey. The journey may be easier in a more liberal political atmosphere but that alone does not ensure a speedy arrival at the table of equality.

Activity 7.3

1 What have been some of the significant factors shaping the development of gay and lesbian politics over the last 40 years in Britain?
2 Which laws regulating homosexual sex remain in force today?

7.4 Justifying discrimination

A number of arguments concerning the need to regulate homosexuality can be identified in contemporary sociopolitical discourse. For the most part these hinge upon different aetiological, or causal, explanations for homosexuality. Generally speaking, there are three explanations most often cited: biological theories, psychoanalytic theories, and environmental/behavioural theories. A brief sketch of each will identify the arguments that underpin political positioning around the regulation of homosexuality. For example, conservative and liberal arguments are the most recognized in western political discourse and as such will also be briefly considered.

Biological theories

Recent biological research has claimed that sexuality is determined by one's genetic makeup (Hamer and Copeland, 1994, also see Byne, 1994). Simon Levay's (1993) study of male twins has attempted to locate a section of the brain that links homosexuality with particular genetic characteristics. Most researchers in this field would add that biology is probably not the determining factor but that it may work in conjunction with social environment, a point we will consider in more detail below. The biological explanation has received attention from both those who support non-discrimination policies and those who do not. On one hand, it is argued that discrimination should not be based on a biologically determined factor, similar to sex or skin colour. On the other hand, those who believe that homosexuality is abnormal or is a disease have welcomed this type of research in hopes that future genetic engineering could be used to detect homosexuality and give the parents the option of abortion.

Psychoanalytic theories

Another explanation for homosexuality is rooted in psychoanalytic theories. Freud's description of the development of sexuality as moving through various stages in which the child learns to reproduce sexual norms locates homosexuality as a type of arrested development, or failure to complete the developmental process (1905). On this and similar analysis, homosexuality could be considered a psychological illness which could be cured through therapy. A feminist interpretation of psychoanalysis maintains that strict heterosexuality is the result of rigid sex role stereotyping so that men are forced by social norms to reject all things socially identified as feminine and vice versa (Mitchell, 1974). This approach recognizes the pervasiveness of gender structure as a social norm without suggesting that alternative interpretations of gender/sex should be seen as abnormal or as a psychological illness. In 1973 the American Psychiatric Association and the American Psychological Association eliminated homosexuality from the list of psychological disorders. However, Freudian theory in its pop-psychology version remains an important part of cultural hegemony concerning homosexuality. Therefore, some continue to argue that it is a disease and policies should support a therapeutic cure (see groups such as Exodus International, www.messiah.edu).

Environmental/behavioural theories

A third explanation for homosexuality can be found in environmental or behavioural theories. Common-sense explanations list any number of things as causes of homosexuality: an unpleasant heterosexual experience, a pleasurable same-sex experience, being separated from members of the opposite sex at school, being seduced or recruited by a homosexual, family relationships – a domineering mother or an absent father. One researcher explains the family relationship in this way: 'the child who becomes homosexual is usually overprotected and preferred by his mother; in other cases he may be under-protected and rejected' (Bieber cited in Blumenfeld and Raymond, 1993: 142). This quote covers all possibilities – both over- and under-protected – and is typical of the unsubstantiated nature of this type of explanation. If environment is the cause of homosexuality, what about siblings who share the same familial environment where one develops as heterosexual and the other as homosexual? Similar cases can be made against most of these theories. Many who have had one same sex experience do not become homosexual. Given the social privilege of heterosexuality, a number of gay men and lesbians have had heterosexual experiences. And homosexuals come from all types of families – 'normal' loving heterosexual ones, unhappy marriages, single-parent families – just as heterosexuals come from all types of families, even same-sex couples.

Conservatism

While each of these theories – biological, psychological, environmental/ behavioural – may offer some insight into the development of sexuality, one thing can be said with certainty: in contemporary western culture the social and political norm is heterosexuality. The reason may stem from the above theories, or it may rest more easily upon the moral belief about the proper sexual conduct and the role of the state in maintaining proper sexual morality. Many believe homosexuality is a sin, an abnormal expression of sexual desire and that heterosexual marriage should be the only place for sexual intercourse. Those who hold such a belief may regard the state as the proper authority to restrict sexual behaviour, protecting the individual from sin and society from the effects of such behaviour. If the state condones such behaviour, it is argued, more people will become homosexual, which will ultimately threaten the centrality of the nuclear family. The belief that decriminalizing homosexual acts or ending discrimination against homosexuals would lead to the breakdown of the nuclear family – and in turn the collapse of British society – is often reiterated by politicians and philosophers, for example Lord Devlin in the 1960s and Thatcher in the 1980s (see discussion in Durham, 1991).

Liberalism

An alternative moral-political belief that appears to represent a more favourable argument lies in liberalism's conception of the separation of the public and the private. Liberalism holds that individuals should decide questions of morality for themselves. Therefore, moral questions regarding sexuality should be left to the individual and should be generally free from state regulation. According to this line of thought, then, the individual who chooses to have consensual adult homosexual sex should be able to do so without state interference. So, it would seem that liberalism supports decriminalization of homosexuality, and generally this is the case. However, this liberal reasoning is built upon the assumption that homosexuality is a choice – or lifestyle choice. Conceived of as a choice, it is not given the same protection from discrimination as other biologically determined identities such as race or sex. If it is not a choice, and the scientific evidence increasingly suggests that it can be influenced by biological factors, then liberalism will need to move beyond just decriminalizing adult private consensual sex and towards pro-active policies which uphold principles of equality (see discussion in Currah, 1993).

Activity 7.4

1 According to the perspectives above, what factors may influence the development of sexual orientation?
2 What are the fundamental differences, and similarities, in the conservative or liberal perspectives on homosexuality?

7.5 Compulsory heterosexuality and enforced homophobia

Above we considered the kinds of arguments that inform debates about the regulation of homosexuality. Theorists such as Michel Foucault, Ken Plummer, Mary McIntosh and Jeffrey Weeks offer an alternative understanding to contemporary sociopolitical discourse. Each of these, in their diverse approaches, maintains that definitions of sexuality, both normal and deviant sexualities, are products of historical social construction. For example, in his influential text, *The History of Sexuality Volume One*, Michel Foucault maps the development of heterosexuality as the privileged social norm (1978). In 1968, Mary McIntosh argued that 'the homosexual role' had emerged in conjunction with the belief that homosexuality was a condition afflicting some citizens. In other words, the regulation of homosexuality necessitated the establishment of a homosexual identity – stereotyped at first as a medical or psychological disease and later by 'homosexuals' themselves as a defining characteristic of individual identity. So, where some believe that desire for the same-sex is either a chosen sin, or a failure to develop appropriate sex/gender norms, these theorists point out that conceptions of sin or gender normality are products of socially constructed definitions. These conceptions are then reinforced through the power structures of the state, church, science, capitalism, and so on. The perpetuation of socially constructed sexuality through normative policies is what Adrienne Rich has labelled 'compulsory heterosexuality' (1980).

This final section will consider the way in which homosexual citizens are excluded through policies that privilege and enforce heterosexuality. As we have noted, Section 28 privileges heterosexuality by maligning gay and lesbian families as 'pretended families'. We will consider other areas of policy that have traditionally excluded gay and lesbian families. In doing so, we will also note a few policy areas that have begun recently to be more inclusive. We will then turn to the most surprising area of direct discrimination, employment policy. The Race Relations Act and the Sex Discrimination Act protect employees from discrimination on the grounds of race and sex. Gay men and lesbians, however, are not legally protected from discrimination. As a result, homosexuality can be legal grounds for dismissal from employment, unequal pay, and harassment at work.

'Pretended families'

As the above sections have shown, some homosexual acts may no longer be considered criminal. However, gay men and lesbians should not confuse decriminalization with social inclusion. Section 28 directly imposes a hierarchy of family structures with gay and lesbian families dismissed as 'pretended families'. This section considers present policies that reinforce this second-class citizenship status as well as ones that are slightly more inclusive and may be taken as a sign of future change. Undoubtedly, fundamental change in the status of gay and lesbian families cannot occur unless gay and lesbian partnerships are legally recognized. This could take the form of legal registration of the partnership, recognized similarly to heterosexual cohabiting or married couples. Until such a time, gay and lesbian couples cannot benefit from laws that privilege cohabiting or married heterosexual couples and as a result are subject to heterosexism in the following areas:

1 Inheritance law makes no provision for a gay or lesbian partner if the deceased dies intestate, without a will. Therefore the biological family (not the gay or lesbian partner) can take the deceased's property – including property for which the surviving partner cannot provide proof of sole payment, for example the house, furnishing, etc.
2 A gay or lesbian partner cannot be considered as next of kin, which normally includes a married heterosexual partner, children, parents, siblings, etc. So the gay or lesbian partner is denied powers of attorney reserved for the next of kin, for example in handling of a person's affairs, authorizing health care, etc.
3 State pensions, superannuation schemes, company pensions can legally discriminate in granting death benefit provisions to a gay or lesbian partner either in the form of lump sum payments or in widow's or widower's benefits such as dependant's pension.
4 Income tax, capital gains tax, and inheritance tax all grant special treatment to married heterosexual couples.

The privilege granted to heterosexual marriage or cohabitation can be seen in the above policies. However, recent changes in two policy areas may signal some shift in at least recognizing gay and lesbian partnerships. First, in Fitzpatrick v. Sterling Housing Association it was agreed that the surviving partner was entitled to succeed the tenancy of a flat formally shared with his deceased partner – because the two men could be regarded as living as a family (3All ER 705). Second, New Labour guidelines on immigration established non-gender specific criteria for non-UK (unmarried) partners of British citizens to settle in Britain (for current guidelines see www.homeoffice.gov.UK/ind.concess.html). Applicants must prove: that they have been 'living together in a relationship akin to marriage' for two years; that the non-UK applicant will be able to maintain him/herself financially without recourse to public funds, and that the couple intend to live together permanently. While the non-gender specific language of this policy offers some recognition of same sex relationships, it does not place them on equal footing with heterosexual married couples. Heterosexual couples, where one is a non-UK citizen, can simply get married. The legal recognition afforded to the marriage contract then enables the non-UK citizen to enter the UK without the stipulations listed above. Under the new guidelines, a same sex couple must prove they have been in a relationship for two years – a feat that is not easily accomplished. For example, a long-term overseas relationship, or one in which the 'visiting' partner is prohibited from working in the UK, is only possible for those with the finances to support such an arrangement. At least one reading of the current immigration policy is that it hesitantly confers partnership privileges upon those who have economic privilege (see Donovan et al. 1999).

Despite gay and lesbian partners' struggle through the various forms of legal discrimination, many raise children despite the secondary status of their 'pretended family'. Historically, discrimination towards homosexual parenting has rested upon myths about an inability to care for children or myths that confuse homosexuality and paedophilia. There are at least three concerns commonly voiced about children of gay or lesbian parents. First, some psychological 'experts' have advised the courts that a child brought up in a household with same sex parents may not develop adequately. The child may not learn the sex-gender roles that are considered normal in society, for example a male child of lesbian parents may not have access to appropriate male role models. Underpinning such concerns are the beliefs that homosexuality is morally wrong and/or that children of homosexuals would not develop 'normal' gender identities (see Rights of Women Custody Group, 1984). This concern entails a number of assumptions about the development of sexuality. For example, most gay men and lesbians are offspring of heterosexual parents, therefore strict gender roles of feminine/mother and masculine/father do not necessarily ensure that a child will be heterosexual. Moreover, children are surrounded with 'normal' or socially acceptable images of sex/gender roles through friends, relatives, and the media, all of which tend to reinforce bipolarized gender roles. A second concern often cited is that gay parents are more likely to sexually abuse their child. This myth persists even though studies show that in the vast majority of cases child sexual assault is committed by heterosexual men (Russell, 1983).

Third, some believe that gay men and lesbians should not be parents because their children will suffer from being teased by their peers. This concern for the child's social environment has been the deciding factor in a number of custody cases for placing the child with the heterosexual parent (Valued Families: The Lesbian Mothers' Legal Handbook, 1984). However, children who are brought up in a loving home and who are taught to have confidence in themselves tend to be able to interact successfully with their peers (see Golombok and Tasker, 1994, 1996; Tasker, and Golombok, 1997; Patterson, 1992; Rafkin, 1990; Saffron, 1996). What this assumption fails to consider is that the heterosexism and homophobia that the child may encounter could be avoided through education about alternative family structures, even through positive images of gay and lesbian parents. It is at least worth noting here that less than 25 per cent of all households in the UK conform to the heterosexual norm of father, mother, and dependent children (General Household Survey, 1996).

Same sex couples may have children through a variety of methods. Perhaps the most common results from the breakdown of a heterosexual relationship where a parent then begins to define his or her sexuality as gay or lesbian. Traditionally the law has assumed that mothers should have custody of children after separation or divorce (see the Guardianship of Minors Act 1973). However, if the mother has been identified as a lesbian, the courts have often questioned her ability to parent. Unlike the heterosexual mother, the lesbian mother is unable, it is reasoned, to adequately care for the child if she has a partner. This reasoning reflects the Freudian understanding of lesbianism as narcissistic or a state of 'arrested development' by equating a lesbian relationship with a juvenile infatuation that renders the adult woman unable to care for her own children – she is incapable of loving both a child and a partner. It also rests upon the myth that all homosexual relationships are casual affairs based on sexual fulfilment only. Gay men seeking custody likewise are dismissed as sexually promiscuous and therefore unable to care for a child. So, courts have utilized a range of 'reasons' for placing custody with the heterosexual parent: either lesbian partnerships are too committed and loving, or gay men are not committed enough to care for a child. As noted above, such conjectures proved to be at odds with academic research about gay and lesbian families.

The Children Act 1989 emphasized the responsibility of each parent for post-divorce childcare. Now judges tend to recognize the child's need to remain a part of the lives of both parents. 'Shared parenting' arrangements reduce the likelihood that legal custody would be granted to one parent only. Alongside this shift in attitudes towards post-divorce childcare, individual judges are beginning to heed the research about gay and lesbian families and are beginning to consider alternative families as a socially acceptable setting for parenting (for more information see Barlow et al., 1999).

Historically the concerns noted above, as well as the myth that homosexuals are paedophiles, have also informed policies regulating adoption, fostering, and fertility treatment (for a comprehensive discussion see Hicks and McDermott, 1999). The Adoption Act of 1976 allowed for adoption either by married couples or by a single person. Unmarried couples cannot make joint applications whether heterosexual or homosexual. Because gay and lesbian couples are not recognized legally as partners, only one can become a legal parent. If the sole applicant is in a relationship, both persons are assessed concerning the child's wellbeing. However, even if a single lesbian or gay man was approved as an adoptive parent, the partner of the applicant could never be a legally recognized parent. Moreover, 'many local authorities remain(ed) reluctant to approve or use lesbian and gay carers for the fear of widespread public and media criticism that this evokes . . . despite evidence that children raised by lesbian or gay parents are no more disadvantaged than those raised by heterosexuals' (Logan et al., 1996: 17). A similar concern was expressed by the 1990 Conservative government when proposed fostering guidelines stated 'the chosen way of life of some adults may mean that they would not be able to provide a suitable environment for the care and nurture of a child . . . No one has a right to be a foster parent. Equal rights and gay rights policies have no place in fostering services' (paragraph 16, proposed fostering guidelines, December 1990). Following a campaign led by Stonewall, the final version of the regulations released in April 1991 did not include the 'equal rights/gay rights' phrase. The 'lifestyles' stipulations remained and, in the shadow of Section 28, most local authorities failed to give serious consideration to potential gay or lesbian carers. Under the Labour government, the winds may be shifting. A recent campaign during National Adoption Week 2000 indicates a change in attitudes amongst adoption panels as the British Adoption Federation hoped to place 1,000 children with gay men and lesbians (see http://www.baaf.org.uk). However, it remains the case that gay and lesbian couples cannot apply to adopt or foster children as a couple. A slight change in guidelines, such as allowing single gay men or lesbians to be considered as applicants, should not been confused with a policy change recognizing gay and lesbian adoptive families.

In the late 1990s, more lesbians and gay men are becoming parents in less traditional ways. For example, lesbians are having children through donor insemination at private fertility clinics. Under current NHS policy lesbians are rarely offered donor insemination treatments. Those able to afford private clinical treatment are subjected to guidelines that assess the appropriate gender influences upon the child (see Human Fertilization and Embryology Act 1990). Away from the normative eye of policy, gay men and lesbians may utilize informal arrangements where the donor is a heterosexual or gay friend. Contractual arrangements may be made, for example surrogacy or co-parenting across two households. However only the biological parent is legally recognized. Under the Children Act 1989 an unmarried (or in a same sex couple, the non-biological) parent can apply for a joint residence order, which grants parental responsibility in such areas as approving medical treatment for the child. Granting joint residence orders depends on the attitudes of individual judges.

The emergence of gay and lesbian family arrangements resonates with the broader cultural changes in heterosexual family structures. Unfortunately much in the area of policies regulating gay and lesbian families remains unclear. This is because the law does not recognize gay and lesbian couples as legal partners, and because most legal arrangements for gay and lesbian families rest precariously upon the attitudes of individual judges. One thing is crystal clear. Given the heterosexism and homophobia articulated in policy, lesbian and gay partners do not have children 'accidentally' or with the blessings of society. The decision to become a gay or lesbian parent must arise from a place of love and commitment to the child.

Discrimination in employment

There is no policy or legal guarantee that ensures against employment discrimination based on homosexuality, or sexual orientation. Homosexuality can be the sole reason for dismissal, harassment, or vetting during application or promotion procedures. Without legal guarantees similar to the Race Relations Act, the Sex Discrimination Act, or the Equal Pay Act, gay men and lesbians are vulnerable to direct discrimination in most jobs. New Labour has stated it will continue to support the sexual orientation discrimination bill. After three years in power, this proposed legislation has yet to become law. If an employee is a union member, and if the union supports gay and lesbian employment rights, it may be possible to challenge discrimination through an industrial tribunal. These are costly for the individual employee and, given the lack of legal obligation on the employer, the outcome is not guaranteed.

According to 'Less equal than others', a Stonewall survey of two thousand people, an alarming percentage of gay, lesbian, and bisexual employees have faced discrimination or harassment at work (Palmer, 1993). The study showed that 22 per cent knew or suspected that they had been denied a job because they were known to be, or suspected to be, gay or lesbian. A similar number, 23 per cent, knew or suspected they had been denied promotion based on their sexuality, while 8 per cent had been dismissed or forced to resign their jobs solely due to their sexual orientation. 'Matthew' was a senior sales representative for a large multinational corporation for 12 years when his partner, Paul, was killed in a car accident. After taking time off work for the funeral, he was asked to attend an interview at the company headquarters where he was asked 'We see you are single, do you have a girlfriend?' Matthew responded, 'No, I'm gay' and the interview was immediately brought to a close. Following this incident, he was consistently downgraded until he was stocking shelves. He eventually resigned and took the company to an industrial tribunal where it could not defend its action (Palmer, 1993: 7). Matthew and others like him who have challenged such discrimination are considered individual cases, and because there is no legal redress, dismissed or harassed employees are not guaranteed that their claims will be even considered as discrimination.

Also in the Stonewall survey, 48 per cent of the respondents had been harassed at work because they were known or suspected to be gay or lesbian. Generally the harassment was in the form of jokes or teasing, homophobic abuse, or aggressive questioning, but in a significant number of cases it had included threats (14 per cent) or physical violence (5 per cent). Little wonder then that many gay men, lesbians, and bisexuals choose to hide their sexuality at work. In fact, as the survey showed, 56 per cent have felt it necessary to hide their sexuality in some jobs, and 33 per cent in all jobs. And 68 per cent hide their sexual orientation to everyone, or someone, at their current job. One person, who is unfortunately representative rather than unique, describes her life in this way, 'I lead a bizarre and stupid double life – out to family, friends and neighbours and firmly in the closet at work.'

Even employers who have equal opportunities guidelines that include sexual orientation still indirectly discriminate against gay or lesbian employees. They do not receive equal pay for equal work. For example, failure to treat a gay or lesbian employee's partner the same as a heterosexual spouse means that more pay is granted to heterosexual employees whose spouse may receive company benefits. In Stonewall's survey 'Less equal than others', of the respondents participating in a pension scheme only 14 per cent could nominate a partner of either sex as lump sum beneficiary, while 27 per cent stipulated that it must be only the spouse (heterosexual married partner). Similarly, of those receiving other benefits – travel expenses, discounts, or special leave, and so on – only 18 per cent were available to all couples. In practice then, and according to current law, gay or lesbian employees do not receive, or have the right to request, equal pay with heterosexual employees. The European Courts in Grant v. South West Trains recently upheld this principle (Grant v. South West Trains). Lisa Grant, employee of South West Trains, argued that her partner should receive the same benefits granted to heterosexual partners, for example, discounted rail fares. The courts decided that South West Trains did not breach the Sex Discrimination Act because it had treated all heterosexual employees the same: for example, if Lisa had been in a heterosexual relationship her partner would have received the benefits. South West Trains therefore had not discriminated on the grounds of sex but on those of sexual orientation, which is legal under UK law.

It is worth noting the potential impact of European Law upon UK policy. While the Grant v. South West Trains case was unsuccessful, others particularly those that make claims under human rights conventions may be more successful. There is evidence that even the threat of a European decision upholding principles of equality moves the government to action. For example, the European court decision in Lustig-Prean et al. v. the UK, declared that the ban on lesbians and gay men in Britain's armed forces was illegal, violating Article 8 of the European Convention on Human Rights. As a result the ban was lifted. Similarly, the age of consent debate may be affected by European directive. An attempt in 1994 to equalize the age of consent for heterosexual and homosexual sex was unsuccessful. The age of consent for gay male sex was lowered from 21 to 18, but it remains unequal to that for heterosexual sex, which is set at 16. Nevertheless, equality may be imposed by the European court, as was the case in Ireland. Similarly, a connection can be made between the recent relaxation of adoption and fostering guidelines and a current case being brought by a French citizen to the European Court around discrimination in adoption policy (Summerskill, 2000). The potential for change, either under the eye of European law or a Labour government, makes social policies regulating homosexuality a captivating study of the relationship between ideology, policy, and shifting public opinion.

Activity 7.5

1 What policies fail to recognize gay and lesbian partnerships as equal to heterosexual partnerships?
2 How have policies regulating gay and lesbian families developed over the past 20 years? What challenges still face gay and lesbian families?
3 How are lesbians and gay men discriminated against in employment?
4 Recap on policy areas of housing, health, education, employment and 'the family' explaining how they continue to discriminate towards, or have become more inclusive of gay men and lesbians.

7.6 Conclusion

This chapter has highlighted the importance of critically analysing normative social policies that regulate homosexuality. A brief examination of the sociopolitical context surrounding the discovery of HIV and AIDS as well as that leading to Section 28 offered a contemporary picture of legislated homophobia. Recalling the history of legal regulation of homosexuality and the subsequent rise of the gay and lesbian movement provided a backdrop for interpreting current policy. The final section of this chapter considered policy areas regulating gay and lesbian partnerships, families, and employment. In each case it was noted that there have been some recent indications that the

UK may be moving towards a place of anti-discrimination. It was also noted that the potential for change does not guarantee a shift in policy. Students of social policy should keep an eye on this area as it will continue to develop interesting and challenging debate upon the role of the state as guarantor of (in)equality through normative policies.

CHAPTER 8

POSTMODERNISM AND SOCIAL WELFARE: A CRITIQUE

Iain Ferguson and Charlie Johnstone

8.1 Introduction

> I define postmodern as incredulity toward metanarratives . . . The narrative function is losing . . . its great hero, its great dangers, its great voyages, its great goal. It is being dispersed in clouds of narrative language elements . . . Thus the society of the future falls . . . within the province of a . . . pragmatics of language particles. There are many different language games – a heterogeneity of elements. They only give rise to institutions in patches – local determinism.
>
> The decision-makers, however, attempt to manage these clouds of sociality according to input/output matrices. (Lyotard, 1984: xxiv)

The above quotation from one of the doyens of postmodernism, while presented in typically convoluted language, indicates at least two of the central tenets of such thinking. The first, and really important, claim that Lyotard is making here is that 'grand theory' in the social sciences ('metanarratives' such as Marxism, but also liberalism and feminism) has lost any of the explanatory powers it may have had. 'Truth' and 'objectivity', which had been central themes in Enlightenment thought since the seventeenth and eighteenth centuries, are no longer useful under postmodern conditions. There are, according to postmodernists, no ultimate truths as knowledge is now regarded as relative and partial. In this sense, postmodernism is sceptical of any universal, or absolute, all-embracing claim to knowledge. There is a sense of losing any unity and certainty to 'knowledge' and 'truth'. Indeed, postmodernists argue that any perspective within the social sciences which makes such claims is open to doubt and contestation. The important consequence, for our purposes, is that it is now regarded as increasingly difficult for individuals and groups to organize or interpret their lives around ideas formed by metanarratives. Thus any social practice, such as welfarism, has no universal validity.

Following on from this Lyotard seems to be suggesting that under postmodern conditions collective political struggle will be abandoned, or at least suspended, as we all progress to participate in 'language games', where discourses around difference and diversity become more significant in terms of an understanding of social reality. Or, as Thompson and Hoggett have suggested:

> Lyotard denies that it is possible to find a universal structure or ground located somehow outside all particular language games on which universal values can be founded. Furthermore, he contends that the attempt to do so – for example, by trying to justify values by reference to a metanarrative of reason – is 'terroristic'; that is, by attempting to create a unity where there is in fact irreducible diversity, that diversity is forcibly suppressed ... The many shapes that language games can take correspond to the diversity of groups and differences between individuals recognized and indeed celebrated by postmodernists. (Thompson and Hoggett, 1996: 24)

Not surprisingly, such ideas have been fiercely contested, and even rejected out of hand by some writers:

> ... it's possible that postmodernity is a chimera – no more than a complex myth – created, perhaps, by an over-zealous playing of obscure language games. If it lacks any concrete reality, well, what else would you expect from a concept devised by philosophers such as Lyotard, who deny that a sense of the real can be arrived at through rational processes? (Tattersall, 1997: 23)

Where there is agreement between adherents and critics of postmodern ideas is that these ideas have profound implications for how we analyse contemporary society and also how we might think about new and changing welfare regimes during the 'lean mean times' that many of us have been living through in recent years. Indeed, and as we will see in more detail in a later section of this chapter, such thinking has particularly profound consequences for welfare policies built around traditional 'universalistic' notions of provision.

The principal purpose of this chapter is to discuss and explore the implications of postmodernist thinking on the broad area of social welfare. The chapter will begin with the seemingly easy task (though it is far from this) of answering the question: what is postmodernism? In order to do this, we must consider what postmodernism is a response to and why it came to garner widespread support within a broad range of academic disciplines when it did. This discussion will be followed by addressing other aspects of recent debates which have had an influence on theoretical debates around social welfare, principally theories of globalization. The concluding sections of the chapter will attempt to outline the extent to which postmodern perspectives provide an adequate understanding of some of the dramatic changes that we have witnessed in the provision of welfare services in recent years.

8.2 What is postmodernism?

> There is hardly a single field of intellectual endeavour which has not been touched
> by the spectre of the 'postmodern'. It leaves its traces in every cultural discipline
> from architecture to zoology, taking in on the way biology, forestry, geography, his-
> tory, law, literature and the arts in general, medicine, politics, philosophy, sexuality,
> and so on. (Docherty, 1993: 1)

Although not mentioned here, it is obvious that postmodernism has eventually, if belatedly (around the early 1990s), had a growing influence on thinking
around social policy and social welfare (see, for instance, Leonard, 1997;
O'Brien and Penna, 1998; and Taylor-Gooby, 1994). However one of the first
problems that we are faced with when trying to define what postmodernism
refers to is to actually pinpoint the moment of its emergence, both as a distinct
historical period (sometimes referred to as postmodernity) and as an important strand of thinking in social scientific debates. This is the problem of
periodization. For instance, Docherty suggests that the term 'postmodernism'
was probably first used by Arnold Toynbee in the 1930s (Docherty, 1993: 1). In
contrast, David Harvey suggests that the publication of the urban critic
Jonathan Raban's book *Soft City* in 1974 was 'a vital affirmation that the postmodernist moment has arrived' (Harvey, 1989: 6). Callinicos, meanwhile, has
suggested that the type of thinking that we now equate with the postmodernist critique of modernity has been around at least since the time of
Nietzsche in the nineteenth century (Callinicos, 1999: 296). Nevertheless,
despite disagreements about when postmodernism emerged as a system of
thought most writers on the subject of postmodernity would probably agree
with Kumar, who stated that:

> ... post-modernism is essentially a 'contrast concept'. It takes its meaning as much
> from what it excludes or claims to supersede as from what it includes or affirms in
> any positive sense. The primary, or at least initial, meaning of post-modernism
> must be that it is not modernism, not modernity. Modernity is over. (Kumar, 1995:
> 66)

The 'end of modernity', or modernism, itself is much disputed but, in order
to understand what is 'post' in postmodernism it is necessary to briefly outline what is meant by modernity. The cultural critic, Marshall Berman, has
offered a compelling and seminal account of these issues and his thinking is
drawn on broadly here to summarize these issues (see Berman, 1982).

In order to provide an outline of the main features of modern times (from
around the eighteenth century onwards) Berman seeks to make a distinction
between three key terms. First, modernization, which refers to the economic,
social, and technological developments which emerged alongside capitalist
society. Secondly, modernism, in the form of experimental movements in the
arts from the futurists at the beginning of the twentieth century through to

various tendencies in modern art in the 1960s. Finally, Berman refers to modernity as the radically transformed character of life under capitalism which began as a philosophical challenge (the Enlightenment) to traditionalism in the eighteenth century but reached its zenith in the major European and American cities of the late nineteenth and early twentieth centuries. Modernity, in its many forms from Baudelaire to Marx, provided a critical engagement with everything from bourgeois norms to 'mass culture' and was part of an ongoing process of critique of all aspects of modern society. As Berman himself put it so clearly:

> . . . To be modern is to find ourselves in an environment that promises adventure, power, joy, growth, transformation of ourselves and the world – and, at the same time, that threatens to destroy everything we have, everything we know, everything we are. Modern environment and experiences cut across all boundaries of geography and ethnicity, of class and nationality, of religion and ideology: in this sense, modernity can be said to unite all mankind. But it is a paradoxical unity, a unity of disunity: it pours us all into a maelstrom of perpetual disintegration and renewal, of struggle and contradiction, of ambiguity and anguish. To be modern is to be part of a universe in which, as Marx said, 'all that is solid melts into air'. (Berman, 1982: 15)

Berman goes on to provide one of the most convincing celebrations of the project of modernity and Enlightenment thinking which, in a different way, only Habermas has come close to. Modernity, for such thinkers, incorporates the scientific, social, and industrial programmes, institutions and artefacts produced by the Enlightenment search for the universal truths which would eventually bring about full human emancipation. Modernity, as Brown suggests, assumed the following:

> (1) The production of objective, demonstrably valid knowledge is both possible and desirable.
> (2) Valid knowledge is based on the production of evidence which in turn is secured through the application of systematic and rigorous methods and procedures by impartial professionals. Valid knowledge can also be used for social engineering purposes, i.e. to identify the causes of social problems and thereby to formulate and implement appropriate social change to alleviate those problems.
> (3) Valid knowledge can extend to whole societies and the various structures and processes which make up those societies. (Brown, 1996: 22)

However, it is this whole 'project of modernity' that postmodernist thinkers seek to challenge and overturn. Postmodernist thinkers reject the notion that valid knowledge only comes through the production of empirical evidence, which was a key characteristic of the modern period. For many postmodernists there are no objective 'truths', as all knowledge is similarly uncertain or unreliable and must be rejected. Bauman, for example, argues that:

> . . . the postmodern time is experienced as living through crisis. What the postmodern mind is aware of is that there are problems in human and social life with no

good solutions, twisted trajectories that cannot be straightened up, ambivalences that are more than linguistic blunders yelling to be corrected, doubts which cannot be legislated out of existence, moral agonies which no reason-dictated recipes can sooth, let alone cure. (Bauman, 1993: 245)

It is for this reason that postmodernists argue that grand theory in the social sciences must be disposed with. The future for social and welfare policy certainly looks rather bleak and uncertain if we were to accept post-modernist discourses. As even those sympathetic to postmodernism have noted, postmodernism can lead to an extreme form of relativism where it becomes impossible to produce knowledge of truth, justice, or freedom – where anything goes (see, for example, Parton, 1996: 17). As we will see later in this chapter, this has profound implications for how we interpret social policy and social welfare. During the period of modernity social scientists did not just believe that they could produce objective 'truth' but also such knowledge could influence social planning and social intervention across a broad range of services. All of this is regarded as inappropriate under postmodern conditions, which has led Brown to make the following pertinent observation: '. . . post-modernism does seem to be rather remote from many of the difficulties which people face in their day-to-day lives – difficulties such as unemployment, poverty and ill-health . . .' (Brown, 1996: 25).

Activity 8.1

What arguments do postmodern thinkers give for rejecting the whole project of modernity? How convincing do you find their arguments?

We will return to these issues in a later section but it is now appropriate to consider another influential theory which has been developed to explain what it is argued are epochal changes in advanced capitalist societies.

Whereas postmodernism is often regarded as a cultural shift in social relations, and in theoretical analysis of these changes, globalization is more specifically related to economic changes which have transformed advanced societies over recent decades; (though we should not ignore the fact that there are also clear political and cultural inputs to developments that are commonly described in terms of the logic of globalization). The next section will explore these issues briefly and make some attempt to assess how these changes affect social policy and social welfare debates.

8.3 Globalization

What should now be clear from the above discussion is that theoretical approaches, particularly Marxism, which sought to explain the world as totality capable of being understood and changed were increasingly challenged in the late 1980s and 1990s by theorists influenced by notions of postmodernism and poststructuralism (for a discussion of the social and material roots of this intellectual and political shift, see Callinicos, 1989). A further aspect of this shift in ideas has been around the notion of the globalization of society. The term globalization has been adopted by a number of writers to refer to the growing integration of societies across the world. Quite simply, globalization means that almost every aspect of our lives in contemporary societies is now influenced by a range of processes and structures operating at a global level (the influence and imposition of dominant American forms of culture should not be underestimated in this context though we do not have the space here to develop this aspect of the debate; but, see Ritzer, 1993 for an interpretation of this aspect of the debate). A clearly obvious aspect of such changes is the enormous developments in information and communications technologies, summed up by the term the 'communications revolution'. Ranging from the global reach of satellite television (dominated by a number of leading companies who control distribution) and the Internet or world wide web (now accessible on WAP operated mobile phones, with e-mail facilities), the latter apparently offering the utopian opportunity of creating a 'global community', the 'information society' is regarded as offering emancipatory possibilities for all of humanity. These developments have been neatly summed up by Robins:

> Globalization is about the dissolution of old structures and boundaries of national states and communities. It is about the increasing transnationalization of economic and cultural life, frequently imagined in terms of the creation of a global space and community in which we shall all be global citizens and neighbours. (Robins, 1997: 2)

or, as Axford puts it:

> . . . The word has become a paradigm for the allegedly uncertain and labile qualities of the times in which we live, an intimation of epochal changes in train, or a neat encapsulation of millenarian hopes and fears of the apocalypse. More prosaically, it is a convenient shorthand for a number of complex processes which, in David Harvey's felicitous expression, are serving to 'compress the world' in terms of time and space, and to redefine all sorts of borders – to taste and imagination as well as to territory and identities. (Axford, 2000: 239–40)

These quotations neatly encapsulate two key aspects of the 'globalization thesis'. First, a rapidly growing literature on globalization has emphasized the apparent shift of social, economic, political, and cultural relations from local-territorial bases (which were evident under modernity) to the stage where time and space have been compressed to such an extent that we are close to global homogeneity in all aspects of life (see, for instance, Appadurai, 1996; Harvey, 1996). Giddens refers to this as 'the "lifting out" of social relations from local contexts of interaction and their restructuring across indefinite spans of time-space' (Giddens, 1990: 21). In this context, it is argued, the nation state which, until recently, made the most important decisions regarding social policy and social welfare provision, no longer has the authority that it once had, as globalizing pressures have disembedded and deterritorialized local social relations, with global flows of cultural influence becoming more pervasive. Second, as the quote from Axford highlights, globalizing forces have helped to produce a number of pessimistic and doom-laden perspectives and movements organized in response to some of the, undoubtedly, immense economic, social, and technological changes that capitalist societies have been going through over the last three decades or so. 'All that is solid' seems to be 'melting into air' again but, for many theorists of globalization, the way in which the historical trajectory of such societies progress in the near future will not be within the grasp of human agents or national states:

> . . . globalization is making it more difficult for social actors like nation-states, localities and individuals to sustain identity without reference to more encompassing global structures and flows. Interconnections globalize the world in a measurable, perhaps even an 'objective' way, but do so mainly because such forces are redefining the experiences and perceptions of more and more actors. So the global is now the cognitive frame of reference for many actors who are aware of the global constraints, although it remains much less so in matters of culture and morality. (Axford, 2000: 243)

Writers who adopt this kind of approach to contemporary social change are suggesting that globalization is the only game in town. Any nation state, individual or community which attempts to remain outwith or against these trends will be left behind in our increasingly 'post-industrial economy'.

There is no doubt that the increased power of finance and banking on a global scale (linked to the dominant neo-liberal economic and political agenda being pursued by most western governments), and the growth of transnational corporations have had substantial effects on the ability of national governments to control their own economic and social policies. However, a cautionary note is required here regarding the supposed impotence of human beings in the face of such an obviously powerful social force, as Spybey indicates:

> . . . human beings do make a difference in the reproduction of social institutions, however routinized they may be. Social institutions that have been globalized are, by definition, global in their extent but the important point is that their reproduction is an active human process. Globalization could not exist without human

beings reproducing the cultural influences on a global scale. In doing so they have an input into the continuing process, and globalization is not the one-way process that it is often portrayed to be. (Spybey, 1998:30)

Alongside this general point about the tendency of globalization theories to treat human activities as processes or objects outwith our control (an example of what the Hungarian Marxist, George Lukacs, (1971) referred to as 'reification'), more specific critiques of globalization theories have also been advanced both by social democratic theorists and by Marxist theorists. As an example of the former, Hirst and Thompson have argued that globalization theories massively understate both the continued dependence of multinational capital on the national state and also the continuing capacity of national states to influence the world economy through, for example, an extension of the use of economic summits (Hirst and Thompson, 1996). They argue therefore that, even within the context of a globalized economy, traditional social democratic reforms are still possible. Harman, by contrast. while emphasizing the continued importance of the national state to capital (not least its military importance, as evidenced by the wars of the 1990s) regards Hirst and Thompson's scenario of governments conducting essentially Keynesian strategies for managing the national economy, albeit tweaked to allow a greater role for international summitry as:

> . . . a pipe dream – and a pipe dream which leads to reactionary conclusions. The economic summits show no sign of being able to regulate the world economy, still less to turn it in a rational direction. They are, in fact, horse-trading sessions in which the rival governments push the interests of the rival firms connected to them . . . More often than not, however, it is not concerted action that results but a failure to agree – the new world disorder. (Harman, 1996: 21)

On the one hand, he argues that globalization will lead to a more dangerous, less stable world order, rather than the 'new world order' prophesied by Fukuyama in the wake of the collapse of the Berlin Wall (Fukuyama, 1992); on the other, that the growing internationalization of production, of communications and of culture, increases and facilitates the possibilities of socialist revolution on an international scale (with the demonstrations in Seattle against the World Trade Organization in 1999 being seen by some as a possible precursor of such upsurges (Charlton, 2000)). The growth of global struggles as a consequence of the globalization of the economy is also noted by Robbins who argues:

> . . . Globalization, in fact, occurs as a contradictory and uneven process, involving new kinds of polarization – economic, social, cultural, political, geographical. Some will clearly win out, but others will lose or be marginalized, and may well react against the disruption and destabalization of global change. The confrontation of social and cultural groups is an inevitable consequence. (Robins, 1997: 6)

The thinking behind the concept of 'globalization' clearly has substantial implications for social policy and social welfare agendas and programmes. The same is true of postmodern thought more generally and it is the specific application of postmodern ideas to social welfare thinking that we shall explore in the remainder of this chapter.

Activity 8.2

1 To what extent has globalization led to the decline in the role of the nation state?
2 Can you identify ways in which the nation state continues to play a key role for capital?

8.4 Postmodern welfare?

Postmodern perspectives have been applied in two main areas of social welfare discourse. First, it has been argued that they are valuable in helping to make sense of the changes that have taken place in the organization and delivery of welfare services since the late 1980s (Williams, 1992; Parton, 1996; Thompson and Hoggett, 1996; O'Brien and Penna, 1998). Secondly, some theorists have argued that postmodern perspectives, at least in their 'weaker' (Pease and Fook, 1999) or 'affirmative' (Rosenau, 1992; Parton and Marshall, 1998) form, can provide a basis for critical or emancipatory practice in social welfare, more radical and thoroughgoing than earlier 'grand narratives' of liberation, particularly Marxism (Penna and O'Brien, 1996; Leonard, 1997; O'Brien and Penna, 1998; Pease and Fook, 1999). Each of these areas will be discussed in turn.

The restructuring of welfare

> The question became . . . 'is there a Thatcherite way we can improve the quality of the welfare state services without the public having to pay for them?' The answer was internal competition. Once you say 'we want the good features of competition, with independent bodies competing, in a service that remains publicly funded', then the internal market just falls out as the conclusion . . . for us 1988, with the Education Reform Act, the NHS Review, the Griffiths report and the Housing Act, was the *annus mirabilis* of social policy. (David Willets, interview, cited in Timmins, 1996: 433)

The 1980s and 1990s were a period of considerable change in the organization and delivery of welfare services in the UK. While different writers have emphasized different aspects of these changes, the four areas identified by Clarke provide a useful starting point for exploring this issue (Clarke, 1996: 45–6). These are:

i)   Marketization. By this Clarke is referring to the introduction of competition between welfare providers and to the deliberate creation of 'internal' or 'quasi' markets which are alleged to mimic real markets;
ii) The introduction of 'mixed economies of welfare'. Alongside the introduction of competition went a conscious attempt, enshrined in law and policy guidance, to shift the balance of provision away from the State towards the 'independent' (i.e. voluntary and private) sector;
iii) The shift in responsibilities from formal to informal care – to 'care by the community'. There is now a substantial literature on the 'familialization' of social welfare since Griffiths, and in particular its implications for women carers. As Clarke notes, the blurring of the link between the public and private spheres entailed in this redrawing of welfare boundaries also has major implications for the regulation and surveillance of families, implications which have become more, not less, pronounced under New Labour with increasing responsibilities being placed on parents (Jones and Novak, 1999);
iv) Managerialization. This refers to the processes and mechanisms involved in the implementation of the above changes, specifically the key role accorded to management in bringing about change. It includes both the principles on which welfare organizations are constructed and also the regimes of power and control existing within such organizations. Again, the issue of managerialization in the restructuring of welfare services has been the subject of considerable discussion and analysis (Clarke et al., 1994; Clarke and Newman, 1997).

As a description of the major changes that have taken place in welfare in recent years, few theorists of whatever ideological persuasion would disagree with Clarke's summary. In terms of the focus of this chapter, however, what is important is the way that writers sympathetic to postmodernism seek to make sense of these changes. For as Clarke himself has argued in a paper critical of postmodern perspectives on welfare, the concern is 'not about whether "something is going on" but that the ways in which changes are being appropriated theoretically are flawed' (Clarke, 1996: 44).

That appropriation by what O'Brien and Penna describe as 'the postmodernization thesis' involves seeing the changes identified above as involving a qualitative break with previous forms of welfare characteristic of 'the modern' (O'Brien and Penna, 1998). The problems in periodizing social change and development in this way have already been discussed in the first part of this chapter. In respect of welfare provision, the core of the thesis is that:

It is possible to detect in the contemporary world patterns of social organization, control and experience that differ both quantitatively and qualitatively from those of the recent past . . . The patterns of change are understood as conforming to emergent trends through which every dimension of social life is being reconfigured. Of particular note are trends towards political-economic decentralization, localization, fragmentation and desocialization. (O'Brien and Penna, 1998: 193)

'Desocialization' or 'desocietalization' in the sense of the decline of the nation state and the growth of international forms of communication and trade has been addressed in an earlier section, while 'localization' and 'fragmentation' in the sense of a new politics concerned primarily with local issues and based on a politics of identity rather than a wider political programme will be discussed in the next section. Decentralization refers to the tendency of bureaucratic organizations to devolve power down to more local units of organization but more generally might be seen to include the areas identified by Clarke above. As an example of such decentralization, O'Brien and Penna cite Parton's discussion of the shift within social work from the ethos and practice of genericism to the administrative specialism of care management (Parton, 1994).

There are two major problems with the postmodernization thesis as a way of making sense of this shift. First, in seeking to demonstrate the break with what has gone before, proponents of the thesis tend to overstate the extent of the changes that are taking place and understate the degree of continuity with what existed previously. In terms of welfare policy, elements of continuity might include: a focus on the poor (with nine out of ten clients of social services, for example, in receipt of state benefits (Becker, 1997)); an emphasis on the rationing of welfare services (with several studies of care management correctly identifying its potential as a mechanism for means testing (Biggs, 1991; McLean, 1989)); a focus on disciplining and regulating the behaviour of the poor (no less pronounced under New Labour governments than under previous Conservative governments (Jones and Novak, 1999)); and resistance by the poor and the organized working class to the attempts of governments to cut the welfare budget and reduce the social wage (Clarke, 1996; Lavalette and Mooney, 2000).

Oliver and Barnes also draw attention to the continuities in welfare policy in their discussion of the application of postmodern perspectives to disability issues:

We are not convinced that modernity can be dismissed or that postmodernity should be embraced in the ways that are now fashionable. We do not see where we are now as somewhere different from where we were 50 or 20 years ago; rather we are confronted with the same issues that we have always been confronted with, even if the circumstances in which we confront them have changed and are changing. For us capitalism continues to rule OK! Even if it is now global rather than based on the nation state. (Oliver and Barnes, 1998: 4)

A second criticism of the postmodernization thesis is that it is quite possible to explain the changes in the form of welfare provision discussed above without resort to the perspectives of postmodernism. The quote from the leading Thatcherite theoretician David Willetts which introduces this section, for example, suggests that these changes might be more convincingly explained in terms of the neo-liberal and neo-conservative agendas which informed the later Thatcher governments (Clarke, 1998: 17). Smith and White (1997), in their critique of the application of postmodern perspectives to social work practice, provide a good example of just what such an analysis might involve. New Right agendas undoubtedly did represent a break with the so-called social democratic, Butskellite consensus which broadly characterized the welfare programmes of both Labour and Conservative governments from the end of the Second World War to the mid-1970s. In our view, however, that break is more fruitfully seen as part of an attempt by ruling classes in Britain and elsewhere to rethink welfare strategy in the wake of the re-emergence of economic crisis in the 1970s than as signifying the 'end of modernity'. In that respect, Clarke's suggestion that a focus on what he calls 'an expanded repertoire of strategies for capital accumulation' is likely to be more productive than a focus on postFordism/flexible accumulation strategies is one which we would share.

Activity 8.3

What are the main limitations of portraying changes in welfare regimes in recent decades as involving a transition from modernity to postmodernity?

Postmodernism – basis of emancipatory critique?

It is now common to distinguish between postmodernism as a means of 'characterizing the present' (Browning et al., 2000) – the 'postmodernization thesis' discussed above – and what O'Brien and Penna refer to as 'social postmodernism' (O'Brien and Penna, 1998: 195), meaning postmodernism as the basis for a new politics. The main elements of this second aspect of postmodernism were outlined in the first part of this chapter. As we saw there, at the heart of such a postmodern politics is a 'radical perspectivism':

> It implies that since there is no factual ground on which to base theory and practice – in other words, there are no factual grounds on which to base true and false interpretations – then all knowledges of the world, including scientific and religious knowledges, are equally ungrounded interpretations of it. Poverty, disability, discrimination, it seems are not facts but interpretations and combating them is the

expression of a value based on interpretation rather than a theory based on fact. (O'Brien and Penna, 1998: 196)

It is in the postmodern challenge to those 'knowledges' or 'grand narratives' that seek to make sense of the world as a totality – which in the field of welfare, tends to mean structuralist theories such as Marxism or feminism – that some writers have seen the possibility of a new 'emancipatory' politics of welfare (Wilson, 1997; Leonard, 1997; Pease and Fook, 1999).

The charge against these overarching theories in the sphere of welfare is twofold. First, it is argued, they are reductionist. In seeking to make sense of the whole, they 'flatten' difference and diversity, in the process reducing and distorting whole areas of social experience. In a critique of class-based explanations in sociology, for example, Bradley argues that:

> The recognition that social inequalities and divisions could not be subsumed under one monolithic theory, that of class, led to a growing appreciation of the complexity of social differentiation in multi-cultural, post-colonial societies, where many sources of difference – class, gender, ethnicity, 'race', age, region, dis/ability, sexual orientation – intertwined to produce multi-faceted and intricate forms of social hierarchy. (Bradley, 2000: 478)

While in the first instance, this critique of Marxist approaches came in the 1980s from feminist and black nationalist writers wishing to stress the 'autonomy' of gender and 'race', it converged neatly with emerging postmodern perspectives which 'saw society in terms of a multitude of social groupings which formed around different potential sources of identity and had their own distinctive cultures, lifestyles and consumption patterns' (Bradley, 2000). A second criticism of the operation of 'grand narratives' in the area of social welfare is that they distort, deny, silence the experience of minorities and consequently, whatever the intentions of their adherents, they function as part of an apparatus of power and oppression which serves the interest of specific privileged groups. Those who wish to develop 'emancipatory practice' on the basis of postmodern perspectives, therefore, would see their role as being to 'give a voice' to those whose voices have historically been ignored or silenced within dominant discourses, including those discourses which portray themselves as discourses of emancipation. The link between such a politics and the wider theoretical premises of postmodernism is summarized by Leonard as follows:

> Because meaning is continually slipping away from us, there can be no essential, certain meanings, only different meanings emerging from different experiences, especially the experiences of those who have been excluded from discourses, whose voices and whose writing have been silenced. In the Western culture of modernity, this has meant especially the excluded voices of women, non-white populations, gays and lesbians and the working classes in general. (Leonard, 1997: 10–11)

The main implication of this approach for the formulation of social policy is an emphasis on 'particularism' as opposed to the 'false universalism' of the postwar welfare state, with its assumption of the white, able-bodied heterosexual male as the norm, an assumption which in practice was used to deny the needs of certain groups, including women and black people. Thompson and Hoggett summarize the postmodernist case in the area of social policy as follows: '[I]n the name of particularism, diversity and difference, such policy should not be formulated within a guiding framework that is universalist in character; it may even question the desirability of incorporating *any* significant element of universalism into social policy' (Thompson and Hoggett, 1996: 23). That many groups in society, including people with disabilities and people with mental health problems, as well as working-class women and members of ethnic minorities, have experienced aspects of the operation of the welfare state as disempowering and oppressive is well-documented. The extent to which a policy based on particularism and informed by postmodern perspectives would challenge that oppression, however, is much less clear. Three particular aspects of postmodern thought must give cause for serious doubt: its individualism, its rejection of structural explanations of poverty and inequality, and its moral relativism.

8.5 A postmodern social policy?

First, let us consider individualism. In a sense the very idea of a postmodern social policy is a contradiction since at the heart of postmodernism is a radical individualism. Postmodernism goes beyond identity politics in rejecting not only class as a basis of common interest and action but all bases of collective identity – whether gender, disability or race – since they are all premised on a wider narrative about how the world works. One might assume that that would disqualify postmodernism from making any contribution to debates about social policy. In fact postmodernism's individualism and emphasis on individual consumption make it quite compatible with social policies which are very far from being radical or emancipatory. As one writer sympathetic to postmodern perspectives has commented: 'In practical policy terms, postmodernism can be seen to fit all too well with a government that denies the existence of society and prioritizes individual expenditure over public welfare' (Wilson, 1997: 349). While Wilson is mainly referring to the social policies of the British Conservative governments of the 1990s, her comments also have relevance for the policies of governments in Britain and elsewhere based on 'third way' notions. For as Jones and Novak note, under New Labour:

> As in contemporary theories of postmodernism, people are identified not by their collective experiences – as workers, as women or black people – but as individuals.

It is not the same individualism as that of the new right, although it draws many parallels, not least with the 'active citizens' that fleetingly formed part of John Major's agenda in the early 1990s. The new right's individualism was of the sink or swim variety. New Labour's individualism is much more actively promoted. (Jones and Novak, 1999: 179)

In fact, core postmodernist themes – the celebration of 'ephemerality, fragmentation, discontinuity', the rejection of structural explanations of poverty and inequality, adoration of all that is new and 'modern', coupled with an ironic disdain for old-fashioned notions of commitment and solidarity – chime in very well with current 'third way' notions of welfare with their stress on the 'end of ideology'.

Secondly, consistent with the individualist emphasis noted above, there is the postmodern rejection of structural explanations of poverty and inequality. In contrast to Marxist approaches, which are primarily concerned with the ways in which one class (comprising a very small number of people) is able to use its economic, political, and ideological power to exploit and oppress another class or classes (comprising a very large number of people), postmodern theorists, and their poststructuralist predecessors like Foucault, see power as omnipresent, as everywhere (and one might argue, nowhere):

> When I think of the mechanics of power, I think of its capillary forms of existence, of the extent to which power seeps into the very grain of individuals, reaches right into their bodies, permeates their gestures, their position, what they say, how they learn to live and work with other people. (Foucault, quoted in Watson, 2000: 68)

As Watson correctly comments on this passage: 'Such a view stands in clear opposition to the notion that the state or capital as a concentrated site of power needs to be overthrown or dismantled for socialism or universal social justice to be achieved' (Watson, 2000). In fact, the implications for social policy potentially go much further than a rejection of the revolutionary socialist case for the overthrow of capitalism. Postmodernism's view of power and resistance as essentially localized and located in the micro-relations between men and women, black and white, and so on is at best likely to lead to a focus on local issues, small-scale studies. Since large-scale societal transformation is neither possible nor desirable, the best that can be hoped for is reform at a local or individual level. Thus, even quite limited reform programmes which require a degree of national structural change, such as those proposed in respect of health inequalities by the Black Committee and more recently the Acheson Committee, are likely to be seen as problematic. Not surprisingly then, as Watson has noted: 'The unwillingness of the postmodernists to conceptualize structured power relations in a traditional way presents problems for those who work with or study disadvantaged groups' (Watson, 2000). In fact, there are indications that the influence of postmodern ideas in welfare thinking is already starting to have a negative impact in this area. In an early critique, Taylor-Gooby expressed the fear that a growth in influence of postmodern perspectives within social policy would lead to a neglect of issues concerning poverty and inequality:

> The implications for social policy are that an interest in postmodernism may cloak developments of considerable importance. Trends towards increased inequality in living standards, the privatization of state welfare services and the stricter regulation of the lives of some of the poorest groups may fail to attract the appropriate attention if the key themes of policy are seen as difference, diversity and choice. (Taylor-Gooby, 1994: 403)

Since then, a number of writers have noted the paradox that at a time when the gap between rich and poor has been shown by numerous studies to be greater than it has ever been (and, according to recent research, in the UK context has continued to grow under a New Labour government), the lack of interest amongst social science academics in exploring class and material inequalities has never been greater (Bradley, 2000; Mooney, 2000). While it would be misleading to attribute the neglect of these issues solely to the growth of postmodernism, not least since this neglect goes back to the 1980s (Becker, 1997), it is nevertheless arguable that the Foucauldian emphasis on 'the specific, the local and the particular' (Watson, 2000: 76) reinforces and legitimizes that neglect.

Finally, there is postmodernism's oft-noted moral relativism. In a previous chapter, one of us has considered some of the implications of that relativism for anti-oppressive social work practice (Ferguson and Lavalette, 1999). Suffice it to say that a metanarrative (for of course, as several critics have noted, postmodernism is itself a metanarrative) which refuses to 'privilege' any discourse over any other scarcely provides a firm foundation for a critical social policy. As Crook has noted:

> When radical social theory loses its accountability, when it can no longer give reasons, something has gone very wrong. But this is precisely what happens to postmodern social theory, and it seems very appropriate to use the over-stretched term 'nihilism' as a label for this degeneration. The nihilism of postmodernism shows itself in two symptoms: an inability to specify mechanisms of change, and an inability to state why change is better than no change. (Crook, 1990: 59)

It would be ironic indeed if social policy as an academic discipline, having finally shaken off the phoney neutrality of the tradition of empiricist social administration, should now opt for the even more pernicious 'ironic detachment' of postmodernism. That said, the willingness of leading social policy academics to write an open letter to the national press in 1999 protesting against the implications of New Labour's 'welfare reform' for the poorest sections of society and arguing for increases in universal benefits suggests that notions of solidarity and a commitment to social justice are still stronger than the scepticism and nihilism encouraged by postmodernism.

Activity 8.4

How valid is postmodernism's claim to provide a more radical basis for an emancipatory welfare than Marxism?

8.6 Conclusion: the alternative to particularism – the radicalized Enlightenment.

In the light of the above discussion, it may seem strange that postmodernism should hold any attractions for social policy theorists, particularly those committed to what Leonard has dubbed 'emancipatory welfare' (Leonard, 1997). It is nevertheless true that many of those who are drawn towards the ideas of poststructuralism and postmodernism see these ideas as more radical than the traditional alternative of Marxism. In explaining that attraction, two factors seem of particular significance. On the one hand, there is a widespread disillusionment with the version of Marxism associated with communist parties internationally, reinforced by the collapse of what are usually (and misleadingly) referred to as the 'state socialist regimes' of the former USSR and Eastern Europe. We have argued elsewhere that Stalinism in theory and practice, not least in its influential Althusserian incarnation, is the antithesis of the genuine Marxist tradition and, rather than repeat these arguments here, would refer readers to a previous publication (Ferguson and Lavalette, 1999). On the other hand, there has been a growing scepticism regarding the 'false universalism' of welfare policy, partly in response to the growth of movements such as the disability movement. It is this latter point which we shall briefly address here.

It is worth noting that the 'false universalism' not simply of the welfare state but more generally of the Enlightenment, is not a new theme. As Callinicos has noted:

> Ever since Marx and Nietzsche in their different ways subjected the Enlightenment to critical scrutiny, the very ideas of universality and rationality have been under suspicion for secreting within themselves hidden particularisms . . . the universal rights and happiness promised by the French and the American revolutions tacitly excluded, among others, slaves, the poor and women. (Callinicos, 1999: 310)

As he goes on to argue, there are really only two ways to respond to these limitations of the Enlightenment's promise of universal emancipation. One is to conclude that every universalism is a masked particularism and then decide which particularism (or coalition of particularisms) one prefers – the postmodern option. In terms of welfare policy, the dangers of such a strategy, particularly during a period of welfare retrenchment, are obvious. At best, it can allow governments, whose overriding concern is limiting welfare expenditure, to play off one group against another as they squabble over the limited resources on offer. At worst, it can contribute to a backlash against oppressed groups whose legitimate demands for affirmative action or positive discrimination can be portrayed as being at the expense of the basic welfare needs of the majority – one factor used in the undermining of the policies of left-wing Labour councils in the 1980s and seen in recent attacks on 'political correctness' (Smith, 1994; Penketh, 2000).

Alternatively, Callinicos argues, one can respond to the failures of the Enlightenment project by seeking a genuine universality, a social and political order from which no one is excluded. A powerful plea for this latter position from the perspective of the disability movement is provided by Oliver and Barnes when they argue that:

> Although versions of the good society vary, for us it is a world in which all human beings, regardless of impairment, age, gender, social class or minority ethnic status can co-exist as equal members of the community, secure in the knowledge that their needs will be met and that their views will be recognized and valued . . . for us, disabled people have no choice but to attempt to build a better world because it is impossible to have a vision of inclusionary capitalism; we all need a world where impairment is valued and celebrated and all disabling barriers are eradicated. Such a world would be inclusionary for all. (Oliver and Barnes, 1998: 102)

In contrast to the pessimism of postmodernism, this view implies the possibility of successful collective action on the basis of opposition to a common enemy – global capitalism – an enemy which, *pace* postmodernism, can be both understood and changed. Significantly, the end of the twentieth century saw the emergence of just such collective action, notably around the meeting of the World Trade Organization in Seattle in 1999. While the 'movement' of those participating is clearly in its very early stages, and is perhaps still more of a mood than a movement, there are indications both in its inchoate philosophy of 'anti-capitalism' (Klein, 2000) and in the wide coalition of interest groups it represents (Charlton, 2000) that it has the potential to transcend both the 'identity politics' of the 1980s and 1990s, as well as the nihilism of postmodernism.

PART THREE

ISSUES AND DEBATES

Any selection of a range of issues deemed to be worthy of inclusion in an undergraduate text of this nature is bound to be arbitrary to some extent. A wide range of candidates for inclusion exists but in selecting poverty, social justice, the universality/selectivity debate, a constellation of issues affecting children and the elderly together with the growth of managerialism within the services, we believe that we are introducing students to ideas and debates that are challenging, complementary, and, in their different ways, reflective of significant questions of continuity and change in social policy. Moreover, they are all about access to, and the distribution of, scarce resources.

In Chapter 9 Brian Lund looks at questions of distributive justice – on what basis, if any, is it right for the state to distribute resources to individuals or groups within society and how should it be done? This is a highly charged and contested area that has taxed various politicians and philosophers from different theoretical traditions. In a thorough review of debates on these questions, Lund looks at the answers provided by the New liberals of the early twentieth century, Fabian socialists, and New Labour politicians today and includes a review of the work of individual philosophers like Rawls, Hayek, Nozick, Walzer and Young.

In Chapter 10 Tony Novak looks at the extent of poverty in modern Britain and the various attempts to label or stigmatize groups of the poor as part of an 'underclass' or the 'socially excluded'. Why are these terms used? What do they mean? What are the consequences of such labelling?

Gerry Mooney in Chapter 11 looks at the increasing levels of 'managerialism' within, and privatization of, the welfare state. He assesses the extent to which these developments reflect the policy goals of the New Labour government as opposed to being the 'inevitable' outcome of longer-term trends of welfare delivery.

Chapters 12 and 13 look at welfare and service delivery issues for two specific user groups – the elderly (Chapter 12) and children (Chapter 13). Although the authors adopt quite different approaches they both look at the way recent developments create problems for sections of these communities. Both chapters start by looking at definitional issues: Who are the elderly? What is childhood? Before proceeding to look at welfare issues as they affect these groups, Lansley looks at changing demographic patterns and the implications this has for the costs of care and pensions. While Lavalette and Cunningham look at the way in which state social policy and welfare services have problematized particular groups of children, trying to regulate their behaviour – emphasizing the extent to which social policy, both historically and today, is often structured by considerations of 'social control'.

Finally, Alan Pratt looks at the major philosophies of resource allocation which have informed social provision in the last half century. In doing so he discusses a variety of concepts and definitions and considers the respective merits of selectivity and universality as allocative mechanisms in the context of developments in the politics and economics of British society. In discussing these themes he brings us back to the questions which structured the first chapter in this part of the book – Lund on distributive justice – emphasizing the link between philosophies of welfare and the practical politics of welfare distribution.

CHAPTER 9

DISTRIBUTIVE JUSTICE AND SOCIAL POLICY

Brian Lund

9.1 Introduction

'Justice' has many meanings. Here we will be concerned with distributive justice or 'how a society or group should allocate its scarce resources or product among individuals with competing needs or claims' (Roemer, 1996: 1). The terms 'social justice' and 'distributive justice' are broadly interchangeable but sometimes social justice has been given a broader meaning to encompass the equal worth of citizens as revealed in political processes and in the respect given to different cultures. 'Distributive justice' has been chosen as the title of this chapter because, although the interaction between political processes, respect for cultures, and distributive outcomes is recognized, its focus is on the allocation of material resources.

Deliberation on distributive justice has a long lineage but, according to David Miller, 'theorizing about social justice became a major concern in the early years of the twentieth century' (Miller, 1999: 4). This awakened interest in the fair distribution of the national product was prompted by the attempts of liberal philosophers to counter Karl Marx's claim that the owners of the means of production exploit the working class. Marx sought an end to capitalism and the creation of a new communist order that produced, and hence distributed, to meet human needs (Heller, 1974; Young, 1990: 15). He believed social justice to be a bourgeois concept constructed to try to harmonize the irreconcilable interests of the bourgeoisie and the proletariat. In contrast to Marx's desire to abolish class society the advocates of distributive justice, wanted to reform the old order by modifying the established links between the acquisition and distribution of resources. They sought to defend some existing property rights but gave the state a role in the redistribution of the social surplus – the economic gains accruing from a co-operative, harmonious society.

9.2 The 'new' liberals and social justice

According to Blaug (1986: 84) Henry George's *Progress and Poverty* (1879) 'was the most widely read of all books on economics in the English-speaking world in the last quarter of the nineteenth century'. George asked why poverty persisted in societies where 'the introduction of improved processes and labour-saving machinery . . . has multiplied enormously the effectiveness of labour' (George, 1979 [1879]: 4–5). He found the answer in the pattern of land ownership arguing that the price paid to use land – its 'rent' – increased with an expanding population and therefore 'rent' absorbed an increasing proportion of gains in productivity. Owners do not deserve the rewards accruing from land because it is the activities of an expanding population, not the efforts of landlords, that increases land values.

> The productive powers that density of population has attached to this land are equivalent to the multiplication of its original fertility by the hundredfold and the thousandfold. And rent, which measures the difference between this added productiveness and that of the least productive land in use, has increased accordingly. Our settler, or whoever has succeeded to his right to the land, is now a millionaire. Like another Rip Van Winkle, he may have lain down and slept; still he is rich – not from anything he has done, but from the increase of population. (George, 1979[1879]: 100)

George's ideal remedy for the 'undeserved' gains derived from land ownership was 'to substitute for the individual ownership of land a common ownership' (George, 1979[1879]: 128) but, as this would promote 'bitter antagonism', he promoted the taxing of all the excess rent gained from the special location of land. Such a tax would represent 'the taking by the community, for the use of the community, of the value that is the creation of the community' (George, 1979[1879]: 139).

The new liberals, anxious to halt the development of a politicized labour movement that might turn the Liberal Party into a 'mere cork on the Socialist tide' (Balfour, 1906 quoted in Pelling, 1993: 16), developed George's notion of a community created 'social surplus'. Leonard Hobhouse (1864-1929) and John Hobson (1858–1940), perhaps the most important new liberal theorists, worked within a paradigm known as 'organic' theory. According to the organic perspective society exists outside individuals and members of society have obligations to ensure society functions in a harmonious and efficient manner. Both Hobhouse and Hobson identified a 'social surplus', generated by the progressive evolution of society, that could be taken from its existing owners for use in the promoting of the rights necessary to enable people to fulfil their duties. They recognized a right to work and a right to receive an adequate income for the fulfilment of the duties of fatherhood and motherhood (Page, 1996: 38). The resources to pay for this living wage would come from the redistribution of the 'undeserved' income derived from land and inheritance. 'We cannot afford to pay £500,000,000 a year', Hobhouse claimed, 'to a number of individuals for wealth that is due partly to nature and partly to efforts of their fathers' (Hobhouse 1893: 78). Hobhouse also believed that, because the resources for the living wage were to be obtained from the collective social surplus then the state had a right to enforce the obligations of citizenship. It could legitimately act as 'over-parent' to secure 'the physical, mental and moral care of children, partly by imposing responsibilities on the parents and punishing them for neglect, partly by elaborating a public system of education and hygiene' (Hobhouse, 1974 [1911]: 25).

Thus, for the new liberals, social justice consisted of taxing the undeserved social surplus for use in promoting the social rights necessary for everyone to contribute to a progressive society. However only 'undeserved' income was legitimately available to the state and the state should have no part in guaranteeing a level of income above that necessary for the fulfilment of obligations. The 'new' liberals linked the notion of obligation to the idea of 'needs' by identifying needs as the requirements necessary for individuals to fulfil societal obligations. In *Poverty: A Study of Town Life* (1901) Seebohm Rowntree used the notion of 'physical efficiency' to connect the needs of the individual to the need of society for an efficient labour force. He defined primary poverty as 'total earnings insufficient to obtain the minimum necessaries for the maintenance of merely physical efficiency' (Rowntree, 1901: 87). Because he wanted to protect his definition of poverty from any accusations of generosity Rowntree made no allowance for expenditure needful for the development of the mental, moral, and social sides of human nature (Rowntree, 1901: 87). His calculation was related to 'the two chief uses of food', that is, 'heat to keep the body warm' and the 'muscular and other power for the work to be done'. Rowntree's clothing standard was based on working-class responses to the question 'What in your opinion is the very lowest sum upon which a man can keep himself in clothing for a year? The clothing should be adequate to keep the man in health, and should not be so shabby as to injure his chances of obtaining *respectable* employment' (Rowntree, 1901: 107–8, emphasis added). By linking the need for national economic efficiency to the public role of the male worker Rowntree – 'throughout his life a "new" Liberal' (Briggs, 1969: 38) – moved the idea of need beyond the mere survival requirements recognized by the Poor Law.

'New' liberal theory underpinned the financing of the Liberal reforms of 1906 to 1911. Lloyd George sought to pay for pensions, school meals, and child welfare partly from the unmerited gains accruing from increases in land prices. He defended his 1908 budget, which included taxes on the development gain of land, by pointing out:

land that not so many years ago was a 'sodden marsh' selling at £3 an acre was now, as result of the commerce that had come through the docks and the consequent demand for accommodation, selling at £8,000 an acre. Who created those increments? Who made the golden swamp? Was it the landlord? Was it his energy? His brains? His forethought? No, it was purely the combined efforts of all the people engaged in the trade and commerce of the Port of London – trader, merchant, shipowner, dock labourer, workmen – everybody except the landlord. (Lloyd George, 1909: 43)

Activity 9.1

Examine the figures on income distribution in 1908 below.

Riches	Number	Income
Persons with incomes of £700 per annum and upwards and their families	1,400,000	£634,000,000
Comfort		
Persons with incomes of between £700 per annum and £160 per annum and their families	4,100,000	£275,000,000
Poverty		
Persons with an income of less than £160 per annum and their families	39,000,000	£935,000,000

Source: Chiozza Money, L.G. (1910) *Riches and Poverty* (London, Methuen)

What do you think were the 'new' liberals' principal objections to this pattern of income distribution?

9.3 Fabian socialism and social justice

The members of the Fabian Society, formed in 1884, expanded the notion of 'undeserved' income to include all forms of income from rent. By 'rent' the Fabians meant 'the differential advantages of any factor of production over and above the worst in use' (Webb and Webb, 1913) such as the extra profit gained from the use of skilled rather than unskilled labour. Fabian economic theory meant more collectivist intervention than desired by the 'new' liberals but their insistence that the capitalist was entitled to some reward for investment (Macfarlane, 1998: 129) justified a more gradual approach to social change than demanded by Marx's followers. Nonetheless many Fabians believed that, even when the 'social surplus' attributed to rent had been harvested, the inefficiency and waste of uncoordinated capitalist activity would remain (Thompson, 1996: 190). Accordingly they supported the common ownership of the means of production although more to promote efficiency than as a route to social justice. Other elements of the socialist movement upheld the common ownership of the means of production as the direct path to social justice irrespective of its merits in promoting national efficiency. The aim of the Independent Labour Party, formed in 1893, was 'to secure the collective ownership of the means of production, distribution and exchange' and clause four of the Labour Party constitution, agreed in 1917, stated the party's objectives as:

> To secure for the workers by hand or by brain the full fruits of their industry and the most equitable distribution thereof that may be possible, upon the basis of the common ownership of the means of production, distribution, and exchange, and the best obtainable system of popular administration and control of each industry or service.

9.4 Social justice and state welfare

According to Tomlinson (1997: 266) Labour's attitude to the social services between 1945 and 1951 was 'conditioned by "fear of insecurity . . ." rather than equality' and the Labour Party, true to its constitution, regarded the common ownership of the means of production as the main road to social justice. Labour's 1945 manifesto stated 'The Labour Party is a socialist party and proud of it' and 'there are basic industries that are ripe and over-ripe for public ownership and management in the direct service of the nation' (Labour Party, 1945: 6). In the 1950s and 1960s, however, the de facto abandonment of nationalization by the party leadership left 'tax and spend' as the only route to social justice deemed feasible (Crosland, 1956, 1974). In a section headed 'Social justice', Labour's October 1974 manifesto stated that 'taxation must be used to achieve a major redistribution of wealth and income' (Labour Party, 1974: 9). It promised to introduce an annual tax on wealth as part of a more progressive tax structure to supply the additional finance for enhanced social security benefits and spending on education, healthcare, and public housing. Academic support for Labour's tax/benefits approach to social justice was provided by John Rawls's *A Theory of Justice* (1971), a book described by Blocker and Smith (1980: vii) as 'initiating a renaissance in social philosophy unparalleled in this century'.

9.5 John Rawls's *A Theory of Justice*

According to Rawls social co-operation 'makes possible a better life for all than any would have if each were to live solely by his own efforts' (Rawls,

1971: 4) but there are potential conflicts about how the fruits of social co-operation are to be shared. Thus 'a set of principles is required for choosing among the various social arrangements which determine this division of advantages' (Rawls, 1971: 4). These principles of social justice provide rules governing the appropriate distribution of the benefits and burdens of social co-operation.

The original position

To establish the basic principles of social justice Rawls invites us to imagine a situation in which we are considering the tenets of a just society behind a 'veil of ignorance' where we have no information about our potential life chances.

> It is assumed, then, that the parties do not know certain kinds of particular facts. First of all, no one knows his place in society, his class position or social status; nor does he know his fortune in the distribution of natural assets and abilities, his intelligence and strength, and the like. (Rawls, 1971: 137)

From this 'original position' potential participants in society construct principles of justice for the allocation of 'primary goods' – the goods necessary for the pursuit of any plan of life whatever that plan may be. These 'primary goods' include rights and liberties, opportunities and powers, income and wealth and a sense of one's own worth (Plant, 1991: 99).

Distributive principles

The principles agreed by the participants in the debate on the just society are, in priority order:

First Principle
each person is to have an equal right to the most extensive total system of equal basic liberties compatible with a similar system of liberty for all.

Second Principle
Social and economic inequalities are to be arranged so that they are both:
(a) to the greatest benefit of the least advantaged . . . and
(b) attached to offices and positions open to all under conditions of fair equality of opportunity. (Rawls, 1971: 102)

Rawls defends the agreement on the primacy of liberty with the argument that all individuals desire self-respect. Liberty is necessary to self-respect and equal liberty is necessary if human beings are to 'express their nature in free social union with others' (Rawls, 1971: 543). The second principle, known as the difference principle, arises because under the conditions of the original position where people discuss the division of the social cake without knowing which slice they will obtain, participants will adopt a 'maximin' strategy. They will attempt to optimize the worst possible outcome because, in the real world, they may receive the smallest slice of the available resources. Rawls starts with the presumption that it will be agreed that all primary goods 'are to be distributed equally unless an unequal distribution of any or all of these goods is to the advantage of the least favoured' (Rawls, 1971: 101). Structuring a society to produce inequalities is legitimate only if such inequalities work to the advantage of the worst off. Thus an individual with natural talents – Rawls regarded natural talents as 'undeserved' – can utilize these abilities and become unequal but the 'maximin' principle provides insurance against the possibility that an individual may suffer because of luck or lack of natural talents.

Rawls argues that in well-ordered society 'it is necessary to set the social and economic process within the surroundings of suitable political and legal institutions' otherwise 'the outcome of the distributive process will not be just' (Rawls, 1971: 275). Accordingly he recommends four branches of government. An allocation branch would keep the price system workably competitive. A stabilization branch would strive to bring about reasonably full employment. A transfer branch to be responsible for the social minimum and a distribution branch would have the task of 'preserving an approximate justice in distributive shares by means of taxation and the necessary adjustments in the rights of property' (Rawls, 1971: 276–7). Thus, using the established techniques of political theory such as the notion of a 'social contract', Rawls produced 'a philosophical apologia for an egalitarian brand of welfare-state capitalism' (Wolff, 1977: 195) a system in evolution in most western industrial democracies since 1945 but, according to Rawls, without a systematic rationale.

Activity 9.2

Explain what Rawls means by:
1 the original position;
2 primary goods;
3 maximin.

Labour's social programme of 1974 to 1976 certainly influenced income distribution to the benefit of the least advantaged. In 1975–76 government expenditure absorbed 48.7 per cent of gross domestic product. The standard rate of income tax was 35 per cent and the highest rate of tax on unearned income was 83 per cent. In 1977 the Gini coefficient (a measure of overall inequality with 100 representing the extreme of inequality) reached a low postwar point of 22 (Johnson, 1999: 21). In the same year the poverty rate (measured as the proportion of the population below half average national income when adjusted for family size) was 6 per cent – a reduction from 11 per cent in 1972 (Burgess and Propper, 1999: 261). However, by 1976, the achievement of social justice via tax and spend was under attack from both inside and outside the government. In February 1976 the Treasury declared that more resources were needed for exports and investment and that such resources could only be made available by restraining public expenditure. Moreover the Treasury asserted that, within total public expenditure, a high priority had to be given to expenditure 'designed to maintain or improve our industrial capacity, and to give us a better chance of success as the economy picks up' (Chancellor of the Exchequer, 1976: 1–2). Meanwhile, outside government, a powerful critique of the pursuit of social justice via taxation and state welfare was developing. Fredrich Hayek was the most important guru of an ideology that came to be labelled the 'New Right'.

9.6 The mirage of social justice

Hayek made a distinction between 'spontaneous' and 'made' orders. A 'spontaneous' order is governed by a rules of conduct that provide a framework within which individuals pursue their own ends but no overall purpose for society is specified. In contrast a 'made' order has a specified purpose and 'order in society is seen as resting upon a relationship of command and obedience. It signifies a hierarchy in which a supreme authority instructs individuals as to how they must behave' (Gamble, 1996: 36–7). Hayek regarded the market as a spontaneous order and, in such an order, the idea of social justice is 'entirely empty and meaningless' (Hayek, 1976a: 11). In a market, there are no principles to apply to individual conduct that would produce a pattern of distribution that can be called just and therefore there is no possibility for the individual to know what he would have to do to secure the 'just' remuneration of his fellows. So, says Hayek, although 'it has of course to be admitted that the manner in which the benefits and burdens are apportioned by the market mechanism would in many instances have to be regarded as very unjust if it were the result of a deliberate allocation to particular people. This is not the case' (Hayek, 1976b: 64).

If Hayek's notion of the market as a 'catallaxy' or spontaneous order, untouched by human design, is accepted then the idea of 'social' allocations, designed to alter the outcomes of market mechanisms in the direction of 'social justice', is at best misguided and at worst dangerous. 'It must lead to the extinction of all moral responsibility' (Hayek, 1976c: 129) and the very idea of social justice becomes a grave threat 'to most other values of a free civilization' being 'the Trojan Horse through which totalitarianism has entered'

(Hayek, 1976a: 66–7, 136). This is so because the achievement of social justice involves imposing a predetermined pattern on the unintended outcomes of market processes and the passing of laws affecting specific forms of behaviour. According to Hayek the only laws compatible with freedom are general, abstract laws concerned with procedures such as 'the rules of the law of property, tort and contract' (Hayek, 1976b: 109).

In Hayek's discourse the philosophical justification of redistribution via state welfare disintegrates. However as Espada (1996: 37) and Kley (1994: 24) have indicated, Hayek runs together the idea that social justice has no meaning in a market system with the notion that social justice is not a legitimate concept to apply to any type of society. Hayek assumes that the market order is the natural order but, because we know about the general outcomes of the market, there is no reason why we should accept such outcomes. We can choose between unfettered markets, regulated markets, a combination of a market with a welfare state or a communist system. Hayek rejects the idea of social justice which creates what Hirsch has called the 'tyranny of small choices'. 'The core of the problem is that the market provides a full range of choice between alternative piecemeal, discrete, marginal adjustments but no facility for selection between alternative states' (Hirsch, 1977: 18).

Activity 9.3

Which of the following laws would Hayek regard as legitimate?
1 a law requiring all local authorities in London to reserve a proportion of their housing stock for homeless people,
2 a law to ensure that contracts are enforced,
3 a law imposing a special tax of 80 per cent on the increased value of land created by the extra demand for houses generated by a movement of population from north to south.

9.7 Robert Nozick and rectification

Robert Nozick (1974) has contributed a further objection to Hayek's insistence that social justice is a mirage. Nozick starts from a similar position to Hayek but reluctantly comes to recognize that historical injustices in acquisition negate the current legitimacy of market outcomes.

In *Anarchy, State and Utopia* (1974) Nozick claimed that 'Individuals have rights, and there are things no person or group may do to them without violating their rights' (Nozick, 1974: ix). Nozick justified a minimal state 'limited to the narrow functions of protection against force, theft, fraud, enforcement of contracts' by constructing a plausible account of how a minimal state, limited to maintaining law and order, may emerge without infringing individual rights (Nozick, 1974: 10–25). However he claimed that a more extensive state, involved in the redistribution of resources already acquired, violates individual rights. This is because current justice in distribution depends on the historical factors that created this distribution. If holdings were gained by creation, free exchange, or as a gift then they are legitimately the property of their current owner. Redistribution of acquisitions according to any 'patterned principle' such as 'equality' or 'social justice' violates the rights of the original holders – hence 'taxation of earnings from labour is on a par with forced labour' (Nozick, 1974: 169). This conclusion seemingly undermines the rationale of a redistributive welfare state and Nozick has been accused of 'proposing to starve or humiliate ten per cent or so of our fellow citizens' (Barry, 1975: 334). However, Nozick is not a heartless libertarian. He recognized that market distributions: 'seem arbitrary unless some acceptable initial set of holdings is specified, or unless it is held that the operation of the system over time washes out any significant effects from the initial set of holdings' (Nozick, 1974: 160). First there is the problem of how individuals can acquire rights to natural resources. Nozick tried hard to reconcile the outcomes of the market with established rights to natural resources but could not find a response to conform with his entitlement theory. He was forced to the conclusion that one is entitled to a part of a natural resource if one leaves 'enough and as good' for others to have some use of it and if the position of others is not worsened by the initial act of appropriation. This concession opened the door to extensive state intervention in the distribution of resources for we must ask 'enough and as good' for what? Because the primary purpose of the use of a natural resource is to satisfy basic needs then 'enough and as good' for needs satisfaction must be the answer to this question thereby giving the state a legitimate role in the redistribution of income and wealth.

Nozick was also concerned by the compounding impact of resources obtained in the past through force and, after much deliberation, he decided that reparations had to be made for historical injustices in acquisition.

> . . . a rough rule of thumb for rectifying injustices might seem to be the following: organize society so as to maximize the position of whatever group ends up least well-off in the society . . . Although to introduce socialism as a punishment for our sins would be to go too far, past injustices might be so great as to make necessary in the short run a more extensive state in order to rectify them. (Nozick, 1974: 152)

Thus, in contrast to Hayek, Nozick identified the problem of rectification and presented an argued case demonstrating why the establishment of free markets, without compensating mechanisms to rectify past injustices, produces unfair outcomes.

9.8 Inequality and social justice

The application of Hayek's principles was the guiding canon of Conservative policy between 1979 and 1997 (Ranelagh, 1991: ix). The collective bargaining rights of trade unions were restricted. Wages Councils were abolished, assistance to the regions reduced, and industries were privatized. Income tax rates were cut in favour of increases in indirect taxation. The value of universal benefits was eroded and earnings related benefits were either scaled down or abolished. State services were brought to the market by privatization and market principles were injected into state welfare via 'quasi-markets' (Bartlett et al. 1998). The outcome of these policies is summarized in Table 9.1 and Table 9. 2.

Table 9.1 Income of selected deciles as a percentage of top decile: two adults with children 1978

	Lowest decile	2nd lowest	3rd lowest	4th lowest
Original income (£)	12	28	34	39
Original income plus cash benefits	24	30	36	40
Disposable income	31	35	39	44
Income after indirect taxation	29	34	37	41
Final income (with value of 'in kind' services)	39	40	43	46

Source: adapted from 'The effects of taxes and benefits on household income: 1978', *Economic Trends*, 315: January 1980, HMSO.

Table 9.2 Income of selected deciles as a percentage of top decile: two adults with children, 1996–97

	Lowest decile	2nd lowest	3rd lowest	4th lowest
Original income (£)	4	7	12	19
Original income plus cash benefits	12	16	20	25
Disposable income	14	20	23	28
Income after indirect taxation	11	17	19	25
Final income (with value of 'in kind' services)	25	29	30	34

Source: adapted from 'The effects of taxes and benefits on household income: 1996/97', *Economic Trends*, 533: April 1998, Stationery Office.

Activity 9.4

Examine Tables 9.1 and 9.2. They give the resources of the lowest decile of households (the poorest 10 per cent with children) as a percentage of the resources of the highest decile (the richest ten per cent with children) at each stage of the redistributive process. Similar figures are given for the second, third, and fourth poorest deciles. Row 1 refers to income from the market, Row 2 adds cash benefits, Row 3 deducts direct taxation such as income tax, Row 4 deducts indirect taxation such as VAT and Row 5 attributes cash value to the use of state services. These figures need to be treated with caution as there are many methodological problems involved in their compilation.

Which stage of redistribution made the greatest contribution to the increase in inequality between 1978 and 1996–7?

In 1996–7 which stage of redistribution helped the poorest most?

Of course an increase in inequality does not necessarily mean a contraction in social justice; remember Rawls argued that inequalities might be just if they produce gains for the least advantaged. Nonetheless it is worth noting that the poorest decile of the population became worse off in absolute terms (after housing costs) between 1978 and 1996 (HM Treasury, 1999: 7) and it is difficult to argue that most of the gainers from increased inequality deserved their enlarged share of the gross national product. The increase in inequality did not enhance the absolute position of the least advantaged – a necessary condition for the justification of inequality under Rawls's conception of justice – and much of the extra inequality was derived from entrenched positions of advantage, not from new entrepreneurial activity in global markets (Hobson, 1999).

9.9 Walzer's spheres of justice

In the 1980s conventional political philosophy was challenged by 'communitarians' who argued that, in its attempt to discover abstract, universal rules of distribution, mainstream political philosophy had ignored the social contexts in which all meaningful notions of social justice must evolve. Advocates of 'identity' and 'recognition' politics added the charge that 'liberal' political philosophy – obsessed by the individual as the basic unit of society – had neglected the institutional frameworks that generate social injustice.

Hayek and Nozick specified principles of distribution to be applied to all goods and services and, although Rawls made a distinction between 'primary' and other goods, his definition of primary goods was so broad that few domains remained in which to apply principles different from his basic tenets of justice. In *Spheres of Justice* (1983: 4–5) Michael Walzer asserted 'justice is a human construction' and 'there has never been a single criterion, or a single set of interconnected criteria, for all distributions'. Moreover he claimed that the recognition of the complexity of justice is essential to achieving equality. Egalitarianism, he says, has its origins in abolitionist politics; its aim has been to eliminate the experience of personal subordination and thereby create a society 'free from domination' (Walzer, 1983: xiii). Freedom from domination can be achieved only by a full recognition that different spheres of life generate different principles of distribution through the shared meanings that come to be associated with varied goods and services. If each separate domain of life is allowed its particular principle of distribution then no single source of power (material wealth for example) can dominate society. Hence medical care, if thought of as a special needed good 'cannot be left to the whim, or distributed in the interest, of some powerful group of owners and practitioners' (Walzer, 1983: 89). Other 'blocked exchanges' for money might include political office, military service in wars, and freedom of speech.

So, against Hayek, Walzer claims that 'A radically laissez-faire economy would be like a totalitarian state, invading every other sphere, dominating every other distributive process. It would transform every social good into a commodity' (Walzer, 1983: 119–20). Walzer promoted the notion of need as one of many principles of distribution but, like the 'new' liberals, he stressed that need had no objective status – other than in relationship to survival needs – outside the shared meanings that have become attached to different goods and services. In *A Theory of Human Need* (1991) Doyal and Gough took the opposite stance arguing that allocation according to need should be the principal criterion in assessing the justice of a distributive system. They were critical of notions of need as relative to cultural contexts or as constructed by discursive communities. Needs, they asserted, are universal and objective in that everyone requires physical health and autonomy.

Activity 9.5

1 In what ways, if any, does healthcare carry 'shared meanings' that suggest it should be distributed in different ways from other goods and services?
2 Is it possible to specify the conditions necessary for individual autonomy that are not related to the specific society in which an individual lives?

9.10 Young and the politics of identity and difference

In *Justice and the Politics of Difference* Iris Young (1990: 3) asked 'what are the implications for political philosophy of the claims of new group-based social movements associated with left politics – such movements as feminism, Black liberation, American Indian movements, and gay and lesbian liberation?' She argued that mainstream political philosophy had proved incapable of accommodating claims from these new social movements because it had attempted to construct a rational notion of social justice 'abstracted from the particular circumstances of social life that give rise to concrete claims of justice' (Young, 1990:4). Moreover it had tended 'to focus thinking about social justice on the allocation of material goods and things, resources, income, and wealth, or on the distribution of social positions, especially jobs'. This restricted concern was inclined to ignore 'decision-making power and procedures, divisions of labour and culture' (Young, 1990: 15) that determine distributive outcomes as well as respect for difference and the self-respect of the members of minority communities.

Young insisted that the empowerment of oppressed groups was the issue. She defined oppression as 'the structural phenomena that immobilise or diminish a group' (Young, 1990: 42) and advocated the award of additional rights to selected groups because oppression had been generally applied to groups, not to individuals. Such enhanced group rights would extend the participation of the people historically excluded from the public sphere and thereby advance the practice of civic self-determination. Habermas puts the matter succinctly in relationship to the involvement of women in the public sphere. 'Rights can empower women to shape their own lives autonomously only to the extent that these rights also facilitate equal participation in the practice of civic self-determination, because only women themselves can clarify the "relevant aspects" that define equality and inequality in a given matter' (Habermas 1996: 420). In *Multicultural Citizenship: A Liberal Theory of Minority Rights* (1994) Will Kymlicka supported the main thrust of Young's argument. He claimed that liberal theorists have had little to say about, for example, 'how the systematic devaluation of the roles of women can be removed' (Kymlicka, 1994: 89). The emphasis in liberalism on individual rights, he argued, does not automatically produce equal rights for minority cultures because the 'viability of their societal cultures may be undermined by economic and political decisions made by the majority. They could be outbid or outvoted on resources and policies that are crucial to the survival of their societal cultures' (Kymlicka, 1994: 109). Group differentiated rights can help to rectify this disadvantage.

Activity 9.6

Paul Kelly claims that Iris Young does not adequately address the issue of the selection of the identity conferring groups who will be allowed additional special representation. He argues that 'not all identities are due public recognition as many of these are the basis of coercive relationships and oppressions ... Young must employ a principle of inclusion which can discriminate among identity-groups but this raises the question of what principle of inclusion' (Kelly 1998: 193).
Which groups, if any, do you think should be awarded extra representational rights?

9.11 New Labour, social justice and social exclusion

In 1996 Tony Blair declared that there was a 'limited but crucial role of government in a modern economy'. This role was to provide:

> A secure low-inflation environment and promote long-term investment; ensure that business has well-educated people to recruit into the workforce; ensure a properly functioning first-class infrastructure; work with business to promote regional development and small and growing firms; seek to open markets for our goods around the world; and create a strong and cohesive society which removes the drag on the economy of social costs. (Blair, 1996: 110)

Blair's endorsement of the market was modified by the promotion of a positive role for the state in promoting 'a strong and cohesive society'. This role was soon presented as meaning that concerted government action was necessary to tackle 'social exclusion', a term embraced by New Labour in late 1997 when a social exclusion unit was set up in the Prime Minister's office. Blair defined social exclusion 'as broadly covering those people who do not have the means, *material or otherwise*, to participate in social, economic, political and cultural life' (Blair, 1998 quoted in Scottish Office, 1998a: 2, emphasis added).

The centrepiece of New Labour's attempt to include the excluded has been its welfare to work programme supported by targeted income support to low income families where at least one parent is in work. In addition help has been concentrated on various 'zones' of deprivation and there has been a strong emphasis on inclusion in mainstream value systems through an insistence that reciprocal obligations – especially the obligation to work – must be attached to welfare rights. This approach has been presented as a vital element of the 'third way' in politics. Advocates of the 'third way' claim that market competitiveness is necessary for success in a global economy but that the state should vigorously promote opportunities for the socially excluded to enable them to participate in this global economy. The 'third way' future for welfare is 'investment in human capital wherever possible, rather than the direct provision of economic maintenance' (Giddens, 1998: 117).

New Labour has linked the attainment of social justice to the creation of 'a community where everyone has the chance to succeed' (Blair, 1999a: 8). In this new, just Britain the socially excluded will be included through work opportunities, better education, the guarantee of a minimum income for those who work and the assurance of 'security for those who cannot work' (Blair, 1998a). This interpretation of a just society can be used to illustrate the ideas on distributive justice outlined earlier in this chapter.

There is a correspondence between New Labour's notion of distributive justice and that of Rawls. New Labour's emphasis on equality of opportunity, with additional help for people living in deprived areas to promote extra opportunities, can be interpreted as conforming to Rawls's notion that inequalities must be attached to positions and offices accessible to all under the principle of fair equality of opportunity (Buckler and Dolowitz, 2000: 102–9). Moreover New Labour appears to favour Rawls's 'least advantaged' in its distributive principles. According to Treasury estimates 1.2 million children will be lifted out of poverty by the minimum wage plus the measures announced in the 1998, 1999, and 2000 budgets (HM Treasury, 2000). Also New Labour's minimum income guarantee and second pension proposals concentrate income on the poorest pensioners. Nonetheless there are important differences between the formulations of social justice presented by Rawls and by New Labour. Rawls started from the presumption of equality arguing that a departure from an equal distribution can be justified only by demonstrating that such a departure will produce gains for the least advantaged above the share they might expect from an equal distribution. In contrast New Labour starts from a position in which the move towards market transactions, characteristic of the period 1979 to 1997, was superimposed on a template of power and wealth forged in earlier times. New Labour has not explained why this historically generated pattern of inequality is 'deserved'. To do so it would have to demonstrate that existing inequalities are necessary to supply the incentives for a dynamic and risk-taking economy that will make the 'least advantaged' better off than in a society where resources are distributed more equally. Because New Labour has not attempted to rectify past injustices in acquisition its notion of distributive justice does not conform to that of Nozick.

Walzer demanded a pluralist society in which different goods and services are distributed according to principles generated by the 'shared meanings' attached to different spheres of life. He was opposed to the domination of a single distributive principle. New Labour's insistence that full social citizenship rights can be obtained only through workforce participation appears to construct a model of 'citizen-worker' and devalue other spheres of citizenship such as parenthood, voluntary activity, and political participation (Phillips, 1997; Helm, 2000).

Certain dimensions of Young's conception of social justice are present in New Labour's stance. The term 'social exclusion' draws attention to the processes involved in distribution whereas poverty can be interpreted as an outcome measure representative of the top-down, cake-slicing approach of the 1970s. Moreover, when in opposition, New Labour granted extra representational rights to women in the form of women only short lists in the selection process for Labour Party parliamentary candidates. Devolution and a new emphasis on pluralism in the delivery of welfare has opened opportunities for representational politics but New Labour has not overtly promoted 'group' politics in public electoral systems, in appointments to public bodies, or in the targets set by the Treasury in public service agreements (Spencer, 2000). This may reflect concerns about the 'politics of difference' as expressed by Kelly and others (see, Phillips, 1999 and Fraser, 1998) but, because class politics has been declared dead (Blair, 1999b), the inference is that New Labour believes that the availability of individual work opportunities for the socially excluded is the criterion on which social justice is to be assessed.

Tony Blair's emphasis on the obligations of the individual to take up the opportunities facilitated by the state is reminiscent of the 'new' liberal stance dominant at the turn of the nineteenth century. However the 'new' liberals qualified these obligations by the insistence that the 'undeserved' social surplus should be redistributed – an insistence absent from the New Labour's notion of distributive justice. Thus, according to Levitas:

> Social inclusion now has nothing to do with distributional equality, but means lifting those poor over the boundary of a minimum standard – or to be more accurate, inducing those who are sufficiently sound in wind and limb to jump over it – while leaving untouched the overall pattern of inequality, especially the rich. (Levitas, 1998: 156)

Even Giddens, the guru of the 'third way', has recognized the link between equality of outcome and equality of opportunity and has endorsed Tobin's statement that 'one generation's inequality of outcome is the next generation's inequality of opportunity' (Giddens, 2000: 89).

9.12 Conclusion

We have seen that distributive or social justice is a contested concept. Disagreement has focused on four dimensions of the idea. First, who are the subjects of distributive justice – individuals or groups? Is Iris Young correct in asserting the priority of groups over individuals and, if so, on what grounds should we select the groups to be assigned special political and social rights?

Second, what is the role of distribution according to need in a theory of justice? Is it possible to identify needs, above the requirements for survival, in an objective way so that a universal criterion of distribution is available? Third, can we apply the same distributive criteria to all goods and services? Are there not some goods and services that, because they embody special characteristics and shared meanings, should be distributed according to their intrinsic or indeed their socially created purposes? Fourth, to what extent do the recipients of unequal shares deserve their portions? Is justice 'historical' and connected to the ways people have acquired their resources or is it 'current' and therefore related to the existing pattern of distribution regardless of how it came about?

CHAPTER 10

WHAT'S IN A NAME? POVERTY, THE UNDERCLASS AND SOCIAL EXCLUSION

Tony Novak

10.1 Introduction

'This is about more than poverty and unemployment. It is about being cut off from what the rest of us regard as normal life. It is called social exclusion, what others call the "underclass"' (Peter Mandelson *Labour's Next Steps: Tackling Social Exclusion*, 1997:1). How we talk about the poor is a matter of great importance. The words that are used not only bring with them their own images – of the poor as a threat, for example, or as a group to be pitied – but they also reflect and influence how we understand and explain poverty. Through history the terminology associated with poverty has changed: from rogues and vagabonds, the idle poor, to the residuum, or the underclass. Such terms, most of them derogatory, are products of their particular historical, economic, social and political contexts. They are forged out of a continual, and mostly unequal, struggle over how this most fundamental of social problems is to be labelled and understood.

Activity 10.1

While it is now widely recognized that many terms used to describe women or black people are derogatory and insulting, there is little such awareness of similar terms that are used to describe the poor. Make a list of as many terms as you can think of that are used to substitute for the word 'poor', and see how many have a positive or a negative image.

This chapter is concerned with two ways of looking at the poor that have emerged over the past decade or so. At the beginning of the 1990s in Britain (although, for example, in the USA considerably earlier) the term 'underclass' came increasingly to be adopted in the media, by politicians, and by some social scientists to describe a significant number of the poor. Like many of its predecessors, the concept had an ugly undertone, and carried with it often explicit moral condemnations that judged the poor as immoral, or more usually, amoral, and responsible for their own deteriorating situation.

Slightly later, and stemming from a continental European rather than a North American origin, a different discourse was to emerge, that of social exclusion. By the end of the 1990s, and in particular with the election and subsequent policy initiatives of the New Labour government elected in 1997, social exclusion was to become the dominant paradigm, largely displacing not only talk of an underclass, but even terms like poverty and the poor themselves.

Yet this chapter will argue that the underclass and social exclusion, far from being radically different concepts, share much in common. Both deny or seek to replace more long-standing concepts of poverty and the poor; both are based on quite problematic conceptions of social order and wellbeing; partly as a result, both place considerable emphasis on the moral culpability of the poor; and both, when translated into government policy and action, fit into a growing authoritarianism in state social policy.

10.2 The problem with poverty

Before we do this, however, we should note that terms like poverty and the poor are not without their problems. Poverty is not a neutral concept, but is laden with images and meanings that reflect its long history. These meanings come from various sources, including from the poor themselves, and can present radically different and conflicting views of the situation. But in the modern era, and especially since the time of the industrial revolution, the experience of poverty – and the meanings attached to it – have been dominated by a state social policy that has for the most part treated the poor with contempt. For generations, to be poor has been to be stigmatized. Subject to beatings and whippings, the Poor Law and its deliberately degrading and feared workhouses, or, more lately, widely criticized as scroungers and benefit cheats, the treatment of those forced to turn to the state for assistance has profoundly shaped not only their own experience of poverty but also the terrain on which the wider society sees the problem (see, for example, Novak 1988; Squires 1990; Dean 1991a).

In such a context few people will readily admit to being poor. This, of course, has major implications for estimating the scale of the problem. It also has important repercussions for the possibilities of creating a common identity and solidarity around poverty. As many studies of people's perceptions of poverty have shown, most people – even those who, objectively, have very little – do not consider themselves to be poor. And where they recognize that a problem of poverty exists, it is usually somebody else, someone worse off than they themselves are, who is seen as really suffering from the problem. In curious ways, of course, such perceptions – that it is 'someone who is worse off than me who is in poverty' – can reflect other sentiments: sentiments of sympathy and of a generosity amongst the poor that puts others first. But this distancing from the problem of poverty that even the poorest exhibit cannot fully be understood in isolation from the wider social practices that treat the poor as pariahs.

Since the end of the nineteenth century this separation of the poor in many people's minds as a group 'out there' has been powerfully reinforced by the development of academic and so-called 'scientific' studies of poverty. Up until the late nineteenth century the issue of poverty, like that of wealth, was most widely understood as an issue of social class. Indeed the two – poverty and wealth – were recognized as intimately related. The nineteenth-century political economist Patrick Colquhoun saw it, in terms with which few of his contemporaries would have disagreed:

> Poverty is a most necessary and indispensable ingredient in society, without which nations and communities could not exist in a state of civilization. It is the lot of man – it is the source of wealth, since without poverty there would be no labour, and without labour there could be no riches, no refinement, no comfort, and no benefit to those who may be possessed of wealth. (Patrick Colquhoun 'A Treatise on Indigence' 1806; quoted Rose 1971: 47)

Seen in these terms, to be poor was to be working class, and to be working class was to be poor. Poverty was thus not a matter of level of income; indeed differences of income within the working class were as great then as they are now. In a much more fundamental sense, poverty was seen and understood as the condition of all of those without property, and who were as a result dependent on the sale of their labour to survive. And in this sense, as another economist, Nassau Senior, recognized, poverty was always seen as something that existed in relation to wealth; talking of 'the unfortunate [sic] double meaning of the word poor', he went on: 'In its widest acceptation it is opposed to the word rich; and *in its most common use* it includes all, except the higher and middle classes' (Senior, 1865: 67, emphasis added).

Such contrasts, not surprisingly, were to excite more than a little concern and anxiety on the part of the rich. Towards the end of the nineteenth century, as Britain came to experience the first Great Depression, with its mass unemployment and deepening levels of poverty and protest, such fears on the part of the wealthy were to be thrown into even starker relief (see, for example, Stedman-Jones, 1971; Harris, 1972, Novak, 1988). Many contemporaries then echoed the fears of the Bishop of Manchester, speaking at the National Association for the Promotion of Social Science in 1879, when he warned of 'the strife of interests; the war of classes widening and deepening day by day . . . The dull desperate hate with which those who want and have not come at last to regard the whole framework of society as but one huge contrivance for their oppression' (cited McGregor, 1957: 154).

It was in this context that social investigators such as Charles Booth and

Seebohm Rowntree were to undertake the first systematic studies of poverty. Their investigations were sparked by a growing concern that, under the pressure of prolonged unemployment, divisions within the working class (divisions that have always played a major role in containing the problem of poverty) were becoming increasingly blurred, and that the usually better off and more skilled workers were coming to identify their own fate with that of their poorer counterparts.

In the face of this situation the activities of social investigators were to seek to establish a dividing line within the working class that would mark a new definition of poverty. According to Charles Booth:

> The question of those who actually suffer from poverty should be considered separately from that of the true working classes, whose desire for a larger share of the wealth is of a different character. It is the plan of agitators and the way of sensational writers to confound the two in one, to talk of 'starving millions', and to tack on the thousands of the working classes to the tens or hundreds of distress. Against this method I protest. To confound these essentially distinct problems is to make the solution of both impossible. It is not by welding distress and aspirations that any good can be done. (Booth 1904: 155)

The so-called 'scientific' study of poverty would thus bring about a radical break in how poverty – and the poor – were to be defined and understood. Rather than see poverty as the condition of a working class, this new definition would seek to define the poor as a minority of the working class, marked off by a certain level of income. Whereas the older understanding and definition had, by its very nature, stressed a common interest amongst workers – both as sharing the same fundamental economic position in society, and as together standing in contrast to the rich – the new definition would establish a dividing line within the working class. It would demarcate the poor only as a minority of workers, and it would substantially narrow the common understanding of poverty.

10.3 The problems of a poverty line

The use of a poverty line as a way both of defining and measuring poverty has ever since dominated studies of the problem. In practice the measurement of poverty has become a substitute for its definition. When we say that the poor are those who have less than £x a week (at whatever level the line is drawn), we end up defining poverty by the way we measure it. In the process we lose any independent definition of what poverty actually is (other than just a certain amount of money), and above all we are left with no way of explaining it (see Novak, 1995).

The problems and limitations of defining poverty by use of a poverty line are many. In the first place it has encouraged a tendency to define poverty at an extremely low level of income. For the most part social scientists, and certainly most politicians and governments, have defined poverty as the absolute minimum level of income necessary to ensure physical survival. Of course, strictly speaking, an absolute measure of poverty – one that will remain the same regardless of social circumstances or the passage of time – is an impossibility. Even the attempt to calculate absolute nutritional requirements for subsistence (on which a number of poverty lines such as that used in the USA are based) fails once we appreciate that even necessary minimum levels of nutrition will vary with such changeable factors as life expectancy. Such measures are even less realistic when we consider the need for clothing or shelter, for what is considered the necessary minimum can never be fixed absolutely, but rises as human society has evolved.

In the face of this reality most social scientists (although not necessarily most politicians) have come to adopt a relative view of poverty: to argue that poverty can never be defined or measured in absolute terms, but is always relative to the society in which it occurs. This approach has also encouraged a wider appreciation of the standards against which poverty is measured: that it is not enough simply to measure the minimum requirements for food, clothing, and shelter in any given society at any given point in time. Poverty must also be measured in terms of other social requirements and necessities, such as the need to be educated and informed, to be healthy, or to take part in social life and interaction. Yet even then the tendency has been to set the poverty line at the lowest possible level.

This brings us to the second problem with a poverty line, which is where and how the line is to be drawn. No British government has ever adopted an official poverty line, so social scientists have had to use other measures. For many years it was common to use the government's minimum level of means-tested benefit as a proxy for an official poverty line. There is of course an immediate problem with this: benefit levels are influenced by political (and not just economic, and even less by scientific) calculations. A government has only to reduce the level of benefit paid out and, by this measure, the number of people counted as in poverty would be reduced, even though the living standards of those now excluded remain the same.

In the attempt to avoid the political susceptibility of benefit levels, other researchers, and most notably Peter Townsend, have sought 'scientific criteria' and 'objective social observation' (Townsend, 1985) as a basis for measuring poverty. Although Townsend's work has done more than anyone else's in Britain to establish the relative nature of poverty and to argue for an approach that encompasses a wide range of social life and participation, the problems of measurement have simply multiplied. Thus his major study of *Poverty in the United Kingdom*, published in 1979, identifies 60 different indicators of poverty, and even then suggests that these are provisional and by no means exhaustive. Trying to define, or even measure, poverty through the infinite number of ways and areas of life in which the poor are deprived may produce a more adequate description of poverty, but still stops short of telling us what it is.

Other researchers have criticized such an approach as imposing the values of 'experts' and their own opinions of what constitutes poverty (who, after all, is to say that 'at least one day in the last fortnight with insufficient to eat' (Townsend, 1987: 141) is a more objective or scientific indicator of poverty than insufficient to eat in the last week or month?). An alternative method, pioneered by Mack and Lansley in their study of *Poor Britain: The Breadline Britain Survey*, sought to develop a poverty line not by asking 'experts' but by using surveys to ask the general population what they thought were the necessities of life. Yet this approach too is beset by problems (for a critique of a number of these approaches see Piachaud, 1987).

Ironically, the failure of social scientists to agree a robust definition of poverty was seized upon by the Conservative government under Margaret Thatcher in 1985. In its Green Paper on the reform of social security it reviewed the debates that had taken place and came to the conclusion that 'there is now no universally agreed standard of poverty' (Department of Health and Social Security, 1985: 12). It then proceeded to introduce reforms that substantially cut the incomes of the very poorest.

The third problem of a poverty line is its tendency to view poverty primarily in material – and most often in monetary – terms. Poverty is of course closely associated with money, or rather the lack of it. But, unlike money, some things are unmeasurable: the worry and stress of never having enough, the effects of living in an unhealthy or overcrowded environment. What is more, poverty is not just a lack of material goods. It is also a matter of social relationships, of the ways in which the poor are treated by those around them. Often these others are in positions of authority and power in their dealings with the poor. They may treat the poor with sympathy, with condescension, with indifference, with suspicion or with hostility. But to be poor is usually to have little or no influence over how you are treated. Such experiences cannot be reduced to or measured by a poverty line. Yet for many people, such experiences are as great if not greater a dimension of poverty than the material standard of living they endure. In one study, for example, conducted amongst some of the poorest villagers in rural Bangladesh, those interviewed put inadequate income low down their list of what it meant to be poor. At the top of the list, the most common and important complaint about being poor was not being treated with respect (Chambers, 1994).

This brings us to a final problem with the poverty line: that it tends to isolate the poor and encourage an understanding of poverty that neglects its relationship with the wider economy and society. Poverty is a continuum. Whether it is measured or defined by level of income, access to a range of goods and services, opportunities to participate in the range of activities that society offers, or the likelihood of being treated with dignity and respect, it is an experience that shades imperceptibly from the poorest and most despised through to the affluent. To impose an often arbitrary cut-off point to mark off some percentage of the population ignores the fact that many people above the line will to some extent experience similar hardships and humiliations. It is not only that many people will at some time in their lives move up or down the continuum, and thus that the number of people who experience poverty will be far greater than a poverty line identifies at any one time, it is also, and more importantly, that the insecurity and stress that disfigure the lives of the poorest also continue to gnaw away at the lives of the majority. The higher up the continuum people find themselves, the less immediate and destructive these pressures might be, but the fear of losing a job, or becoming sick or disabled, the requirement to submit to the authority of employers or others, are aspects of life which few, except the rich, fully escape. To define poverty as something only affecting a minority, and to ignore the threat that poverty poses to a majority of people, is not only to underestimate the problem. It is also to encourage those higher up the continuum to distance themselves from those below: to see themselves as different rather than having something in common.

10.4 Increasing poverty

Understanding poverty requires much more than the very limited insights which current definitions and measurements of poverty allow. Yet even in their own terms, these indicators of poverty have shown a dramatic increase in recent years. Between 1979 and the mid-1990s the number of people living in poverty (measured as below half average income) increased from one in ten to one in four of the population, with the number of children in poverty seeing an even greater rise to one in three. At the same time while the incomes of the poor stagnated, and those of the poorest actually fell by some 13 per cent, the incomes of the richest increased: by 1993 they were 63 per cent better off than they had been some 15 years earlier. This growth in inequality was greater than in any other industrialized country (many, although by no means all, of which also saw inequality increase), and its effect was to more than wipe out all the progress towards greater equality of income and wealth that had been made since the Second World War. This was not, of course accidental (see Jones and Novak, 1999). Although government policy was not alone responsible for this unprecedented rise in poverty and inequality (the market economy and employers themselves playing a major role, for example, in increasing unemployment or lowering wages) government action played a decisive and deliberate part. For the Conservative governments in power between 1979 and 1997 inequality was seen as a necessary, and indeed valuable, mechanism of economic motivation. Indeed it was the pursuit of equality (albeit something that was very far from ever realized) embodied in the expansion of the postwar welfare state that was, for the New Right, the cause of Britain's economic (and, they argued, moral) decline. By introducing a greater degree of security for the poor, for example, through its commitment to full employment or the provision of benefits, the welfare state was seen as having shifted the balance of power in society too far in favour of the poor. It had, they believed, reduced the incentive to work, undermined the patriar-chal nuclear family, and eroded the sense of deference and respect for authority amongst the poor. If private enterprise was to flourish, and the rich were to reap what they considered to be their just rewards, then the role of the state as a provider of welfare would have to be drastically changed, if not abolished altogether.

Accordingly, the Conservative governments led by Margaret Thatcher, and subsequently by John Major, set about reducing the entitlements of the poor. Benefit levels were reduced, access to them was made more difficult and demanding, while some were abolished altogether. At the same time, reduc-tions in levels of direct taxation, and a shift in tax policy towards the taxation of consumption, were to boost significantly the incomes of the rich, while increasing the tax burden on the poor. The state's role in provision, espe-cially of housing, was drastically reduced. Under the impact of new legislation, and the introduction of market mechanisms and new managerial controls, other public services on which the poorest most depended became more punitive and less supportive. This is not the place for a detailed study of these events, but their cumulative impact, together with those changes taking place within the labour market, was not only dramatically to increase levels of poverty and inequality, but to inflict immense economic, social and psychological damage on some of the poorest and most vulnerable people in Britain.

10.5 The construction of an 'underclass'

It was in this context that, in the early 1990s, public attention was focused on what was rapidly to become a new dominant image of the poor: that of an 'underclass'. Although the term had been widely used in the USA for a number of years, where it had developed as a coded way of talking about the black American poor, it was not until *The Sunday Times* began in 1990 to seri-alize a report by Charles Murray on *The Emerging British Underclass* that the concept was catapulted into national attention. Murray, a new right academic who had contributed significantly to the growing literature on the underclass in the USA, was paid by *The Sunday Times* to spend a year studying in Britain to see if the same phenomenon could be identified here.

'I arrived in Britain earlier this year,' he reported, 'a visitor from a plague area, come to see whether the disease is spreading' and his conclusions were as dramatic as they were predictable: 'Britain has a growing population of working-aged, healthy people who live in a different world from other Britons, who are raising their children to live in it, and whose values are now contaminating the life of entire neighbourhoods.' (Murray, 1990: 4)

Images of disease and contagion were to be an important part of the way the concept of the underclass was to attempt to mould perceptions of the poor. According to Murray, and others, the underclass were poor, not because of their material circumstances (to say nothing of the devastating effects of market forces and government policy) but because of their abnormal values and behaviour. Three groups of poor people were singled out for particular attention: those who, it was argued, had rejected the 'normal' values of marriage and family life, and whose growth was evidenced in the rise in single parenthood; those who had rejected the work ethic, and who consequently had been responsible for the rise in long-term unemployment; and those who had no respect for law and authority, and who had as a result fed a growth in crime. *The Sunday Times,* in one period of particularly acute national self-examination into the state of Britain that followed the murder of the toddler James Bulger by two young children in Liverpool, summed up this combination of fears over the family, work, and crime in an editorial widely reflecting the views of the media:

> The past two decades have witnessed the growth of whole communities in which the dominant family structure is the single-parent on welfare, whose male offspring are already immersed in a criminal culture by the time they are teenagers and whose daughters are destined to follow in the family tradition of unmarried teenage mothers. It is not just a question of a few families without fathers; it is a matter of whole communities with barely a single worthwhile male role-model. No wonder the youths of the underclass are uncontrollable by the time (sometimes before) they are teenagers . . . In communities without fathers, the overwhelming evidence is that youngsters begin by running wild and end up running foul of the law. (*The Sunday Times*, 28 February 1993)

Such values, it was argued, were in danger of infecting others; hence the need for urgent and drastic action.

Central to the idea of an underclass is the attempt to mark off the poor as qualitatively distinct and different from the rest of the population. It was the blurring of this distinction during the era of the postwar welfare state, argued Charles Murray, that had itself contributed to the growth of the problem:

> Henceforth the poor were to be homogenized. The only difference between poor people and everyone else, we were told, was that the poor had less money. More importantly, the poor were all alike . . . Poor people, *all* poor people, were equally victims, and would be equally successful if only society gave them a fair shake. (Murray, 1990: 2)

The concept of the underclass was to reintroduce this division with a vengeance. Members of the underclass were to be seen not only as different from the rest of the supposedly law abiding, family centred and working population, but their active choice of what was seen as an anti-social lifestyle meant that there was little positive that could be done to alter their situation. This was particularly true in terms of welfare provision. Whereas the postwar welfare state had offered a range of welfare initiatives in the attempt to reduce, if not solve, problems of juvenile delinquency, crime, or other so-called social problems, for the New Right such initiatives, far from being solutions, were themselves seen as a major part of the problem: a standpoint summed up by the Conservative Home Secretary Kenneth Clarke when he argued that 'it is no good permanently finding excuses for a section of the population who are essentially nasty pieces of work' (cited in *The Independent* 28 February 1993). Others were even less compromising in their stand, according to Bruce Anderson, adviser to successive Conservative Prime Ministers in the 1980s and 1990s: 'We are in the grip of the post-modern vagabond. We have expensively constructed slums full of layabouts and sluts whose progeny are two-legged beasts. We cannot cure this by family, religion and self-help. So we will have to rely on repression' (cited in Davies, 1997: 303).

Despite (or, perhaps more accurately, because of) its diatribe against the morals and character of the poor, the concept of the underclass quickly built a huge resonance. Newspaper articles, television documentaries, conferences, seminars and speeches by politicians and other leading figures warned of the growing threat that an expanding underclass posed to Britain's economic and social fabric. In part, like earlier and equally vitriolic depictions of the poor, it was a concept that served to deflect attention away from the structural causes of growing poverty and inequality. In blaming the poor themselves for their situation it conveniently shifted the public gaze away from government policy. It equally offered a quick and seemingly simple explanation for the evidence of social breakdown and the cumulative effects of long-term poverty – of unemployment, urban riots and unrest, the disaffection of young working-class people, and the stresses imposed on poor families and com-munities – that other explanations struggled to achieve. In this sense the concept of the underclass fed importantly on people's fears. In laying the blame on those who were often the poorest and most vulnerable, it encour-aged others, often themselves only slightly less poor and insecure, to keep their distance.

The idea that Britain was about to be engulfed by a growing underclass was not, of course, without its critics. Few serious social scientists gave the concept much credibility, and many questioned both the terms in which it was con-structed and the empirical evidence on which it was supposedly based (see, for example, Dean, 1991b; MacNicol, 1987; Morris 1994).

It was in this context that the concept of social exclusion emerged to offer an alternative perspective. As we shall see, however, it is not one that offers a radically different interpretation of the problem.

10.6 Social exclusion

Unlike the concept of the underclass, which came to prominence first in the USA and which drew on a particular Anglo-American tradition of attitudes and policies towards the poor, the concept of social exclusion has its origins in continental Europe. In the most immediate sense, social exclusion was pushed to the forefront of the social policy agenda as a result of its adoption by the European Commission in the early 1990s to frame a series of European Union funded initiatives. Previously the Commission had embarked upon a series of anti-poverty programmes, but it has been argued that opposition to any extension of these, in particular from the Conservative government who argued that poverty in Britain was largely a thing of the past, led to a change in terminology: 'social exclusion emerged as the compromise concept from the ensuing political debate' (Parkinson, 1998: 1).

For many of those in Britain who found the concept of the underclass irrelevant, unconvincing, or at the very least distasteful, the concept of 'social exclusion' appeared to offer a much more sympathetic and potentially constructive analysis. Not only was it less pejorative than the term 'underclass'; it also seemed to many to be preferable to the more traditional concept of poverty. To talk about social exclusion was to talk about much more than just money. Instead it pointed to the multidimensional aspects of deprivation. It also hinted at a process: if people were excluded, then someone or something was responsible for excluding them. It also promised to widen the narrow understanding of more traditional accounts of poverty, to look at social relationships, including relations of race and gender. For some, social exclusion was seen as representing a 'new' form of poverty (Room, 1995); for others, including for the New Labour government, it would become a substitute for addressing the issue of poverty. As Tony Blair argued: 'It is a very modern problem, and one that is more harmful to the individual, more damaging to self-esteem, more corrosive for society as a whole, more likely to be passed down from generation to generation, than material poverty' (Blair 1997c: 4). This counterposing of social exclusion against material poverty has been one important way in which the issues of poverty and inequality have been quietly dropped from much of the political agenda. This has happened in two ways: both explicitly and implicitly. Explicitly, the focus on social exclusion has allowed the government to argue that tackling social exclusion is a greater priority than more immediate ways of raising the incomes of the poor. Indeed, according to Tony Blair, 'governments can all too easily institutionalise poverty rather than solving it. They give money out not because it is the right thing to do but because it is the easy thing to do' (Blair, 1997b). Or as Peter Mandelson argued:

Let us be crystal clear on this point. The people we are concerned about, those in danger of dropping off the end of the ladder of opportunity and becoming disengaged from society, will not have their long term problems addressed by an extra pound a week on their benefits. (Mandelson, 1997: 7)

With such a perspective it was not difficult for the government to justify, at least to itself, its decision within weeks of taking office to press ahead with cuts in benefits to lone parents, or subsequently to substantially raise the level of benefit paid to other claimants.

But poverty and inequality have also been squeezed from the political and public agenda in more indirect and implicit ways. These come as a consequence of the nature of the concept of social exclusion itself, and of the particularly narrow way it has been interpreted as a guide to social policy.

Although the concept of social exclusion owed much to its adoption by the European Commission, in a more general sense social exclusion stems from a European, and in particular French, tradition of sociology (Levitas, 1998). As a concept its roots lie in a theory of society, most clearly articulated by the French sociologist Emile Durkheim, that sees the potentially disintegrative individualism of modern societies as held together by the integrating institutions of the family, the community, and the labour market. A breakdown in social order – a rise in crime, for example, or of protest – is seen as indicative of a breakdown in the integrative role of these institutions. In essence it is a conservative theory of society: one in which such basic institutions as the family or the labour market are seen as generally benign, and in which conflict and dissent is seen as pathological.

As a concept social exclusion implies that the major fault line and division in society is between two groups: an excluded minority and the included majority. What it suggests is that the included share a common situation and a common interest. Yet all the available evidence on inequality shows that inequalities, whether of income and wealth, or of education, health, housing, life chances and so on, run throughout the whole population. The 'included' are not a homogeneous group: the division between the rich and the great majority of the population overrides any similarities they may have in common.

The adoption, moreover, of social exclusion as a framework for social policy has been carried out on a particularly narrow definition of the term. Although academic studies might look at the range of ways in which the poor are excluded, for government policy social exclusion has come to mean one thing: exclusion from the paid labour market. It is lack of employment (and usually a consequent dependence on state benefits) that is seen as the key problem, and the key objective in government policy has been to get the excluded off welfare and into work. What kind of work they will go into, and whether they will be materially worse or better off as a result, is a less pressing issue.

In some important ways, the politics of New Labour are different from those of the New Right governments of Thatcher and Major that it replaced in 1997; but there are also more important similarities and continuities. Similarly, while the concept of social exclusion marks a break with the concept of the underclass, it also carries with it many of the same assumptions, explanations, and implications for social policy.

Like the New Right, New Labour accepts the dominance of the market over economic, and ultimately social, life. While for the New Right the operation of the market was ideally to be completely unfettered, for New Labour the market is to be welcomed so long as it is 'fair'. In practice the degree of regulation imposed on the market has been extremely slight: the government's most significant intervention being the introduction of a national minimum wage. This was a development which already had the support of a significant section of big business, who saw in it some protection from the threat of cutthroat competition on labour costs from smaller rivals. The low level at which it is set, however, while benefiting a number of extremely low-paid workers, does little to overcome the wider problem of the working poor.

Where New Labour does differ significantly from its New Right predecessors is in its willingness to use the power of the state to address what it sees as contemporary social problems. For the New Right, at least in ideological terms, the state was seen as an unnecessary and harmful intrusion, both into the free operation of the market and in the freedom of choice of individuals (although this did not prevent the new right governments of the 1980s and 1990s overseeing a massive centralization of state power). For New Labour, while state intervention directly in the economy has to be kept to a minimum, the state has a clear and legitimate role in organizing the social infrastructure that will allow the economy to flourish. Hence social policy (particularly in areas like education and training for work) is pushed to the forefront of the government's agenda. 'This will be the welfare to work government' announced Tony Blair on his election victory in 1997, and since then a successive range of initiatives have been put into place to attempt to bring this about.

If the government's view is that the state has a responsibility to ensure inclusion (within, as we have seen, its particularly narrow understanding of that), it also takes the view that those who are excluded have a duty to make use of the opportunities that are provided. This language of duty and opportunity is the hallmark of the new form of social policy that is being developed. There is very little talk of the rights of citizens, and especially of the rights of the poor. Instead the notion of rights is replaced by one of responsibility. As the government's Green Paper setting out its plans for welfare reform argued:

> The responsibilities of individuals who can provide for themselves and their families to do so must always be matched by a responsibility on the part of government to provide opportunities for self advancement . . . The government's commitment to expand significantly the range of help available therefore alters the contract with those who are capable of work. It is the government's responsibility to promote work opportunities and to help people take advantage of them. It is the responsibility of those who can take them up to do so . . . For example, the New Deal for Young People provides high quality options, all of which include education and training, designed to attract accredited qualifications. Those who unreasonably

refuse an offer or fail to take up a place will be sanctioned. (DSS *New Ambitions for Our Country: A New Contract for Welfare* 1998 quoted in Lavalette and Mooney, 1999: 40)

The use of sanctions – in the case of benefit recipients, usually a suspension of their income – thus becomes an important part of the strategy against exclusion. Ironically, such measures when applied have the effect of further increasing the exclusion the government aims to prevent, as those denied an income turn to other and, most likely, illegal ways of making a living. But the 'tough discipline' that is called for 'to break the culture of hopelessness and cynicism which a concentration of hard-core unemployment has bred in many estates throughout Britain' (Peter Mandelson quoted Deacon, 1996: 68) also reflects a belief that, like the underclass, the socially excluded are themselves at least in part responsible for their situation, and require a firm hand to put them back on the straight and narrow. As the example of the USA has shown, when it marked the new millennium by jailing its two millionth prisoner to stand out as the most heavily incarcerated nation in the so-called 'free' world, tough discipline as a response to the problem of poverty risks embarking on a spiral of incarceration that makes poverty a criminal offence.

CHAPTER 11

NEW LABOUR AND MANAGERIALISM: PRIVATIZING THE WELFARE STATE?

Gerry Mooney

11.1 Introduction

This chapter sets out to consider some of the key elements of New Labour's plans to 'reform' the welfare state. Since coming to power in 1997, Labour has presented the modernization of the welfare state as one of its key political objectives. Indeed in its first three years in government Labour has proved to be just as enthusiastic about welfare reform as the Conservatives were during their 18 years of rule between 1979 and 1997. Central to the Conservative approach was an attack on 'welfarism', the idea that welfare creates a dependency culture and an undeserving underclass of the poor (see Jones and Novak, 1999). However, this was combined with an assault on state welfare provision as unproductive, inefficient, ineffective, bureaucratic and primarily serving the interests of the professional groups involved in its delivery. This anti-public sectorism paved the way for the opening-up of welfare provision to competition from a range of statutory, voluntary, and corporate agencies. 'Rolling back the state' and reducing the costs of welfare provision were pivotal elements of the Conservative approach to welfare.

By the mid-1990s such shifts in welfare delivery had led to a diminishing of the scale and significance of state provision while enhancing the role of the private sector (that is delivery by for-profit organizations). But 'the private' was also celebrated in another way: individual and family responsibility for care and support also became a Conservative mantra. Taken together this stress on both senses of 'private' helped to alter the landscape of welfare delivery during the 1980s and 1990s.

Welfare reform continues to be on the agenda of many governments in the western world. Growing demand for welfare provision, not least across Western Europe and in North America, reflects rising unemployment, the growth and spread of labour market flexibility with its attendant problems of low wages, and irregular earnings, shifts in family and household formation together with other demographic changes and new patterns of migration. Alongside this there appears to be less willingness on the part of many governments to resource sufficiently publicly provided welfare to meet these new demands as they pursue policies of no tax increases and minimizing non-wage labour costs in the drive to attain competitiveness and attract investment. As governments have sought to reduce the 'costs of welfare' and control public expenditure, new opportunities have been provided for corporate organizations to become more involved in provision. What are termed the modernization of welfare delivery and the reform of welfare states have become central political platforms of governments in many countries.

This chapter focuses in particular on the extent to which New Labour has followed the Conservatives and increasingly looked to the private and non-statutory sectors as a means of delivering public services, especially in health, housing, and education. As leading New Labour architect Peter Mandelson once put it: 'New Labour's mission is to move forward from where Margaret Thatcher left off, rather than dismantle every single thing she did' (quoted in Mandelson and Liddle, 1996: 1). How far is this reflected in New Labour's programme of welfare state modernization? Certainly New Labour appears to have adopted many of the premises of neo-liberalism, as well as the language and rhetoric of the market: choice, competition, performance targets, customers, improvements, and performance related pay. But has a new welfare consensus emerged in which non-state forms of provision, cost control, managerialism and individual responsibilities are the key elements? Has Labour continued to open up important areas of public sector provision to the market? At the time of writing this chapter there are important ongoing controversies surrounding New Labour's plans to privatize further important areas of what remains of the public sector. Included here are the proposals for the partial privatization of the London Underground system, so roundly rejected by London voters in the mayoral elections in 2000. Elsewhere, despite widespread opposition and concerns about safety, plans to privatize the National Air Traffic Control Service are still in place while hardly a week passes without some announcement of the latest privately funded and operated prison, private financed roads, as well as the contracting out of important areas of defence related work. This is not to mention proposals for the health, education, and housing sectors. At the same time across the length and breadth of Britain trade unionists, campaigning groups, and service users have combined to oppose such policies.

This chapter explores important aspects of New Labour's welfare reforms, its view of the role of the state and the market in the provision of welfare. The chapter highlights particular areas of welfare provision where the private sector has begun to enjoy unparalleled opportunities for involvement and for profit maximization. Before proceeding any further something should be said about the term 'privatization' itself. As one would expect there is no universal agreement as to what this means as it carries considerable ideological and political baggage. It is a term that is bandied about both by critics of welfare reform, as well as those who seek to embrace and support such reform by denying that any privatization is taking place. In a narrow sense privatization can refer simply to the replacement of public sector service delivery by a private firm or non-statutory agency. More generally, and this is the sense used in this chapter, privatization is taken to signify a process through which the private sector (the market) is provided with an opportunity to take on a more extensive role in the financing, operation, and management of health, housing, education and welfare services which may or may not include wholesale replacement of public provision. In the section that follows, the legacy of Conservative welfare reform and the development of New Labour's approach is examined.

11.2 From New Right to New Labour: the Conservative inheritance

While direct use of privately provided social welfare services remains limited and outside the reach of the majority of people in Britain, the last two decades of the twentieth century witnessed a significant shift away from state welfare provision towards a greater role for the market. This took a number of diverse forms: a shift in the welfare 'mix' in which public sector provision was diminished or steadily replaced by both voluntary and for-profit agencies. That this was uneven across the public sector does not detract from the major inroads that were made in the marketization of the public sector. For the Conservatives the right to buy legislation introduced under the 1980 Housing Act, the Assisted Places Scheme brought in under the 1980 Education Act, and tax relief for private pensions and private health care insurance, would reduce welfare dependency while opportunities for the exercise of individual choice would be maximized.

Increased welfare pluralism had become the order of the day by the early 1990s. This was accompanied by a gradual, though widespread, introduction of management and business strategies for coordinating welfare delivery. One of the most significant examples of this was in the distinction between provider and purchasing roles that became so central to Conservative reforms for the NHS in the 1980s and 1990s. This allowed for the mimicking of competition between the different components of the internal, or 'quasi', market. Additionally new providers were encouraged to bid for contracts, particularly in the field of social care where there has been a proliferation of private sector nursing and care establishments in recent decades, or for the running of schools, prisons, and so on.

An important element of the Conservative approach to welfare was to transform those state agencies that remained significant providers (such as social work/services) into more business-like organizations. Through this it was argued more efficient forms of delivery could be developed, offering better value for money. Contracting out services and compulsory competitive tendering (CCT) opened up important sectors of local government to the market, while in many areas driving down the costs of labour and eroding conditions of employment. Key to this was the claim that more and better management was the route to a more cost effective welfare system.

The growth of managerialism in the public sector during the 1980s and 1990s has been well documented (see Clarke, et al., 1994; Clarke and Newman, 1997; Clarke et al., 2001). Public services in both Britain and the USA were, in the language of New Right critics, lacking 'proper management'. Managerialism as an ideology became established as the means through which public sector agencies would become more effective service providers. Importantly, while this was to lead to a significant growth in the numbers of public sector managers, all members of the organization were to become infused with the managerialist rhetoric and language: clients were now customers and public services were now businesses with mission statements, objectives, and contracts. All workers were to behave differently as a result. Social workers would become, for instance, care managers. Budget control, cost effectiveness, and efficiency were now the key bywords. Through improved management, therefore, more could be had for less.

Taken together these changes have, as has been noted, led to major shifts in welfare delivery and in the prevailing view about the role of the welfare state. There is an ongoing debate as to whether these changes led to the 'end of the welfare state' or represented the restructuring of an otherwise 'resilient' welfare system. While opposition remains to all forms of what has generally been termed privatization, a number of past critics of Conservative welfare reforms, particularly in the Parliamentary Labour Party, have now embraced many of the changes previously introduced, as well as now themselves operating within discourses that see managerialism as the key method of achieving particular goals. However, it is important to distinguish between rhetoric and reality here. We cannot simply take a New Right (or indeed a New Labour) perspective on what was achieved during the period of Tory rule without question. One of the first points to make in relation to this is that despite claims that a more cost effective welfare system had been introduced, Conservative policies had little impact on overall public expenditure on welfare spending in general. As Burchardt and Hills point out, welfare spending accounted for a higher percentage of government spending towards the end of the Conservative period in government compared to 1979, despite all their attempts to reduce it (Burchardt and Hills, 1999). As the Conservatives sought to shift the costs of welfare further on to the poor and disadvantaged, through changes in taxation and the benefits system, this served only to increase the numbers who were in need of state support. This was further exacerbated by policies that sought to achieve wage discipline through mass unemployment. Further, although a key goal of the Conservative agenda was to 'roll back the state', this was not achieved in any simple way. Indeed in relation to income maintenance and social security (not to mention policing strategies and immigration policies) the state became even more interventionist and oppressive. In any case 'roll back' was hindered by opposition and by the growing awareness, even among Conservative politicians and policy makers, that cherished welfare institutions such as the NHS would have to remain largely as public sector organizations, not least for reasons of electoral support.

The Conservatives then were able to introduce major changes in relation to health and welfare, albeit ones that were partial, uneven, ambiguous, and, at times, contradictory. However, they did succeed to a significant extent in securing legitimation for the role of the market in the delivery of heartland social and welfare services, and in the role of management in securing cost effectiveness. More importantly for the purposes of this chapter, they also created a new culture around welfare which New Labour was to embrace.

Much has already been written about the New Labour political project, and its approach to welfare and the welfare state (see for example Anderson and Mann, 1998; Clarke and Newman, 1998; Clarke et al., 2001; Driver and Martell, 1998; Jones and MacGregor, 1998; Jones and Novak, 1999; Lavalette and Mooney, 1999; Powell, 1999). One of the key themes to have emerged in the ongoing debates about the basis of the New Labour ideology is the extent to which it is founded upon ground already secured by the New Right. In other words, how much continuity or difference is there between New Labour and the New Right/Conservatives, or indeed 'old Labour? There are a number of different threads in this debate about New Labour's project, if indeed it is possible to talk of a single, coherent project at all. These include the concern with New Labour's apparent pragmatism and emphasis on style and presentation, its reassertion of the social and communal over the rampant individualism of neo-liberalism, the support for European notions of 'social exclusion' and its close relationship with the Clinton administration in the USA which has been influential on Labour policies, particularly in relation to welfare to work. In addition to this controversy there is New Labour's own story about its political trajectory and how it seeks to transcend the 'old differences' between left and right in constructing a 'third way' in British politics. Blair contrasts the political commitments of old Labour/the left, as pro-state and anti-market, with the pro-market and anti-state position of the Right (Blair, 1998b). For Blair and for New Labour's leading theoretician Anthony Giddens, these represent two 'failed pasts', based upon the state or the market or, to borrow the language of the 1998 Green Paper on health, *Our Healthier Nation* (Secretary of State for Health, 1998), 'nanny state engineering' on the one hand, and 'individual victim blaming' on the other. Between these two sharply polarized positions, it is claimed, a new pragmatic and modern approach to politics can be developed. But before considering the key elements of this 'third way', it is useful to explore some of the key shifts in Labour thinking since the late 1980s.

In its 1997 general election manifesto, the Labour Party committed itself to keeping within Tory spending limits for at least the initial two to three years of any period in government. The manifesto clearly signalled Labour's desire to distance itself from the old tax and spend policies that it was so closely associated with in the past. As Blair himself put it:

I want a country in which people get on, do well, make a success of their lives...We need more successful entrepreneurs, not fewer of them. But these life chances should be for all the people. And I want a society in which ambition and compassion are seen as partners not opposites – where we value public service as well as material wealth . . . but we must recognize also that the policies of 1997 cannot be those of 1947 or 1967. (Labour Party, 1997: 2)

Elsewhere in the manifesto there were further signs of the general approach New Labour would take on public spending:

New Labour will be wise spenders, not long spenders. We will work in partnership with the private sector to achieve our goals. We will ask about public spending the first question that a manager in any company would ask – can existing resources be used more effectively to meet our priorities? And because efficiency and value for money are central, ministers will be required to save before they spend. Save to invest is our approach, not tax and spend. (Labour Party, 1997: 12)

The seeds of New Labour's thinking were evident long before the publication of the 1997 manifesto. During the Conservatives' second period of office, between 1983 and 1987, Labour had been anti-market and was clearly opposed to privatization in any shape or form. But under Neil Kinnock in the late 1980s there were already signs of a major shift in the party's approach. This reached new heights in the early 1990s under the leadership of John Smith. The party's 1992 manifesto, for instance, interpreted the role of the government as one of supporting the market as opposed to replacing it through direct provision. Elsewhere Smith's Commission on Social Justice signalled support in principle for the private funding of services, as well as a commitment to developing a partnership between the public and private sector. The market, it was argued, could be harnessed to the pursuit of social justice. Thus 'the ethics of community and the dynamics of a market economy' could be combined (Commission on Social Justice, 1994: 95). The commission also appeared to accept other important tenets of New Right thinking by accepting that greater levels of inequality were inevitable and that welfare spending was a drain on resources. The Commission on Social Justice marks how far Labour had retreated from its previous position in defence of the 1945 welfare state. With Blair there were to be further major shifts in Labour ideology: one of the most cherished elements of Labour's constitution, Clause 4, which committed the party to public ownership and state control, was revised, providing a clear indication of the party's growing willingness to embrace a neo-liberal market agenda. Not only did Blair and other Labour leaders spend considerable time wooing the business lobby and corporate leaders, but they also provided opportunities for business and management consultants to work on redrafting party policy.

This brings us back to the issue of the 'third way'. This has already received considerable attention (see Blair, 1998b; Giddens, 1998, 2000; Glennerster, 1999; Lavalette and Mooney, 1999; Le Grand, 1998; Rose, 1999).

The intention here is to consider its main features as they impinge on New Labour's approach to reforming the welfare state. The 'third way' represents the clearest attempt to provide New Labour with an intellectual basis (see Giddens, 1998, 2000). For Giddens the 'third way' provides a 'framework of thinking and policy making that seeks to adapt social democracy to a world that has changed fundamentally over the past two or three decades' (Giddens, 1998: 26). What links the 'third way' and the approach outlined in the 1997 manifesto is a shared view of a changing world. To quote Blair again, 'the policies of 1997 cannot be those of 1947 or 1967'. So just what has changed according to this perspective? New Labour shares with the US Democrats a view of the world shaped by globalization – one where the inexorable forces of the global market render the nation state unable to moderate its effects except in the most limited of ways. A world in which mobile capital is taken as given. In this new globalized world, competition is the order of the day. In order to achieve global competitiveness and to enhance Britain's economic performance, flexible labour markets are to be encouraged as well as the reskilling and education of a new workforce to cope with the requirements of knowledge and information based employment. However, the drive for economic competitiveness also requires a far reaching programme of 'national renewal', a key element of which is the modernization of major institutions, such as the welfare state, local government, and the role of the state itself.

For proponents of the 'third way' there are other changes that make this new approach to politics both necessary and feasible. These include increasing individualism and detraditionalization along with the pursuit of self-fulfilment. Related to these is what Giddens refers to as the decline in collectivism, reflected in the decreasing salience of class politics (see Lavalette and Mooney, 1999: 35).

Modernization is, therefore, central to the overall goal of economic competitiveness and in this respect welfare plays an important role. Welfare strategies that enhance competitiveness, such as welfare to work, are to be welcomed. In his speech to the Trades Union Congress in 1997, Blair claimed that there were two crucial elements in the process of modernization:

> The first is to create an economy fully attuned to a new global market; one that combines enterprise and flexibility with harnessing the creative potential of all our people. The second is to fashion a modern welfare state, where we maintain high levels of social inclusion based on values of community and social justice, but where the role of government changes so it is not necessary to provide all social provision, and fund all social provision but to organize and regulate it most efficiently and fairly. (Blair, 1997a)

Only through the 'third way' for social and welfare policy could Britain build a twenty-first century welfare system. Against critics who have attacked his plans as bringing about the end of the welfare state he claimed that New Labour:

is not dismantling welfare, leaving it simply as a low-grade safety net for the destitute; nor keeping it unreformed and under performing; but reforming it on the basis of a new contract between citizen and state, where we keep a welfare state from which we all benefit, but on terms that are fair and clear. (Blair, 1998b: v)

Both these comments imply a fundamental rethinking of the role of the state in general, and in relation to welfare provision in particular. The 'third way' approach questions the extent to which services should be provided by the state and emphasizes instead the contribution that non-state agencies can make, albeit in partnership with the state. This is an issue to which we return. What emerges from this though is the idea that the state takes on an enabling role, rather than the role of mass provider that characterized the social democratic state. As Giddens put it: 'Investment in human capital wherever possible, rather than direct provision of economic maintenance. In place of the welfare state we should put the social investment state, operating in the context of a positive welfare society' (Giddens, 1998: 117).

In this regard Blair and other architects of the 'third way' project have much in common with both Thatcher and Major. Thus the state is to be harnessed in the drive for global competitiveness. In place of a role as large-scale provider, a myriad of partners and providers will be steered from the centre through regular audits, inspections, and appraisal systems conducted by a range of elected and non-elected governmental agencies. For Blair:

> Governments . . . now need to learn new skills: working in partnership with the private and voluntary sector; sharing responsibility and devolving power . . . answering to a much more demanding public . . .
>
> In the key public services, the third way is about money for modernization – new investment of £40 billion over the next three years driving reform and higher standards . . . In all areas, monitoring and inspection are playing a key role, as an incentive to higher standards and as a means of determining appropriate levels of intervention. (Blair, 1998b: 7 and 16)

The further managerialization of welfare, and local government in particular, with the introduction of competitive practices and the stress on partnerships, undermines the traditional role of local state agencies in service delivery. For New Labour, however, these methods will ensure value for money, efficiency, flexibility, and responsiveness among service providers.

Although Labour is keen to downplay the role of the state, and emphasize instead monitoring and regulation, this itself reflects centralizing and controlling tendencies in government. Moreover, in important ways the power of the state has been extended, in, for example, initiatives like the 1998 Crime and Disorder Act. The government has extended processes of criminalization through curfews, parenting orders, and the forced removal of the homeless from the streets of some towns and cities. The stress on combating crime and disorder reflects the moral authoritarianism at the heart of New Labour and signifies the greater disciplinary involvement of the state. In this respect Jones and Novak argue that the state is not being 'rolled-back', rather it is being 're-tooled' (Jones and Novak, 1999: Chapter 5).

The 'third way' is presented by Labour as something that is new and distinctively modern, distinct from old Labour methods of service delivery on the one hand, and the rampaging market of neo-liberalism on the other. The 'third way' is offered above all as a project of 'modernization'. This is, as Clarke and Newman point out (1998), crucial for New Labour's political project of constructing a new relationship between the state, market, and civil society. Rose asks some important questions about the notion of modernization:

> This is the appeal to 'modernization' as if it in itself provided the guidelines for the justification and the rationale for specific policy and organizational changes: become modern or face the destiny of the obsolete – the scrap heap of history. But what is it to be modern? Have we ever been modern? Why should we want to be modern? (Rose, 1999: 471)

The idea of a 'third way' has been widely criticized (see, for example, Jones and Novak, 1999; Rose, 1999). There is little that is novel about the idea of a 'third way' itself, while it can be argued that Labour has always sought to tread a path between the state on the one hand and the market on the other (Lavalette and Mooney, 1999). It is an extremely slippery notion, reflecting as it does a diverse range of ideological traditions. However, the 'third way' represents an acceptance that the market is the most effective way of organizing economic activity, albeit with some role for the state as regulator. Through this there is an attempt to marry for-profit services with a never to be defined elusive public interest. For Jones and Novak:

> In the third way capitalism is not challenged: rather it is embraced. New Labour's acceptance of the market differs little from that of the new right, echoing its predecessor's claim that 'there is no alternative' . . . The global market is seen as the final and unchallengeable arbiter in economic – and ultimately in social – life. But the market is not only accepted as setting the agenda and imposing constraints which national governments are powerless to resist. It is also embraced as the main provider. (Jones and Novak, 1999: 181)

The jury is still out on the question of the distinctiveness of the New Labour project. We have seen that for some critics the New Labour approach represents the wholesale acceptance of the market as the best method of delivering services, in tune with a neo-liberal agenda. However, there are important signs that this is not simply the continuation of the neo-liberal agenda of the Conservatives. Blair has argued that 'social-ism' is something worth pursuing (Blair, 1998a) and the desire for social justice is presented as a key element in New Labour's discourse, though this appears to be secondary to the goal of limiting public expenditure. However, New Labour has sought to tie the pursuit of social justice and social inclusion to economic growth and

competitiveness. In this respect modernization has an important social element with support for the market and the 'entrepreneurial' ideal, closely
interwoven with a language of equal opportunity, as opposed to equality per
se, partnership, responsibility and community. Further, Blair and other leading Labour politicians have been keen to stress New Labour's pragmatism –
transcending the 'old' ideological battles between left and right – refusing to
make a judgement about the relative merits of the state or the market. This is
tied-up in New Labour's buzz- phrase, 'what counts is what works' (Labour
Party, 1997: 4).

There are important continuities between the New Labour project and that
of the Conservatives. But there are also significant differences, notably in the
greater emphasis given to 'the social' and the recognition, against Thatcher,
that there is something called 'society'. However, there are also significant
contradictions in this project, primarily in relation to the goal of integrating
the pursuit of social justice with the drive for economic competitiveness.

In this section key elements of New Labour's general political agenda have
been considered. In the discussion that follows we explore how this approach
is directly reflected in its social and welfare policy, focusing on health, housing, and education.

Activity 11.1

What are the key elements of the 'third way'? How do these contrast with
the two failed pasts of old Labour and neo-liberalism?

11.3 New Labour in power: modernizing the welfare state?

> Reform is a vital part of rediscovering a true national purpose, part of a bigger pic-
> ture in which our country is a model of a 21st century developed nation: with
> sound, stable economic management; dynamism and enterprise in business; the
> best educated and creative nation in the world; and a welfare state that promotes
> our aims and achievements. But we should not forget why reform is right, and why,
> whatever the concerns over individual benefits, most people know it is right. Above
> all, the system must change because the world has changed, beyond the recognition
> of Beveridge's generation . . . We need a system designed not for yesterday, but for
> today. (Blair, quoted in IPPR, 1998: iii–iv)

As we have seen in the 1997 election manifesto Labour was at pains to stress
that the days of 'tax and spend' had gone and in its place the key objective
was reforming and modernizing the welfare state: A 'modern' welfare state
for a 'modern world' as Blair put it. Towards the end of the previous section

it was noted that New Labour's project combined a mix of continuity with, and divergence from, the neo-liberal agenda of the Conservatives. This is clearly evident in the 1997 manifesto. On the one hand there was a commitment to keep to Conservative public spending plans and to avoid increases in income tax. In the first Queen's speech made within weeks of the general election, Blair claimed that 'we have reached the limit of the public's willingness simply to fund an unreformed welfare system through ever higher taxes and spending'. However, there would be a one-off 'windfall' tax on the privatized utilities that would raise upwards of £3.5 billion to fund the New Deal for Employment ('welfare to work'). Elsewhere there was a commitment to reducing NHS waiting lists, an issue that would return to haunt Labour in its first four years in power. The NHS itself would be reformed with the abolition of the internal market, though the purchaser/provider split (now designated as commissioning and service management) would remain, along with devolved budgetary responsibility. In education the Conservatives' Assisted Places Scheme was to be abolished but there were to be new opportunities for the private sector to become involved through the Education Action Zones programme and in the direct management of schools.

In local government CCT was to be replaced by 'Best Value'. Local authorities were now required to introduce strategies that stressed objective setting, performance management, partnership, consultation and service improvement. However, marketization and competition were to remain as key elements of this approach and, as with the Conservatives, there was a continuing emphasis on value for money, efficiency, and effectiveness. In this renewed stress on managerialist approaches, the language of efficiency, benchmarking and, a goal that New Labour was to continually stress, quality, were to become important ideas. Additionally outcomes were emphasized rather than the relative merits of the public or private sector in delivering services, in line with 'third way' thinking.

Another feature of New Labour's discourse was the prominence accorded to 'partnerships'. This is reflected across the policy spectrum: there are partnerships in delivering healthcare, education programmes, housing, in social work, youth policy and urban regeneration among others. Once more it is important to note that such a concern with 'partnership' is hardly new, particularly in relation to urban social policy and urban regeneration programmes. However, under New Labour it has been given renewed vigour. One of the obvious attractions for the Blair government is that partnership can take a number of different forms. Public Private Partnerships (PPPs) – the new name for the Private Finance Initiative – are attractive as they work to blur the distinction between public and private. Partners would work together to ensure projects were well managed and targets met, with the threat of regular inspection and audit by government agencies.

These developments were part and parcel of welfare reform. Reform had become something of a mantra among leading Labour politicians and policy makers, with the modernization of the £90 billion per annum welfare system a key target. In the general election campaign Labour had, after all, constructed itself as 'the party of welfare reform'. We have already noted the role that the discourse of modernization has played in New Labour's political agenda. But it is important to acknowledge once again that there is little that is new in the desire for 'modernization'. The rhetoric of modernization has been an appealing discourse for successive governments, albeit mobilized in different ways in different periods.

The extension of managerialism and the increased role for the private sector in delivering public services were crucial elements of New Labour's platform as we have seen. These were accompanied by two key flagship policies: Welfare to Work and the Social Exclusion Unit (see Jones and Novak, 1999; Lavalette and Mooney, 1999; Levitas, 1998). The task of modernizing welfare was given to Frank Field, Minster for Welfare Reform, who was charged with 'thinking the unthinkable' about welfare reform (Secretary of State for Social Security and Minister for Welfare Reform, 1998). For Field this would involve combining public and private provision wherever possible. 'Modernization', then, was directly tied to marketization.

Activity 11.2

What role does the discourse of 'modernization' play in New labour's political project?

11.4 New Labour and PFI: 'profits from illness'?

The Private Finance Initiative was one of the most contentious strategies through which the Conservatives sought to promote the role of the market in the provision of public services. Although the seeds of PFI were evident in the late 1980s, it was introduced in the 1992 budget speech as a way of encouraging the private sector to invest in public infrastructure, such as new roads and hospitals. At its simplest, private funding would be used to construct and manage facilities that would then be leased back by the public sector. Guarantees are made to the firms involved that they will be reimbursed in some way. One obvious attraction for the Conservatives was that it provided an opportunity for the increasing use of private sector management techniques in the delivery of public goods and services. More importantly it also appeared to address the need for improved public services without resorting to increased taxation – or escalating the public sector borrowing requirement. Indeed there is a great deal of political expediency involved in PFI schemes. They offer political advantages today while the costs are borne in the future.

Many Labour politicians had opposed PFI under the Conservatives but by

1997 support for PFI/PPP had become a central element of New Labour policy and in any case it was increasingly being adopted by hard-pressed Labour councils who were searching for capital funds for large-scale public projects. By early 2000, over £16 billion of PFI projects had been agreed by the government which has enthusiastically embraced PFI as a means of delivering its promises of improved public services, new hospitals, better transport links and a wide range of schemes across the range of public services, without resorting to increased taxation. The Treasury Financial Statement and Budget Report in July 1997 stated that:

> The Government sees productive public/private partnerships as being key to delivering high quality public services that offer the taxpayer value for money . . . Effort will be focused where it will achieve results, cutting costs for the public and private sectors alike . . . The Government is committed to make PFI work where appropriate.

Elsewhere in the same report former Paymaster General Geoffrey Robinson was to claim that:

> The success of PFI is vital for Britain. Our infrastructure is dangerously run down. Our schools and transport networks are seriously neglected and all too often our urban environment has been allowed to deteriorate. In an age of tight public spending, value for money public/private partnerships will be at the heart of a much-needed renewal of our public services. (Treasury Taskforce on Private Finance, 1997)

Value for money was a repeated message used to present PFI in a positive guise. There were already widespread concerns about PFI following well-publicized cases where PFI was shown to be a very costly way of providing public services and infrastructure. One of the most notorious examples of this was the Skye road bridge project. This was a type of PFI scheme that allowed for the private sector to charge users thereby securing a return on investment – and a healthy profit for the financers and operators, The Bank of America. Originally quoted at £10.5 million, the final estimated cost to the public of this one bridge (with the highest tolls in Western Europe) is around £128 million. However, it is in relation to the NHS where some of the strongest criticisms of PFI have been voiced. For health services trade unions and organizations such as the British Medical Association, PFI means little more than 'profits from illness'. Labour is extremely sensitive to its position in relation to the NHS. It has historically portrayed itself as 'the party of the NHS' and argued in opposition that it would save the NHS from the legacy of Conservative under-funding. It has increasingly looked to PFI to build new hospitals and to finance other health related projects. Since the early 1990s most major capital projects in the NHS have been through PFI schemes of one kind or another. The private sector is not only involved in building but in a range of activities ranging from the designing of new hospitals through to running them, which are then leased back to the NHS for periods of up to 60 years. A whole industry of advisers, consultants, banks, brokers, managers, and so on, has built up around PFI in the NHS. In the case of the new Worcester Royal Infirmary, for example, financing costs through PFI included £30 million in fees to agents alone, as well as in interest on loans during construction. Researchers from the Health Services Policy Unit at University College London have closely studied the case of the Worcester PFI. They estimated that the costs of the new hospital jumped by 118% during PFI negotiations from £49 million in 1996 to £108 million in 1999. They concluded that 'much of the 118 per cent cost increase was due to the extra costs of financing that would not have been incurred under a public sector option' (Pollock et al., 2000: 3). In Edinburgh the construction of the new 850-bed Royal Infirmary has attracted even more attention. Due to open in 2003 this is one of the 'flagship' PFI schemes in Scotland. This project will be financed in a 30-year programme costing over £900 million which the local NHS trust has claimed is almost £700,000 cheaper per year than traditional public sector financing. Unison has argued that through PFI the cost is actually £6–£10 million pounds greater (Unison, 2000). In addition there have been well-publicized claims that the new infirmary, as in Worcester, will have insufficient beds and space for all the necessary services.

Not only has PFI been attacked for its higher costs but for many critics the whole PFI ethos is founded on the belief that 'private is better'. PFI is presented as the 'best option' against the public sector where there are in-built negative assumptions. Further, PFI has also resulted in cutbacks in services and, importantly, deteriorating conditions of employment for many thousands of public sector workers who become effectively 'privatized', all this at a time when concerns about lengthening waiting lists have been widespread.

11.5 Privatizing housing?

On coming to power in 1997, Labour inherited a housing environment that was markedly different from when it was last in power in 1979. In 1981 council housing accounted for 30 per cent of all housing in Britain, but by 1996 this had declined to 19 per cent. Over the same period owner occupation increased from 56 per cent to 67 per cent. From its opposition to the Conservatives' right to buy policy in the early 1980s, Labour now appears to have accepted many of the policy prescriptions of the Conservatives in relation to social housing (Kemp, 1999: 172). One particular shift in its approach is in relation to the provision of public sector housing itself. Once more Labour has embraced the market as the means through which demand for more and better housing will be addressed. To quote Housing Minister, Hilary Armstrong:

Our over-riding aim is to make the housing market work for all the people. If the housing market worked perfectly there would be no need or rationale for government intervention but the free market cannot accommodate the needs and aspirations of all. Government must intervene – but that intervention must be limited and strategic, empowering and enabling, not centralizing and controlling. [New Labour] will make no preference between public or private sectors . . . I have no ideological objection with the transfer of local authority housing. If it works, and it is what tenants want, transfer maybe an appropriate option. What matters is what works. (Armstrong, 1998: 3–4)

The limited role provided here for the state is very much in line with both previous Conservative policies and 'third way' thinking. While Armstrong has sought to emphasize that she is in line with New Labour's pragmatism by singing the 'what matters is what works' song, New Labour has gone further than the Conservatives in favouring the demunicipalization of housing stock, and its transfer to a plethora of partnerships, cooperatives, and housing associations, along with the transfer of management responsibilities. Once more this transfer has been couched in terms of promoting choice, self-reliance, and responsibility. According to the National Campaign to Defend Council Housing, between 1997 and 2000 over 140,000 homes were removed from the public sector housing stock through transfer schemes, more than the Conservatives achieved during their last decade in office (National Campaign to Defend Council Housing, 2000). On 24 January 2000, *The Guardian* ran with the headline 'Prescott plans to abolish council housing' as the housing Green Paper was published announcing proposals to transfer up to 200,000 more council houses each year for the next decade.

The Scottish Executive has earmarked £300 million for the creation of new housing partnerships that would see the transfer of stock from the public sector. Here the desire of New Labour, both in the Scottish Parliament and at local authority level, to offload as much of socially rented housing as possible is all the more significant given the historic importance of this sector in the Scottish housing market. In both Scotland and England these moves signal a comprehensive break with one of the central elements of the Beveridgean welfare state. But they are not without opposition. While this is evident in a number of major towns across Britain, it is in Glasgow, long associated with struggles and campaigns over state housing provision, that this has been most pronounced.

In the Scottish Office's Green Paper on housing policy in Scotland in 1999, the Scottish Housing Minister claimed that: 'The time has come to move beyond the "municipal paternalism", which resulted in large single tenure estates' (Scottish Office, 1999b: para.7). Stock transfer and demunicipalization were to be encouraged across Scotland, not least in Glasgow. For the Labour dominated Scottish Parliament, this was the only option through which Scotland's council housing debt of £4 billion could be addressed. With the largest stock of council houses in Britain, the political significance of Glasgow Council's plans for stock transfer should not be underestimated.

With a housing debt of almost £950 million alone, Glasgow's housing situation is appalling. Fifty five pence in every £1 of rent goes in debt servicing charges, some 47 per cent of the total housing revenue account (Danson et al., 2000: 18). Eighty-five per cent of its tenants are in receipt of housing benefit while the stock of almost 100,000 houses is estimated to be worth only £13 million given its relatively poor condition. Glasgow City Council and the Scottish Executive have promised a £1.6 billion ten-year programme of investment, including wiping-out the housing debt. However, this would only be implemented if tenants voted to accept far-reaching changes including stock reduction, to be achieved mainly through substantial demolition programmes, and the transfer of all remaining houses to a new social landlord – Glasgow Housing Association. This single take it or leave it option has led to widespread protests among public sector trade unions and tenants' organizations.

The government has been at pains to present the proposals for housing as very much in line with its social inclusion objectives. However, in Glasgow as elsewhere there seems to be a major contradiction between its desires to demunicipalize yet continue to meet the housing needs of a significant proportion of the population, many of whom are economically disadvantaged. Glasgow's plans to cut stock from 100,000 to 75,000 units will mean fewer houses than the number of households currently in receipt of housing benefit. There are major questions then about the market's ability to deliver quality housing for all who will need it, particularly for the homeless and other socially excluded groups.

11.6 Marketizing education?

New Labour has placed considerable importance on 'modernizing' Britain's education sector. It has closely linked education and employment/employability in its eagerness to increase Britain's capacity to compete effectively in the global marketplace. In the government's enthusiasm to promote the 'knowledge economy', education plays a significant role. The relationship between education and the economy extends to adopting business and managerial practices in the delivery of education and in the running of schools and other educational institutions. Labour's distrust of local education authorities is evidenced by the commitment of Education Minister (for England) David Blunkett to 'making PPPs (in education) attractive to the private sector' (Blunkett, 1997), through the Education Action Zones (EAZs) programme. For Blunkett, EAZs represent '. . . the beginning of an entirely new way of delivering the education service. It is about partnership based on success rather than outdated dogma on either side' (quoted in Gewirtz, 1999). For New Labour EAZs would address problems of underfunding (though few additional resources are available) while tackling social exclusion in the localities concerned, through strategies such as those to reduce truancy rates. But it was clear from the outset that the private sector would have a considerable role in running the zones (Whitfield, 1999). Parental choice remains as do league tables detailing each school's performance and there may also be some academic selection and marketization (Gewirtz, 1999: 148).

For both Gewirtz and Whitfield through EAZs the way is open for a full privatization of school education. In what Whitfield refers to as the 'commodification and marketization of education', the opportunities for business are immense. Again we can look to Glasgow for a prime example of this. The Glasgow Secondary Schools PPP is one of the largest in Britain and the largest in British education. According to Glasgow City Council this PPP will create: '. . . a stimulating and supportive learning environment in all of the City's secondary schools by August 2002' (Glasgow City Council, 2000).

Through a new education 'consortium', '3 Ed Glasgow Ltd', which includes the Miller Construction Group, Hewlett Packard, Amey and Mitel, the local education authority plans to refurbish all existing secondary schools as well as building 12 new ones. Eight thousand computers will be provided and each of the schools electronically networked. In turn '3ED' will be paid £40.5 million in 2003 rising each year to £58.4 million in the final year, 2032. The total cost is estimated at £1.2 billion. In addition to concerns about the price tag that comes with this PPP, which is estimated to cost over £34 million more than by the public sector route, teaching and other unions have complained that the proposals will lead to a reduction in capacity, the loss of important sports facilities including 6 fewer swimming pools, fewer classrooms and staff rooms. The plan also involves transferring cleaning and janitorial staff to the private sector-led consortium. As with the stock transfer of houses, much valuable publicly owned land would now become available to private developers.

One problem facing those opposed to PPPs and PFI is the absence of financial clarity and the difficulty in assessing the true costs involved. Often the private sector is provided with hidden subsidies and in many of the projects to date there has been a reluctance on the part of those putting forward proposals to release funding details, often under the excuse of commercial confidentiality.

Activity 11.3

What are the common features of New Labour's policies in relation to health, housing, and education?

11.7 New Labour's social policy: a new welfare settlement?

In education, housing, and the health service, as in other public services, there is an ongoing struggle between two competing discourses: the New Labour sanctioned view that the increasing use of the private sector in the delivery of public services is to be welcomed as more cost effective and efficient while delivering better quality services, and the position being adopted by an increasing number of trade unions, professional organizations, and user groups, and indeed among a growing number of Labour voters, that despite the rhetoric of 'reform' and 'modernization' the government has continued to privatize large swathes of the public sector leading to deteriorating services and worsening conditions for public sector workers. As we pointed out above Labour committed itself to Tory spending plans for the first three years in office. This resulted in a further reduction in public spending, estimated by *The Guardian* to be at its lowest for 40 years at 39.4 per cent of GDP. It says much about Labour's attitude to the public sector when it can be claimed that 'Thatcher was more lavish than Labour' (*The Guardian*, 25 August 1999). A succession of public outcries about the lack of funding in education and the NHS in particular forced the government to act. However, the indication is that Labour is only partially prepared to redress funding shortfalls. In its much heralded Spending Review and new NHS plan in 2000, for example, the government promised £13 billion for the NHS in a five-year reform plan. But once more there are signs that Labour is increasingly looking to the private sector, as well as to PFI, to help deliver its plans.

While Labour has thus far baulked at the idea of a large-scale attack on the public sector, unlike the Conservatives, it has, at times almost by stealth, gone further than them in the objective of removing from the public sector what remains of large swathes of local authority housing, an increasing number of schools and organizations such as air traffic control. Where there is an opportunity, it would appear, Labour is committed to providing the private sector with all the encouragement it needs to get involved in delivering public services. The following comments from Gordon Brown and Tony Blair display the government's fondness for the private sector:

> Through the Private Finance Initiative, the private sector is able to bring a wide range of managerial, commercial and creative skills to the provision of public services, offering potentially huge benefits for the Government. We are keen to see the Private Finance Initiative and other public/private partnerships succeed in delivering the necessary investment the country needs, on terms it can afford. (Gordon Brown, quoted in Treasury Taskforce on Private Finance, 1997)

In July 1999 Blair informed the British Venture Capitalist Association that,

'One of the things I would like to do, as well as stimulating more entrepreneurship in the private sector, is to get a bit of it into the public sector as well' (*The Guardian*, July 7 1999). In the same speech he also attacked Britain's public sector workers for being deeply resistant to change. Identified by Blair as one of the key 'forces of conservatism' in the country, leading Labour politicians have not been slow in criticizing public sector workers for failing to embrace modernization and reform. Teachers, for long a target of the Conservatives, have continued to be denounced by sections of the government for their opposition to EAZs and a number of other educational policies being adopted by the government. One important sign of the government's attitude to public sector workers has been its refusal to fund pay increases that would see the public sector regaining some of the ground lost in comparison with private sector pay awards during the 1980s and 1990s. In its 1997 manifesto Labour committed itself to a policy of public sector pay restraint. Further, it has presented performance related pay (PRP) as a key element of its reform of the public sector. Plans for the introduction of PRP are well advanced in education while in other sectors the government has made it clear that it wishes to abolish national pay bargaining.

The increasing involvement of business in the delivery of public services has for the government brought with it badly needed managerial and financial skills. For many workers it has brought changes in working practices and employment status, at times mounting to little more than the effective casualization of work. In addition there have been major job losses in the public sector in recent years, with the promise of more to follow.

This leads to the question of whether Labour's reforms are creating a new welfare settlement. There is no one simple answer to this. There are signs that Labour is seeking to continue with Conservative policies – not to mention attitudes – in relation to the public sector. But it has also gone further than the Tories in extending managerialism and privatization across the public sector. Labour has, albeit in the language of the 'third way', interpreted the role of the state as enabler, not the provider of services, in line with the approach adopted by the Conservatives. However, once again it is important to highlight that this does not mean that the state has gone away, as we can observe in its oppressive attitude to policing and refugees – more that Labour has continued with the Tory project to reconstruct the public sector in a more limited way but one that opens up new opportunities for the market (see Hughes et al., 1998). New Labour have travelled far from the commitment to the welfare state that was characteristic of what is now defined as old Labour. There is now a stress on individual and family responsibility and a downplaying of rights to public goods and services.

Despite the competing ideological influences in the New Labour project, like the Conservatives before them they have stressed that there is no alternative to the market. Where they diverge is, in the Labour view, that public services, and social welfare in particular, can be harnessed to the drive of creating a 'modern, dynamic, economy'. How many would now accept without question that what remains of the public sector is 'safe in New Labour's hands'?

Activity 11.4

What signs are there that a new welfare settlement has emerged around New Labour's social policy agenda?

CHAPTER 12

AGEING: POPULATION AND PENSIONS

John Lansley

12.1 Introduction

When Old Parr died in 1635, the great William Harvey, the discoverer of the circulation of the blood, was called in to carry out the post mortem examination. For Parr was a person of great interest. He was, he had claimed, 152 years old, and had done penance for adultery at 105. His contemporaries did not question his claims, nor those of Henry Jenkins, who died in 1670 at the supposed age of 169 (Thomas, 1976: 234–5). In a society where written records were only slowly replacing people's memories, and where the status of age was based on wisdom and economic power, rather than just family affection or religious custom, similar, if less extreme claims, must have been made quite often, and in many villages and small towns the role of village 'elder' would have been one of considerable informal consequence.

Our attitudes have undergone a great change in the last hundred or so years. In high-tech society the memories and wisdom of older people are ignored, while few people rely on inheriting a family farm or business from their parents (Arensberg and Kimball, 1940; Brody, 1973). Ninety-year-olds and centenarians no longer have rarity value (Bury and Holme, 1991), indeed, it has been reported that the Queen is cutting down on her birthday card list for those over 100 on grounds of expense – there are just too many of them. And here we have a hint of two paradoxes which have developed in this century. First, while most of us would like to live for as long as possible, we fear old age. (For an early account of this fear see Swift's *Gulliver's Travels* [1726], Book 3, Chapter 10.) And secondly, as a society we fear that the costs of preserving so many older people will be an insupportable drain on the economy – so-called apocalyptic demography.

This chapter will look at the ways in which the lives of older people have changed over time, their present position in society, and the reasons why their growing numbers have caused concerns to most western governments – and increasingly to governments in other parts of the world. Can we afford so many old people? What quality of life can we offer them? Is their later life their own responsibility, that of their families, or a duty of the state? And all the time the nagging personal question is 'What about when I am old?'

Students are often doubtful about topics like ageing and population growth, regarding statistics with anxiety and old age as, at best, a far off country. However, studying ageing can tell us a great deal about how we live in societies and the relationships between different groups – here, generational relations in particular, but also issues of gender, class, and race. Gerontology (the study of ageing) can be a very valuable form of applied social science, showing how different disciplines can be brought together to illustrate a common theme.

12.2 Who is old, when?

First, let us consider what it means to be an older person in Britain today. We start with a problem of definition: what does being old imply? We can look at this from a variety of viewpoints.

First, we may start from a chronological approach: old age begins at a given age, usually retirement age. This is used for many administrative purposes, such as entitlement to pensions or other benefits. But retirement age tells us little about a person's employment status (many people have left work before they reach 60 or 65, while others may continue beyond that point (see Fennell et al., 1988: 84–8, or Johnson and Falkingham, 1992: 84–5) and still less about whether they are able to perform a job. People in their seventies may be highly dependent on others for support, while others in their nineties may be active and fiercely independent.

Secondly, we may suppose that being old is to do with biological dependency, and changes in people's physical and mental conditions as they get older. But we need to be careful here, too. While people's bodily capacities can influence their lives greatly, the analysis of this is by no means unproblematic (Twigg, 1997, 2000). We also need to remember that physical ageing can take place at very different rates from one person to another, and that some aspects of physical ageing (white hair, wrinkled skin) have no significance at all for people's levels of independence, while other conditions can be perfectly well compensated for with appropriate treatment or appliances. And while dementia in later life can be a major and so far irremediable condition, it should be remembered that depression (which may be treatable) is more common in later life than dementia, with which it is sometimes confused. Certainly, we should not treat all people of a given age as dependent on any biological grounds.

Why, then, do we group old people together and make them special objects of social policy? One very influential answer, from the end of the 1970s, was made in terms of the political economy of ageing (Estes, 1979; Minkler and Estes, 1984, 1998; Townsend, 1981; Walker 1981; Phillipson, 1982, 1998; Phillipson and Walker, 1986, and, for a critique, Wilson 1997, 2000). This approach involves analysing how political, economic, and social structures interact with one another, and is used to show how ageing is a socially constructed condition. On this analysis, our present concepts of old age derive from the idea of retirement, which exists primarily in the interests of the economy, as a means of controlling the size of the labour force. In order to justify excluding older people from the labour market, the belief has to be maintained that people beyond a certain age are no longer capable of working efficiently, while the fact of their exclusion requires the development of pension systems, provided, or regulated by the state (Phillipson, 1982, 1998). Dependency on pensions and other forms of income not related to earnings may be reinforced by social dependency (Walker 1980; Townsend, 1981), whereby older people's inability to achieve economic independence is met by the provision of services which reinforce their dependency on others for their care. From this develops the 'ageing enterprise' (Estes, 1979), an industry of health and welfare providers who have a vested interest in the maintenance of this dependency. On this analysis we thus have an increasingly large number of people who have been moved out of mainstream society, lumped together under the term 'old' and treated as inferior, because they are unproductive members of society. Such ageism (see Bytheway, 1995) is a form of social discrimination just as demeaning to individuals and damaging to society as sexism or racism, though it is seldom taken as seriously (see Activity 12.1 below).

However, analysing social relations in later life simply in terms of dependency may itself be a form of ageism. Wilson (1997) argues from a postmodern perspective that applying a form of analysis to the lives of people who do not recognize it or acknowledge its validity can itself become a form of oppression. The political economy analysis does not correspond to the experience and self-image of many older people – indeed, they will often go out of their way to stress that they are not dependent, and fear the time when they may have to rely on welfare services or enter residential care. 'I don't feel old', they say, and this response is both a true boast of their personal capacities and an expression of fear of how they may be treated if they are labelled 'old' by the rest of society (Thompson et al., 1990). Moreover, where they are in need of support, it may often come from their contemporaries, rather than from younger generations or from the state. A recent study of two very deprived areas of Liverpool found that older people suffered as much as any other groups from general social exclusion. They did not interpret this in terms of age deprivation or dependency, but as part of the wider problems of their neighbourhoods, and they clearly relied heavily on one another for mutual support. (Munck et al., 1999; Lansley forthcoming).

And meanwhile the rest of society is developing an increasingly ambivalent attitude to its older members. The certainties of the traditional welfare state, in which older people seemed to be assured of general sympathy and support in theory, even if in practice things fell far short (Townsend, 1962; Robb, 1967) have been lost with so many other moral certainties in the last two decades. As Phillipson has put it, 'while providing the basis – through changes to patterns of fertility and mortality – for developing an ageing society, we seem to have undercut a language and moral space which can resonate with the rights and needs of older people as a group' (Phillipson, 1998: 51). It is to this ageing society that we now turn.

Activity 12.1

Collect examples of ways in which older people are commonly depicted in the media for a week. What may this tell us about how they are viewed and treated by the rest of society? Why do you think this is?

12.3 Ageing societies

As we have already seen, old age, which was a rarity in the past, has become a relative commonplace today. This does not mean that the maximum age for humankind has increased: there were always some people who lived to a great age, even if Parr and Jenkins were over exuberant with the truth. Rather, what it means is that the proportion of older people in the population has increased. We can see this if we compare the population structure of Great Britain in 1891 and 1991 (see Figure 12.1), in which the size of each five-year age group is indicated by a horizontal bar, males coming out to the left of the central column and females to the right. In 1891 the distribution of the population was pyramidal, with a large number of young children, and with each age band smaller than the one below. This represented a society with quite a high birth rate, and with death affecting every age group infant mortality was still common, and young people and adults died at all ages. Survival to old age was exceptional, as can be seen by the very thin peak of the pyramid.

The picture in 1991 is very different. The pyramid has been replaced by a column, which bulges in and out according to the incidence of baby 'booms' and 'busts', and which is topped by a shorter, fatter pyramid which represents the effects of mortality beyond the age of 70. Variations in the column are the result, not of the death rate, but of the birth rate. The children of one baby boom become the parents of the next boom, so that a bulge in the column will repeat itself 20 or so years later. Note that the number of live births in 1991 was not very different from that a hundred years earlier: most of the extra numbers in the population – and total size increased during the century from 29 million to 55 million – appear in the upper part of the diagram. In particular, the percentage of people over retirement age increased from 6.1 per cent to 18.7 per cent.

Figure 12.1   Population in 1891

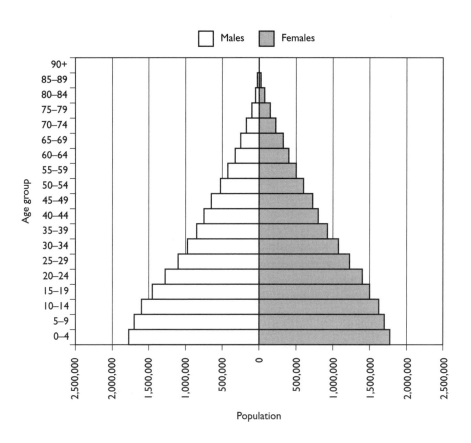

Activity 12.2

Compare the population figures for 1891 and 1991 in Figures 12.1 and 12.2. What factors account for the differences between them? How would you explain the differences between age cohorts in the 1991 figures?

These population shifts are not, of course, unique to Britain. All industrialized societies have gone through this process, and in the future resource issues for older people are likely to be much more severe (Tout, 1989; Johnson and Slater, 1993: 339–57; Wilson 2000). Populations go through four stages (Warnes, 1982; Mullan, 2000: 33). At the first stage, both fertility (birth rates)

Figure 12.2   Population in 1991

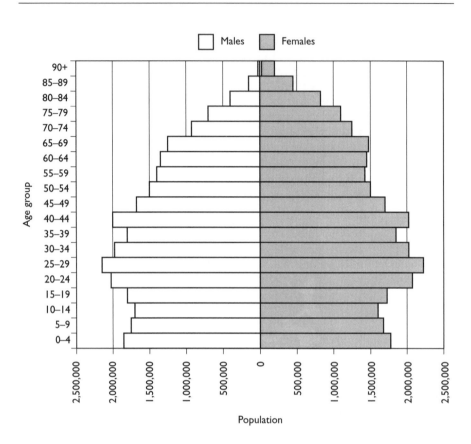

and mortality are high, and the population size is relatively stationary. At the second stage, mortality begins to drop as the general standard of living improves: in the short run, this means there will be a younger, larger population. In the third stage, this improvement in mortality reaches the older generations, and by this time the birth rate will also have begun to drop – now that more children are surviving, there is no need to have so many – and consequently the overall structure shifts towards becoming an ageing population. In stage four the population once again becomes relatively stationary, but now with low fertility and mortality, and with a much higher percentage of older people than at the start of the process. It should be noted at this stage that the UK has gone further down this road than many other western countries, and with fewer dramatic effects (Walker and Maltby, 1997). Thus, although it is often claimed that the 'crisis' of ageing is common to all western countries, it is less problematic for the UK than for many other countries.

Another interesting thing about Figure 12.1 is that there were actually fewer people in the 65–75 age band in 1991 than there were in 1981: this is because of the low birth rate in the 1930s. However, the number of over 75s has been increasing throughout the century, so that by 2025 there are projected to be 5.9 million over-75s in the population (9.7 per cent) compared with 3.3 million (5.9 per cent) in 1981 (Tinker, 1996: 13–15). Since it is generally these older people who make most use of health and welfare services, the concern is often expressed that the burden on these services will be insupportable by the working population.

12.4 Dependency ratios

The argument which has developed from this proportionate change in ageing populations has been that a relatively smaller number of workers is having to support an increasing number of retired people, and that this burden will prove too great, both for the economy and in terms of the willingness of the working population to shoulder such high tax levels. The relationship of the working to the non-working population is usually expressed in terms of the dependency ratio (Tinker, 1996: 14–15). At its simplest, this is expressed as the ratio of the working to non-working population, that is, all those aged from 16 to 59–64, compared with those aged 0–15, and over 60–6. Mathematically,

$$\text{dependency ratio} = \frac{\text{children aged 0–15+ men over 65+ women over 60}}{\text{men 16–64 + women 16–59}}$$

But this, of course, is a serious over-simplification. What we are actually dealing with is the proportion of those in paid (and tax-paid) employment, and the rest of the population – children, full-time students, women engaged wholly in caring and domestic activities, unemployed, sick and non-working disabled people, and pensioners (Falkingham, 1989). The equation thus becomes

$$\text{dependency ratio} = \frac{\text{children + unemployed + sick + non-employed women + retired, etc.}}{\text{working men and women}}$$

But even this is to miss the point, because it is by no means only those who are working who pay taxes. Most occupational pensioners, for example, will be paying income tax on their pensions, while all members of the population are paying indirect taxes, such as VAT.

If we go a stage further we become concerned not merely with the numbers of tax payers, but the amount of tax which they are paying. As always, the issue for social policy is how resources are to be distributed. It was explicit in the enterprise culture of the 1980s and 1990s that the rewards of productivity should lie with those who generated them. The implication of this was that the social inequalities generated in society (and which expanded rapidly during those decades) would continue into retirement. If those are the pre-suppositions of social policy, then clearly there will be problems in sustaining into retirement those who spent long periods of their adult lives unemployed, or on low and irregular earnings. By contrast, a more equal distribution of resources could generate substantial sums to support the retired population as a whole. The dependency ratio, in short, is not just a matter of inter-generational dependencies, but of the underlying philosophies which determine how resources are to be distributed in society. Britain adopted the recommendations of Beveridge and others for the creation of the welfare state, with much larger implications for redistribution, at a time when the economy was in much worse shape than it is today.

12.5 Social divisions of ageing

It will already have become clear that we must not lump all older people together as one group: they differ enormously in age, health, wealth and family and social contacts. As with the analysis of other social policies, we must also be aware that age is only one social division which affects them. Their lives will also be profoundly influenced by their social class, gender, and ethnic background. Each of these divisions has its own relevance to the social policies which we shall consider. Social class, in so far as it relates to employment history, is obviously of direct relevance to people's pension entitlements, while the life history of people's living and working conditions is likely to be relevant to their health in later life.

Gender is relevant to ageing for a variety of reasons (Arber and Ginn, 1991, 1995). The most obvious one is that their greater life expectancy means that there are many more older women than men. In 1991, the UK population of people over 65 was 8.8 million, split 40 per cent men and 60 per cent women. The over 75 population (3.9 m) was split 34:66, and by the time we get to over 85s (831,678) the ratio is 25:75. This difference is also reflected in marital status. Even in the 85–9 cohort, there are as many men married as there are widowed or divorced, whereas widowhood is the most likely marital status for women: nearly two thirds of women over 75 are widows, compared with less than a third of men. Widows are likely to face particular forms of financial dependency: at best, they may hope to inherit half their late husbands' occupational pensions, while their own independent occupational pensions are likely to be a lot lower (so a man whose wife dies will not be so adversely affected). They may also have relied on their husbands for physical support: women are more likely than men to suffer from limited ability to perform the normal activities of daily living (Arber and Ginn, 1991: 108–20). On the other hand, women are more likely to maintain links with other members of their families, especially with daughters (Lewis and Meredith, 1988). Consequently, inter-generational caring is also a gendered issue (Ungerson, 1990; Dalley, 1996), though we must not forget the mutual caring roles of spouses of both genders (Green, 1988; Wenger, 1990).

When we look at the position of older people from minority ethnic groups (Blakemore and Boneham, 1994; Atkin, 1998) we find that they may be heavily dependent on their families. This can arise for two reasons. On the one hand, if they are recent immigrants, they will not have had time to build up pension contributions, and they may also be excluded from claiming other welfare benefits: they are thus dependent on their children financially. At the same time, there has been an assumption on the part of health and welfare providers that immigrant families have brought with them a sense of duty of caring for their elders which means that alternative provision is not required. This simplistic, racist assumption has been widely challenged, but a residue of failure to make appropriate provision for ethnic elders remains, and much still needs to be done to build up services for them.

Activity 12.3

How relevant is a person's class, gender, or ethnic group likely to be at age 65, 75 or 85?

12.6 The financial situations of older people today

The previous discussion tells us that there are going to be no simple answers to questions about the financial position of older people – their income and wealth, the adequacy of their pensions, the support which they receive from other people, and any special outgoings which they may incur as a result of physical or mental dependency.

In 1989 John Moore, then Secretary of State for Social Security made a speech to a Help the Aged conference in which he stated: 'It is simply no longer true that being a pensioner tends to mean being badly off . . . For most it is a time to look forward to with confidence. The modern pensioner has a great deal to contribute and a great deal to be envied' Falkingham and Victor (1991: 471). If we set aside the politician's weasel words ('tends' to mean . . ., for 'most' . . .) the implications are clear, and the claims Moore was making may well have resonated with the experience of some of his audience. Some of them would be in receipt of good occupational pensions. They had paid off their mortgages, and in any case the value of their houses had increased substantially over the last 20 years. They had the leisure and the money to afford good holidays and an agreeable lifestyle. Yes, things were a lot better for pensioners than they were in the old days.

Some of this is undoubtedly true, and the sheer increase in numbers has meant that well-off retired people are much more visible, and are indeed being pursued by producers and advertisers eager to capture the 'grey pound'. But is this true for the majority of the retired population?

Table 12.1   The components of single pensioner gross incomes 1994–5 by quintile (£s)

	Lowest 20%	2nd	3rd	4th	Top 20%	Average
Benefit income	65.40	75.50	87.60	93.60	89.80	82.40
Occupational pensions	3.00	8.10	12.00	25.50	94.50	28.60
Investment income	4.00	5.10	5.50	11.20	84.10	21.90
Earnings	0.20	0.50	0.50	2.30	41.20	8.90
Gross Income	72.90	89.70	106.20	133.80	311.60	142.70
Benefit income as % of total gross income	90	84	82	70	29	58

Table 12.2   The components of pensioner couple gross incomes 1994–5 by quintiles (£s)

	Lowest 20%	2nd	3rd	4th	Top 20%	Average
Benefit income	101.80	120.00	126.90	125.00	116.00	119.30
Occupational pensions	8.00	22.60	44.60	89.20	219.00	76.70
Investment income	5.10	9.60	15.00	31.30	128.80	37.90
Earnings	0.60	4.70	5.50	13.20	77.80	20.30
Other income	0.80	0.30	3.10	1.00	3.00	1.60
Gross income	123.30	157.20	195.10	259.70	544.60	255.90
Benefit income as % of gross income	88	76	65	48	21	58

Sources (both tables): Hansard Written Answers, 14 February 1997, cols. 345–6; Phillipson (1998: 75)

The easiest way to answer this is by studying the figures in Tables 12.1 and 12.2, which divide pensioners into five equal groups (quintiles) and compare the average incomes of each group. A number of points stand out. First, that the income for the bottom four quintiles in the single pensioner group, and the bottom two for couples, is basically dependent on state benefits. (We should also notice here that the majority of single pensioners are women.) They have no earnings, and have not in the past been able to contribute meaningfully to occupational or private pension schemes, nor have they built up any savings to bring them investment income.

By contrast, the top quintile has a totally different profile. Although their benefit income is not particularly high (they will not qualify for means-tested benefits), their occupational pensions comfortably outweigh their state pension, while they also have substantial investment income and some earnings. The contrast is so acute that Falkingham and Victor (1991) carried out a study, using government general household survey data, to analyse the characteristics of the 'woopie' (*well off older person* – one of a series of acronyms coined to describe this group by advertisers and others: see Falkingham and Victor (1991: 472) and Meade (1989: 12)). They defined woopies as 'those elderly persons whose incomes place them in the top quintile of the total income distribution of Great Britain' (Falkingham and Victor, 1991: 478) – thus a rather higher income group than those in our tables – and identified other characteristics of this group. These were not wholly surprising: woopies were more likely to be male, under 75, married, owner occupiers, with an occupational pension and asset income, and to possess a wide range of consumer durables. Interestingly, they were also likely to be in possession of good health, and to make little if any use of state health and welfare services. This challenges the argument that because older people are now better off, there is less need for state services, or that those services which are provided should be charged for at economic prices: those who could afford to pay those rates are not using the services anyway.

We might conclude from this that those in the bottom quintiles will have the opposite characteristics: they are more likely to be women (especially if single), they will be older, in poorer health, in worse, rented, housing, and with few resources other than their state pension and other benefits. The whole picture reinforces Titmuss's claim in 1955 that there are two nations in retirement: one increasingly benefiting from occupational pensions and the other, larger, group, depending on state benefits of declining value.

12.7 Pensions

Given the low income levels of the majority of older people, pensions are clearly a matter of great importance. Although the first state pension scheme in Britain was introduced in 1908, the present scheme takes its origins from the Beveridge Report of 1942. This, like Beveridge's other proposals, was to be a universal benefit, available to all contributors to the National Insurance scheme, and payable on a flat-rate, subsistence basis. This in itself raised the question of what the subsistence level should be. Beveridge used the poverty line developed by Seebohm Rowntree for his 1936 study of poverty in York (Rowntree, 1941), but there is a great difference between a poverty line designed for research purposes to ensure that all those counted are inescapably poor, and one to be used by the state to set a maximum above which help would not be given (Veit-Wilson, 1992). Consequently, the basic state pension has always been too low to provide adequate support in retirement, and the poorest pensioners have needed to top it up from means-tested benefits – even if large numbers have failed to do so.

This invalidates a claim made by Beveridge in the report:

> Any Plan of Social Security worthy of its name must ensure that every citizen, fulfilling during his working life the obligation of citizenship according to his powers, can obtain as of right when he is past work an income adequate to maintain him. This means . . . a pension . . . which is enough for subsistence, even though the pensioner has no other resources whatever. (Beveridge, 1942: para. 239)

Moreover, the tell-tale use of 'he' in the text indicates the style of pension which Beveridge had in mind. It assumed that for the most part workers were male, and that women would be covered by their husbands' contributions. Consequently, it did not consider the special issues which affected women's capacity to build up a contribution record in their own right.

That particular problem was left to 1975, and the introduction of the State Earnings Related Pension Scheme (SERPS). This scheme recognized that while many people were benefiting from occupational pensions schemes their benefits were not available to those with broken employment records, those who changed jobs frequently, and those whose earnings might be highest in their early, rather than later working life. Occupational schemes also failed to meet adequately the needs of widows of pensioners. The SERPS scheme sought to bring the benefits of occupational pensions to low-paid workers, and in particular to women. It allowed members up to 20 years' absence from the workforce for purposes of childcare or similar duties, gave full entitlement to pensions for widows, and calculated the pension on the best 20 years' earnings during membership of the scheme (thereby giving a better deal to such people as manual workers who might be able to undertake a lot of overtime in their twenties and thirties, but who were no longer fit enough to do so in their fifties). Although the scheme had its critics at the time, particularly over the earnings related nature of the scheme, so that those on very low incomes got least out of it, it was an imaginative approach which made a real effort to take into account the actual working conditions of many lower paid people. Sadly, it was never allowed to come into full effect. On the grounds that the actuarial calculations for the scheme had underestimated its costs, the Fowler review of the Social Security System (DHSS, 1985c) cut SERPS savagely, and it was further reduced in 1995, so that many of the key features of the scheme were lost or severely reduced in value. (For an analysis of the continued relevance of SERPS see NPC, 1998: 11–17.)

Nor was this the only loss of income for the poorer pensioner in the 1980s. In 1980 the Thatcher government cut the automatic index link between the state pension scheme and earnings, which had been introduced in 1975, and linked it only to price increases, thus preventing pensioners from sharing any increase in the standard of living over time. This means that over time the real value of the basic pension will decline – from 16 per cent of average male earnings in 1990 to 10 per cent by 2020, and 7 per cent by 2050 (Johnson and Falkingham, 1992: 143). Those affected by the downgrading of the two government pension schemes would have two options: to rely on means-tested benefits or to turn to the private market.

The government was keen to see a shift from state to private pension provision, and in the late 1980s encouraged private pension companies to develop alternatives to state occupational schemes for workers in bodies like the NHS. It later transpired that many unscrupulous and false claims had been made for some schemes, and that those who took them up came out a great deal worse off: a report by the Office of Fair Trading (1997) found that up to £4 billion had been lost by pensioners, in what *The Times* described as 'the greatest financial scandal of the century' (16th July 1997, quoted in Phillipson 1998: 82). On top of this came the discovery, after the death of Robert Maxwell, that he had siphoned off £400 million. from his companies' pension schemes.

12.8 What are pensions?

It is not surprising, in the wake of so many assaults on both state and private pension provision, that there should be widespread concern about the nature, organization, and costs of pensions. Before we look at some more recent proposals, and return to our initial question of what we can afford as a country, we should pause to consider what pensions are, what they should achieve, and how they can best be organized.

We start with two main ways of conceptualizing pensions. When Beveridge was drawing up his plan, pensions were part of a raft of social security measures. People needed to insure against the risks of not working, including those created by retirement. Pensions were thus a basic means of income support, backed up by supplementary means-tested pensions for those who had earned no income, or had low and irregular earnings during their lifetime. The state pension should be an equal reward for all citizens.

There is, however, a quite different way of viewing pensions. We now live in a society where retirement is not a risk but a near certainty: most of us can expect 20 or more years of retirement as life expectancy increases and the number of working years decreases. We thus should make our own provision for retirement by saving, and since we may not do this voluntarily, the state lays down regulations to ensure that this saving takes place. In effect, pensions are a means of ensuring that money earned over a short number of years is spread across a growing lifetime. This is an individualistic approach, and fails to allow for those unable to work and save.

The organization of pension schemes is potentially quite different, depending on which of the above models we adopt. If we go for the social security model, then there is in principle nothing wrong with sticking with a 'pay as you go' system: that is, that sufficient money is collected from tax payers to cover the costs of paying for pensions in any given year. In essence, current working generations are expected to pay for those who are no longer working, just as today's pensioners did in their turn for the generation before: it is a long reciprocal chain. In practice, as we have already seen, it is not quite as simple as that, because these contributions are part of a broader system whereby taxpayers support dependent members of society.

The drawback with this approach, for many people, is that it either results in a flat rate, subsistence, pension, or, if it is earnings related, it fails to redress the inequalities which continue through life into retirement. Nor, in an individualistic society, does it take account of personal achievement. The second model, spreading an individual's earnings over a lifetime, by contrast, seeks to do just that. Ideally, every contributor would have his or her own identifiable pension fund, which would reflect exactly what they had saved over time. This, however, suffers from the reverse disadvantages. It does not provide for those who cannot save, nor does it redress lifetime inequalities, so that, while it may be satisfactory for individuals, it does not provide a complete answer for a state which must ensure at least a minimum income for all its members.

It also raises a further question. Are pensions to be paid according to the amount of money saved, or the number of years worked? A private pensions scheme works on the former principle, whereas many occupational schemes are in effect based on the latter: a typical scheme may provide a final pension calculated as a proportion of one's final salary – typically a sixtieth or an eightieth – times the number of years one has contributed to the scheme. For many people this can provide a very satisfactory arrangement, providing certainty about the level of one's final pension, but it may not be so easy to transfer from one job to another. In this respect, we should note that if the trend to flexible employment continues, with people moving more rapidly from one job to another, and sometimes having more than one job at a time, then a personal pension rather than membership of a company pension fund is likely to be desirable. The downside is that the flexible working patterns forecast may mean that people will not be receiving pension contributions or any other benefits from their 'employers', which will also make it harder to forecast one's earning capacity from one year to another. Pension funds will therefore need to allow for differential payment levels over time.

The final issue is who is to run pension schemes? The first model is clearly part of the task of government. The second may well be done by private insurance companies – but it requires a willingness on their part to take on lower paid workers, and needs a capacity to reduce costs far below those which had such a disastrous effect on the private pensions schemes of the late 1980s. An additional point is that private schemes may be trusted to invest to maximize income both for policy holders and for themselves, whereas there is a fear that governments would be unable to resist the temptations to raid pension funds for political ends – a fear acknowledged by Frank Field when he was a junior social security minister, who argued against government involvement on these very grounds. However, the need to support those unable to subscribe to private schemes means that government will need to be involved in some sort of mixed economy of pension provision.

Activity 12.4

The foregoing section describes two different models of pensions. Which groups of pensioners would benefit most from the social security model, and which from the individualistic model? (Bear in mind the divisions listed in Activity 12.3).

12.9 Current government proposals

Many of these points are recognized by the government in its Green Paper *A New Contract for Welfare: Partnership in Pensions* (DSS, 1998). It proposes, first, a scheme whereby the state will be responsible for those earning less than £9,000 per annum, with the basic pension topped up with a means-tested scheme, the minimum income guarantee, which will be index linked to earnings. This scheme will make specific provision for carers or people with disabilities who are unable to work. Secondly, there will be a short-term state second pension for those in the income band £9–18,000, which will ensure that all contributors will have the benefits of an occupational pension. As and when the private pension sector brings out 'stakeholder' pensions of equal value, the state scheme will be run down. This will provide a better deal than the present attenuated SERPS, which it will replace. It is hoped that the size of the stakeholder pensions market will enable schemes to be developed which will benefit from economies of scale and flexibility of movement to a point where the failures of the 1980s will be avoided. Thirdly, all those earning over £18,000 will be expected to belong to a private or occupational scheme, and all pension schemes will be more tightly regulated than in the past.

These proposals have not satisfied the pensioners' lobby, who want to see the present basic pension uprated to a decent level, and once again indexed to earnings. Whereas government claims that this would be too expensive an option, pensioners point out that the present costs are well within the capacity of government to achieve, and could remain so in the future (National Pensioners Convention, 1998, 1999). The government also argues that to increase the basic pension is to give money to those who do not need it – a repetition of the woopie thesis. By contrast, it is argued, the minimum income guarantee for the poorest pensioners will target money to those most in need faster and more generously than a return to standard of living index linking would achieve (Toynbee, 2000b). However, as we have seen, the woopie part of the pensioner population is quite small, and a progressive tax system could ensure that at least a part of such increases could be clawed back. Other targeting arguments have also been made: Field (2000), for example, has recently argued that higher pensions for older pensioners, whose incomes are commonly lowest, would be a means of supporting the poorest, without the problems associated with the uptake of means-tested benefits. Ever since the 1966 report on the Financial and Other Circumstances of Retirement Pensioners (MPNI, 1966) there has been a steady figure of around 850,000 pensioners who were entitled to means-tested benefits but who have not claimed them.

12.10 What can we afford?

As Mullan (2000) argues, success in health and survival rates has led to more of our social resources being concentrated on the older sectors of the population. Properly, this should be seen as a major achievement for humanity; instead, it is too often construed in terms of older people being a burden which the rest of society cannot afford. If we go back to Figure 12.1, we can see how mortality, and hence its preceding potential health costs, were spread throughout the population. Indeed, when we consider how closely poverty was associated with the death of wage earners in working-class families (Rowntree, 1901), the true social burden of early mortality would have been significantly greater than just the medical costs. If we now turn to Figure 12.2 we can see that the younger population is now far healthier, at least as far as mortality goes. Consequently, a higher proportion of ill-health, and thus of health costs, is concentrated among the older members of society.

But while illness is more common among older people, and death is universal, this is by no means the same thing as to say that all older people are unhealthy. Most people over 65 are in good health, and in terms of acute illness their prevalence rate is little different from that of younger people (Victor, 1991: 74). The picture with chronic diseases and disabilities is at present rather different, but there are considerable debates as to how this pattern will develop in the future. Whereas Figure 12.1 is a pyramid, reflecting deaths right through the age bands, Figure 12.2 is rather a cylinder, unaffected by mortality, with a much smaller and shallower pyramid on top. The debate on the future pattern of mortality is essentially about how far this pyramid will flatten out further in the future.

A medical scientist who has pursued this idea is J.F. Fries (1980, 1989). He has developed two concepts: the 'rectangularization of mortality' – that is, that ultimately, in terms of our diagram, models of mortality will cease to appear as a pyramid and will rather resemble a rectangle, with the great majority of older people living to their maximum lifespan (Fries suggests around age 85) and then dying within a short period of one another; and 'the compression of morbidity' – that increases in medical science will lead to people remaining healthy until their last few years of life.

Both of these ideas have been disputed (see Bury, 1988; Victor 1991). But two points are relevant to our argument here. First, that although healthcare costs are rising consequent on developments in medical technology we are a much healthier nation than we were a century ago, and that the higher proportion of older people in the population bears testimony to this. And secondly, that to complain that older people are a burden on the NHS is a classic case of blaming the victim. We all die, and, barring nuclear catastrophes, most of us will cost the NHS quite a lot of money during our final illnesses. That is what health services are there for. To suggest that we should be more parsimonious in our spending on healthcare because it is mostly directed at the very old (and the very young) is an act of selfishness on the part of younger generations as breathtaking as it is short sighted: we too shall need those services eventually.

12.11 Conclusion

Success in improving the standard of living and, to a lesser extent, medical advances, over the last two centuries have led to substantial changes in the structure of the population. Most people can now expect to live well into a period which a hundred years ago was thought of as the preserve of a few 'very old'. Further, the physical quality which these older people (we, ultimately) can expect is, or should be, one in which we can hope for high levels of personal independence, subject to adequate illness and appropriate healthcare. The development of industrialization during this same period has created a situation in which we have to work less strenuously, and for a much shorter period than before. This has resulted in a new phenomenon over the last 50 years of virtually universal and extensive retirement.

But social inequalities are carried over into retirement, leading to the creation of two types of pensioners. On the one hand there are those whose lifetime earnings have been such that they have been able to save and spread their incomes sufficiently for an enjoyable lifestyle throughout their lives. On the other hand are those people, including very many existing pensioners, who have had consistently low wages, or who have experienced long periods out of the labour market, whether unemployed or engaged in domestic tasks, who lack the resources to build up savings of this kind. The current state of the labour market, and the history of unemployment over the last 20 years, suggest that there will continue to be many such new pensioners in the foreseeable future.

We thus have two types of pensions policies. Since the mid-1980s it has been government policy to urge people towards personal pensions, based on savings, without acknowledging that many will not be able to afford this. This residualized group are gradually shifting from National Insurance pensions, to which they have contributed as of right, to means-tested provision, for which they must prove need. Whereas the owners of personal pensions can anticipate the levels of their pensions, based on their individual earnings, state pensioners are dependent on political decisions about the value of their pensions.

Population change has been called in to provide an excuse for low levels of state pensions. It is the argument of this chapter that this claim is invalid. Increases in the number and proportion of older people are not at a level where low pensions, or health services, can be justified in terms of any 'scientific' economic approach. As a society we can afford – better than in the past, and better than many other countries – to provide pensions for all which will keep pensioners in touch with average levels of spending for the rest of the population. There are indeed difficult technical decisions to be made about the relationship between different types of pensions, and the fine tuning of particular schemes, but the primary issue is one of political will.

Activity 12.5

'Will you still need me, will you still feed me, when I'm 64?' (Lennon and McCartney, 1967) – or 74? or 84?

CHAPTER 13

CHILDREN, SOCIAL POLICY, AND THE STATE

Michael Lavalette and Stephen Cunningham

Twelve year olds should not be on the street at night[1]

[In the city there are] constantly increasing numbers of vagrant, idle and vicious children[2]

How do you feel now you little bastards[3]

[Delinquents must] gradually be restored to the true position of childhood . . . in a *family*[4]

We [cannot] build a society fit for our children to grow up in without making a moral judgement about the nature of that society . . . Any decent society is founded on duty [and] responsibility. A philosophy of enlightened self interest in which opportunity is extended . . . [and there is] greater security, safer streets [and] motivated young people.[5]

> ### Activity 13.1
>
> Look at the quotations given above. They all relate to children. From which decade do you think they come? (Full references are given at the end of this chapter.)

13.1 Introduction

Over the last 20 years politicians, journalists, and various social commentators have seemingly come to the conclusion that 'childhood is in crisis' (Scraton 1997). On the one hand this crisis reflects the fact that large numbers of children in Britain are being brought up in the most desperate circumstances. In the final quarter of the twentieth century child poverty has increased more in Britain than in almost any other developed society. According to a UNICEF report published in June 2000 approximately 47 million children in the rich 29 countries of the OECD live below nationally-defined poverty lines. But:

> the most shaming fact is that while child poverty remained stable or increased only slightly across most OECD countries in then last twenty years, it tripled in Britain . . . Child poverty in Britain is twice as high as France or the Netherlands and five times higher than Norway or Sweden. (UKPHA, 2000: 1, 12)

To put this into figures, halfway through New Labour's first term in office some 3.4 million children were living in poverty *(The Guardian,* 14 July 2000) (see Chapters 4 and 10). The childhood these children endure is significantly detached from the ideal many of us hold on to.

On the other hand, children are increasingly portrayed as unruly, uncontrollable, amoral and even evil. As Bob Franklin notes:

> Ideologically, children have become the focus of a moral panic . . . [P]resentations of children have metamorphosed them from . . . innocent 'sugar and spice' angels . . . into inherently evil demons who, typifying Britain's declining moral standards, seem incapable of distinguishing right from wrong. (1995: 4–5)

Despite the growing problem of child poverty, it is this latter issue that is increasingly dominant within political debates – though there is a link between these two concerns. For it is the children of the poor who are the targets of the new moral agenda embraced by the two major political parties in Britain. Thus, when Tony Blair says children under 12 should not be on the streets after 8pm he does not mean middle-class children playing cricket in the park, going to the cinema, or leisure centre, or cycling on their streets during the long summer evenings. These children are neither portrayed nor perceived as a threat. Rather, it is the poor working-class children in inner city areas or desolate council estates who instil fear and loathing. The victims of poverty and the gross inequalities that structure British society are increasingly portrayed as a group who need to be controlled by police and state social service agencies.

The focus on these problem children is part of a wider attack on the moral malaise of particular sections of the community that has developed at a time when the certainties of the postwar welfare state have been questioned by both major political parties in Britain (Lavalette and Mooney, 1999). For both Conservative and New Labour governments state welfare provision is both uneconomic and morally questionable leading to a welfare dependent or socially excluded sub-stratum of the population (see Chapter 10). We will suggest that the recent focusing on poor children cannot be separated from these wider ideological justifications for welfare restructuring.

But we will also suggest that the existent problem of children is not particularly new. During other periods of economic, political, and social crises, children – or more specifically poor working-class children – have become an object of attention by commentators, welfare workers, and state legislators. Thus, we suggest, the recent policy directions of governments are merely the latest phase of an attempt to regulate, or control, poor children in Britain in the face of welfare crisis.

We start, however, by asking two deceptively simple questions: what is childhood and who are children? The answer seems obvious – everyone knows what a child is; everyone knows what childhood is. After all, this is an experience or life period we have all lived through. But over the last 20 years there has been a growing recognition that both children and childhood are, to some extent, socially constructed concepts rather than merely biological or natural ones. This means that what we consider childhood to be, or whom we consider to be children, will vary cross-culturally and historically and will be affected by the class, gender, and race into which someone is born.

13.2 What is childhood?

The last 20 years has witnessed the development of a new paradigm for the sociological study of children and childhood. Developing the work of the French historian Philippe Ariés, whose book *Centuries of Childhood* was first published in 1962, sociologists have challenged the notion of a universal or 'natural' childhood. Instead they argue that the experiences of children, and indeed those who are considered children, will vary across time and space.

The sociological perspective is one that challenges the dominant common-sense picture of childhood as a time of unrestricted free time, protected from the cares and concerns of the outside world where the best interests of the child are served by being encased in what Holt (1974) terms a 'walled garden' of purely childish concerns. The walled garden represents an idealized world free from oppression and exploitation (which does not exist for most children). However, it also acts as a barrier to the outside world where children, because they are children, are denied access to activities which adults take for granted. The fact of biological immaturity is utilized to determine a presumed social, political, and economic incompetence and so children find themselves excluded from decision-making at all levels of society, subjected to various forms of punishment (including physical chastisement) to control their behaviour, and represented by parents and a range of welfare professionals who, it is assumed, know what is best for them.

The socially inferior position of children is assumed to be natural. The problem, however, is that young people have not always been treated in this way. Numerous historical and cross-cultural studies portray societies where children were not encased within the 'walled garden' but were much more active participants in family, productive, and social life. Within the sociological literature, it is now recognized that children's experiences will be affected and shaped by a range of interacting social divisions and will be mediated by a range of social institutions put in place to control, direct, or meet the perceived needs of young people. The result is that childhood has been revealed as a period of flux and development shaped by social and political factors as much as by biological and psychological ones. Consequently, in reality, there is no single experience 'childhood' but instead a number of 'childhoods' through which children from different social situations will live.

In Britain, for example, the experience of children from bourgeois and working-class backgrounds was (and remains) radically different. Looking at the eighteenth and nineteenth centuries, Davin (1990) has noted that for bourgeois children life experiences were highly gendered. For boys, childhood was shaped by a life trajectory that took them through nursery, preparatory school, public school, and then university, army, church, or business. For their female counterparts life was far more restrictive. The nursery was gradually replaced by education within the home and preparation for coming out as a debutante where an offer of marriage would see them replace the confines of the parental home for those of their husband. The lives of working-class children in the seventeenth, eighteenth, and early nineteenth centuries was completely different. Their experiences were shaped by poverty and the struggle for survival, labour (both domestic and paid), childcare responsibility with younger siblings, the streets of their developing and expanding urban environment and a much quicker integration into the adult world.

Yet as we shall show, by the end of the nineteenth century the life stage 'childhood' had been imposed on to working-class children and their life experiences had been radically altered. Central to this process were changes to the labour market and employment structure and state social policy which increasingly focused on children as both a problem and a potential national asset to be educated and socialized to meet the goals of an increasingly organized capitalism. To paraphrase the historian Edward Thompson (1968), in the latter half of the nineteenth century we can witness the making of a working-class childhood. It is to this process we now turn.

Activity 13.2

What was your childhood like? Did it match the ideal we are supposed to live through?

13.3 The state and the construction of working-class childhood

For much of the nineteenth century childhood was considered to be a brief, relatively unimportant stage of life. For the most part, children were treated as little adults and exposed to the responsibilities and demands of adulthood at a very early age. As the following analysis of the state's changing response to both juvenile delinquency and child labour will illustrate, childhood simply did not exist for the vast majority of children, and it was not until the latter third of the nineteenth century that state legislation began to recognize their 'special' and distinct physical, social, and psychological needs.

The state and the treatment of child offenders in the nineteenth century

At the beginning of the nineteenth century, Britain's legal system granted few concessions to age and, invariably, the full range and force of criminal sanctions were applied to adults and children equally. In the case of child offenders aged over 14 there was no question of leniency; they were simply deemed to be able to discern between good and evil and faced the same forms of trial and punishment as adults. Those aged between 7 and 14 were, theoretically, held to be in doli incapax. That is, they were presumed innocent unless strong evidence of 'mischievous discretion' could be proven (May, 1973: 9). However, proof that children had acted with malicious intent was frequently forthcoming and in such cases their behaviour was seen to be the result of a conscious devotion to vicious habits. Thus, it was felt that child offenders needed to be held wholly accountable for the consequences of their actions. As one judge explained after condemning a 10-year-old boy to death for stealing letters at Chelmsford Post Office, there was a need to avoid the 'infinite danger' of it 'going abroad into the world that a child might commit . . . a crime with impunity, when it was clear that he knew what he was doing' (quoted in Hammond and Hammond, 1917: 13).

Children could be – and on frequent occasions were – sentenced to death for what were, even by contemporary standards, relatively minor offences. For example, at the Old Bailey, in 1814, on one day alone, five children under 14 were condemned to death after being found guilty of theft and burglary (Pinchbeck and Hewitt, 1973: 352). In all, 103 children under 14 received capital sentences at the Old Bailey between 1801–36. Nor were children spared other forms of adult punishment. For instance, between 1812–17, 780 males and 136 females under the age of 21 were transported to Australia (May, 1973: 9). The following extract, taken from the Registers of Stafford Prison for 1834, provides an illustration of the sort of crimes that were deemed to warrant such a penalty:

William Biglen: Aged 14, for stealing one silk handkerchief – sentenced to transportation for seven years . . . Matilda Seymour: Aged 10, for stealing one shawl and one petticoat – sentenced to transportation for seven years . . . Thomas Bell: Aged 11, for stealing two silk handkerchiefs – also sentenced to transportation for seven years. (Pinchbeck and Hewitt ,1973: 352)

Transportation was often portrayed by its advocates as a reformative punishment for children, because, it was argued, it extracted them from their immoral surroundings, and gave them a new start in life. However, the regimes that greeted juveniles dispatched to the colonies stood in stark contrast to these claims. Child convicts were seen primarily by their guardians or masters as an economic resource and the apprenticeships into which they were bound constituted little more than a system of convict slave labour. Children were compelled to undertake hard, physical work for little or no reward, and at the same time were forced to endure savage disciplinary regimes where floggings and other forms of physical (and sexual) abuse were administered routinely. Of course, the severity of the experience of transportation was not entirely incidental. On the contrary, ill treatment was tolerated, and even encouraged, in order to appease contemporaries such as Lord Ellenborough (Chief Justice of the King's Bench), who were concerned that the prospect of 'a summer's excursion, in an easy migration, to a happier and better climate' might act as an inducement for juveniles and others to commit crime (Radzinowicz and Hood, 1986: 474).

In Britain, prior to the introduction of the first penal institution for juveniles, offenders of all ages and types were herded together, detained, and subjected to the same forms of restraint and discipline. The establishment of a specialist boys prison at Parkhurst in 1838, did little to mitigate the fate awaiting juvenile offenders. The authorities, influenced by the Poor Law principle of less eligibility, feared that humane and reformative conditions would place a premium on the commission of crime, and encourage parents to succumb to the temptation to allow their children to be supported, educated, and reformed at the public's expense. The Parkhurst regime was shaped by a determination to ensure that the position of the juvenile offender was not made 'more eligible' than that of the honest law-abiding child. Thus, boys were forced to wear manacles, the diet provided to inmates was sparse, and a code of silence was enforced.

It was not until the 1850s that the state came under sustained pressure to alter the way it treated juvenile offenders. Foremost among those campaigning for change was the social reformer, Mary Carpenter. Her 1853 book, *Juvenile Delinquents: Their Conditions and Treatment* (cited in Carpenter, 1995), attacked the regime at Parkhurst boys prison, accusing it of attempting 'to fashion children into machines through iron discipline, instead of self-acting human beings'. She called for the introduction of educational, 'home-like' reformatory schools, the principal aim of which would not be to punish, but to restore the child offender to its 'true position of childhood' (quoted in Muncie, 1984: 36). Within a year after the publication of Carpenter's book, the Youthful Offenders Act (1854) empowered judges and magistrates to sentence offenders under 16 to separate voluntary run juvenile reformatory schools. This went some way towards acknowledging that child offenders had specific mental and physical needs, and should not necessarily be dealt with in the same manner as adult prisoners. However, the architects of the 1854 Act, and those subsequently responsible for implementing its provisions, were as concerned to preserve elements of control, deterrence and less eligibility as they were with child welfare considerations.

Once in reformatory schools, children found the conditions uniformly harsh and strict. School managers adhered unswervingly to the Reverend Sydney Turner's suggestion that the daily regime should consist of exposure to weather and cold, a diet that was studiously plain, and a system of 'manly training in obedience, regularity, industry and self-control' (cited in Weiner, 1994: 138). The hard, gruelling labour children were required to perform in the schools could rarely be regarded in any sense as training, and in most cases was determined by the economic exigencies of the institutions and the desire of their managers to make a profit. Indeed, in many cases economically productive children were detained longer than necessary because they were seen by those responsible for the institutions as a positive asset (Muncie, 1984: 39).

By the 1880s, leading politicians began to express disillusionment over the severity and effectiveness of the punishments meted out to young offenders. For instance, in 1884, the Liberal Home Secretary, Vernon Harcourt, condemned the inappropriate detention of children in reformatory schools. The managers of these schools, he argued, regarded themselves 'as a sort of earthly providence' and thought that the more children they could 'get and keep from the parents the better' (quoted in Hurt, 1984: 55). In a surprisingly frank private letter to a colleague, he acknowledged the profoundly unjust – and class bias – nature of the juvenile justice system over which he presided:

> Many if not most of the cases in these schools are now those of children who for some petty act of naughtiness (such our own children commit every day) are seized upon, hauled off by the Police before the Magistrate, who without inquiry into the character of the home of the parents commits them to Prison and takes them away from good or happy homes for seven or eight years. (cited in Weiner, 1994: 290)

In the years following Harcourt's criticisms, a number of reforms were introduced, the effect of which was to gradually set in motion a process of differentiation between the treatment of child and adult offenders. The Liberal government finally established the principle that juvenile offenders should be tried and punished separately from adults in 1908, when its Children Act set up a system of specialist juvenile courts and abolished the imprisonment of children under the age of 14. Herbert Samuel, the minister who introduced the children bill into Parliament, insisted the courts 'should be agencies for the rescue as well as the punishment of children', and child offenders 'should receive at the hands of the law a treatment differentiated to suit his special needs' (Hansard, Vol. 183, c. 1436).

What concerns motivated those responsible for initiating reform of the juvenile justice system at the turn of the nineteenth century? Herbert Samuel claimed that its provisions were 'saturated with the rising sprit of humanitarianism'

(Radzinowicz and Hood, 1986: 633). Some historians share this view today. For example, in their seminal analysis of the evolution of childhood, Pinchbeck and Hewitt (1973: 612) claim that the second half of the nineteenth century was characterized by 'a general awakening, a "quickening" of social ... conscience over neglect and cruelty of all kinds'. For authors such as these, then, altruism and intolerability were the master cards. This was an age when philanthropists, such as Mary Carpenter, and campaigning organizations, such as the Howard Association, discovered a 'new and barbarous world', and the Christian consciences of the general public and politicians of all political shades were touched by the excesses exposed (Roberts, 1969: 318).

In fact as Muncie (1984) argues, the trend towards treating child offenders separately and differently from their adult counterparts was influenced by far less altruistic concerns. In part, it represented an attempt to reduce the populations of expensive, notoriously overcrowded jails. More importantly, though, it reflected growing evidence that suggested that the experience of imprisonment neither deterred nor rehabilitated. On the one hand, prisons exposed children to the promiscuous, contaminating influences of hardened adult criminals. On the other, they 'scarred the young with a life-long stigma which prevented respectable, honest employment and forced children back into criminal life' (May, 1973: 12). The improvement of conditions in reformatory schools also owed less to humanitarian sentiment and more to the realization that the harsh, penal regimes found in them were inhibiting rehabilitation. However, in order to understand more fully the state's changing response to juvenile crime, it is important to acknowledge the significance of concurrent moves which were made towards the separate classification and treatment of children in other areas of social policy.

Education and child labour reform

Prior to 1870, working-class educational provision was wholly inadequate and many children received no schooling whatsoever. As late as 1861, the Newcastle Commission, which was appointed to inquire into 'what measures, if any, were required for the extension of sound and cheap elementary instruction', discovered that only one child in 7.7 attended school. Moreover, it found 'overwhelming evidence' that not more than 25 per cent of these received what could be described as a 'good education'. Despite this, the Commission concluded that the level and standard of schooling provided to children of the labouring classes was sufficient and that the chief features of the system – no central control over education, no compulsory school attendance and no direct state provision – should remain in place.

Why, in the face of overwhelming evidence of inadequate educational provision for working-class children, was so little emphasis placed upon the need to improve it? In part, the lack of concern stemmed from a widely held fear that schooling might render future generations of workers 'insolent to their superiors'. David Giddy MP in 1807, in response to the introduction of a Parliamentary bill designed to enhance educational provision for working-class children, made the following comments:

> [Giving] education to the labouring classes of the poor . . . would, in effect, be found to be prejudicial to their morals and happiness; it would teach them to despise their lot in life, instead of making them good servants in agriculture, and other laborious employments to which their rank in society had destined them; instead of teaching them subordination, it would render them factious and refractory, as was evident in the manufacturing counties; it would enable them to read seditious pamphlets, vicious books and publications against Christianity. (cited in Dyson and Lovelock, 1975: 45)

The educational needs of working-class children were, however, also deemed subordinate to the demands of the rapidly growing industrial economy. Of course, children were employed by their own families in the domestic economy prior to the industrial revolution (Hutt, 1963; Hayek, 1963). However, as E.P. Thompson (1968: 366) argues, the industrial revolution, and the factory system it spawned, did lead to a 'drastic increase in the intensity of exploitation of child labour'. Precise estimates of the numbers of children drawn into the labour market vary, but recent analyses of household budgets between 1787–1872 suggest that approximately 70 per cent of children whose fathers worked in factories were employed between 1840–72 (Horrell and Humphries, 1999). According to Thompson (1968: 384 and 370) 'the exploitation of little children, on this scale and with this intensity, was one of the most shameful events in our history'. Certainly, most historians of childhood would agree with his conclusion that the factory system 'systematized child labour, pauper and free, and exploited it with persistent brutality'. For those such as Cunningham (1995) and Walvin (1982), the comparison made by contemporaries such as Richard Oastler between the lot of the child factory worker and that of the slave on the sugar plantation was not without foundation.

It was not until the 1870s that the first serious steps were made towards protecting children from economic exploitation and expanding working-class educational provision. How can we explain the state's growing willingness to intervene to reinforce and protect childhood?

Once again, there are those who argue that reform was motivated primarily by humanitarian impulses. Governments, it is argued, were genuinely shocked and surprised at the compendium of long forgotten or overlooked inhumanities uncovered by commissions of inquiry, and once abuses were exposed, no doctrine or interest could resist the 'single trumpet cry' for reform. The 'instinctive reaction' of governments was to legislate social evils out of existence (MacDonagh, 1958: 58). However, as Cunningham (1995: 195) has argued, the introduction of compulsory schooling and the imposition of restrictions on child labour were not motivated by an altruistic desire to provide working-class children with an experience of 'childhood'. On the contrary, the state's acceptance of greater responsibility for children's health and welfare must be understood in the context of concerns over political instability and national efficiency. For instance, the passage of the 1870 Education Act just three years after the Franchise Act of 1867 was not coincidental. With the extension of the vote to one million artisans, universal education had become a political necessity: 'Education was to be the means by which the mass of the people, the "labouring poor", would be brought up to understand their identity of interest with capital' (Simon, 1965: 11). In the words of James Kay-Shuttleworth, a contemporary advocate of working-class schooling, public education would teach future workers 'sound economic opinions' and induce them 'to leave undisturbed the control of commercial enterprises in the hands of the capitalists' (cited in Simon, 1960: 356–7). The role of education was now perceived as being beneficial to maintaining social order – rather than a threat to it as David Geddy feared in 1807.

Prevailing fears about Britain's relative economic performance and military standing were also significant in encouraging the state to intervene more directly to protect 'childhood'. From the 1870s onwards, Britain was finding it increasingly difficult to maintain its traditional economic and military supremacy, and the period marked a decisive shift in the European balance of power. Contemporaries witnessed the 'sudden transformation of the leading and most dynamic industrial economy into the most sluggish and conservative in the short space of thirty or forty years' (Hobsbawm, 1969: 178). The emergence of a broad based national efficiency 'movement', which placed great emphasis on the need to reconstruct the nation's economy and to 'regenerate' the 'race', was one response to the growing awareness of economic decline (Searle, 1971). Those involved in this 'movement' insisted that if the country was to remain a world economic power then it could no longer afford to ignore the needs of its human capital. Moreover, it was argued that a laissez-faire, minimalist state was incapable of stimulating or achieving the far reaching programme of reforms necessary to restore Britain's national and international economic and military status, and that a more interventionist approach was needed. Naturally, in the battle for social and economic efficiency the treatment, health, and education of children took on a new importance. With regard to child labour, politicians of all political shades began to question the economic wisdom of allowing the educational and welfare needs of the next generation of workers to be sacrificed through premature employment, and calls were made for the imposition of similar restrictions to those adopted in other countries. Opponents of child labour reform had traditionally defended the status quo by arguing that regulation would lead to increased 'costs' and thereby expose Britain's industries to unfair competition. Now, though, advocates of reform could point to the economic 'benefits' of child labour regulation. The Conservative MP, Robson, made the following comments in defence of his Parliamentary bill, which increased the minimum age for half-time employment from 11 to 12:

> Everybody admits that the foreigner in this matter is well ahead of us. He has pre-
> ferred very deliberately to leave us without competition in the employment of child
> labour . . . I do not think that humanity has been the only motive. The statesmen of
> Germany are intensely keen on the national development of their country, and it
> would take a great deal to make German statesmen do anything which would be
> detrimental to the present commercial rivalry which prevails between them and
> England. But the fact is that they are not missing a point, but they are making a
> point when they guard the physical and intellectual development even of the poor-
> est people. (Hansard: Vol. 67, c. 923, 1/3/1899)

The disastrous experiences of the Boer War led to an even greater level of concern over the state of the nation's human capital, serving to accentuate the
latent doubts and feelings of insecurity which had already gathered pace in
the previous two decades (Hay, 1975: 31). The poor physical state of working-
class recruits led to a searching re-examination of domestic economic and
social policy. As large numbers of volunteers were rejected as physically unfit
for service, the social consequences of laissez faire individualism became
increasingly clear. Contemporaries, well aware of the political, social and
economic developments going on around them, recognized that the 'horrify-
ing . . . picture of a working-class stunted and debilitated by a century of
industrialism' could no longer be tolerated (Hobsbawm, 1969: 164). It is
within such a context that we must locate changing conceptions of childhood
at the turn of the century.

Activity 13.3

1 What role did the state play in shaping childhood?
2 What motivated the changes in the dominant attitude to childhood?

---

13. 4 'Care and control' – legislation in the twentieth century

In accounting for the state's increased willingness to assume greater responsibility for children's welfare at the turn of the twentieth century, the
discussion has so far concentrated on contemporary fears over Britain's social
and economic efficiency. However, a desire on the part of the state to exert
greater control over the behaviour of working-class children and their families shaped, and has continued to shape, the state's regulation of childhood.
Despite frequent allusions to 'children's rights', the notion that 'deviant',
poorly socialized working-class youths posed a threat to public order, and
needed to be subjected to strict, coercive methods of control, remained an

important influence on both juvenile justice and child labour policy right throughout the twentieth century.

In some respects, the failure of a number of commentators on twentieth-century social policy to acknowledge the influence of social control concerns on child-related legislation is understandable. Punitive policies have frequently been introduced alongside 'progressive' measures, and when this has occurred, the rhetorical emphasis politicians have placed on 'positive', 'caring' proposals has had the effect of 'cloaking' retributive policies in a discourse of liberal reform (Muncie, 1990b). It is perhaps for this reason that Pinchbeck and Hewitt's suggestion, that the twentieth century heralded the emergence of 'more generous and liberal provisions for children in all walks of life', has rarely been challenged in 'mainstream' social policy texts. Such interpretations of history have, however, not remained entirely uncontested. Muncie (1998: 178), for example, has drawn attention to the extent to which social control concerns influenced the shape of child related legislation introduced during the first two decades of the twentieth century. He points out that the 1908 Children Act removed a child's right to trial by jury and to legal representation. He also highlights the fact that it empowered the courts and the state to act upon not only the delinquent, but also the 'neglected' child. The legal definition of the latter category was left deliberately vague, so that it encompassed children found begging and those whose parents were deemed to be 'incapable', 'unworthy', or 'immoral'. Because the conditions constituting neglect were so broad, the Act effectively enabled the state (in the name of welfare) to intervene and control working-class family life to a much greater extent than was ever before possible.

The attention subsequently devoted to the assumed progressive effects of early twentieth-century child related legislation has also served to divert attention away from the simultaneous introduction of coercive, punitive measures. For example, the Prevention of Crime Act, passed in the same year as the 1908 Children Act, was directly influenced by social control concerns, providing, as it did, for the setting up of Borstal institutions for young offenders. Despite official claims that these were designed to foster 'training' and 'reformation', the Borstal regime was influenced primarily by a desire to deter and control 'inappropriate' modes of behaviour among working-class youths. It was based on 'stern and exact discipline' and the sentences of those committed to the institutions were indeterminate (up to a period of three years). Youthful offenders, it was argued, needed to be removed from the demoralizing influences of their families and communities for a significant period (Newburn, 1995: 130).

It is worth noting here the continued emphasis contemporary policy makers placed on what they felt were the moral causes of crime. As was the case in the nineteenth century, delinquency was seen to be the result of selfish criminal tendencies and/or immorality, bad parenting, and poor socialization within working-class families. The possibility that certain relatively minor misdemeanours – for example, the stealing of coal, food, and items of clothing – may have been necessitated and indeed justified by extreme poverty and the struggle for survival was ignored. In fact, as Humphries (1981: 153) points out, this type of offence – 'simple and minor larceny' – constituted the single most important category of juvenile crime during this period. Juvenile crime was often merely a symptom of wider structural problems such as worklessness, deprivation, and inadequate social support. However, the juvenile justice system continued to be shaped by the belief that delinquency was due primarily to contaminating, immoral surroundings and/or intrinsically egotistical anti-social behaviour.

Juvenile justice was not the only area where state social policy was shaped by a concern to regulate or negate the potentially rebellious behaviour of working-class children. For example, Cunningham (1999 and 2000) has shown how similar concerns influenced the state's response to calls for children's out-of-school work to be more tightly regulated. Until recently, it was commonly assumed that by the end of the nineteenth century children were no longer significant workers and that they had instead become consumers of education. Children, it was thought, were gradually protected from the worst rigours of employment characteristic of earlier decades, and sheltered from the burdens, worries, and responsibilities of adulthood. However, recent historical research has contested this conception of child employment. First, despite the introduction of compulsory education, it is now clear that large numbers of children continued to work excessively, to the detriment of their education and health, right throughout the twentieth century (Lavalette, 1994 and 1999; Cunningham 1999 and 2000). Secondly, and more importantly for our purposes here, research has highlighted the fact that child labour policy was a contested terrain, and that state officials deliberately sought to frustrate and block reform. In short, the Home Office, the government department responsible for children's employment (and, crucially, combating crime and delinquency) viewed it as a 'functional' activity – as an effective means of disciplining working-class youths and keeping them 'out of mischief'. The following comments, taken from a 1924 Home Office memorandum on child labour, highlight the continuing influence of a 'public order conception' of child labour well into the twentieth century:

> It is urged that in the absence of other occupation, street-trading at least finds youth something to do . . . Boys so occupied are at least removed from the temptations to mischief arising out of sheer idleness . . . Further, it is represented that the physical benefit derived from running long distances in the distribution of newspapers must be considerable and must produce such a state of fatigue as to leave little energy for the prosecution of undesirable forms of recreation. (Home Office, 1924, cited in Cunningham, 2000: 184)

There can, then, be little doubt that social control considerations were a significant influence on early twentieth-century child related social policy. To what extent, though, did such concerns continue to influence policy as the century progressed? The immediate post Second World War period is often seen as marking a watershed, in that it is said to have heralded a further movement towards an explicitly welfare orientated approach on the part of the state towards children. Pinchbeck and Hewitt (1973) point out that the 1944 Education Act raised the school leaving age from 14 to 15 and established the principle of secondary education for all. They also draw attention to the introduction of family allowances and the 1948 Children Act, which provided for the setting up of specialist local authority children's departments. Certainly, the rhetoric that surrounded the introduction of these policies was uniformly positive and 'reformist'. More recently, however, social policy historians and theorists have drawn attention to the gap between the progressive rhetoric that accompanied these measures and their failure to deliver the promised 'new Jerusalem' for children. For example, the view that the tripartite structure of the 1944 Education Act was designed as a springboard for future advances in equality of opportunity in education has been challenged. As the failings of the Act became ever more evident, critics drew attention to its role in maintaining and reinforcing, rather than reducing, prewar social inequalities (Simon, 1986; Thom, 1986). With regard to the impact of family allowances, it is now clear that they too failed to achieve their aim – a significant reduction in the incidence of child poverty.

As was the case at the beginning of the twentieth century, the emphasis that was placed on the 'reformist' motives underpinning postwar child related reforms also served to disguise the simultaneous introduction of measures designed to control and regulate the behaviour of working-class children more stringently. For example, whilst most mainstream social policy texts applaud the introduction of the 1945–51 Labour government's care orientated 1948 Children Act, its Criminal Justices Act that was passed in the same year is rarely mentioned. Influenced by the perceived success of the glass house during wartime, this latter measure allowed courts to sentence children aged 14 and above to a 'short, sharp punishment' in purpose-built detention centres (Muncie, 1990a: 53). Despite being presented as experimental, and as a humane alternative to prison, the detention centres that eventually emerged proved to be neither temporary nor reformative. In fact, the 'experiment' lasted some 40 years, and, throughout this period, its rehabilitative record was extremely poor. For instance, a 1959 study found that 45 per cent of junior inmates (14–16) and 56 per cent of seniors (17–21) offended within two years of leaving. Despite this, the 1961 Criminal Justice Act paved the way for an expansion of the system. The number of children and young persons detained subsequently increased from 2,000 at the end of the 1950s to 6,000 by the mid-1960s. By 1974, when over 10,000 passed through detention centres, the futility of the experiment – vividly illustrated by a 73 per cent reconviction rate for junior inmates – was clearly evident to criminal justice professionals. However, failure was not allowed to stand in the way of what was proving to be a populist political initiative. Indeed, a series of largely unjustified moral panics about juvenile delinquency, mugging, and football hooliganism in the late 1970s, served to reinforce the arguments of those calling for juvenile miscreants to be subjected to harsher, more retributive modes of punishment. What followed, argues Muncie (1990a: 60), was 'a new onslaught on the rehabilitative ideal and a shift towards an ideology based on punishment and an obsession with vindictiveness'. In October 1979, William Whitelaw, the newly appointed Conservative Home Secretary, announced that the detention centre experiment would be extended and that its regime would be tightened still further:

> [Life] . . . will be conducted at a brisk tempo. Much greater emphasis will be put on hard and constructive activities, on discipline and tidiness, on self-respect and respect for those in authority . . . These will be no holiday camps and those who attend them will not ever want to go back. (cited in Muncie, 1990a: 60)

How successful was this new, tougher regime? In 1984 government sponsored research found that it 'had no discernable effect on the rate at which trainees were reconvicted'. Even the right-wing Conservative group, the Monday Club, dismissed the policy as 'gimmickery', arguing that little could be achieved with young offenders 'by shouting at them, giving them meaningless tasks and trying to make them feel as humiliated, isolated and worthless as possible'. However, it was perhaps the human consequences of the new, 'tougher' approach that were most disturbing. Records show that there were 175 known cases of deliberate self-injury between 1979 and April 1988 and at least two suicides in detention centres. Faced with opposition from the Prison Reform Trust, the Prison Officers Association, NACRO and the Howard League, detention centres were formally abolished in 1988, and thereafter the numbers of children given custodial sentences fell significantly (Muncie, 1990a: 63–4 and Muncie and McLaughlin, 1993: 176). However, as in the late nineteenth century, the gradual movement away from a retributive approach was not driven by altruism or humanitarian sentiment. Rather, it represented a long overdue acknowledgement of the failure of custodial sentences to rehabilitate young offenders (in 1989, the Children's Society calculated that 84 per cent of those sent into youth custody reoffended within two years). The shift was also influenced by concerns over the costs of juvenile detention. For instance, studies showed that a three-week custodial sentence was more expensive than a year of supervision or community service (Muncie, 1998: 196 and 197). To a government as ideologically committed to cutting public expenditure as Margaret Thatcher's neo-liberal administration (see Chapter 3), the fiscal attraction of a shift to non-custodial modes of dealing with child offenders must have been considerable.

At the same time, though, it is important to acknowledge that the late 1980s was a period when children's rights were being placed firmly at the forefront of the national and international political agenda. On the domestic front, the Conservative government passed a Children Act in 1989, which, it claimed, extended children's rights in a number of areas. In the international sphere, the United Nations (UN) adopted a Convention on the Rights of the Child in 1989, and, subject to certain reservations it was ratified by Britain in 1991. For many academics, child welfare organizations and childcare professionals the British Conservative government's apparent willingness to acknowledge certain basic minimum rights for children was a welcome, but long overdue development. It was hoped that the 1990s would see a new settlement for children, not just in relation to juvenile justice, but also in welfare provision generally.

13.5 Children's rights

Over the last 20 years there has been increasing regard for children's right's within society in general and welfare institutions in particular. Within academia, the focus on rights has had the effect of moving the debate towards a position where children, as social actors, are treated seriously as subjects shaping their own lives, rather than passive objects to be studied by adults. It has also pushed practitioners in legal, welfare, and educational settings to address the issue of children's participation and empowerment in institutional processes that affect them (Cloke and Davies, 1995). At the level of political debate there is no doubt that the turn towards rights has been a positive step motivated by a 'progressive politics of inclusion'. In this regard, it is surely appropriate that children's wishes are recognized in a range of legal and welfare situations where traditionally they had been unheard. The demand for children's rights in a range of institutional settings (children's homes, schools, within the criminal justice system, and so on) is a clear acknowledgement that they, as much as any 'expert' carer or educator, have opinions about how the institution should be run and should have the opportunity to make significant choices over these issues.

However, the extent to which any of these demands have actually been met (or is even being considered beyond academic and activist circles) is open to question. In this regard the claim for rights is an agenda. That is, it is a series of political demands that challenge orthodox prescriptions regarding child-rearing and dominant perceptions of children and their abilities; it is a critique of the social roles ascribed to children by the dominant paradigm of childhood. In its place it puts forward a reform platform aimed at prioritizing children's needs and promoting the idea that children are a group whose voice should be heard and their opinions taken seriously.

Yet, the 'rights' agenda represents a far from homogeneous or unified politics. The demand for rights has been utilized in a number of different ways with a variety of implications, which can often be contradictory in application. Within what Franklin and Franklin (1996) term the 'children's rights movement', the discussion of rights reflects the input of a number of different perspectives for change. First, the focus on rights has been given great impetus by the increased interest in this issue within the international political community over the last 20 years or so. The International Year of the Child was held in 1979 and, on the initiative of the Polish government in that year, a UN Convention on the Rights of the Child was proposed and eventually adopted by the UN General Assembly in 1989. The British government ratified the Convention in December 1991 (with three reservations). The Convention sets out basic values regarding the treatment, protection, and participation of children within society and makes a claim for equality for children (between all children and with adults) combined with a recognition 'that childhood is valuable in itself' (Hammarberg, 1995: ix). The Convention, therefore, embodies claims for a mixture of protective, welfare, moral, and liberty rights and, according to Franklin and Franklin, it has become 'akin to a manifesto for the Children's Rights Movement' (1996: 102), encapsulating the three ps of children's rights: provision, protection and participation. They go on to claim that the Convention's 54 articles provide: 'a wide range of rights entitlements including the most basic rights to life, the right to adequate health care, food, clean water, shelter, rights to protection against sexual abuse, neglect and exploitation, rights to education, privacy and freedom of association and thought' (1996: 102). Clearly this list covers issues that, as a minimum, should be freely available to the world's children, but the question is surely how are these admirable demands to be met or fulfilled?

There are several issues worth considering in this regard. First the Convention embodies certain assumptions about meeting children's rights. It aims to balance and promote the 'best interests of the child' within existing institutions but, by so doing, makes de facto assumptions about the best location for child rearing and protection (for example, within families), about both appropriate and inappropriate activities for children to undertake (for example, education as opposed to labour) and encapsulates a demand that children should have the right to a protected childhood. The variety of rights promoted in this way often pull in different directions with, for example, the commitment to liberty and equality for children often clashing with protectionist concerns of (adult) professionals and state officials seeking to pursue children's best interests.

Second, the Convention requires states to become the agents of progressive social legislation and change. Yet states are not neutral entities pursuing the best interests of all their citizens. Rather states exist, operate, and organize within particular socio-economic structures and formations and pursue interests and objectives aimed at maintaining social relations and optimizing the economic priorities of capitalism. Of course, sometimes, for a variety of reasons and in certain situations, this may include a reform agenda but the major priorities of states are always broadly socio-economic ones. Further, as was noted above, the state in Britain was central to the promotion of a restricting, oppressive childhood for working-class children in the late nineteenth century, a process that had more to do with maintaining existing social relations and structuring working-class family life than it had with promoting child welfare.

Third, as Guy Standing has noted, we should be wary of Conventions and international proclamations which become mere idealized 'social policy blue-prints'. Standing is particularly critical of the tendency among some social scientists: 'to analyse "policies" and make liberal policy presentations whilst ignoring the social context into which these policies are supposedly addressed' (1982: 611). Policy prescriptions, in other words, which avoid the difficult issues of how Articles should be operationalized in class divided societies located within the international capitalist system. For example the Convention on the Rights of the Child has been signed by many countries who are at present subject to stabilization and structural adjustment pro-grammes (SSAPs) orchestrated by the major international financial institutions, the World Bank and the International Monetary Fund. SSAPs require, as a matter of course, governments to cut public expenditure, in effect to cut education and welfare programmes, to reflect the economic pri-orities of the neo-liberal paradigm dominant within international finance institutions. But by following the SSAPs these states undermine their ability to fulfil both the letter and spirit of the Convention, emphasizing once again that the economic priorities of competing within the international capitalist system undermine and deprioritize the goals of social reform. But it is not just in countries facing SSAPs that the Convention comes up against entrenched and institutionalized interests. The US government despite being heavily involved in framing the Convention has refused to sign, while the British gov-ernment has been heavily criticized by the UN Committee for not implementing the Articles of the Convention within its policy portfolio. Further, as Lansdown notes, in Britain the legal changes that have started for-mally to take place since the Convention was signed have 'in reality . . . had little impact on children's status in society' (1995: 21). This issue will be addressed further in the next section.

However, the issue of 'rights' has not simply been framed in terms of the possibilities and limits contained within the Convention. For some writers (for example, Holt 1974; Franklin 1986, 1995) the recognition that modern childhood is a social construct which devalues children as social, political, and economic actors and ascribes an inferior status on to their actions, activi-ties, and abilities, has meant that the banner of children's rights has been raised to counter all manifestations of their oppression. As Franklin argues childhood is a 'cocoon [which] can stifle and oppress as well as comfort' (1995: 7). The radical rights of children are proclaimed as a liberating mechanism – to free children from childhood and obtain equal citizenship rights with adults. Within this paradigm the liberation of children from childhood includes demands that children, of whatever age, should be free to make all relevant decisions about their lives normally enjoyed by adults. For Holt (1974), this includes the right to vote, work, and own property; in essence, full modern cit-izenship rights should be made available to the socially excluded child.

At this level, radical rights represent a philosophical commitment to, and mechanism to achieve, child liberation. However, there are problems with this. First, as noted above, it ignores the nature of the state (the vehicle to deliver 'rights') within capitalist societies: the state is not a neutral entity, something which exists in a vacuum, free from the divisions that wrack society. Rather it embodies and reflects the priorities of society as a whole and reinforces and re-creates the divisions that exist in society. Second, rights discourse, in effect, treats abstract individuals as the key political constituent, but by so doing, the full range of social divisions are either ignored or underestimated. Thus, the right to own property and dispose of it as one wishes, which Holt (1974) demands for children, is, in reality, not a right that will affect the vast majority of children. Third, as has been shown by studies of the municipal, equal opportunities and rights-based feminist and anti-racist movements within local government and various state institutions, the adoption of legally enshrined rights and policies does not automatically lead to changes in social practices (Penketh, 1998, 2000; Bruegel and Kean, 1995). The oppression of women, black people, and children, for example, is embedded within the structure of modern capitalist social relations and the mere provision of formal rights to these groups will not in itself overcome that position.

More particularly, an abstract, essentialist commitment to rights is vulnerable to 'counter claims' (for example, the right for children to be liberated from restrictive sexual codes of conduct and the right of paedophiles to have sex with children) and ignores the context into which rights, once obtained, will be operationalized (for example, the right of children to work cannot be separated from the right of employers to exploit children as a cheap source of labour power). This is not to dismiss claims for 'rights' but to argue that we must be aware of the context of the demand and its consequences. Thus whether rights are advocated should not be an abstract principle but a contingent, specific political question dealt with in particular contextual settings.

Finally, for rights advocates there is a question of how they should be obtained. Ironically, for liberationists committed to the perspective that children are active social agents capable of shaping and reforming their world, there is an apparent consensus that adult legislators will secure children's rights and adult advocates will undertake ombudsman's work (Franklin, 1995). Such a conclusion reflects a contradiction, that children's access to liberal democratic citizenship rights are being advocated within societies which historically have constructed childhoods which oppress children and restrict their rights.

Activity 13.4

1 Should children ever be smacked?
2 What rights should adults have but children be denied?
3 Who, and what mechanisms, should police children's rights?

13.6 The 'children's rights' backlash?

At the close of the 1980s it appeared that children's rights had been placed firmly at the forefront of the political agenda. With the passage of the Children Act in 1989 and the subsequent adoption of the UN Convention on the Rights of the Child, it seemed possible that Britain's Conservative government might be prepared to pay more than lip service to demands that children should be protected from harm, and that legislation would be introduced to protect their development and wellbeing. At a rhetorical level, the political climate certainly appeared to have changed.

It did seem that in one area at least – juvenile justice – a new welfarist approach was subsequently pursued. As Rutherford (1999: 47) notes, the futility of retributive forms of punishment for child and young offenders was increasingly acknowledged, and 'concerted efforts were made at the level of both policy and practice to fashion an approach to youth justice that was rational, reflective and humane'. Consequently, much greater use was made of 'diversionary' measures such as informal warnings and cautions, and the result was a dramatic fall in the number of children and young persons given custodial sentences – between 1983–92 the number of males aged 14–18 sentenced to immediate custody declined from 13,500 to 3,300 (Goldson, 2000). This new approach seemed to have much in common with the children's rights agenda. However, that the government was less committed to the extension of children's rights than its rhetoric implied soon became evident. First, within the space of no more than two years the Conservative government had dismantled most of the progressive juvenile justice reforms it had implemented. Secondly, its record of extending children's rights to other areas – most notably, in the words of Article 27 of the UN Convention, to 'the right of every child to a standard of living adequate for the child's physical, mental, spiritual, moral and social development' – was, as will be shown below, woefully inadequate (UN, 1989).

The volte face on juvenile justice policy occurred between 1992–3, after a series of high profile crimes involving children led to a ferocious backlash against rehabilitative methods of dealing with young offenders. Paradoxically, the blame for the apparent breakdown in youth discipline and morality was placed on the diversionary strategies of the 1980s and early 1990s that had, in fact, been extremely successful in curbing juvenile crime – between 1983–94, the period when children were increasingly diverted away from custodial sentences, the numbers of young people aged 17 or under convicted or cautioned declined by 34 per cent (Muncie, 1998: 195 and 206). However, influential right-wing commentators such as Charles Murray (1994) continued to insist that the cause of the apparent upsurge in juvenile crime lay in the 'coddling' of habitual young criminals. In the moral panic that ensued, the achievements of the welfarist approach were ignored, and politicians and lurid media coverage portrayed informal warnings and cautioning as unacceptably lenient means of dealing with 'yobs' (Goldson, 2000: 36). This, in turn, led to pressure for harsher sentences to be imposed on juvenile miscreants. Some, such as Lord Justice Woolf, sought to draw attention to the emphatic failure of custodial sentences to rehabilitate. However, encouraged by sensational populist journalism, right-wing elements in his own party, and an opposition Labour Party seeking to make political capital out of the emergence of a 'yob culture', Kenneth Clark, the Conservative Home Secretary, announced his intention to introduce new powers to lock-up 'really persistent nasty little juveniles' (Moore, 2000: 116).

The 1994 Criminal Justice and Public Order Act, with its creation of new, harsher penalties for child offenders, represented the pinnacle of this policy reversal. As Bandalli (2000: 81) argues, it 'systematically eroded much of the "special status" of childhood in criminal law and produced a matrix of provisions to facilitate and increase the criminalization of children'. Consequently, the number of young offenders under 21 in prison increased by 30 per cent between June 1993 and June 1996 (Moore, 2000: 118). As for the conditions found in the institutions in which children were detained, the government's own Chief Inspector of Prisons, Sir David Ramsbotham, was appalled at what he discovered in 1997. It seemed to him that the 'majority of establishments holding children and young adults' were operating 'as human warehouses rather than reforming institutions', and that 'criminal attitudes, rather than being challenged', were 'in too many cases being reinforced'. He concluded that the conditions were 'in many cases . . . far below the minimum conditions . . . required by the Children Act 1989 and the UN Convention on the Rights of the Child'. Once again, it was the human consequences of the denial of basic fundamental rights that were most disturbing – between 1994–7 there were 41 suicides and 4,112 reported cases of self harm among young inmates (Home Office, 1997a).

Clearly, the acknowledgement of children's 'rights' in the juvenile justice arena proved to be a temporary, short-lived experiment. Was the Conservative government's record on promoting children's rights in other areas of policy any better? In fact, as Micklewright and Stewart (2000: 23) argue, by the mid-1990s the UK was 'a serious contender for the title of worst place in Europe to be a child'. Between 1979–93 the percentage of UK children living in poverty rose from 10 per cent to 32 per cent, a level higher than that found in any other country in the European Union. In fact, in the final years of John Major's Conservative government, levels of child poverty in the UK rose still further, reaching 35 per cent in 1997–8 (DSS, 2000: 87). Nor was the UK's record on other key child related indicators any better. For instance, by the end of the Conservatives' final term in office more children in the UK were living in households without a working adult than in any other European country – 19.5 per cent compared with a European average of 10.5 per cent. Furthermore, these households were forced to rely on a residualized social security system, which, as the TUC (1998) noted, now offered the lowest levels of unemployment benefit out of all OECD countries. In short, in the light of Micklewright and Stewart's detailed findings on the relative wellbeing of British children (see the Table 13.1 below), it is difficult to disagree with their conclusion, that successive Conservative governments in the 1980s and 1990s emphatically failed to promote children's rights.

Table 13.1   Indicators of child wellbeing in the European Union

	Children (0–15) in households with below half the national average income (%) 1993	Households with children (0–14) without working adult (%) 1996	Enrolment of 16-year-olds in education (%) 1994
Austria	–	4.9	90
Belgium	15	11	100
Denmark	5	–	92
Finland	–	11.8	92
France	12	8.8	92
Germany	13	8.6	96
Greece	19	4.5	79
Ireland	28	15.4	91
Italy	24	7.6	–
Luxemburg	23	3.8	77
Netherlands	16	9.3	89
Portugal	27	3.3	78
Spain	25	10.1	89
Sweden	–	–	95
UK	32	19.5	82
EU	20	10.5	90

(*Source*: Micklewright and Stewart, 2000: 19)

The failure to advance the material wellbeing of children in the UK in the 1980s and 1990s serves to reinforce the points made earlier about the problematic nature of social policy blueprints, such as the 1989 UN Convention, that proclaim children's right's, whilst ignoring the political and economic context within which they are supposedly to be implemented. As Chapter 3 showed, between 1979–97 successive Conservative governments in the UK sought to impose a neo-liberal project that aimed to break with the postwar welfare settlement and 'to transfer the balance of economic, social and political power decisively in favour of capital and its allies' (Jones and Novak, 1999: 133). Clearly, the dismantling of rights and entitlements to social provision that this project entailed was not conducive to the welfare of the millions of children whose living standards depended on the availability of a reasonable level of state support. To a large extent, the Labour Party's May 1997 General Election victory represented a rejection of the neo-liberal ideas and philosophies that had, in the words of Robin Cook, then a senior shadow minister, created a society in which 'so many children begin their lives in families excluded from the stimulus, the security, the pleasures of life that the rest of society takes for granted' (Shrimsley, 1996). To what extent, though, did May 1997 represent the beginning of a new, more progressive agenda for children?

13.7 New Labour: a new agenda for children?

As Robin Cook's comments illustrate, the Labour Party condemned the detrimental impact of Conservative policies on the nation's children during its period in opposition. Hence, those interested in child welfare welcomed the landslide general election victory of New Labour in May 1997, and looked forward to the adoption of a more constructive approach in relation to both juvenile justice and child welfare generally.

With regard to juvenile justice, whilst some commentators had become alarmed at the tone of the law and order rhetoric emanating from Labour in opposition, it was hoped that the new government would distance itself from custodial methods of dealing with juvenile offenders (Moore, 2000: 121). Certainly, during the passage of the 1994 Criminal Justice and Public Order Bill, Tony Blair, then Shadow Home Secretary, criticized Conservative ministers for their uncritical embrace of the 'prison works' slogan, describing it as 'a sham'. Blair also differed from his Conservative counterpart, Michael Howard, in that he sought to draw attention to social rather than the moral causes of juvenile crime:

> Let us be clear. No one . . . but a Tory would deny the influence that . . . social conditions can have on the way in which our young people develop. That is why we need to remedy not just the faults of the criminal justice system but the culture of despair, hopelessness, drugs, violence, instability, poor education and poor job prospects that characterize elements of our young people today. To achieve that, we do not need or want lectures from Ministers on the responsibilities of everyone else but themselves. (Hansard, 11/1/94, c. 41)

However, in government New Labour has pursued a similar agenda to that of its Conservative predecessors. No longer does it seek to link juvenile crime to structural inequality. Indeed, academics, criminal justice groups, and child welfare organizations that do seek to establish such a connection are now accused by the government of promoting a culture that 'too often excuses the young offender . . . implying that they cannot help their behaviour because of their social circumstances' (Home Office, 1997b: 2). Instead, Labour's juvenile justice policy is driven by a 'new moralism', which locates the blame for offending in intrinsically egotistical anti-social behaviour and bad parenting (Lavalette and Mooney, 1999). The solution, therefore, lies not in the eradication of structural inequalities, but in the introduction of coercive social control mechanisms to deter criminal behaviour and reinforce parental responsibility. Hence, in the name of deterrence, child offenders continue to face imprisonment 'despite the fact that the treatment they will receive is likely to harm them further and compound their problems' (Moore, 2000: 125). In addition, a new penalty, the parenting order, has been introduced to reinforce parental responsibility. Thus, parents can now be forced by the courts to attend counselling or guidance sessions; they can be required to see that their children get to school every day, and to ensure that they are home by a certain time at night (Home Office, 1997b). However, as Drakeford and McCarthy, (2000: 102) note, what both these solutions conveniently mask is the extent to which juvenile crime and ineffective parenting are themselves merely 'a symptom of more fundamental problems and pressures, including poverty, social exclusion and structural inequality'. Working-class parents and their children have, according to Drakeford and McCarthy, become convenient political scapegoats, and the government's own responsibility for ensuring families have access to adequate housing, worthwhile educational provision, and a decent income have been sidestepped. From this perspective, the solution to juvenile crime lies not in the harassment and stigmatization of those already living on the margins of society, but in the eradication of the deep structural inequality generated by two decades of neo-liberal government.

New Labour, though, has shown little enthusiasm for the sort of redistributive policies that will be needed to reverse the structural inequality it has inherited. Indeed, as with juvenile crime, poverty is invariably portrayed as an individual, behavioural problem rather than a structural one, and policy is therefore focused on creating a more coercive, rather than a more generous social welfare system. Consequently, inequality remains as firmly entrenched today as it did when New Labour entered government in May 1997. Indeed, the gap between rich and poor widened during Labour's first two years of power, reaching its highest level since 1990 (White, 2000). During the same two years, the number of children living in poverty rose to 3.4 million, an increase of 100,000 (Elliot et. al., 2000). In the light of more recent findings, which show that two million British children are today being brought up in such poverty that they lack at least two of the items considered by most people to be basic necessities of life (for example, adequate food, clothing, or housing), we can only conclude that New Labour, like previous Conservative administrations, has failed to promote adequately children's rights and opportunities (Carvel, 2000).

13.8 Summary and conclusion

The dominant ideology of childhood portrays it as a 'walled garden', a period of life free from worries and oppression. We have shown that this conception of childhood has not always existed. Our case studies emphasize that in the spheres of juvenile justice, education, and labour the last third of the nineteenth century saw the imposition of childhood on to working-class children – the result of a variety of factors relating to Britain's economic and imperial requirements and investment in future resources for the nation.

Even today the mythical childhood stands in stark contrast to the lives of millions of children in Britain who live and are brought up in severe hardship. Yet for recent governments in Britain, solving the problem of child poverty has become secondary to their prime objective to control these children and regulate their lives. Britain remains one of the wealthiest countries in the world and one of the wealthiest in the European Union, yet, as Table 13.1 emphasized, Britain's record of dealing with children living in poverty is the worst in the EU. We can only understand Britain's woeful record by recognizing it as a direct consequence of the neo-liberal politics that have dominated Britain for the last 25 years – and which have continued under New Labour (see Chapter 10).

Notes

1 Tony Blair, *Observer* 5 September 1999.
2 Chief of Police, New York 1849 in Cunningham (1995).
3 *Daily Star* headline 25 November 1993 after two young boys were convicted of the murder of James Bulger.
4 Philanthropist Mary Carpenter writing in the 1850s in Cunningham (1995).
5 Jack Straw, quoted in *The Guardian*, 15 October 1996.

CHAPTER 14

UNIVERSALISM OR SELECTIVISM? THE PROVISION OF SERVICES IN THE MODERN WELFARE STATE

Alan Pratt

14.1 Introduction

Once the political decision is taken to remove, wholly or in part, the allocation of a limited range of commodities from the sole ambit of market operations, governments are faced with a new set of problems. If command over income is not to determine the population's access to education, heathcare, replacement income and the other goods whose distribution, in one way or another, lies at the heart of most welfare states, then what is? More specifically, what criteria do governments use? Who gets what and why?

This chapter is devoted to an examination of the concepts of universality and selectivity together with hybrids such as positive discrimination. It attempts to establish their precise meaning and their strengths and weaknesses against a range of characteristics (such as cost, effectiveness in meeting ostensible policy objectives, impact on labour market participation, stigmatization, and so on). Following this, attention is focused on the historiography of the debate since the reconstruction of the 'welfare state' in the 1940s. Since the early 1950s the debate has often been dormant (though never extinct), has sometimes been dismissed as 'the most misleading of trivial dichotomies', and as a conflict between ideological ghosts (Pinker, 1971).

That these ideas are still at the very heart of the politics of social policy was vividly demonstrated by the activities of the Commission on Social Justice set up in December 1992, almost exactly 50 years after the publication of the Beveridge Report, *Social Insurance and Allied Services*, on the initiative of the late John Smith, then Leader of the Labour Party. Whether the work contained in individual issue papers published for the Commission by the Institute for Public Policy Research (for example, Papers 1 and 2, November 1993) and in the Commission's own final report, *Social Justice: Strategies for National Renewal* (1994) is any more successful in resolving these possibly intractable questions remains to be seen, but what cannot be denied is the political controversy it generated within the Labour Party.

Thus the main aims of this chapter are:

1 to develop a clear understanding of the meaning of universalism and selectivism;
2 to examine protagonists' claims about their respective and relative merits;
3 to become familiar with changes in the academic debate; and
4 to locate these intellectual exchanges in the real world of British economics and politics since the 1940s.

14.2 Concepts and definitions

Given that these contested concepts have periodically generated intense debate and disagreement among and between their respective supporters, it is, perhaps, rather surprising that the literature does not offer many sustained or lengthy attempts to define them with any degree of precision. It may be, of course, that their meaning is so self-evident that any such attempt would be superfluous.

One approach to the problem of definition is to ignore it completely, to say that there can never be any truly universal or selective services because they are differentially used and financed (thus healthy people will not use the NHS; those with no dependent children will not receive Child Benefit; everyone pays a different amount of taxation depending on their income levels and patterns of expenditure). This approach is a little disingenuous. Child Benefit is only intended to be received by parent(s) with one or more dependent children. The real question facing government is that once having recognized the extra demands placed on family income by the presence of dependent children, what programme employing what techniques of allocation is best suited to assist the state in the execution of its accepted responsibility of helping families in the critical task of rearing the next generation? By definition, childless families will not receive any benefit designed to deliver assistance to families with dependent children. To argue that because families without dependent children do not receive Child Benefit makes this particular programme selective and not universal is bizarre and almost wilfully neglects the real practical and philosophical issues necessarily attached to questions of the allocation of scarce public resources.

Given the significance of his contribution to the development of the entire discipline of social policy we are almost compelled to go to the work of Richard Titmuss for at least the beginnings of enlightenment. Although he was often regarded as the high priest of universalism and as an unswerving critic of selectivity, Titmuss's position was in reality rather more complex, as will become apparent as this chapter unfolds. (For an excellent analysis of the development of Titmuss's work see Reisman, 1977.) For the moment, though, it is enough to consider his understanding of what the terms mean. In one of his most important collections of essays Titmuss (1976) offered a view of universalism which goes beyond a simple definition but which identifies many of the themes central to the debate. Having asserted that universalism was the principle embodied in such legislation as the 1944 Education Act, the 1946 National Insurance Act, the 1945 Family Allowances Act and the 1946 National Health Service Act, he argues that:

> One fundamental historical reason for the adoption of this principle was the aim of making services available and accessible to the whole population in such ways as would not involve users in any humiliating loss of status, dignity or self-respect. There should be no sense of inferiority, pauperism, shame or stigma in the use of a publicly provided service; no attribution that one was being or becoming a 'public burden'. Hence the emphasis on the social rights of all citizens to use or not to use as responsible people the services made available by the community in respect of certain needs which the private market and the family were unable or unwilling to provide universally. If these services were not provided for everybody by everybody they would either not be available at all, or only for those who could afford them, and for others on such terms as would involve the infliction of a sense of inferiority and stigma. (Titmuss, 1976: 129)

In contrast, selectivity, which could mean many different things to most critics of 'welfare statism', denoted an individual means test, some enquiry into resources to identify poor people who should be provided with free services or cash benefits, be excused charges, or pay lower charges (Titmuss, 1976: 115).

Perhaps one of the clearest attempts to define both universalism and selectivity can be found in a brief essay by Collard (1971) for the Child Poverty Action Group. Collard argues that the criterion of need as the basis of resource allocation should not be income but a range of relatively objective criteria such as the need for medical attention, pregnancy, having dependent children and so on. 'That is to say, there will, for any type of benefit, be a *trigger criterion* which, if satisfied, entitles a person to that benefit regardless of income' (1971: 38, emphasis in original). Selectivists had always argued that this relatively simple needs based approach represented a waste of resources and that a more efficient, more clearly targeted, method ought to be employed. Thus selectivists, 'wish to impose a double criterion for free benefits: first a trigger criterion of the objective sort that has just been mentioned and, secondly, *a low income criterion*. Only those people satisfying both criteria actually get the benefit' (Collard, 1971: 38, emphasis in original).

Davies's examination of the school meals service represents a rigorous and powerful investigation into the theory and practice of selectivity, in the course of which he necessarily tests universalists' objections to the residualist model of welfare. We will have good cause to refer to it consistently in much of what follows. Thus it might not seem unreasonable to expect Davies to have offered some definition of the terms in the way that Collard and Titmuss did. That he does not do this is perhaps a reflection of the earlier observation that the meaning of the respective allocative systems is so obvious that one need not waste valuable time in explicating one's position. He contents himself by arguing that:

> The essence of the selectivist prescription is that charging should be applied more widely as an instrument of resource allocation in social policy; but that the commodities thus allocated are judged by society to be of a 'merit' character when their recipients are those most vulnerable in markets, so that the consumption of the poor must be safeguarded by the remission of charges. Since the vulnerability of the consumer is due to poverty, it is logical that a means test should be used as the criterion of eligibility for the remission. (Davies, with Reddin, 1978: 7)

Davies's understanding of universalism, as a concept, has to be inferred from his exposition of the case that its promoters have developed over the years. Basically, it is very much the same as Collard's: universal services are available on the basis of a single, trigger criterion.

Activity 14. 1

1 How would you define universalism and selectivism?
2 Which of the following do you think the state should provide,
   (a) universally, (b) selectively, (c) not at all?
   (i) health care, (ii) child benefit, (iii) dental care, (iv) free
   public transport, (v) access to leisure facilities.

14.3 The case for selectivism

On the surface at least, the selectivist argument is both attractive and powerful. In a world whose reality is described and circumscribed by the existence of scarce resources and, in effect, unlimited demands on those resources, it would be sensible, efficient, and just to construct public policy in such a way that these scarce resources go to those people who could derive most benefit from their consumption. All that government has to do is to decide on the appropriate volume of resources available, identify those whose needs are greatest and devise service programmes and delivery systems to direct the right benefit to the right people. Common sense and compassion demand no less. In what follows immediately, this simple cameo is developed in more detail and in slightly more technical language, but the essence remains the same: it is wrong on every count to treat unequal need equally.

Arguments for selectivity have been set down in many places and on many occasions by the committed, such as Harris, with Seldon (1963, 1965) (Seldon, 1967; Seldon and Gray, 1967), but one of the most rigorous, coherent, and objective expositions of the core of these arguments can be found in Davies's (1978) analysis of the school meals service. For Davies the selectivist position rests on a number of key assumptions which need to be understood before the details of the analysis can be properly evaluated.

First the goods and services whose allocation lies at the heart of the modem welfare state, such as healthcare, income maintenance entitlements, housing, education and what in Britain are called the personal social services, are indistinguishable in character and nature from those goods and services usually distributed through market mechanisms (clothing, consumer durables, and so forth). Unlike defence and law and order, they are not truly public goods; that is, there is no free rider principle involved in their allocation and consumption and therefore their distribution through normal market procedures would be entirely appropriate. Moreover, it is probably true to say that these markets should be natural and autonomous, arising out of spontaneous association, rather than quasi-markets.

Secondly, the price mechanism within the market is fulfilling its primary task of acting as an efficient signalling device to well-informed consumers and suppliers.

Thirdly, demand is not extremely inelastic, so that if the price was at a level not reflecting the true costs of production to society of producing a commodity an inefficient allocation of resources would result.

Fourthly, consumers behave in a rational manner and make rational judgements about costs and benefits. This assumption of rationality is probably the most fundamental of all of the assumptions about human behaviour which lie at the heart of the neo-liberal project, and in this context it is interesting to note the findings of some recent research in the USA which appears to provide solid empirical evidence casting doubt on this centrepiece of neo-classical political economy (Hutton, 1995).

Fifthly, Davies offers an interesting addition to the orthodox account of selectivist philosophy when he suggests that 'at the heart of the selectivist argument lies the assumption that consumers face sets of opportunities and incentives which they will seize, in order to make the best of diverse circumstances' (1978: 9). He argues that the implication of this position is that the cultural obstacles to grasping the opportunities referred to above, including the claiming of benefit, are great for only a small minority of the target population. 'It is therefore neither necessary nor right in principle to subordinate the choice of policy instruments to the needs of those whose culture imposes such obstacles' (1978: 9). In fact, since their culture is believed to be a significant feature in their experience of poverty its modification should be a major policy objective.

Armed with these assumptions it is now possible to set down the major features of the selectivist case. Thus:

1 Charging should be used more widely as a technique of resource allocation in the arena of social provision, but once these 'services' come within

the ambit of state intervention their distribution should take on the character of 'merit' goods 'when their recipients are those most vulnerable in markets so that the consumption of the poor must be safeguarded by the remission of charges' (Davies, 1978: 7). Since the consumer is vulnerable because of poverty it is logical that entitlement to 'free' benefits or the remission of charges should be determined by the application of a means test as the eligibility criterion (the secondary criterion in Collard's definition of selectivity noted above).

2   The supply of services made available should reflect the costs to society of making them available and so provide an incentive to potential consumers to behave rationally, thus securing a more efficient allocation of scarce social resources. Charges deter; they are meant to deter.

3   Market operations provide an incentive and an environment within which suppliers have to operate efficiently. They cannot do this when allocations are made through administrative and political processes.

4   The evidence, from opinion surveys, shows that there was no general consensus in favour of universalism. One such survey claimed to show that there were almost twice as many people in favour of selective benefits as of universal benefits (Houghton, 1967).

14.4 The case for universalism

Universalists approach the question of the distribution of scarce resources from a different perspective than selectivists and use a very different set of concepts and language. Against the claims of efficiency, of cost, of market supremacy and of calculating individuals they counterpose a collectivity in which citizens and their families are often the victims of the rapid change that characterizes modern industrial societies in an increasingly integrated global economy. Economic change creates losers as well as winners, and consequently one of the central problems facing us is the question of where the costs of this progress ultimately lie. The fundamental fact was 'that for many consumers the services used are not essentially benefits or increments to welfare at all; they represent partial compensations for disservices, for social costs and social insecurities which are the product of a rapidly changing industrial-urban society' (Titmuss, 1976: 133).

It was becoming more and more difficult to identify the causal agency or agencies responsible for these diswelfares and so, impossible to seek redress through the courts. Thus we have to consider the potential of universalist and selectivist social services for meeting the problems of 'multiple causality and the diffusion of disservices'. For Titmuss the response was relatively clear: 'Non-discriminating universalist services are in part *the consequence of unidentifiable* causality. If disservices are wasteful (to use the economists' concept of waste) so welfare has to be wasteful' (1976: 133; emphasis added).

Universalists reject each of the assumptions on which the selectivists' case is based, and in so doing necessarily replace them with their own. Thus:

1   The nature of the goods at the heart of social provision is such that their distribution through market mechanisms is inappropriate. Access to, and experience of, healthcare, education, income maintenance, housing and so on is so important in determining the nature and quality of everyone's life experiences that allocation cannot be left to command over resources in markets. There is a collective responsibility and a mutual interest in attempting to ensure the guarantee of a certain level of consumption, a level determined by political and administrative judgement. The social services then are properly to be regarded as merit goods.

2   For a variety of psychological and organizational reasons, individuals' ability to claim entitlement to what for them are merit goods is more limited than generally thought. As Titmuss observed, selectivists overestimated 'the potential of the poor, without help, to understand and manipulate an increasingly ad hoc society' (Titmuss, 1976).

3   The receipt of a means-tested service could be regarded as symbolic of the clash between the social policy ethic (described by Boulding as 'that which is centred in those institutions that create integration and discourage alienation' (1967: 7) and the work ethic, a conflict which, according to Davies, means that the '"evil repute" of the means test is in some circumstances powerful, pervasive and ineradicable' (1978: 11). The receipt of a means-tested service necessarily involves a loss of self-esteem and consequently stigmatization by others 'because it creates a conflict between the work ethic and obtaining benefits which the potential claimant thinks that he (or the dependants for whom he is claiming) needs' (Davies, 1978: 11).

Social cohesion and integration demanded the provision of universal services, concerns that were imprinted on the minds of those who shaped the reconstruction of the British welfare state in the 1940s, conscious as they were of the systematic degradation represented by administrative devices such as the household means test. Trade union leadership was even willing to accept the quintessentially regressive poll tax of flat rate National Insurance contributions as the primary funding mechanism of Beveridge's income maintenance proposals if it appeared to guarantee subsistence level benefits without means testing (Pratt, 1988).

Activity 14.2

In what ways do the assumptions on which universalists and selectivists base their arguments differ? How might these differences be reconciled?

14.5 From principle to practice

Thus far our discussion has been pitched at the level of general principle. It is now time to switch to a consideration of the philosophies in action at programmatic level to see how they fare in practice. What does experience in the real world of policy implementation tell us and what can we learn from it?

Because universal services are made available through the application of a relatively objective trigger criterion (illness or unemployment, or the presence of dependent children in a family), it is not too difficult to set up administrative structures to deliver the appropriate service, be it healthcare, cash transfers, education or whatever to the relevant target population. All of the evidence suggests that take-up rates are high and administrative costs low. Consequently, opposition to universalism in social provision rests on opinions about financial costs and what is held to be the waste involved in providing services to those who allegedly do not need them. These opinions are necessarily subjective in nature and reflective of political preference and value judgement. Given this, and the fact that British social policy has become increasingly selective in nature, especially, though not exclusively, over the last 20 years, it would seem appropriate to concentrate on selectivism in action. Moreover, it should also be noted that since the foundation of the Institute of Economic Affairs in 1957 the intellectual pace has been set by selectivist theoreticians.

The main elements of a general critique of means-tested social provision have been well established for many years and include a consideration of the following: stigma, take-up rates, administrative costs, the creation of poverty traps and a poverty plateau and, finally, the impact of economic and social change. It is to each of these that we now turn.

Stigma

Stigma has been well defined as 'a loss of self-respect and personal dignity, a sense of guilt, of shame, of personal fault or failure. It means the sensation of second class citizenship that results from discrimination' (Reisman, 1977: 45). More than anyone else Titmuss believed that stigma was an inherent characteristic of selective social provision, a characteristic that provided much of the moral case for universalism. To claim means-tested benefits constituted a self-declaration of failure, of inadequacy, of poverty; it represented a demonstration that the claimant was unable to cope in a competitive market economy. Apart from the incalculable psychological damage this inflicts on people, universalists have taken it as an article of faith that the reality of stigma acts as a deterrent to the take-up of welfare entitlements. That take-up rates are low, very low in some cases, is not in doubt, but what is more problematic is the significance of stigma as a factor in this outcome. The evidence is not conclusive (Davies, 1978; Page, 1984).

Take-up rates

Means-tested benefits have always been characterized by low take-up rates. All of the evidence shows this clearly. Although the proportion of a particular target population claiming particular benefits varies, only rarely does it reach over 50 per cent of those eligible. Governments have always accepted that such benefits will never be claimed by the whole of a relevant group and have budgeted accordingly. When the Family Income Supplement (FIS) was introduced in 1971 the government only made financial provision available for an estimated take-up figure of 85 per cent and committed itself to a very elaborate take-up campaign to achieve even that figure. Take-up campaigns can be successful in raising awareness of the availability of means-tested benefits and, if advertising and other publicity campaigns are intensive and maintained over a long period of time, then take-up rates can be increased.

Such campaigns are expensive, though, and obviously add to administrative and operating costs and so cannot be maintained indefinitely. They demonstrate the prescience of Collard's observation that the marginal cost of raising the efficiency ratio will increase as efficiency rises; that is, it is relatively easy to increase the efficiency ratio from 10 per cent to 20 per cent, but very difficult to raise it from 80 per cent to 90 per cent (Collard, 1971). Governments of all parties have tried to combat this very real problem through initiatives which have sought to simplify what is a highly bureaucratic and complex process of claiming benefit entitlements. Most notable among these initiatives has been the introduction and gradual refinement of what is usually referred to as a passport system. In essence, this means that individual claimants, through applying for, and being granted, a particular benefit, automatically secure entitlement to a range of other benefits without having to undergo separate means tests. Such procedures, because they simplify the existing complex generality, do increase overall take-up rates but, ironically, in so doing they run up against what American authors refer to as the 'notch' problem. That is, as more of the potential target population are successful in claiming benefits for which entitlement is usually determined through the application of a secondary, low-income criterion, they face the possibility that as earned income increases their entitlement to benefit is extinguished.

FIS take-up rates never exceeded 50 per cent throughout its existence, and its successor as the main instrument through which the Conservative government sought to subsidize the low earnings of full-time workers with dependent children, Family Credit, was not claimed by nearly 40 per cent of those with a theoretical entitlement. The Working Families Tax Credit, which is the Blair government's replacement for Family Credit, has a higher take-up rate than both earlier versions of wage subsidization but does not approach 100 per cent. Income Support, the major source of social assistance, is still characterized by unacceptably low levels of take-up, especially by the elderly. Given that the present government is placing so much faith in the Minimum Income Guarantee (in fact a renamed Income Support for the elderly) as the best way of targeting resources on to the poorest retired households, it is difficult to have too much confidence in the success of such a strategy. As the final report of the Commission on Social Justice has noted, means-tested benefits, which cannot prevent poverty, are also remarkably inefficient at relieving it (Commission on Social Justice, 1994).

Administrative costs

Notwithstanding the simplification achieved through passport schemes, a social welfare system increasingly characterized by means-testing must mean that individuals seek entitlement to targeted benefits through making individual claims which have to be processed and evaluated as individual claims by the bureaucracy. There is no other way. Evidence from the whole range of selective services has consistently demonstrated that such benefits are inherently more expensive to administer than their universal equivalents. Whereas a leading selectivist, somewhat defensively perhaps, felt able to dismiss such fears as a minor quibble about mundane administrative costs (Seldon, 1967), Titmuss wrote in scathing terms about the extraordinary and frightening administrative naivety of such an attitude (Titmuss, 1976). The apparently simple task of identifying the most needy and of delivering appropriate levels of resources to them might not be so simple after all. Certainly means-tested benefits are expensive to administer.

Concern about the reality of administrative complexity and expense, together with low take-up rates, has led to a search for a delivery system that could target help precisely and selectively without these associated problems. This search usually focuses on the merits of some scheme of negative income tax (NIT) which would cover the entire population and be used either to raise revenue from taxation or to pay out benefits in a totally integrated taxation/benefits system. A number of such schemes have been advanced over the years and, although there are important differences of detail between them, they all involve looking at the difference between income and the tax threshold appropriate to an individual: if income is below the tax threshold a negative income tax would be used to pay an individual whatever percentage of this difference the particular version of NIT allowed for. The majority of such schemes use a 50 per cent payment figure.

Support for this technique has spanned the intellectual and political spectrum, although in general terms support is more likely to come from the right than anywhere else. Indeed, in the late 1960s and early 1970s, some version of NIT was the preferred solution of the Conservative Party to the problem of family poverty. The party's commitment went so far that in 1973 the Conservative government introduced a Green Paper containing proposals for a Tax Credit Scheme (TCS) which, although not purely a negative income tax, had many similarities. Although opposed by the Labour Party and academics such as Townsend and Atkinson, the TCS was welcomed by other left-leaning academics like David Piachaud as being the most radical statement on income maintenance since the Beveridge Report in 1942 and, significantly for our purposes, as representing the end of the selectivity – universality debate. Whatever the merits of Piachaud's claim, the TCS was killed by the incoming Labour government in February 1974, which announced in its stead a system of child benefits. Although there is some continuing residual support for NIT the weight of opinion is that its introduction would be fraught with a variety of administrative problems which would be both expensive and difficult to resolve.

Poverty traps and poverty plateaux

The concept of the rational, income-maximizing individual pursuing pleasure rather than pain is a fundamental of liberal political economy. There is, therefore, some irony to be found in the way that opponents of means testing have used this idea to undermine selective social provision further. Critics of universal benefits have pointed to the alleged disincentive characteristics of the high levels of marginal tax rates generated by the financial demands of quality universal provision, and a reduction of these marginal tax rates, especially of income tax, has been the cornerstone of economic policy since 1979.

As the distributional consequences of the welfare state became clearer, researchers began to take seriously the impact of the overlap between benefits and taxation on people at the bottom of the scale of income distribution. It was quickly demonstrated that a rise in earnings for low-paid workers could, because of increased liability to higher taxation and insurance contributions, together with loss of entitlement to income-related benefits, lead to a marginal tax rate of over 100 per cent (see Lees (1967), Field and Piachaud (1982), Bradshaw and Wakeman (1972) and Meacher (1972)). If one assumes that rational economic calculation is not the sole prerogative of the well-to-do and that high marginal tax rates do have disincentive implications for labour market behaviour, then the case for means-tested selectivity is significantly weakened. Over the years governments of both major parties have responded to this criticism by structuring the nature of means-tested benefits in ways which allow for a more gentle and drawn out 'tapering' as earned income rises. Thus, particularly as qualification periods have been extended before a new application needs to be made, loss of entitlement to benefit along with reductions in the amount of benefit are less sudden and dramatic. Consequently the disincentive implications of selectivity have been muted. Nevertheless, there will, and must always be, at least a theoretical disincentive character to selective benefits. This would be true even if we applied an 'affluence' test rather than a means test as the qualifying criterion. Given New Labour's emphasis on wage subsidization and better, more effective targeting there is a real possibility that these arrangements might lead to a significant section of the population becoming permanently dependent on means-tested welfare benefits for the whole or part of their income: their pauperization is inherent to the system.

The impact of economic and social change

Changes in family structure, the labour market and the wider economy have made means testing increasingly complex and irrelevant. Because means-tested benefits are based on an assessment of family income it is rarely worthwhile for a claimant's partner to enter or remain in the labour market. Married women's labour-market activity is especially sensitive to the benefits system (McLaughlin, 1994). Moreover, as more people live together without marrying, means testing demands increasingly complicated rules which become particularly difficult to enforce in situations where partners sometimes live together and sometimes separately. Means-tested benefits intensify insecurity: they assume stable earnings from employment at a time when the labour market is becoming more and more deregulated and is generating employment income that is insecure and unpredictable. In contrast, a woman who knows that she has a guaranteed right to Child Benefit has a firmer basis on which, for example, she can consider the possibility of leaving a violent partner. Entry into even this insecure labour market becomes less unattractive given the guarantee of at least some income from continuing Child Benefit. This complex, confusing and insecure world is harshest for the most vulnerable and marginal in society. Members of minority ethnic communities are very exposed to the vicissitudes of a system in which, despite some improvements (such as the Benefit Agency's introduction of a code of practice on discrimination and racial harassment), it is still by no means universal to provide appropriate information for people whose first language is not English (Commission on Social Justice, 1994).

The observations and conclusions of this section are summarized and presented in tabular form below.

Table 14. 1   **Universalism and selectivism: a summary of their characteristics**

Characteristic	Universalism	Selectivism
Effectiveness	High/very high take-up rates	Variable (usually low) levels of take-up
Meeting policy objectives	Wasteful of resources (benefits go to those who do not necessarily need them)	Effective use of resources (targeting)
Administrative costs	Low administrative costs	High administrative costs
Public expenditure implications	Relatively demanding of public expenditure	Lessens pressure on public spending
Social costs and social benefits	1 No stigmatization 2 Promotes social integration 3 Egalitarian	1 Considerable stigmatizing propensities 2 Socially divisive 3 Equitable
Labour market implications	Promotes work incentives	High marginal tax rates theoretically damaging to work initiatives (the poverty trap)

Activity 14.3

Make a list of those benefits/services which you think are (a) selective, (b) universal. What features do they possess which help you decide which category they belong to?

14.6 The intellectual and political context

The allegedly institutional character of the reconstructed welfare state of the 1940s had barely been established when it came under attack from the political right. In 1950 a number of young Conservative MPs, including some, such as Edward Heath, Iain Macleod, and Enoch Powell, who were to become leading figures in the party over the next three decades, produced an unofficial statement on Conservative social policy whose title – rather ironically given its general philosophical orientation – incorporated echoes of the party's Disraelian past (Conservative Political Centre, 1950). 'One Nation' is important on a number of counts, but for present purposes perhaps its most interesting aspect is its identification of what is perceived to be the crucial difference between the two major parties on social policy. Thus: 'Socialists would give the same benefits to everyone, whether or not the help is needed, and indeed whether or not the country's resources are adequate. We believe that we must first help those in need' (Conservative Political Centre, 1950: 9).

This general observation was developed in more detail in a later pamphlet written by Macleod and Powell in 1952. 'The social services: needs and means' is a sustained critique of the then existing pattern of social provision in Britain. It rejects the argument that the British welfare state was, in fact, universal to any significant degree and argues for a rational and consistent approach to the allocation of resources on a selectivist basis. Given that redistribution was an essential characteristic of social provision, the general presumption had to be that services would be provided on the basis of the evidence of need, otherwise 'the process is a wasteful and purposeless collection and issue of resources, which leaves people in the enjoyment of the same facilities as before, or rather, worse off, to the extent of the waste involved in the administrative process' (Macleod and Powell, 1952, revised by Powell, 1954: 9).

Notwithstanding its internal coherence and intellectual rigour, Macleod and Powell's position failed to find significant support from the party leadership whose 'official' line remained one of public support for the main contours of the postwar settlement. The Conservatives' reluctance to tamper with this settlement after they were returned to power following the 1951 general election not only surprised the now Labour opposition, which confidently expected them to renege on their conversion to full employment and an expanded welfare state, but was also consistent with the economic prosperity and apparent ideological consensus characteristic of the 1950s and early 1960s (see Lowe, 1990, 1993; Sullivan, 1992).

The rediscovery of poverty during this age of affluence was part of a more general reappraisal of the success of the Keynesian-Beveridgian welfare state in meeting its broad objectives. Titmuss (1962) and Abel-Smith and Townsend (1965) all asked searching questions about the extent to which existing welfare institutions secured a significant amount of vertical income redistribution, and the failures they identified quickly infiltrated the wider political debate. Labour's return to office in 1964 was accompanied by a long and agonized review of its social policy commitments, one which was given a new urgency by the financial crisis leading up to the 1967 devaluation of sterling. As this protracted review went on a number of figures from the centre and right of the party, including Douglas Houghton (1967), then regarded as one of the most authoritative commentators on social security, Ray Gunter (1967), David Owen (1967) and David Marquand (1967) all argued publicly in favour of greater selectivity, while a similar debate raged in the Cabinet. The ostensible Labour/universalist and Conservative/selectivist dichotomy, even if it had never been as clear and simple as political myth would have it, became even more difficult to sustain as the 1960s progressed, and it was within the Labour Party that the shift was most obvious. Significant sections of the party were much more willing to embrace notions of giving most help to those presumed to be in greatest need, especially if acceptable delivery mechanisms could be devised. Houghton's (1967) discussion of a negative income tax is a particularly good example of this.

Perhaps the most significant manifestation of this conflict is provided by the struggle that took place over the shape of family income support policy. A general increase in universal family allowances would have been too expensive for a Treasury desperate to keep public expenditure under control while the trade unions, together with some sympathetic MPs, frustrated Jim Callaghan's (then Chancellor of the Exchequer), attempt to bounce the Cabinet into accepting what later, under the next Conservative government, became the Family Income Supplement scheme. The complicated compromise that finally emerged was the 'clawback' mechanism which reduced income tax allowances in respect of dependent children by an amount exactly sufficient to negate the increase in family allowance scale rates. This was the scheme described by Roy Jenkins, Callaghan's successor as Chancellor, as 'a civilized and acceptable' form of selectivity (Pratt, 1976).

Townsend (1972) explains this shift towards selectivity on three grounds – the increasing dominance of economic policy over social policy, a move away from social equality as a national objective, and the degeneration of large-scale planning into piecemeal improvization – but, whatever the truth of Townsend's analysis, that there was a significant intellectual as well as political change is undeniable. Economic failure, particularly when accompanied by a spectacular crisis on the foreign exchange markets as in 1967, tends to concentrate minds wonderfully. From 1967 onwards a sea change is evident in the work of left leaning theoreticians of social policy, and the development of Titmuss's thought provides powerful testimony to this. It shows the most important theorist of the institutional model of the welfare state, one of the key components of which is the availability of high quality universal services, engaged in a self-conscious attempt at reconciling his commitment to social justice with the reality of scarce resources. His response to these dilemmas was typically creative:

> The challenge that faces us is not the choice between universalist and selective social services. The real challenge resides in the question: what particular infrastructure of universalist services is needed in order to provide a framework of values and opportunity bases within and around which can be developed socially acceptable services aiming to discriminate positively, with the minimum risk of stigma in favour of those whose needs are greatest. (Titmuss, 1976: 135)

This plea by Titmuss for non-stigmatizing positive discrimination must be one of the most quoted pieces in the whole of the academic literature of social policy. It has a profound significance, one which was quickly recognized by Titmuss's neo-liberal equivalent, Arthur Seldon. After sardonically noting Titmuss's earlier, eloquent support for universalism (Titmuss, 1950), Seldon develops a merciless and pointed critique. It merits lengthy quotation.

> The academic advocates of unqualified universalism on principle are in an intellectual

dilemma from which they cannot escape except by concession of error. If selectivity is, at last, morally acceptable, there can be no moral reason for insistence on a substructure of wasteful universal benefits. Economic circumstance, intellectual argument and the belated recognition that generalized benefits are inhumane have destroyed the case for universalism. Nor should refuge be taken in attempts to pay lip service to both principles, formerly regarded as moral opposites, now joined in an administrative 'mariage de convenance'. (1967: 50)

His analysis of Titmuss's preference for allocating resources on a group, categorical or territorial basis is prescient, as later research on positive discrimination programmes such as Educational Priority Areas was to demonstrate. Positive discrimination abandoned the moral case for universalism and still failed to help individuals in need. Seldon's judgement could just as easily be applied to Pinker's examination of positive discrimination as a way out of the increasingly barren debate between the ideologies of universalism and selectivism as 'alive in principle, but dead in practice, just as the nineteenth-century struggle between collectivist and individualist doctrines was largely the invention of an intellectual minority' (Pinker, 1971: 108).

The public spending implications of high quality universal social provision and the problems associated with means-tested selectivity continue to attend the politics of social policy. An important example of this in the 1980s, with a lasting impact, can be found in the publication of a three volume Green Paper, the *Reform of Social Security* (DHSS, 1985b). Constrained from the outset by the Treasury's 'stipulation that the exercise must not increase social security spending, regardless of whatever unusual need it might identify' (Social Security Consortium, 1986: 3), the review found its solution in the concept of 'targeting', the idea 'that resources must be directed more effectively to areas of greatest need notably low income families with children' (DHSS, 1985b: 2).

We must ask whether targeting, thus defined, obviates any of the problems of traditional forms of selectivity. If targeting as a principle is to deliver extra help to the most needy how is it to be done? What is to be the basis of allocation? Can appropriate policy instruments be created to translate intent into reality? Means-tested selectivity continues to be the vehicle through which targeting is operationalized, and remains at the heart of the social security system.

Titmuss's plea for the development of non-stigmatizing positive discrimination has been used by Williams (1992) in her application of postmodernist theory to the analysis of social policy. Postmodernism leads to a distrust of uniformity and universalism, and Williams argues that bottom-up work around gender, race, disability, age and sexuality has exposed 'the "false" universalism of the post-war welfare state – that is, the extent to which social policies have been, and continue to be, built on a white, male, able-bodied, heterosexual norm, living within a supportive nuclear family form' (Williams, 1992: 206). She suggests that postmodernism can assist in retrieving the idea of positive discrimination (understood as a form of selectivity), and in developing it through the notion of diversity which 'suggests a more subjective and self-determined approach to need' (Williams, 1992: 209). In this way the universality/selectivity debate is taken on to new ground and selectivity is replaced by the idea of diversity, which creates the possibility of 'people articulating their own needs'. For Williams the crucial question is, 'how are we to have welfare provision which is universal in that it meets all people's welfare needs, but also diverse and not uniform, reflecting people's own changing definitions of difference, and not simply the structured differentiation of the society at large?' (Williams, 1992: 209). She concludes by suggesting that Titmuss's classic statement could be rephrased thus: 'perhaps the real challenge resides in the question how can government at local, national, and international levels facilitate the universal articulation and provision for diverse welfare needs?' (Williams, 1992: 209). Apostles of difference and diversity sporadically criticize the 'false' universalism of the classic welfare state, ignoring the fact that it was founded on the politics of solidarity, a politics which is not easily reconciled with the current passion for the claims of diversity (Wolfe and Klausen, 2000). Meanwhile governments still have to decide on the principles and techniques governing their allocation of scarce resources.

In a world freed from the depressing reality of scarce resources Williams's liberating notions of self-articulated need would present no problems, but whatever else postmodernist theory might have achieved it has not abolished scarcity: choices still have to be made and the notion of opportunity cost is still relevant.

We are still no nearer to a resolution of these problems. The thoughts of Titmuss and Pinker are echoed in the work done by and for the Commission on Social Justice, work which, essentially, addresses the philosophical and political issues involved by defining them away. The Commission's staff accused politicians and commentators of frequently posing a choice between 'universalist' and 'targeted' (selective) benefits, and suggested, perhaps anachronistically given the comments made above, that 'those on the right [favoured] a shift towards targeting and those on the left usually defend[ed] universality' (Commission on Social Justice, 1993). However, for the Commission this simple dualism was inappropriate both in describing the existing complex system and in developing new proposals. The solution was easy because both terms had been abused so much they should be abandoned completely and replaced by a different classification system. In future, benefits should be categorized as contributory (based on National Insurance contributions), means-tested (based on a test of income and savings), or categorical (awarded to a particular group of people without a test of either contributions or means). The Commission's concluding thoughts on the matter are worth noting. 'This is not simply a matter of terminology: the choice before us is not a crude one between means-tested and non-means-tested benefits, but a complex one between a wide variety of different kinds of provision' (1993: 6). The line of descent from Titmuss is obvious but whether it provides any more of an answer must remain conjectural.

What has changed in the second half of the 1990s is the extent and pace of social democracy's further move from its principled commitment to universalism. According to Vandenbroucke (1999) neither universalism nor selectivism are to be regarded as core social democratic principles. What matters now is what works best in any given situation: pragmatism is all. This is nowhere more apparent than in the actions of the New Labour government since it took office in 1997. In two key areas as we have seen, family income support policy and the incomes of the retired, the government has combined a catholic mixture of universal and selective approaches. The war on family poverty has been prosecuted through the biggest ever increases in the universal Child Benefit and the introduction of the selective Working Families Tax Credit, whilst for the retired a similar duality is present in the form of increases in the universal basic state pension together with a much larger increase in the selective Minimum Income Guarantee. There is a certain irony in the Conservative Party's criticism of the government's greater use of selective instruments like the Minimum Income Guarantee because of the difficulties potential claimants have in finding their way through its complex administrative procedures. Political differences between the two major parties on the question of how best to allocate scarce resources are now smaller than ever and this is unlikely to change in the foreseeable future.

Activity 14.4

In what ways, if any, does targeting overcome the problems associated with the universal/selective debate?

14.7 Summary and conclusions

In this chapter we have considered the most important non-market approaches to the allocation of a number of services, access to which is generally agreed to be vital in determining quality of life in an urban industrial society. Universalism and selectivism have been defined as concepts, had their respective strengths and weaknesses examined in theory and practice, been located in the intellectual and political context of Britain since 1945, and been analysed in the setting of a society whose economic and social structure has been changing at an increasingly rapid and bewildering rate. What general conclusions can be drawn from this exercise?

First, this is a significant debate which should not be reduced to a barren shouting match between the competing claims of 'social justice and cohesion' on the one hand and 'giving most help to those whose needs are greatest' on the other. Simple and beguiling though each of these positions might be, they are of little use in helping us unravel what in reality is a complex problem of public policy. Each of the approaches is reflective of different theoretical models of welfare, possessing conflicting views about what are the most relevant and valid mechanisms for the allocation of a vital range of resources. Is it to be the state or the market? In this sense the universality-selectivity debate can also be seen as one dimension of a perennial, profound fault line in western political thought: the relationship between state and civil society, between the market and the state.

Second, it is a mistake to believe that there is a clear and simple political dichotomy between Conservative/selectivists and Labour/universalists. No such set of relationships exists any longer, although in the past, certainly in the immediate postwar years, left-of-centre political opinion tended to be rather more inclined to universalism and right-of-centre towards selectivism.

Third, both philosophies, and the delivery systems associated with them, have important weaknesses. Whereas universal benefits might encourage work incentives and be more successful in reaching relevant target populations, there is no denying the fact that they do demand a huge commitment of public expenditure and, as Titmuss admitted, by their nature they are wasteful.

In contrast, although selective benefits are more economical in the demands they place on scarce resources, there are very real problems of take-up, stigma, disincentives and costs of administration. It may well be that these problems are intractable no matter how ingenious and subtle policy instruments might become in future.

Fourth, is a 'perfect' solution possible at all, or will we have to recognize that something like the present admixture of fudge and compromise will continue into the foreseeable future – a compromise, moreover, which will accord with no theoretical ideal type and therefore be continuously vilified by ideologues of all persuasions?

Fifth and finally, a point not directly concerned with the substance of the debate at all, but rather more with questions of general intellectual procedure. It can be argued that the issues dealt with in this chapter, which in the first instance appear to be simple and non-problematic, soon reveal themselves as difficult and controversial in nature. As such they can stand as a powerful encouragement to students always to go beyond superficial certainties and to explore the stimulating reality of context.

BIBLIOGRAPHY

Abel-Smith, B. and Townsend, P. (1965) *The Poor and the Poorest*. London: George Bell and Sons.

Adonis, A. and Pollard, S. (1997) *A Class Act: The Myth of Britain's Classless Society*. Harmondsworth: Penguin.

Alcock, C., Payne, S. and Sullivan, M. (2000) *Introducing Social Policy*. (London: Prentice Hall).

Alcock, P., Erskine, A. and May, M. (1998) *The Student's Companion to Social Policy*. Oxford: Blackwell.

Ali, T. (ed.) (2000) *Masters of the Universe?* London: Verso.

Anderson, P. and Mann, N. (1998) *Safety First: The Making of New Labour*. London: Granta.

Appadurai, A. (1996) *Modernity at Large: Cultural Dimensions of Globalization*. Minneapolis: University of Minnesota Press.

Arber, S. and Ginn, J. (1991) *Gender and Later Life*. London: Sage.

Arber, S. and Ginn, J. (1995) (eds) *Connecting Gender and Ageing: A Sociological Approach*. Buckingham: Open University Press.

Arensberg, C.M. and Kimball, S.T. (1940) *Family and Community in Ireland*. Cambridge, MA: Harvard University Press.

Ariés, P. (1962) *Centuries of Children*. Edinburgh, J. and J. Gray.

Armstrong, H. (1998) *Speech to the Annual Conference of the Chartered Institute of Housing*. Harrogate, June.

Atkin, K. (1998) 'Ageing in multi-racial Britain: demography, policy and practice', in M. Bernard and J. Phillips (eds), *The Social Policy of Old Age*. London: Centre for Policy on Ageing.

Atkinson, D. and Elliott, L. (1999) 'Reflating Keynes: a different view of the crisis', *International Socialism 82*.

Axford, B. (2000) 'Globalization', in G. Browning A. Halcli and F. Webster, *Understanding Contemporary Society: Theories of the Present*. London: Sage.

Aziz, R. (1992) 'Feminism and the challenge of racism: deviance or difference?', in H. Cowley and S. Himmelweit (eds), *Knowing Women*. Oxford: Polity.

Bacon, R.W. and Eltis, W.A. (1976) *Britain's Economic Problem: Too Few Producers*. London: Macmillan.

Baldock, J. et. al. (eds) (1999) *Social Policy*. Oxford: Oxford University Press.

Bandalli, S. (2000) 'Children, responsibility and the new youth justice', in B. Goldston (ed.), *The New Youth Justice*. Lyme Regis: Russell House Publishing.

Barker, M. and Beezer, A. (1983) 'The language of racism – an examination of Lord Scarman's report on the Brixton riots', *International Socialism*, 18.

Barlow, A., Bowley, M. and Butler, G. (1999) *Advising Gay and Lesbian Clients: A Guide For Lawyers*. London: Butterworth.

Barrett, M. and McIntosh, M. (1980) 'The "family wage": some problems for socialists and feminists', *Capital and Class 11*.

Barrett, M. and McIntosh, M. (1985) *The Anti-Social Family*. London: Verso.

Barrett, M. and Phillips, A. (eds) (1992) Destabilizing Theory: Contemporary Feminist Debates. Cambridge: Polity Press.

Barry, B. (1975) 'Review of "Anarchy, State and Utopia"', *Political Theory*, 3: 330–3.

Bart, P. (1971) 'Depression in middle-aged women', in V. Cornick and B. Moran (eds), *Women in Sexist Society*. New York: Basic Books.

Bartlett, W., Roberts, J.A. and Le Grand, J.A (1998) *Revolution in Social Policy: Quasi-Market Reforms in the 1990s*. Bristol: Policy Press.

Bauman, Z. (1993) *Postmodern Ethics*. Oxford: Blackwell.

Becker, S.(1997) *Responding to Poverty*, London: Longman.

Beechey,V. (1985) 'Familial ideology' in V. Beechey and J. Donald (eds), *Subjectivity and Social Relations*. Milton Keynes: Open University Press.

Bennett, F. (1993) *Social Insurance. Reform or Abolition?* Commission on Social Justice,Vol 1, London: IPPR.

Berman, M. (1982) *All That is Solid Melts Into Air:The Experience of Modernity*. London:Verso.

Bernard, J. (1973) *The Future of Marriage*. New York: Souvenir Press.

Beveridge,W. (1942) *Social Insurance and Allied Services*, (Cm. 6404). London: HMSO.

Biggs, S. (1990/91) 'Consumers, case management and inspection: obscuring social deprivation and need ?', *Critical Social Policy* (10) 30: 23–8.

Birchill, I. (1986) *Baling Out the System*. London: Bookmarx.

Black, M. and Coward, R. (1981) 'Linguistic, social and sexual relations', *Screen Education, 39*, Summer.

Blackburn, R. (1997) *The Making of New World Slavery*. London:Verso.

Blair,T. (1996) *New Britain: My Vision of a Young Country*. London: Fourth Estate.

Blair,T. (1997a) 'The modernisation of Britain', speech to the 1997 Trades Union Congress.

Blair,T. (1997b) Speech at the Aylesbury estate, Southwark, 2 June (http://www.open.gov.uk/co/seu.more.html/speech by the prime minister).

Blair,T. (1997c) Speech at Stockwell Park School, Lambeth, 8 December (http://www.open.gov.uk/co/seu.more.html/speech by the prime minister).

Blair,T. (1998a) *New Britain: My Vision of a Young Country*. London: Fourth Estate.

Blair, T. (1998b) *The Third Way*. London:The Fabian Society.

Blair, T. (1998c) Foreword to *New Ambitions For Our Country: A New Contract For Welfare*, Cm. 3805, Department of Social Security, London: Stationery Office.

Blair,T. (1999a) 'Beveridge revisited: a welfare state for the twenty-first century', in R.Walker (ed.), *Ending Child Poverty: Popular Welfare for the Twenty-first Century*. Bristol: Policy Press.

Blair,T. (1999b) Speech to Labour Party Conference, September.

Blakemore, K. and Boneham, M. (1994) *Age, Race and Ethnicity*. Buckingham: Open University Press.

Blaug, M. (1986) *Great Economists before Keynes:An Introduction to the Lives and Work of One Hundred Great Economists of the Past*. Brighton:Wheatsheaf.

Blocker, H.G. and Smith, E.H. (1980). *John Rawls's Theory of Justice: An Introduction*. Columbus, Ohio: Ohio University Press.

Blumenfeld,W. and Raymond, D. (1993) *Looking at Gay and Lesbian Life*. Boston: Beacon Press.

Blunkett, D. (1997) *PPP's Key to Tackling Crumbling Schools*. London: Department for Education and Employment, Press Release 152/97, 23 June.

Booth, C. (1904) *Life and Labour of the People in London*. London: Macmillan.

Bosanquet, N. (1983) *After the New Right*. London: Heinemann.

Boulding, K.E. (1967) 'The boundaries of social policy' *Social Work* (12) 1.

Bradley, H. (2000) 'Social inequalities: coming to terms with complexity', in G. Browning, A. Halcli and F. Webster (eds), *Understanding Contemporary Society:Theories of the Present*. London: Sage.

Bradshaw, J. and Wakeman, I. (1972) 'The poverty trap up-dated', *The Political Quarterly*, 43: 459–69.

Branson, N. (1979) *Popularism*. London: Lawrence and Wishart.

Briggs,A. (1969) 'The welfare state in historical perspective', in C. Schottland (ed.), *The Welfare State*. New York: Harper and Row.

Bright, M. (2000) 'Youth jails "must be closed"', in *The Guardian*, 19 November 2000.

Bristow, J. and Wilson,A. (eds) (1993) *Activating Theory: Lesbian, Gay, Bisexual Politics*. London: Lawrence and Wishart.

Brody, H. (1973) *Inishkillance: Change and Decline in the West of Ireland*. London: Allen Lane.

Brown, C. (1984) *Black and White Britain: The Third PSI Survey*. London: Heinemann.

Brown, P. (1996) 'Modernism, post-modernism and sociological theory', *Sociology Review*, 5 (2).

Browning, G., Halcli, A. and Webster, F. (2000) 'Theory, theorists and themes: a user's guide to understanding the present', in G. Browning, A. Halcli and F. Webster (eds), *Understanding Contemporary Society: Theories of the Present*. London: Sage.

Bruegal, I. and Kean, H. (1995) 'The movement of municipal feminism', *Critical Social Policy*, 44/45.

Bryson, L. (1992) *Welfare and the State*. Basingstoke: Macmillan.

Buckler, S. and Dolowitz, D. (2000) 'New Labour's ideology: a reply to Michael Freeden', *Political Quarterly*, February 2000: 102–9.

Bull, D. (ed.) (1971) *Family Poverty*. London: Duckworth.

Burchardt, T. and Hills, J. (1999) 'Public expenditure and the public/private mix', in M. Powell (ed.), *New Labour, New Welfare State?* Bristol: Policy Press.

Burgess, S. and Propper, C. (1999) 'Poverty in Britain', in P. Gregg and J. Wadsworth (eds.), *The State of Working Britain* Manchester: Manchester University Press.

Bury, M. (1988) 'Arguments about ageing, long life and its consequences', in N. Wells and C. Freer (eds), *The Ageing Population: Burden or Challenge?* London: Macmillan.

Bury, M. and Holme, A. (1991) *Life after Ninety*. London: Routledge.

Butler, J. (1990) *Gender Trouble: Feminism and the Subversion of Identity*. London: Routledge.

Byne, W. (1994) 'The biological evidence challenged', *Scientific American*, May 1994: 50–5.

Bytheway, B. (1995) *Ageism*. Buckingham: The Open University Press.

Callinicos, A. (1983) *The Revolutionary Ideas of Karl Marx*. London: Bookmarks.

Callinicos, A. (1987a) *Making History*. Oxford: Polity.

Callinicos, A. (1987b) 'The "new middle class" and socialist politics', in A. Callinicos and C. Harman, *The Changing Working Class*. London: Bookmarks.

Callincos, A. (1989) *Against Postmodernism*, Cambridge: Polity Press.

Callinicos, A. (1993) *Race and Class*. London: Bookmarks.

Callinicos, A. (1999) *Social Theory: A Historical Introduction*. Oxford: Polity Press.

Callinicos, A. (2000) *Equality*. Cambridge: Polity.

Campbell, B. (1984) *Wigan Pier Revisited: Poverty and Politics in the 80s*. London: Virago.

Campbell, B. (1987) *The Iron Ladies: Why Do Women Vote Tory?* London: Virago.

Carvel, J. (2000) 'Basics denied to 2m children, *The Guardian*, 11 September 2000.

CCETSW (1991) *Rules and Requirements for the Diploma in Social Work (Paper 30)* (second edn). London: CCETSW.

Chambers, R. (1994) 'Poverty and livelihood: whose reality counts?', United Nations Stockholm Round Table on Global Change.

Chancellor of the Exchequer (1976) *Public Expenditure to 1979–80*, Cm. 6393. London: HMSO.

Charlton, J. (2000) 'Talking Seattle', *International Socialism*, 2:86: 3–18.

Cheetham, J. (1987) 'Racism in practice', *Social Work Today*, 27 September.

Chiozza Money, L.G. (1910) *Riches and Poverty*. London: Methuen.

Chodorow, N. (1978) *The Reproduction of Mothering*. London: University of California Press.

Clarke, J. (1996) 'After social work?', in N. Parton (ed.), *Social Theory, Social Change and Social Work*. London: Routledge.

Clarke, J. (1998) 'Consumerism', in G. Hughes (ed.), *Imagining Welfare Futures*. London: Routledge/Open University.

Clarke, J. and Newman, J. (1997) *The Managerial State*. London: Sage.

Clarke, J. and Newman, J. (1998) 'A modern British people? New Labour and welfare reform', Paper to Discourse Analysis and Social Research Conference, Copenhagen, September.

Clarke, J., Cochrane, A. and McLaughlin, E. (eds) (1994) *Managing Social Policy*. London: Sage.

Clarke, J., Gewirtz, S. and McLaughlin, E. (eds) (2001) *Reinventing the Welfare State: From New Right to New Labour*. London: Sage.

Cloke, C. and Davies, M. (eds) (1995) *Participation and Empowerment in Child Protection*. Chichester: Wiley/NSPCC.

Collard, D. (1971) 'The case for universal benefits', in D. Bull (ed.), *Family Poverty*. London: Duckworth.

Commission on Social Justice, Staff Paper (1993) 'Making Sense of Benefits', *Commission on Social Justice*, Vol. 2. London: IPPR.

Commission on Social Justice (1994) *Strategies for National Renewal*. London: Vintage/IPPR.

Conservative Political Centre (1950) *One Nation*. London: CPR.

Cook, D. (1998) 'Racism, immigration policy and welfare policing: the case of the Asylum and Immigration Act', in M. Lavalette, L. Penketh and C. Jones (eds), *Anti-Racism and Social Welfare*. Aldershot: Ashgate.

Cooper, D. (1994) *Sexing the City: Lesbian and Gay Politics within the Activist State*. London: Rivers Oram Press.

Coote, A. (1999) 'The helmsman and the cattle prod', in A. Gamble, and T. Wright, 'The New Social Democracy', *Supplement to the Political Quarterly*. Oxford: Blackwell.

Corby, B. (2000) *Child Abuse: Towards a Knowledge Base* (second edn). Milton Keynes: The Open University Press.

Creighton, C. (1980) 'Family, property and relations of production in western Europe', *Economy and Society*, 9.

Creighton, C. (1985) 'The family and capitalism in Marxist theory', in M. Shaw, (ed.), *Marxist Sociology Revisited*. Basingstoke: Macmillan.

Crook, S. (1990) 'The end of radical social theory? Notes on radicalism, modernism and postmodernism' in R. Boyne and A. Rattansi (eds.), *Postmodernism and Society*. London: Macmillan.

Crosland, A. (1974) *The Teacher of Sociology*. London: Jonathan Cape.

Crouch, C. (1999) 'The parabola of working class politics', *Supplement to The Political Quarterly*. Oxford: Blackwell.

Croucher, R. (1987) *We Refuse to Starve in Silence*. London: Lawrence and Wishart.

Crowley, H. and Himmelweit, S. (eds) (1992) *Knowing Women*. Oxford: Polity.

Cunningham, H. (1990) 'The employment and unemployment of children in England, c. 1680–1851', *Past and Present*, 126.

Cunningham, H. (1995) *Children and Childhood in Western Society Since 1500*. London: Longman.

Cunningham, S. (1999) 'The problem that doesn't exist? Child labour in Britain, 1918–1970', in M. Lavalette (ed.), *A Thing of the Past? Child Labour in Britain in the Nineteenth and Twentieth Centuries*. Liverpool: Liverpool University Press.

Cunningham, S. (2000) 'Child labour in Britain 1900–1970', PhD dissertation, University of Central Lancashire.

Currah, P. (1993) 'Searching for immutability: homosexuality, race and rights discourse,' in A. Wilson (ed.), *A Simple Matter of Justice?* London: Cassell.

Dalley, G. (1988) *Ideologies of Caring*. London: Macmillan.

Dalley, G. (1996) *Ideologies of Caring: Rethinking Community and Collectivism* (second edn). Basingstoke: Macmillan.

Daly, M. (1978) *Gyn/Ecology: The Metaethics of Radical Feminism*. Boston: Beacon Press.

Daly, M. (1994) 'A matter of dependency: gender in British income maintenance provision', *Sociology*, 28 (3), Exeter: BSAP.

Danson, M., Fleming, I., Gilmore, K., Sternberg, A. and Whittam, G. (2000) *Glasgow City Council Proposed Housing Stock Transfer: Final Report*. Glasgow: Unison Scotland.

Davies, B. (with Reddin, M.) (1978) *Universality, Selectivity and Effectiveness in Social Policy*. London: Heinemann.

Davies, N. (1997) *Dark Heart*. London: Chatto and Windus.

Davin, A. (1990) 'When is a child not a child?', in H. Carr and L. Jamieson (eds), *The Politics of Everyday Life*. Basingstoke: Macmillan.

Davis, A. (1991) 'Hazardous lives – social work in the 1980s: a view from the left', in M. Loney, B. Bocock, J. Clarke, A. Cochrane, P. Graham and M. Wilson, (eds.), *The State or the Market*. London: Sage.

de Ste Croix, G.E.M. (1981) *The Class Struggle in the Ancient Greek World*. London: Duckworth.

Deacon, A. (1996) 'Welfare and character', in A. Deacon, *Stakeholder Welfare*. London: Institute for Economic Affairs.

Deacon, A. (2000) 'Learning from the US? The influence of American ideas upon "New Labour" thinking on welfare reform', *Policy and Politics* 18 (1).

Deacon, A. and Mann, K. (1999) 'Agency, modernity and social policy', *Journal of Social Policy*, 28 (3): 413–35.

Dean, H. (1991a) *Social Security and Social Control*. London: Routledge.

Dean, H. (1991b) 'In search of the underclass', in P. Brown and R. Scase, *Poor Work: Disadvantage and the Division of Labour*. Milton Keynes: The Open University Press.

Department of Health (1997) *The New NHS: Modern, Dependable*. London: The Stationery Office.

Department of Health (1998) *Modernising Social Services*. London: The Stationery Office.

Department of Health and Social Security (1985a) *Reform of Social Security*, Vol. 1, Cm. 9517. London: HMSO.

Department of Health and Social Security (Dec 1985b) *Programme for Action*, Cm. 9691. London: HMSO.

Department of Health and Social Security (1985c) *Reform of Social Security*, Vol. 1, Cm. 9517; Vol. 2, *Programme for Change*, Cm. 9518; Vol. 3, *Background Papers*, Cm. 9519. London: HMSO,.

Department of Social Security (1998a) *A New Contract for Welfare: Partnership in Pensions*, Cm. 4179. London: The Stationery Office.

Department of Social Security (1998b) *Households Below Average Income: A Statistical Analysis, 1979–1995/96*. London: The Stationery Office.

Department of Social Security (2000) *Opportunity for All: One Year On* (second annual report). London: HMSO.

Derrida, J. (1994) *Spectres of Marx*. London: Routledge.

Dinnerstein, D. (1976) *The Rocking of the Cradle and the Ruling of the World*. (second revised edn 1987). London: The Women's Press.

Divine, D. (1991) 'The value of anti-racism in social work education and training', in CCETSW (eds), *Northern Curriculum Development Project*. London: CCETSW.

Docherty, T. (ed.) (1993) *Postmodernism: A Reader*. Hertfordshire, Harvester: Wheatsheaf.

Donovan, C., Heaphy, B. and Weeks, J. (1999a) 'Partners by choice: equality, power and commitment in non-heterosexual relationships', in G. Allan (ed.), *The Sociology of the Family: A Reader*. Oxford: Blackwell.

Donovan, C., Heaphy, B. and Weeks, J. (1999b) 'Everyday Experiments: narratives of non-heterosexual relationships', in E. Silva and C. Smart (eds), *The New Family?* London: Sage.

Donzelot, J. (1980) *The Policing of Families*. London: Hutchinson.

Downs, A. (1957) *An Economic Theory of Democracy*. London: Harper and Row.

Doyal, L. (1985) 'Women and the National Health Service: the carers and the careless', in E. Lewin and V. Olesen (eds.), *Women's Health and Healing*. London: Tavistock.

Doyal, L. and Gough, I. (1991) *A Theory of Human Need*. Basingstoke: Macmillan.

Drakeford, M. and McCarthy, K. (2000) 'Parents' responsibility and the new youth justice', in B. Goldston (ed.), *The New Youth Justice*. Lyme Regis: Russell House Publishing.

Draper, H. (1966/1996) *The Two Souls of Socialism*. London: Bookmarks.

Driver, S. and Martell, L. (1998) *New Labour: Politics After Thatcherism*. Cambridge: Polity.

Duberman, M. (1991) *Hidden from History*. London: Penguin.

Durham, M. (1991) *Sex and Politics: The Family and Morality in the Thatcher Years*. London: Macmillan.

Dyson, A.E. and Lovelock, J. (eds.) (1975) *Education and Democracy*. London: Routledge and Kegan Paul.

Eichenbaum, L. and Orbach, S. (1982) *Outside In, Inside Out*. Harmondsworth: Penguin.

Eisenstein, H. (1984) *Contemporary Feminist Thought*. London: Unwin.

Elliott, L., Denny, C. and White, M. (2000) 'Poverty gap hits labour boasts, *The Guardian*, 14 July 2000.

Engels, F. (1845/1976) *The Condition of the Working Class in England*. London: Lawrence and Wishart.

Espada, J.S. (1996) *Social Citizenship Rights: A Critique of F.A. Hayek and Raymond Plant*. Basingstoke: Macmillan.

Esping-Anderson, G. (1990) *The Three Worlds of Welfare Capitalism*. Oxford: Polity Press.

Estes, C. (1979) *The Aging Enterprise*. San Francisco, CA: Jossey Bass.

Evans, D. (1993) *Sexual Citizenship: The Material Construction of Sexualities*. London: Routledge.

Falkingham, J. (1989) Dependency and ageing in Britain; a re-examination of the evidence, *Journal of Social Policy*, 18 (2): 211–33.

Falkingham, J. and Victor, C. (1991) 'The myth of the woopie? Incomes, the elderly and targeting the elderly', *Ageing and Society*, 11 **(4)**: 471–93.

'Family secrets: child sex abuse', *Feminist Review*, Special Issue, 28, 1988.

Fennell, G., Phillipson C. and Evers, H. (1988) *The Sociology of Old Age*. Stony Stratford: The Open University Press.

Ferguson, I. and Lavalette, M. (1999) 'Postmodernism, Marxism and social work', *European Journal of Social Work*, 2 (1): 27–40.

Ferguson, I., Lavalette, M. and Mooney, G. (forthcoming) *Marx, Neoliberalism and Welfare*. London: Sage.

Field, F. (2000) 'Pay off the oldest ones', *The Guardian*, 26 May.

Field, F. and Piachaud, D. (1982) *Poverty and Politics*. London: Heinemann: (first published in the New *Statesman*).

Finch, J. (1988) 'Whose responsibility? Women and the future of family care', in J. Allen, M. Wicks, J. Finch and D. Leat (eds), *Informal Care Tomorrow*. London: Policy Studies Institute.

Finch, J. and Groves, D. (1983) *A Labour of Love: Women, Work and Caring*. London: Routledge and Kegan Paul.

Finkelhor, D. (1983) 'Common features of family abuse', in D. Finkelhor, R.J. Gelles, G.T. Hotaling and M. Straus (eds), *The Dark Side of Families*. London: Sage.

Finlayson, A. (1999) 'Third way Theory', in A. Gamble and T. Wright (eds) 'The New Social Democracy', *Supplement to the Political Quarterly*. Oxford: Blackwell.

Finlayson, A. (1999) 'Third Way Theory' *The Political Quarterly*, Vol. 70, 3.

Firestone, S. (1970) *The Dialetic of Sex: The Case for Feminist Revolution*. New York: Bantam Books.

Foucault, M. (1978) *The History of Sexuality*, Vol. 1 trans. R. Hurley. Harmondsworth: Penguin.

Foucault, M. (1987) *The History of Sexuality: Volume 1, An Introduction*. Harmondsworth: Penguin.

Franklin, A. and Franklin B. (1996) 'The developing children's rights movement in the UK', in J. Pilcher and S. Wagg (eds), *Thatcher's Children*. Bristol: Falmer Press.

Franklin, B. (1986) *The Rights of Children*. Oxford: Blackwell.

Franklin, B. (ed.) (1995) *The Handbook of Children's Rights*. London: Routledge.

Franks, S. (1999) *Having None of It. Women, Men and the Future of Work*. London: Granta.

Fraser, D. (2000) 'The post-war consensus: a debate not long enough?', *Parliamentary Affairs*, 53.

Fraser, N. (1998) 'From redistribution to recognition? Dilemmas of justice in a "Post-socialist" age', in C. Willett (ed.) *Theorising Multiculturalism: A Guide to the Current Debate*. Oxford: Blackwell.

Freud, S. (1905) 'Three essays on the theory of sexuality', in *On Sexuality* (1976) (PFL 7). Harmondsworth: Penguin.

Friedan, B. (1963) *The Feminine Mystique*. Harmondsworth: Penguin.

Fries, J.F. (1980) 'Aging, natural death and the compression of morbidity', *New England Journal of Medicine*, 303: 130–6.

Fries, J.F. (1989) 'The compression of morbidity: near or far?', *Milbank Quarterly* 67 (2): 208–32.

Frow E. and Frow, R. (1970) *The Half-Time System in Education*. Manchester: E.J. Moxton.

Fryer, P. (1984) *Staying Power: The History of Black People in Britain*. London: Pluto.

Fryer, P. (1988) *Black People in the British Empire*. London: Pluto.

Fukuyama, F. (1992) *The End of History and the Last Man*. London: Hamish Hamilton.

Gaffney, D. and Pollock, A.M. (1998) *Putting a Price on the PFI: The Illusionist Economics of the PFI*. London: Unison.

Gamble, A. (1987) 'The weakening of social democracy', in *Politics and Welfare in Contemporary Britain*, M. Loney, R. Bocock, J. Clarke, A. Cochrane, P. Graham, and M. Wilson et al. (eds), *The State or the Market*. London: Sage.

Gamble, A. (1996) *Hayek: The Iron Cage of Liberty*. Cambridge: Polity Press.

Gavron, H. (1966) *The Captive Wife: Conflicts of Housebound wives*. Harmondsworth: Penguin.

Geiger, T. (1979) *Welfare and Efficiency*. London: Macmillan.

General Household Survey (1996). London: HMSO.

George, H. (1979) [1879] *Progress and Poverty*. London: Hogarth Press.

George, S. (1999) *The Lugano Report*. London: Pluto.

George, V. and Wilding, P. (1994) *Welfare and Ideology*. London: Harvester Wheatsheaf.

Geras, N. (1983) *Marx and Human Nature*. London: Verso.

German, L. (1989) *Sex, Class and Socialism*. London: Bookmarx.

Gewirtz, S. (1999) 'Education action zones', in H. Dean and R. Woods (eds), *Social Policy Review 11*. Luton: University of Luton/Social Policy Association.

Giddens, A. (1990) *The Consequences of Modernity*. Cambridge: Polity Press.

Giddens, A. (1998) *The Third Way: The Renewal of Social Democracy*. Oxford: Polity Press.

Giddens, A. (2000) *The Third Way and Its Critics*. Cambridge: Polity.

Gil, D. (1973) *Unravelling Social Policy*. New York: Schenkman.

Gilbert, B.B. (1970) *British Social Policy 1914–1939*. London: Batesford.

Gilligan, C. (1982) *In a Different Voice: Psychological Theory and Women's Development*. London: Harvard University Press.

Ginsburg, N. (1992) *Social Divisions of Welfare*. London: Sage.

Gittins, D. (1985) *The Family in Question*. London: Macmillan.

Glasgow City Council (2000) *Project 2002: Glasgow's Secondary School Public/Private Partnership*. http://www.glasgow.gov.uk

Glennerster, H. (1999) 'A third way?', in H. Dean and R. Woods (eds), *Social Policy Review 11*. Luton: University of Luton/Social Policy Association.

Goldson, B. (2000) 'Wither diversion? Interventionism and the new youth justice', in B. Goldston (ed.), *The New Youth Justice*. Lyme Regis: Russell House Publishing.

Golombok, S. and Tasker, F. (1994) 'Children in lesbian and gay families: theories and evidence', *Annual Review of Sex Research* 4: 3–100.

Golombok, S. and Tasker, F. (1996) 'Do parents influence the sexual orientation of their children? Findings from a longitudinal study of lesbian families', *Developmental Psychology* 32 (1): 1–9.

Gore, C. (1998) 'Inequality, ethnicity and educational achievement', in M. Lavalette, L. Penketh and C. Jones (eds), *Anti-Racism and Social Welfare*. Aldershot: Ashgate.

Gough, I. (1979) *The Political Economy of the Welfare State*. Basingstoke: Macmillan.

Graham, H. (1987) 'Being poor: perceptions and coping strategies of lone mothers', in J. Brannen and G. Wilson (eds), *Give and Take in Families*. London: Allen and Unwin.

Grant v. South West Trains, C249/96 [1998] ECR 1-0621.

Gray, J. (1993) *Beyond the New Right*. London: Routledge.

Gray, J. (1994) 'On the Edge of the Abyss', *The Guardian* 18 July

Green, H. (1988) *Informal Carers.* OPCS Series GHS, No. 15, Supplement A. London: HMSO.

Grmek, M. (1990) *History of AIDS: Emergence and Origin of a Modern Pandemic,* trans. Russell C. Maulitz and Jacalyn Duffin. Princeton, NJ: Princeton University Press.

Gunter, R. (1967) *The Sunday Times,* 19 August.

Habermas, J. (1996) *Between Facts and Norms.* Cambridge: Polity Press.

Hall, S. (1984) 'The rise of the representative/interventionist state', in G. McLennan et al. (eds), *State and Society in Contemporary Britain.* Oxford: Polity Press.

Hall, S. and Jacques, M. (eds) (1989) *New Times.* London: Lawrence and Wishart.

Hamer, D. and Copeland P. (1994) *The Science of Desire: The Search for the Gay Gene and the Biology of Behavior.* New York: Simon and Schuster.

Hammarberg, T. (1995) 'Preface', in B. Franklin, (ed.), *The Handbook of Children's Rights.* London: Routledge.

Hammond, J.L. and Hammond, B. (1917) *The Town Labourer: The New Civilisation.* London: Longmans and Co.

Hansard: , Various Volumes & Dates

Harman, C. (1996) 'Globalisation: a critique of a new orthodoxy', *International Socialism,* 73: 3–34.

Harman, C. (1999) *A People's History of the World.* London: Bookmarks.

Harman, C. (2000) 'Anti-capitalism: theory and practice', *International Socialism* , 88.

Harman, C. (2001) 'Beyond the boom', *International Socialism,* 90.

Harris, J. (1972) *Unemployment and Politics: A Study in English Social Policy 1886–1914.* Oxford: Oxford University Press.

Harris, R. (with Seldon, A.) (1963/1965) *Choice in Welfare.* London: IEA.

Hartmann, H. (1979) 'The unhappy marriage of Marxism and Feminism – towards a more progressive union', *Capital and Class.*

Harvey, D. (1989) *The Condition of Postmodernity.* Oxford: Blackwell.

Harvey, D. (1996) 'Globalisation in question', *Rethinking Marxism,* 8 (4): 1–17.

Hassan, R. (2000) 'Riots and urban unrest in Britain in the 1980s and 1990s' in M. Lavalette and G. Mooney (eds), *Class Struggle and Social Welfare.* London: Routledge.

Hay, J.R. (1975) *The Origins of the Liberal Welfare Reforms 1906–1914.* Basingstoke: Macmillan.

Hayek, F.A. (1944) *The Road to Serfdom.* London: Routledge and Kegan Paul.

Hayek, F.A. (ed.) (1963) *Capitalism and the Historians: A Defence of the Early Factory System.* Chicago: University of Chicago Press.

Hayek, F.A. (1976a) *Law, Legislation and Liberty, vol. 1, Rules and Social Order.* London: Routledge.

Hayek, F.A. (1976b) *Law, Legislation and Liberty, vol. 2, The Mirage of Social Justice.* London: Routledge.

Hayek, F.A. (1976c) *Law, Legislation and Liberty, vol. 3, The Political Order of a Free People.* London: Routledge.

Healey, E. and Mason, A. (1994) *Stonewall 25: The Making of The Lesbian and Gay Community in Britain.* London: Virago.

Health Matters (2000) *Globalisation and Health* www.healthmatters.org.uk.

Heller, A. (1974) *The Theory of Need in Marx.* London: Allison and Busby.

Helm, S. (2000) 'It's easier to work than to mother', *New Statesman,* 19 May.

Her Majesty's Treasury (1999) *The Modernisation of Britain's Tax and Benefit System, Number Four: Tackling Poverty and Extending Opportunity.* London: HM Treasury.

Her Majesty's Treasury (2000) *Prudent for a Purpose: Working for a Stronger and Fairer Britain: Financial Statement and Budget Report.* London: Stationery Office.

Hicks, S. and McDermott, J. (eds), (1999) *Lesbian and Gay Fostering and Adoption – Extraordinary Yet Ordinary.* London: Jessica Kingsley Publishers.

Hirsch, F. (1977) *The Social Limits to Growth.* London: Routledge and Kegan Paul.

Hirst, P. and Thompson, G. (1996) *Globalization in Question: The International Economy and the Possibilities of Governance.* Cambridge, Polity Press.

HMSO (1994) *Social Trends* 24. London: HMSO.

Hobhouse, L.T. (1893) *The Labour Movement*. London: Harvester.

Hobhouse, L.T. (1974) [1911] *Liberalism*. New York: Galaxy Books.

Hobsbawm, E. (1969) *Industry and Empire*. Harmondsworth: Penguin.

Hobsbawm, E. (1977) *The Age of Capital 1840–1875*. London: Sphere.

Hobson, D. (1999) *The National Wealth: Who Gets What in Britain*. London: HarperCollins.

Holdsworth, A. (1988) *Out of the Doll's House*. London: BBC Publications.

Holt, J. (1974) *Escape From Childhood*. Harmondsworth: Penguin.

Home Office (1997a) *Young Prisoners: A Thematic Review by HM Chief Inspector of Prisons for England and Wales – Thematic Report*. London: HMSO.

Home Office (1997b) *No More Excuses: A New Approach to Tackling Youth Crime in England and Wales*, Cm. 3809. London: HMSO.

hooks, b. (1984) *Feminist Theory: From Margin to Center*. Boston, MA: South End Press.

Horne, L., Rights of women (eds) Valued Families: The Lesbian Mothers' Legal Handbook. London: The Womens' Press.

Horrell, S. and Humphries, J. (1999) 'Child labour and British industrialisation' in M. Lavalette (ed.), *A Thing of the Past? Child Labour in Britain in the Nineteenth and Twentieth Centuries*. Liverpool: Liverpool University Press.

Houghton, D. (1967) 'Paying for the social services', *Occasional Paper* 16. London: Institute of Economic Affairs.

Hughes, G., Clarke, J., Lewis, G. and Mooney, G. (1998) 'Reinventing the public?', in G. Hughes (ed.), *Imagining Welfare Futures*. London: Routledge.

Humphries, S. (1981) *Hooligans or Rebels? An Oral History of Working Class Childhood and Youth 1889–1939*. Oxford: Basil Blackwell.

Hurt, J. (1984) 'Reformatory and industrial schools before 1933', *History of Education*, 13 (1).

Husband, C. (1980) Culture, context and practice: racism in social work', in R. Bailey and M. Brake (eds), *Radical Social Work*. London: Edward Arnold.

Husband, C. (1991) 'Race, conflictual politics and anti-racist social work: lessons from the past for action in the 1990s', in Northern Curriculum Development Project (ed.), *Setting the Context for Change*. London: CCETSW.

Hutt, W.H. (1963) 'The factory system of the early nineteenth century' in F.A. Hayek (ed.), *Capitalism and the Historians: A Defence of the Early Factory System*. Chicago: University of Chicago Press.

Hutton, W. (1995) *The State We're In*. London: Jonathan Cape.

Hyde, H.M. (1970) *The Love that Dared not Speak its Name: A Candid History of Homosexuality*. Boston, MA: Little Brown.

Institute for Public Policy Research (1993) 'Making sense of benefits' *Staff Paper*, vol.2. London: IPPR.

IPPR (1998) *Leading the Way: A New Vision for Local Government*. London: Institute for Public Policy Research.

Jayasuriya, K. (2000) 'Capability, freedom and new social democracy', in A. Gamble and T. Wright (eds) 'The New Social Democracy', *Supplement to the Political Quarterly*, 71 (3) Oxford: Blackwell.

Jeffery-Poulter, S. (1991) *Peers, Queers and Commons: The Struggle for Gay Law Reform from 1950 to the Present*. London: Routledge.

Jeffreys, S. (1986) *The Spinster and Her Enemies*. London: Pandora Press.

Jeffreys, S. (1990) *Anti-Climax*. London: The Women's Press.

Jenkins, R. and Solomos, J. (1989) *Racism and Equal Opportunity Policies in the 1980s* (second edn) Cambridge: Cambridge University Press.

Johnson, J. and Slater, R. (eds) (1993) *Ageing and Later Life*. London: Sage.

Johnson, N. (1990) *Reconstructing the Welfare State*. London: Harvester Wheatsheaf.

Johnson, P. (1999) 'Inequality, redistribution and living standards in Britain since 1945', in H. Fawcett and R. Lowe (eds), *Welfare Policy in Britain: The Road from 1945*. Basingstoke: Macmillan Press.

Johnson, P. and Falkingham, J. (1992) *Ageing and Economic Welfare*. London: Sage.

Jones, C. and Novak, T. (1980) 'The state and social policy', in P. Corrrigan (ed.), *Capitalism, State Formation and Marxist Theory*. London: Quartet.

Jones, C. and Novak, T. (1999) *Poverty, Welfare and the Disciplinary State*. London: Routledge.

Jones, H. and MacGregor, S. (eds) (1998) *Social Issues and Party Politics*. London: Routledge.

Joseph, K. and Sumption, J. (1978) *Equality*. London: J. Murray.

Joseph, K. and Sumption, J. (1979) *Equality*. London: John Murray.

Kavanagh, D. (1990) *Thatcherism and British Politics. The End of Consensus?* (second edn). Oxford: Oxford University Press.

Kearns, K. (1997) 'Social democratic perspectives on the welfare state', in M. Lavalette and A. Pratt (eds), *Social Policy: A Conceptual and Theoretical Introduction* London: Sage.

Kelly, E. (1988) *Surviving Sexual Violence*. Cambridge: Polity Press.

Kelly, P. (1998) 'Contractarian social justice: an overview of some contemporary debates', in D. Boucher and P. Kelly (eds), *Social Justice from Hume to Walzer*. London: Routledge.

Kemp, P.A. (1999) 'Making the market work? New Labour and the housing question', in H. Dean and R. Woods (eds), *Social Policy Review 11*. Luton: University of Luton/Social Policy Association.

Keynes, J.M. (1936) *The General Theory of Employment, Interest and Money*. London: Macmillan.

King, D.S. (1987) *The New Right: Politics, Markets and Citizenship*. London: Macmillan.

Klein, N. (2000) *No Logo*. London: Flamingo.

Klein, R. (1993) 'O'Goffe's tale', in C. Jones (ed.), *New Perspectives on the Welfare State in Europe*. London: Routledge.

Kley, R. (1994) *Hayek's Social and Political Thought*. Oxford: Clarendon Press.

Kumar, K. (1995) *From Post-Industrial to Post-Modern Society: New Theories of the Contemporary World*. Oxford: Blackwell.

Kymlicka, W. (1994) *Multicultural Citizenship: A Liberal Theory of Minority Rights*. Oxford: Clarendon Press.

Labour Party (1945) *Let Us Face The Future*. London: The Labour Party.

Labour Party (1974) *Let Us Work Together – Labour's Way out of the Crisis*. London: The Labour Party.

Labour Party (1997) *New Labour: Because Britain Deserves Better*. London: The Labour Party.

Lansdown, G. (1995) 'Children's rights to participation: a critique', in C. Cloke and M. Davies (eds), *Participation and Empowerment in Child Protection*. Chichester: Wiley/NSPCC.

Lansley, J. (forthcoming) 'Older people in the city', in R. Munck (ed.), *Reinventing the City: Liverpool in Comparative Perspective*. Liverpool: Liverpool University Press.

Latham, M. (1998) *Civilising Global Capital*. Sydney: Allen and Unwin.

Lavalette, M. (1994) *Child Employment in the Capitalist Labour Market*. Aldershot: Avebury.

Lavalette, M. (ed.) (1999) *A Thing of the Past? Child Labour in Britain in the Nineteenth and Twentieth Centuries*. Liverpool: Liverpool University Press.

Lavalette, M. and Mooney, G. (1999) 'New Labour, new moralism: the welfare politics and ideology of New Labour under Blair', *International Socialism*, 85: 27–47.

Lavalette, M. and Mooney, G. (eds.) (2000) *Class Struggle and Social Welfare*. London: Routledge.

Law, I. (1998) 'Sharpening the conceptual tools – racial and ethnic inequalities in housing policy', in M. Lavalette, L. Penketh and C. Jones (eds), *Anti-Racism and Social Welfare*. Aldershot: Ashgate.

Lees, D. (1967) 'Poor families and fiscal reform', in *Lloyds Bank Review*, October.

Le Grand, J. (1998) 'The third way begins with CORA', *New Statesman*, 6 March.

Leonard, P. (1997) *Postmodern Welfare: Reconstructing an Emancipatory Project*. London: Sage.

Lerner, G. (1979) *The Majority Finds its Past: Placing Women in History*. New York: Oxford University Press.

Levay, S. (1993) *The Sexual Brain*. Cambridge, MA: MIT Publishing.

Levitas, R. (1998) *The Inclusive Society: Social Exclusion and New Labour*. Basingstoke: Macmillan.

Lewis, G., Gewirtz, S. and Clarke J. (eds) (2000) *Rethinking Social Policy*. London: Sage.

Lewis, J. (1992) *Women in Britain since 1945*. Oxford: Blackwell.

Lewis, J. (1993) *Women and Social Policies in Europe, Work, Family and the State*. London: Edward Elgar Publishing.

Lewis, J. and Meredith, B. (1988) *Daughters who Care: Daughters Caring for Mothers at Home*. London: Routledge.

Lister, R. (1990) 'Women, economic dependency and citizenship', *Journal of Social Policy*, 19 (4): 445–68.

Lloyd George, D. (1909) *The New Liberalism: Speeches by the Right Hon. David Lloyd George*. London: Daily News.

Logan, J. et. al. (1996) *Confronting Prejudice*. London: Ashgate.

Loney, M., Bocock, R. Clarke, J., Cochrane A., Graham, P. and Wilson, M. (eds) (1991) *The State or the Market. Politics and Welfare in Contemporary Britain*. London: Sage.

Lorde, A. (1984) *Sister Outsider: Essays and Speeches*. New York: The Crossing Press.

Lowe, R. (1990) 'The second world war, and the foundation of the welfare state', *Twentieth Century British History*. 1 (2).

Lowe, R. (1993) *The Welfare State in Britain since 1945*. London: Macmillan.

Lukacs, G. (1971) *History and Class Consciousness*. London: Merlin.

Luttwak, E. (1999) *Turbo-Capitalism*. London: Texere Publishing.

Lyotard, J.F. (1984) *The Postmodern Condition: A Report on Knowledge*. Manchester: Manchester University Press.

MacDonagh, O. (1958) 'The nineteenth-century revolution in government: a reappraisal', *The Historical Journal*, 1 (1).

Macfarlane, L.J. (1998) *Socialism, Social Ownership and Social Justice*. Basingstoke: Macmillan.

Mack, J. and Lansley S. (1985) *Poor Britain*. London, Allen and Unwin.

Macleod, H. and Saraga, E. (1988) 'Challenging the orthodoxy: towards a feminist theory and practice', *Feminist Review*, 28: 16–25.

MacLeod, I. and Powell, E. (1952) *The Social Services: Needs and Means*. London: Conservative Political Centre (updated by Powell, 1954).

Maclure, J.S. (1968) *Educational Documents: England and Wales 1816–1967*. London: Methuen.

MacNicol, J. (1987) 'In pursuit of the underclass', *Journal of Social Policy*, 16 (2).

Madrick, J. (1997) *The End of Affluence*. New York: Random House.

Mandelson, P. (1997) *Labour's Next Steps: Tackling Social Exclusion*. London: Fabian Society.

Mandelson, P. and Liddle, R. (1996) *The Blair Revolution*. London: Faber and Faber.

Mann, K. (1992) *The Making of an English 'Underclass'?* Milton Keynes: The Open University Press.

Mann, M. (1987) 'Ruling class strategies and citizenship' *Sociology*, 21 (3): 339–54.

Marfleet, P. (1999) 'Nationalism and internationalism in the new Europe', *International Socialism*, 84.

Marquand, D. (1967) 'Change gear', in *Socialist Commentary*, October.

Marquand, D. (1987) *The Unprincipled Society*. Fontana: London.

Marquand, D. (1996) 'Moralists and hedonists', in D. Marquand and A. Seldon (eds), *The Ideas that Shaped Post-War Britain*. London: Fontana.

Marshall, T.H. (1950) *Citizenship and Social Class*. Cambridge: Cambridge University Press.

Marshall, T. H. (1975) *Social Policy in the Twentieth Century*. London: Hutchinson (first edn 1965).

Marshall, T.H. (1981) *The Right to Welfare*. London: Heinemann.

Marx, K. and Engels, F. (1848/1998) 'The manifesto of the communist party', (Communist Manifesto), in *Marx and Engels Classics in Politics*. London: ElecBook.

Mason, D. (2000) *Race and Ethnicity in Modern Britain* (second edn). Oxford: Oxford University Press.

May, M. (1973) 'Innocence and experience: the evolution of the concept of juvenile delinquency in the mid-nineteenth century', *Victorian Studies*, September 1973.

McGarr, P. (2000) 'Why green is red: Marxism and the threat to the environment', *International Socialism*, 88.

McGregor, O. (1957) 'Sociology and welfare', *Sociological Review Monograph*, 4.

McIntosh, M. (1968) 'The homosexual role', *Social Problems*, 16 (2): 182–92, reprinted in K. Plummer (ed.), (1981) *The Making of the Modern Homosexual*. London: Hutchinson.

McIntosh, M. (1998) 'Dependency culture? Welfare women and work', *Radical Philosophy* 91, September/October: 5.

McLaughlin, E. (1994) 'Flexibility in work and benefits', *Commission on Social Justice*, Vol. II, London: IPPR.

McLean, U. (1989) *Dependent Territories: The Frail Elderly and Community Care*, London: NPHT.

Meacher, M. (1972) 'The malaise of the low-paid worker', in J. Hughes and R. Moore, *A Special Case: Social Justice and the Miners*. London: Penguin.

Meade, C. (1989) *The Thoughts of Betty Spital*. Harmondsworth: Penguin.

Melling, J. (1983) *Rent Strikes*. London: Polygon.

Meszaros, I. (1970) *Marx's Theory of Alienation* (fourth edn). London: Merlin.

Micklewright, J. and Stewart, K. (2000) 'Child well-being and social cohesion: is the UK the oddball in Europe?', in *New Economy*, March 2000.

Middlemas, K. (1980) *Politics in Industrial Society*. London: Macmillan.

Miles, R. (1982), *Racism and Migrant Labour*. London: Routledge.

Miles, R. (1989) *Racism*. London: RKP.

Miles, R. (1993) *Racism After Race Relations*. London: Routledge.

Miles, R. and Phizacklea, A. (eds) (1979) *Racism and Political Action in Britain*. London: RKP.

Miles, R. and Phizacklea, A. (eds) (1984) *White Man's Country*. London: Pluto.

Millar, J. and Gendinning, C. (1987) *Women and Poverty in Britain*. Brighton: Wheatsheaf.

Miller, D. (1999) *Principles of Justice*. Cambridge, MA: Harvard University Press.

Millett, K. (1971) *Sexual Politics*. New York: Avon Books.

Minford, P. (1987) 'The role of the social services: a view from the new right' in M. Loney, R. Bocock, J. Clarke, A. Cochrane, P. Graham and M. Wilson (eds), *The State and the Market: Politics and Welfare in Contemporary Britain*. London: Sage.

Ministry of Pensions and National Insurance (1966) *The Economic Circumstances of Retirement Pensioners*. London: HMSO.

Minkler, M. and Estes, C. (eds) (1984) *Readings in the Political Economy of Aging*. New York: Baywood.

Minkler, M. and Estes, C. (eds) (1998) *Critical Gerontology: Perspectives from Political and Moral Economy*. New York: Baywood.

Mishra, R. (1984) *The Welfare State in Crisis*. London: Harvester Wheatsheaf.

Mitchell, J. (1974) *Psychoanalysis and Feminism*. Harmondsworth: Penguin.

Mooney, G. (2000) 'Class and social policy', in G. Lewis, S. Gewirtz, and J. Clarke (eds), *Rethinking Social Policy*. London: Open University/Sage.

Moore, S. (2000) 'Child incarceration and the new youth justice', in B. Goldston (ed.), *The New Youth Justice*. Lyme Regis: Russell House Publishing.

Morris, L. (1994) *Dangerous Classes: The Underclass and Social Citizenship*. London: Routledge.

Mullan, P. (2000) *The Imaginary Time Bomb*. London: I.B. Tauris.

Muncie, J. (1984) *The Trouble With Kids Today: Youth and Crime in Post-War Britain*. London: Hutchinson.

Muncie, J. (1990a) 'Failure never matters: detention centres and the politics of deterrence', in *Critical Social Policy*, 28, Summer 1990.

Muncie, J. (1990b) 'Juvenile delinquency', in R. Dallos, and E. McLaughlin (eds), *Social Problems and the Family*. London: Sage.

Muncie, J. (1998) 'Give em what they deserve: the young offender and youth justice policy', in M. Langan (ed.), *Welfare: Needs, Rights and Risks*. London: Routledge.

Muncie, J. and McLaughlin, E. (1993) 'Juvenile delinquency' in R. Dallos and E. McLaughlin, *Social Problems and the Family*. Milton Keynes: The Open University Press.

Munck, R., Andersen, H., et al. (1999) *Neighbourhood Images of Liverpool*. York: Joseph Rowntree Foundation.

Murray, C. (1990) *The Emerging British Underclass*. London: Institute of Economic Affairs.

Murray, C. (1994) *Underclass: The Crisis Deepens*. London: Institute of Economic Affairs.

Myrdal, G. (1972) 'The place of values in social policy', *Journal of Social Policy*, 1 (1).

National Campaign to Defend Council Housing (2000) *Defend Council Housing*. www.defendcouncilhousing.org.uk/

National Pensioners Convention (1998) *Pensions, not Poor Relief*. London: NPC.

National Pensioners Convention (1999) *Pensions: Who Pays?* London: NPC.

Newburn, T. (1995) *Crime and Criminal Justice Policy*. London: Longman.

Norton-Taylor, R. (1999) *The Colour of Justice*. London: Oberon.

Novak, T. (1988) *Poverty and the State: A Historical Sociology*. Milton Keynes: The Open University Press.

Novak, T. (1995) 'Rethinking poverty', *Critical Social Policy* 15(44/45): 58–74.

Nozick, R. (1974) *Anarchy, State and Utopia*. London: Blackwell.

Oakley, A. (1974) *The Sociology of Housework*. London: Martin Robertson.

O'Brien, M. and Penna, S. (1998) *Theorising Welfare: Enlightenment and Modern Society*. London: Sage.

O'Connor, J. (1973) *The Fiscal Crisis of the State*. New York: St Martin's Press.

Offe, C. (1984) *Contradictions of the Welfare State*. Cambridge, MA: MIT Press.

Office of Fair Trading (1997) *Inquiry into Pensions*. London: OFT.

Oliver, M. and Barnes, C. (1998) *Disabled People and Social Policy: From Exclusion to Inclusion*. London: Longman.

Oppenheim, C. and Harker, L. (1996) *Poverty: The Facts*. London: CPAG.

Owen, D. (1967) 'Change gear', *Socialist Commentary*, October.

Page, R. (1984) *Stigma*. London: Routledge and Kegan Paul.

Page, R.M. (1996) *Altruism and the British Welfare State*. Aldershot: Avebury.

Pahl, J. (1965) *Private Violence and Public Policy*. London: Routledge and Kegan Paul.

Pahl, J. (1985) *Private Violence and Public Policy* 2nd ed.. London: Routledge.

Palmer, A. (1993) *Less Equal than Others*. London: Stonewall.

Parkinson, M. (1998) *Combating Social Exclusion: Lessons From Area-Based Programmes in Europe*. Bristol: Policy Press.

Parton, N. (1994) 'Problematics of governance: (post) modernity and social work', *British Journal of Social Work*, 24 (1): 9–32.

Parton, N. (ed.) (1996) *Social Theory, Social Change and Social Work*. London: Routledge.

Parton, N. and Marshall, W. (1998) 'Postmodernism and discourse approaches to social work', in R. Adams, L. Dominelli and M. Payne (eds), *Social Work: Themes, Issues and Critical Debates*. Basingstoke: Macmillan.

Pateman, C. (1988) *The Sexual Contract*. Cambridge: Polity.

Pateman, C. (1992) 'The patriarchal welfare state', in L. McDowell and R. Pringle (eds), *Defining Women, Social Institutions and Gender Division*. Oxford: Polity.

Patterson, C. (1992) 'Children of lesbian and gay parents', *Child Development* 63: 1025–42.

Payne, S. (1991) *Women, Health and Poverty: an Introduction*. Hemel Hempstead: Harvester Wheatsheaf.

Pease, B. and Fook, J. (1999) *Transforming Social Work Practice*. London: Routledge.

Pelling, H. (1993) *A Short History of the Labour Party*. Basingstoke: Macmillan Press.

Penketh, L. (1998) 'Anti-racist policies and practice: the case of CCETSWs Paper 30', in M. Lavalette, L. Penketh and C. Jones (eds), *Anti-Racism and Social Welfare* Aldershot: Ashgate.

Penketh, L. (2000) *Tackling Institutional Racism*. Bristol: The Policy Press.

Penketh, L. and Ali, Y. (1997) 'Racism and social welfare', in M. Lavalette and Alan Pratt (eds), *Social Policy: A Conceptual and Theoretical Introduction*. London: Sage.

Penna, S. and O'Brien, M. (1996) 'Postmodernism and social policy: a small step forwards?', *Journal of Social Policy*, 25 (1): 39–61.

Phelan, S. (ed.) (1997) *Playing With Fire: Queer Politics, Queer Theories*, London: Routledge.

Phillips, A. (1999) *Which Equalities Matter?* Cambridge: Polity.

Phillips, M. (1997) 'Workfare for lone mothers: a solution to the wrong problem', in A. Deacon (ed.), *From Welfare to Work*. London: Institute of Economic Affairs.

Phillipson, C. (1982) *Capitalism and the Construction of Old Age*. London: Macmillan.

Phillipson, C. (1998) *Reconstructing Old Age*. London: Sage.

Phillipson, C. and Walker, A. (1986) *Ageing and Social Policy: A Critical Assessment*. Aldershot: Gower.

Piachaud, D. (1971) 'Poverty and taxation', *The Political Quarterly*, January, March.

Piachaud, D. (1987) 'Problems in the definition and measurement of poverty', *Journal of Social Policy* 16 (2).

Pinchbeck, I. and Hewitt, M. (1973) *Children in English Society, Volume II*. London: Routledge and Kegan Paul.

Pinker, R. (1971) *Social Theory and Social Policy*. London: Heinemann.

Pinker, R. (1999) 'Social work and adoption: a case of mistaken identities', in T. Philpot (ed.), *Political Correctness and Social Work*. London: IEA.

Plant, R. (1985) *Equality, Markets and the State*, Fabian Trust 495. London: Fabian Society.

Plant, R. (1990) 'The New Right and social policy: a critique', in M. Manning and C. Ungerson (eds), *Social Policy Review 1989/90*. London: Longman.

Plant, R. (1991) *Modern Political Thought*. London: Blackwell.

Plewis, I. (2000) 'Educational inequalities and educational action zones', in C. Pantazis and D. Gordon (eds), *Tackling Inequalities*. Bristol: Polity.

Plummer, K. (ed.) (1981) *The Making of the Modern Homosexual*. London: Hutchinson.

Pollock, A., Price, D. and Dunnigan, M. (2000) *Deficits Before Patients*. London: University College London.

Pope, R., Pratt, A. and Hoyle, B. (1986) *Social Welfare in Britain, 1885–1985*. Beckenham: Croom Helm.

Powell, M. (ed.) (1999) *New Labour, New Welfare State?* Bristol: Policy Press.

Powell, V. (2000) 'Fears for future of Section 28 repeal', *Gay Times* 258, March: 37–8.

Pratt, A. (1976) 'The family income supplement: origins and issues', MA dissertation, University of Salford.

Pratt, A. (1988) 'The Labour Party, family income support policy, and the labour market, 1940–79' PhD. dissertation, University of Bradford.

Pringle, R. and Watson, S. (1992) 'Women's interests and the post-structuralist state', in M. Barrett, and A. Phillips (eds), *De-establishing Theory*. Cambridge: Polity, p. 65.

Radzinowicz, L. and Hood, R. (1986) *A History of English Criminal Law and its Administration From 1750, Vol. 5, The Emergence of Penal Policy*. London: Stevens.

Rafkin, L. (1990) *Different Mothers: Sons and Daughters of Lesbians Talk about their Lives*. Pittsburgh, PA: Cleis Press.

Ramdin, R. (1987) *The Making of the Black Working Class in Britain*. Aldershot: Gower.

Ranelagh, J. (1991) *Thatcher's People*. London: Fontana.

Ransome, P. (1999) *Sociology and the Future of Work*. Aldershot: Ashgate.

Rapp, R. (1979) 'Household and family', in R. Rapp, R. Ross and R. Bridenthal, 'Examining family history' *Feminist Studies* 181, Spring.

Rawls, J. (1971) *A Theory of Justice*. Oxford: Oxford University Press.

Rees, J. (1998) *The Algebra of Revolution*. London: Routledge.

Reisman, D. (1977) *Richard Titmuss. Welfare and Society*. London: Heinemann.

Rendall, J. (1985) *The Origins of Modern Feminism: Women in Britain, France and the United States, 1780–1860*. London and Basingstoke: Macmillan.

Rich, A. (1977) *Of Women Born: Motherhood as Experience and Institution.* London: Virago (first published New York, Norton, 1976).

Rich, A. (1980) 'Compulsory heterosexuality and the lesbian existence', *Signs*, 5 (4) Summer: 389–417.

Richardson, D. (1993) *Women, Motherhood and Childhood.* London: Macmillan.

Rights of Women Custody Group (1984) *Lesbian Mothers' Legal Handbook.* London: Womens Press.

Ringen, S. (1986) *The Possibility of Politics: A Study in the Political Economy of the Welfare State.* Oxford: Clarendon.

Ritzer, G. (1993) *The McDonaldization of Society: An Investigation Into the Changing Character of Contemporary Social Life.* California: Pine Forge Press.

Robb, B. (1967) *Sans Everything: A Case to Answer.* London: Nelson.

Roberts, D. (1969) *The Victorian Origins of the British Welfare State.* London: Archon Books.

Robertson, R. (1993) *Globalization: Social Theory and Global Culture.* London: Sage.

Robins, K. (1997) 'What is globalisation?', *Sociology Review*, 6, 3 (2): 2–6.

Roemer, J.E. (1996) *Theories of Distributive Justice.* London: Harvard University Press.

Rogers, A. (1993) 'Back to the workhouse?', *International Socialism* 59.

Room, G., (ed.)(1995) *Beyond the Threshold.* Bristol: Polity Press.

Rose, M. (1971) *The English Poor Laws 1780–1930.* David and Charles: Newton Abbott.

Rose, N. (1999) 'Inventiveness in politics', *Economy and Society*, 28 (3): 467–93.

Rosenau, P.M. (1992) *Post-Modernism and the Social Sciences: Insights, Inroads and Intrusions.* Princeton NJ: Princeton University Press.

Rowbotham, S. (1969) *Women's Liberation and the New Politics.* Pamphlet.

Rowbotham, S. (1974) *Hidden from History: Three Hundred Years of Women's Oppression and the Fight Against It.* London: Pluto Press.

Rowbotham, S. (1989) *The Past is Before Us: Feminism in Action since the 1960s.* Harmondsworth: Penguin.

Rowntree, B.S. (1901) *Poverty: A Study of Town Life.* London: Macmillan.

Rowntree, B.S. (1941) *Poverty and Progress.* London: Longman.

Ruddick, S. (1980) 'Maternal thinking', *Feminist Studies*, 6 (2): 342–67

Russell, D. (1983) 'Instances and prevalence of intrafamilial and extrafamilial sexual abuse of female children', *Child Abuse and Neglect*, 7, pp. 133–46.

Rutherford, A. (1999) The new political consensus on youth justice in Britain', in G.L. McDowell and J.S. Smith (eds), *Juvenile Delinquency in the United States and the United Kingdom.* London: Macmillan.

Saffron, L. (1996) *What About the Children? Sons and Daughters of Lesbian and Gay Parents Talk About Their Lives.* London: Cassell.

Sapsford, R. and Abbott, P. (1988) 'The body politic, health, family and society' in *Family, Gender and Welfare.* Milton Keynes: The Open University Press.

Saraga, E. (1993) 'The abuse of children', in R. Dallos and E. McLaughlin (eds), *Social Problems and the Family.* London: Sage.

Sassoon, D. (1996) *One Hundred Years of Socialism: The West European Left in the Twentieth Century.* London: I.B. Tauris.

Scarman, Lord (1981) *The Scarman Report: The Brixton Disorders.* Harmondsworth: Penguin.

Schumpeter, J.A. (1943/1976) *Capitalism, Socialism and Democracy.* London: George Allen and Unwin.

Scottish Office (1999) *Investing in Modernisation – An Agenda for Scotland's Housing.* Edinburgh: The Stationery Office.

Scottish Office (1999) *Social Exclusion in Scotland.* Edinburgh: Stationery Office.

Scraton, P. (ed.) (1997) *Childhood in Crisis.* London: UCL Press.

Searle, G.R. (1971) *The Quest for National Efficiency.* London: Basil Blackwell.

Secretary of State for Health (1998) *Our Healthier Nation: A Contract for Health.* Cm. 3852. London: The Stationery Office.

Secretary of State for Social Security and Minister for Welfare Reform (1998) *A New Contract for Welfare: New Ambitions for our Country*. Cm. 3805. London: The Stationery Office.

Segal, L. (1987) *Is the Future Female? Troubled Thoughts on Contemporary Feminism*. London: Virago.

Segal, L. (1993) 'A feminist looks at the family', in M. Wetherell, R. Dallos and D. Miell (eds), *Interactions and Identities*. Milton Keynes: The Open University.

Segal, L. (1999) *Why Feminism?* Cambridge: Polity.

Seldon, A. (1967) 'Taxation and welfare' *Research Monograph* 14. London: IEA.

Seldon, A. (1977) *Charge*. London: Temple Smith.

Self, P. (1993) *Government by the Market? The Politics of Public Choice*. London: Macmillan.

Self, P. (2000) *Rolling Back the Market Economic Dogma and Political Choice*. London: Macmillan.

Senior, N. (1865) *Historical and Philosophical Essays*. London: Longman Green.

Shaw, M., Dorling, D., Gordon, D., and Smith, G.D. (1999) *The Widening Gap*. Bristol: Policy Press.

Shilts, R. (1988) *And the Band Played On: Politics, People and the AIDS Epidemic*. Harmondsworth: Penguin.

Shrimsley, R. (1996) 'Cook tells Labour not to forget the poor', *The Daily Telegraph*, 18 April 1996.

Simon, B. (1965) *Education and the Labour Movement 1870–1920*, London: Lawrence and Wishart.

Simon, B. (1960) *Studies in the History of Education 1780–1870*. London: Lawrence and Wishart.

Simon, B. (1986) The Education Act: a conservative measure? *History of Education*, (15 (1).

Sivanandan, A. (1981) 'From resistance to rebellion: Asian and Afro-Caribbean struggles in Britain', *Race and Class*, 23 (2–3).

Sivanandan, A. (1982) 'Waiting for Scarman', *Race and Class*, 23 (2–3).

Sivanandan, A. (1991) 'Black struggles against racism', in Northern Curriculum Development Project (ed.), *Setting the Context for Change*. London: CCETSW.

Skellington, R. and Morris, P. (1992) *'Race' in Britain Today*. London: Sage.

Smith, C. and White, S. (1997) 'Parton, Howe and postmodernity: a critical comment on mistaken identity', *British Journal of Social Work*, 27 (2): 275–95.

Smith, S. (1994) 'Mistaken identity – or can identity politics liberate the oppressed?', *International Socialism*, 62: 3–50.

Smith, S. (1999) 'The trickle up effect', *Socialist Review*, November.

Social Security Consortium (1986) *Of Little Benefit, A Critical Guide to the Social Security Act*. London: SSC.

Social Trends (2000) Social Trends 30 (edited by J. Matheson and C. Summerfield). London, Stationery Office.

Spencer, S. (2000) 'Making race equality count: measuring progress towards race equality', *New Economy*, 7 (1) March, 35-41.

Spybey, T. (1998) 'Globalisation or imperialism?', *Sociology Review*, 7, (3): 29–33.

Squires, P. (1990) *Anti Social Policy*. London: Harvester Wheatsheaf.

Standing, G. (1982) 'State policy and child labour: accumulation versus legitimation', *Development and Change* 13.

Stedman-Jones, G. (1971) *Outcast London: A Study of the Relationship Between Classes in Victorian Society*. Oxford: Oxford University Press.

Sullivan, M. (1992) *The Politics of Social Policy*. Hemel Hempstead: Harvester Wheatsheaf.

Summerskill, B. (2000) 'Adoption drive set to target more gay parents', *Observer*, 1 October 1.

Swift, J. (1726) *Gulliver's Travels*. London: Motte.

Tasker, F. and Golombok, S. (1997) *Growing Up in a Lesbian Family – Effects on Child Development*. London: Guilford Press.

Tattersall, M. (1997) 'From punk to pastiche: are Oasis postmodernists?', in *Sociology Review*, 6 (3): 20–3.

Tawney, R. (1931) *Equality*. London: Unwin Books.

Tawney, R. (1951) *Equality* 2nd ed. London: Unwin Books.

Taylor-Gooby, P. (1994) 'Postmodernism and social policy: a great leap backwards?', *Journal of Social Policy*, 23 (3): 385–405.

Thom, D. (1986) 'The 1944 Education Act: the "art of the possible"?', in H.L. Smith (ed.), *War and Social Change: British Society in the Second World War*. Manchester: Manchester University Press.

Thomas, K. (1976) 'Age and authority in early modern England', *Proceedings of the British Academy*, 62, 205–48.

Thompson, E.P. (1968) *The Making of the English Working Class*. Harmondsworth: Penguin.

Thompson, N. (1996) *Political Economy and the Labour Party*. London: UCL Press.

Thompson, P., Itzin, C. and Abendstern, M. (1990) *I Don't Feel Old*. Oxford: Oxford University Press.

Thompson, S. and Hoggett, P. (1996) 'Universalism, selectivism and particularism', *Critical Social Policy*. 46, 211–43.

Thomson, R. (1993) 'Unholy alliances: the recent politics of sex education', in J. Bristow and A. Wilson (eds), *Activating Theory*. London: Lawrence and Wishart.

Timmins, N. (1996) *The Five Giants: A Biography of the Welfare State*. London: HarperCollins.

Tinker, A. (1996) *Older People in Modern Society* (fourth edn). London: Longman.

Titmuss, R.M. (1950) *Problems of Social Policy*. London: HMSO.

Titmuss, R.M. (1955) 'Pension systems and population change', *Political Quarterly* 26 (2): 152–66, reprinted in R.M. Titmuss (1958) *Essays on The Welfare State*. London: Allen and Unwin.

Titmuss, R.M. (1962) *Income Distribution and Social Change*. London: George Allen and Unwin.

Titmuss, R.M. (1974) *Social Policy*. London: Allen and Unwin.

Titmuss, R.M. (1976) *Commitment to Welfare*. London: George Allen and Unwin (first published 1968).

Tomlinson, J. (1997) *Democratic Socialism and Economic Policy: The Attlee Years, 1945–1951*. Cambridge: Cambridge University Press.

Tout, K. (1989) *Ageing in Developing Countries*. Oxford: Oxford University Press.

Townsend, P. (1962) *The Last Refuge*. London: Routledge and Kegan Paul.

Townsend, P. (1972) 'Selectivity: a nation divided', in *Sociology and Social Policy*. London: Penguin, pp. 122–3.

Townsend, P. (1979) *Poverty in the United Kingdom*. Harmondsworth: Penguin.

Townsend, P. (1981) 'The structured dependency of the elderly: the creation of social policy in the twentieth century', *Ageing and Society*, 1 (1): 5–28.

Townsend, P. (1985) 'A sociological approach to measuring poverty: a rejoinder to Professor Anartya Sen', *Oxford Economic Papers* 37 (4): 649–58.

Townsend, P. (1987) 'Deprivation', *Journal of Social Policy*, 16 (2): 125–46.

Toynbee, P. (2000a) 'Give them hope', *The Guardian*, 24 November.

Toynbee, P. (2000b) 'Pensioner power', *The Guardian*, 26 May.

Treasury Taskforce on Private Finance (1997) *Partnerships for Prosperity: The Private Finance Initiative*. London: HM Treasury.

Troyna, B. (1992) 'Can you see the join? A historical analysis of multicultural and anti-racist education policies', in D. Gill, B. Mayor and M. Blair (eds), *Racism and Education – Structures and Strategies*. London: Sage.

Troyna, B. and Hatcher, R. (1992) 'Racist incidents in school: a framework for analysis' in D. Gill, B. Mayor and M. Blair (eds), *Racism and Education – Structures and Strategies*. London: Sage.

TUC (1998) *Economic Inequality and Benefit Levels*. Internet reference http://www.tuc.org.uk/vbuilding/tuc/brouse/brouse.exe

Turner, B. (1990) 'Outline of a theory of citizenship', *Sociology*, 24 (2): 189–217.

Twigg, J. (1997) 'Deconstructing the "social bath": help with bathing at home for older and disabled people', *Journal of Social Policy*, 26 (2): 211–32.

Twigg, J. (2000) 'Social policy and the body', in G. Lewis, S. Gewirtz and J. Clarke (eds), *Rethinking Social Policy*. London: Sage.

UKPHA (2000) Report: Newsletter of the UK Public Health Association, 4, Summer.

Ungerson, C. (ed.) (1990) Gender and Caring: Work and Welfare in Britain and Scandinavia. Hemel Hempstead: Harvester Wheatsheaf.

Unison (1999) Report of the Unison Working Group on PFI. London: Unison.

Unison (2000) Local Government PFI Newsletter, 5. http://www.unison.org.uk/

United Nations (1989) Convention on the Rights of the Child. Geneva: UNO.

United Nations Development Programme (1999) Human Development Report. New York, UNDP.

Vandenbroucke, F. (1999) 'European social democracy: convergence, divisions and shared questions', in A. Gamble, and T. Wright, (eds), The New Social Democracy – Supplement to the Political Quarterly, Oxford: Blackwell.

Veit-Wilson, J. (1992) 'Muddle or mendacity? The Beveridge Committee and the poverty line', Journal of Social Policy, 21 (3): 269–303.

Victor, C. (1991) Health and Health Care in Later Life. Buckingham: The Open University Press.

Walby, S. (1988) 'Gender politics and social theory', Sociology, 22, (2): 215–32.

Walby, S. (1994) 'Is citizenship gendered?', Sociology, 28 (2, 3): 79–395.

Walker, A. (1980) 'The social creation of poverty and dependency in old age', Journal of Social Policy 9 (1): 45–75.

Walker, A. (1981) 'Towards a political economy of old age', Ageing and Society, 1 (1): 73–94.

Walker A. and Maltby, T. (1997) Ageing Europe. Buckingham: The Open University Press.

Walker, A. and Walker, C. (eds) (1998) Britain Divided. London: Child Poverty Action Group.

Walkowitz, J. (1980) Prostitution in Victorian Society: Women, Class and State. Cambridge: Cambridge University Press.

Walvin, J. (1982) A Child's World: A Social History of English Childhood 1800–1914. Harmondsworth: Penguin.

Walzer, M. (1983) Spheres of Justice. Oxford: Martin Robertson.

Warland, B. (ed.) (1992) Inversions. London: Open Letters.

Warnes, A. (ed.) (1982) Geographical Perspectives on the Elderly. Chichester: John Wiley.

Watney, S. (1987) Policing Desire: Pornography, AIDS and the Media. London: Methuen/Comedia.

Watson, S. (2000) 'Foucault and the study of social policy', in G. Lewis, S. Gewirtz and J. Clarke (eds), Rethinking Social Policy. London: Open University/Sage.

Webb, S. and Webb, B. (1913) 'What is socialism?', New Statesman, 10 May.

Webster, G.G. (1986) 'Putting father back at the head of the table', Press Conference Speech, 14 March.

Weeks, J. (1977) Coming Out: Homosexual Politics in Britain from the Nineteenth Century to the Present. London: Quartet.

Weeks, J. (1981) Sex, Politics and Society: The Regulation of Sexuality since 1800. London: Longman.

Weeks, J. (1985) Sexuality and its Discontents. London: Routledge.

Weiner, M.J. (1994) Reconstructing the Criminal – Culture, Law and Policy in England 1830–1914, Cambridge: Cambridge University Press.

Wenger, G.C. (1990) 'Elderly carers: the need for appropriate interventions', Ageing and Society, 10 (2): 197–219.

Wheen, F. (1999) Karl Marx. London: Fourth Estate.

White, M. (2000) 'Poor lost ground in Labour's first years', The Guardian, 13 April.

White, S. (1999) 'Rights and responsibilities: a social democratic perspective' in A. Gamble, and T. Wright, (eds), The New Social Democracy – Supplement to the Political Quarterly Oxford: Blackwell.

Whitfield, D. (1999) 'Private finance initiative: the commodification and marketisation of education', Education and Social Justice, 1 (2): 2–13.

Wicks, M. (1991) 'Family matters and public policy', in M. Loney, R. Bocock, J. Clarke, A. Cochrane, P. Graham and M. Wilson (eds), The State or the Market. Politics and Welfare in Contemporary Britain. London: Sage.

Williams, F. (1992) 'Somewhere over the rainbow: universality and diversity in social policy', in N. Manning and R. Page (eds), *Social Policy Review*, 4. London: SPA.

Williams, W. (1985) 'Redefining institutional racism', *Ethnic and Racial Studies*, 8 (3).

Wilson, A. (ed.) (1994) *A Simple Matter of Justice*. London: Cassell.

Wilson, E. (1989) 'In a different way', in K. Grieve (ed.), *Balancing Acts: On Being a Mother*. London: Virago.

Wilson, G. (1997) 'A postmodern approach to structured dependency theory', *Journal of Social Policy*, 3: 341–50.

Wilson, G. (2000) *Understanding Old Age: Critical and Global Perspectives*. London: Sage.

Wolfe, A. and Klausen, J. (2000) 'Other people', *Prospect*, December.

Wolff, R. (1977) *Understanding Rawls*. Princeton, NJ: Princeton University Press.

Woodroffe, J. and Ellis-Jones. M. (2000) *States of Unrest* (World Development Report) http://www.wdm.org.uk/cambriefs/DEBT/unrest.htm

Woodward, K. (1997) 'Motherhood: identities, meanings and myths', in K. Woodward, (ed.), *Identity and Difference*. London: Sage, pp. 239–98.

Woodward, K. (1999) 'Representing reproduction; reproducing representation', in G. Kirkup, L. Janes, F. Hovendon, and K. Woodward (eds), *The Useful Cyborg*. London: Routledge.

Wright, E.O. (1979) *Class Crisis and the State*. London: Verso.

Yilo, K. and Bograd, M. (eds) (1988) *Feminist Perspectives on Wife Abuse*. London: Sage.

Young, I.M. (1990) *Justice and the Politics of Difference*. Chichester: Princeton University Press.

INDEX